United States Army Military Commission

The Conspiracy Trial for the Murder of the President

And the Attempt to Overthrow the Government by the Assassination...

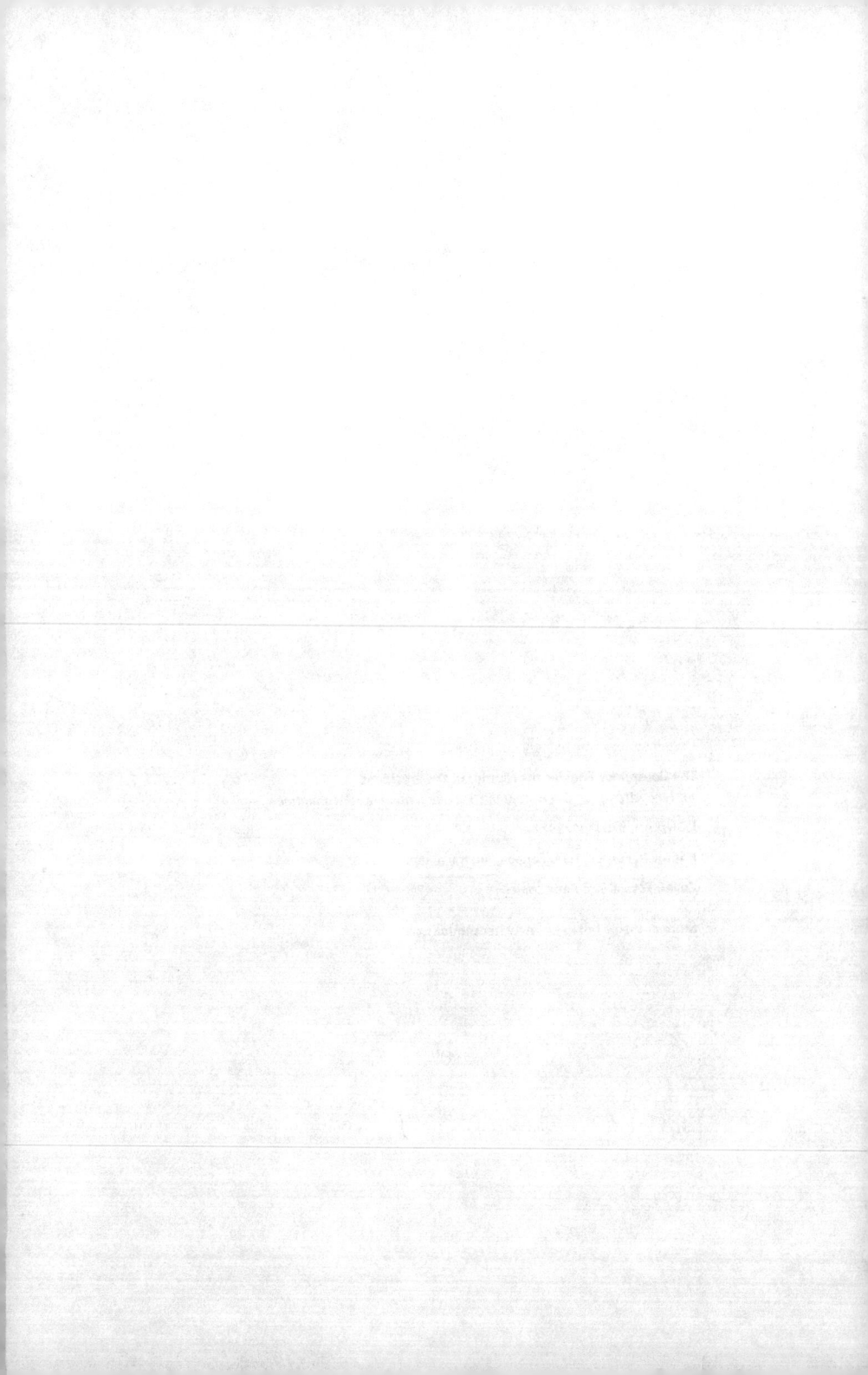

United States Army Military Commission

The Conspiracy Trial for the Murder of the President
And the Attempt to Overthrow the Government by the Assassination...

ISBN/EAN: 9783744729741

Printed in Europe, USA, Canada, Australia, Japan

Cover: Foto ©Suzi / pixelio.de

More available books at **www.hansebooks.com**

THE

CONSPIRACY TRIAL

FOR THE MURDER OF

THE PRESIDENT,

AND THE ATTEMPT TO OVERTHROW THE GOVERNMENT BY THE ASSASSINATION OF ITS PRINCIPAL OFFICERS.

EDITED, WITH AN INTRODUCTION,

BY BEN: PERLEY POORE.

———◆———

BOSTON:

J. E. TILTON AND COMPANY.

1865.

STEREOTYPED BY C. J. PETERS AND SON,

13, Washington Street, Boston.

PRESS OF GEO. C. RAND & AVERY.

THE TRIAL.

THE assassination of ABRAHAM LINCOLN was a military crime. While actually in command of the national forces, he was killed in a city which was his headquarters, strongly fortified and garrisoned, with a military governor, and a provost-marshal whose patrols were abroad day and night arresting all persons found violating the "rules and articles of war." Not only was the murdered commander-in-chief, to use the words of the Constitution, "*in actual service in time of war,*" but it was a time of "*public danger,*" in which the assassins were constitutionally excluded from any right to a trial in the civil courts. Peace had not then been conquered; there was a powerful enemy in arms, to whom "aid and comfort" could be given; the leader of the Rebellion was still at large; many loyal men were becoming disheartened by the conscription, and by the prolonged expenditure of blood and treasure; and there are good reasons for believing that the rebel authorities, having traversed all the stages of crime, confidently hoped by this assassination to inaugurate anarchy at the North, and to thus prepare the way for a dictator. Fortunately for the cause of freedom throughout the world, the Government of the United States proved its sovereign strength by not even halting in its onward march, as the assassins struck down its head, and cruelly assaulted one of its principal officers. Majestically moving on in accordance with the provisions of the Constitution, the Government at once asserted its supreme power by providing for the apprehension and the trial of those who had conspired to commit the Great Crime, so infamous in name, and so impotent in effect.

Before the martyr-president had ceased to live, Mr. Secretary Stanton directed a search for the recognized assassin, and an investigation into the circumstances connected with the perpetration of

3

the bloody deed. The next day, in a letter to the Hon. Charles Francis Adams, Mr. Stanton said, " The murderer of the President has been discovered, and evidence obtained that these horrible crimes were committed in execution of a conspiracy deliberately planned and set on foot by rebels, under pretence of avenging the South and aiding the rebel cause." Subsequently the Secretary of War announced, in an official bulletin, that all persons who had harbored or secreted Booth, Atzerodt, or Herold, or who had aided or assisted their escape, should be "subject to trial before a military commission ; and the punishment is death." The bulletin concluded by saying, " Let the stain of innocent blood be removed from the land by the arrest and punishment of the murderers ! All good citizens are exhorted to aid public justice on this occasion. Every man should consider his own innocence charged with this solemn duty, and rest neither night nor day till it is accomplished."

Secretary Stanton faithfully performed his share of this work ; and he was ably seconded by the Provost Marshal of the War Department, Colonel L. C. Baker. The discovery by Fouché of the celebrated French conspiracy, headed by Pichegru, for the assassination of the first Emperor Napoleon, has been regarded as the greatest triumph of detective-police skill on record ; but it will be eclipsed by Colonel Baker's report of his operations. It was not long after the commission of the Great Crime before he was thoroughly conversant with the associations and habits of the chief actor's acquaintances in Washington, Baltimore, Montreal, and other cities. Some were promptly arrested ; a careful espionage was established over others ; confidential agents were sent far and wide, some of them in disguise ; the magnetic telegraph and the photographer's camera were called into the service for the transmission of intelligence, and for the multiplication of portraits for identification ; and it was not long before the proofs of a conspiracy, organized at Richmond and perfected in Canada, were overwhelming. The finger of an avenging Providence appears to have tracked the principal conspirators, and to have furnished abundant proofs that the rebel leaders — already known to be guilty of perjury, treason, theft, cruelty to Union prisoners, desecration of the Union dead, incendiarism afloat and ashore, the propagation of deadly diseases,

and other diabolical crimes — had crowned their detestable labors
with assassination, base in its cowardice, dark in its accomplishment,
and effectual for the perpetration of its terrible purpose.

President Johnson, after having considered the reports of the
officials charged with the preliminary examinations of the testimony,
and obtained the opinion of Attorney-General Speed on the manner
in which those of the suspected conspirators who had been arrested
should be tried, issued the following special order: —

EXECUTIVE CHAMBER,
Washington City, May 1. 1865.

Whereas the Attorney-General of the United States hath given
his opinion —

"That the persons implicated in the murder of the late President,
Abraham Lincoln, and the attempted assassination of the Hon.
William H. Seward, Secretary of State, and in an alleged con-
spiracy to assassinate other officers of the Federal Government at
Washington City, and their aiders and abettors, are subject to the
jurisdiction of and legally triable before a Military Commission:"

It is ordered, 1st, That the Assistant Adjutant-General detail
nine competent military officers to serve as a Commission for the
trial of said parties, and that the Judge Advocate General proceed
to prefer charges against said parties for their alleged offences, and
bring them to trial before said Military Commission; that said trial
or trials be conducted by the said Judge Advocate General, as
recorder thereof, in person, aided by such assistant or special
judge advocates as he may designate; and that said trials be conducted with all diligence consistent with the ends of justice; the
said Commission to sit without regard to hours.

2d, That Brevet Major-General Hartranft be assigned to duty
as special Provost Marshal General for the purposes of said trial
and attendance upon said Commission and the execution of its
mandates.

3d, That the said Commission establish such order, or rules of
proceeding, as may avoid unnecessary delay, and conduce to the
ends of public justice.

ANDREW JOHNSON.

Judge Advocate General Holt is a loyal Kentuckian, who has rendered signal political services to the Union since the commencement of the Rebellion. After having acted as Judge Advocate at the trial of General Fitz John Porter, he was invited to organize the "Bureau of Military Justice," established by Act of Congress, and was commissioned as Judge Advocate General, a position for which he is eminently fitted. Familiar in a marked degree with military law, with a quick and keen intellect, unwearied industry, and an impressive style of oratory, General Holt is an inflexibly upright administrator of justice; yet the humanities have a large place in his heart. He is tall, with an imposing presence, gray hair, and a manner which not only imposes respect, but wins admiration.

Hon. John A. Bingham, a member of the House of Representatives, from Ohio, has had some experience as a Judge Advocate, and enjoys a high reputation as a criminal lawyer. While Judge Holt is calm and contemplative, Judge Bingham is energetic and impulsive; watching the movements of opposing counsel, unravelling the tangled skeins of testimony, and eviscerating truth from masses of conflicting evidence.

Colonel H. L. Burnett, the second Assistant Judge Advocate, is a young officer, who prepared and conducted the trial for treason at Indianapolis, which disclosed the plans for establishing a Northwestern Confederacy; and also the trial of the Chicago conspirators against the Union. The first-named case occupied in its trial three months and two days; and the latter, four months. The great ability displayed by Colonel Burnett in the prosecution of these cases commended him to Mr. Secretary Stanton, by whose order he was summoned here, and specially assigned to duty in connection with Judge Holt. He was the executive officer, so to speak, of the trial; seeing that the witnesses were in readiness, and infusing into the proceedings order, industry, and promptness.

Before the Commission assembled, President Johnson, after consultation with his Cabinet, issued the following proclamation, offering large rewards for five named individuals reported to him as implicated in the awful crime of assassination and attempted murder. This proclamation forms a part of the history of the trial, as much evidence was introduced to verify its assertion.

BY THE PRESIDENT OF THE UNITED STATES OF AMERICA.

A PROCLAMATION.

Whereas it appears, from evidence in the Bureau of Military Justice, that the atrocious murder of the late President, ABRAHAM LINCOLN, and the attempted assassination of the Honorable WILLIAM H. SEWARD, Secretary of State, were incited, concerted, and procured by and between JEFFERSON DAVIS, late of Richmond, Va., and JACOB THOMPSON, CLEMENT C. CLAY, BEVERLY TUCKER, GEORGE N. SAUNDERS. WILLIAM C. CLEARY, and other rebels and traitors against the Government of the United States, harbored in Canada : —

Now, therefore, to the end that justice may be done, I, ANDREW JOHNSON, President of the United States, do offer and promise for the arrest of said persons, or either of them, within the limits of the United States, so that they can be brought to trial, the following rewards : —

One hundred thousand dollars for the arrest of JEFFERSON DAVIS.

Twenty-five thousand dollars for the arrest of CLEMENT C. CLAY.

Twenty-five thousand dollars for the arrest of JACOB THOMPSON, late of Mississippi.

Twenty-five thousand dollars for the arrest of GEO. N. SAUNDERS.

Twenty-five thousand dollars for the arrest of BEVERLY TUCKER.

Ten thousand dollars for the arrest of WILLIAM C. CLEARY, late clerk of CLEMENT C. CLAY.

The Provost Marshal General of the United States is directed to cause a description of said persons, with notice of the above rewards, to be published.

In testimony whereof, I have hereunto set my hand, and caused the seal of the United States to be affixed.

Done at the city of Washington, this second day of May, in the year of our Lord one thousand eight hundred and sixty-five, and of the independence of the United States of America the eighty-ninth.

[L. S.]

ANDREW JOHNSON.

By the President :

W. HUNTER, Acting Secretary of State.

The persons arrested as conspirators were at first confined on board of the monitors, anchored off the Washington Navy Yard; whence they were removed to the building originally used as the Penitentiary of the District of Columbia, now within the limits of the United-States Arsenal, on Greenleaf's Point. This is at the junction of the Potomac and the Anacostia, or Eastern Branch; and, as the channels of the two rivers run near the shores, the tract of land was purchased, when Washington was first laid out as a metropolis, by a Mr. Greenleaf. He hoped that it would become the business portion of the future city, which General Washington expected would be the tide-water depot of the Great West, by the improvement of the Potomac River as a channel of transmontane transportation. Mr. Greenleaf's "great expectations" were not realized; and he became so involved, that several houses which he erected and nearly completed actually fell gradually to pieces, and were carried away for fire-wood. The name of "Greenleaf's Point," however, remains.

The extremity of the point has been used as a United-States arsenal since the last war with Great Britain. When the British troops occupied the metropolis, the retreating Americans undertook to conceal a large quantity of powder in a dry well, and then burned the buildings. The next day, a detachment of two hundred British grenadiers, with several officers, was sent by General Ross to complete the work of destruction; and, by some accident, a lighted port-fire was thrown into the dry well which contained the powder. An explosion took place, killing and wounding many of the invaders, and precipitating the retreat from the capital, as the British thought that a mine had been purposely fired.

Soon afterwards, Colonel Bomford, of the engineer-corps, commenced the erection of the present substantial arsenal-buildings, which include a museum of weapons and of artillery, many of them trophies of the Revolutionary, English, and Mexican wars. The workshops have gradually been increased; and, since the breaking-out of the war for the suppression of the Rebellion, it has been an important depot for field-artillery, muskets, and ammunition.

The old Penitentiary was erected in 1836, but has since been enlarged and improved. It is on the northern side of the old

Arsenal, toward Pennsylvania Avenue, from which it is over a mile distant; Four and a Half Street running directly from the City Hall and Court House, across the avenue, down to the old Penitentiary gate. At the breaking-out of the Rebellion, however, it was found imperatively necessary to enlarge the arsenal-grounds; and their limits were extended quite a distance toward Pennsylvania Avenue, including the Penitentiary. The convicts were taken to Albany, N.Y., where they were incarcerated; and all adult criminals who have subsequently been convicted have also been sent here. Juvenile offenders are sentenced to confinement in the House of Refuge at Baltimore.

Brevet Major-General Hartranft, the special provost-marshal detailed for the trial, had placed under his orders a brigade of volunteers, and a detachment of the Veteran Reserve Corps. Strong guards were so posted as to render the rescue or escape of the prisoners impossible; and there was in addition a detective force who exercised a watchful surveillance. Each prisoner was manacled, and confined in a separate cell, attended by a guard; and the heads of the male prisoners were enveloped in mufflers, as one of them, while on board of the monitor, had endeavored to commit suicide by dashing out his brains.

A large room in the north-east corner of the third story of the old Penitentiary, near the cells in which the prisoners were confined, was fitted up for the trial. It is about thirty by forty-five feet square, with a ceiling about eleven feet high, supported by three wooden pillars. Four windows, with heavy iron gratings, afforded tolerable ventilation; and there are two ante-rooms for the accommodation of the court and of the witnesses. The room was whitewashed and painted for the occasion, a prisoner's dock was constructed along the western side, the floor was covered with cocoa-nut matting, and the tables and chairs were new. Gas was introduced, in case the court should protract its sittings until after dark.

WEDNESDAY, May 10.

The Commission, convened by Special Order No. 216, met at ten o'clock, A.M., consisting of the following detail: —

Major-General David Hunter, U. S. V.

Major-General Lew Wallace, U. S. V.

Brevet Major-General August V. Kautz, U. S. V.

Brigadier-General Alvin P. Howe, U. S. V.

Brigadier-General Robert S. Foster, U. S. V.

Brevet Brigadier-General James A. Ekin, U. S. V.

Brigadier-General T. M. Harris, U. S. V.

Brevet Colonel C. H. Tompkins, U. S. A.

Lieutenant-Colonel David R. Clendenin, Eighth Illinois Cavalry.

Brigadier-General Joseph Holt, Judge Advocate and Recorder, assisted by Judge Advocates Burnett and Bingham.

The members of the Court, who were all in full uniform, took their seats around a large table parallel with the north side of the room; General Hunter, the President, sitting at the eastern end. General Hunter has had much experience as a member of courts-martial, and is an admirable presiding officer, giving the most careful attention to every word spoken by the witnesses; and, when the Judge Advocate and the prisoner's counsel differ on any question, the General has the uncommon faculty of holding his judgment in perfect abeyance until he has heard both sides, and then forming it with inflexible firmness. At the right of General Hunter sit Generals Wallace and Ekin, with Colonel Tompkins; at his left sit Generals Kautz, Foster, Harris, and Howe, with Colonel Clendenin.

At the foot of the table at which the Court sat was another, occupied by Judge Advocate General Holt, with his assistants, Hon. Mr. Bingham and Colonel Burnett. On this table, as the trial progressed, were deposited the weapons identified by witnesses, the machine used by the Rebel War Department as a key to communications written in cipher, the articles found on the dead assassin's person, with a mass of law-books, notes of testimony, &c.

In the centre of the room was a stand for witnesses, who were required to face the Court while being examined; although many of them would persist in turning towards the prisoners' counsel while undergoing cross-examination, provoking sharp reprimands from General Hunter.

Behind the witness-stand, and parallel with the southern side of the room, was a long table, which was occupied by reporters and correspondents during the public sessions of the Court. At the foot of this table sat the counsel for the prisoners after they had been introduced.

The prisoner's "dock" was a platform raised about one foot from the floor, and about four feet broad, with a strong railing in front of it. Along this "dock" sat the prisoners. Mrs. Surratt had the left-hand corner to herself; a passage-way to the door leading to the cells intervening between her and the seven male prisoners, who sat sandwiched with six soldiers who wore the light-blue uniform of the Veteran Reserve Corps. Dr. Mudd wore hand-cuffs connected with chains; but the "bracelets" of the other male prisoners were joined by wide bars of iron ten inches long, which kept their hands apart. All of the prisoners, including Mrs. Surratt, wore anklets connected by short chains, which hamper their walk; and heavy iron balls were also attached by chains to the limbs of Payne and Atzerodt, attendants carrying them as they go to and from their cells. As the prisoners entered and left the room, their fetters clanking at every step, they formed an impressive procession. As seen by the Court and the gentlemen of the press, they sat in the following order : —

Samuel Arnold, a young Baltimorean, had a rather intelligent face, with curly brown hair and restless dark eyes. He was a schoolmate of the President's assassin; and, at the breaking-out of the Rebellion, he joined the rebel army. An original conspirator, his courage failed him; and he went some weeks before the assassination to Fortress Monroe, where he was clerk to a sutler when arrested.

Samuel A. Mudd, M.D., was the most inoffensive and decent in appearance of all the prisoners. He was about forty years of age, rather tall, and quite thin, with sharp features, a high bald forehead, astute blue eyes, compressed pale lips, and sandy hair, whiskers, and mustache. He took a deep interest in the testimony, often prompting his counsel during the cross-examinations.

Edward Spangler was a middle-aged man, with a large, unintelligent-looking face, evidently swollen by an intemperate use of ardent spirits, a low forehead, anxious-looking gray eyes, and brown hair. He was born in the interior of Pennsylvania, where he has respectable connections; and, after having been employed at Ford's Theatre in Baltimore as a stage-carpenter, came to Washington with Mr. Ford when he built the house in which Mr. Lincoln was assassinated. Doleful as Spangler looked when in Court, the guards declared that he was the most loquacious and jovial of the prisoners when in his cell.

Michael O'Laughlin, like Arnold, was a Baltimore friend of the principal assassin, and at one time a soldier in the rebel army. He was a rather small, delicate-looking man, with rather pleasing features, uneasy black eyes, bushy black hair, a heavy black mustache and imperial, and a most anxious expression of countenance, shaded by a sad, remorseful look.

George B. Atzerodt was a type of those Teutonic Dugald Dalgettys who have taken an active part in the war for the suppression of the Rebellion, — sometimes on one side, and sometimes on the other, as bounties, or chances to pillage, were presented. He was born in Germany, but was raised and lived among the " poor white trash " in Charles County, Md.; working as a blacksmith until tho war broke out, when he became a blockade-runner. He was a short, thick-set, round-shouldered, brawny-armed man, with a stupid expression, high cheek-bones, a sallow complexion, small grayish-blue eyes, tangled light-brown hair, and straggling sandy whiskers and mustache. He apparently manifested a stoical indifference to what was going on in the Court, although an occasional cat-like glance would reveal his anxiety concerning himself. Evidently crafty, cowardly, and mercenary, his own safety was evidently the all-absorbing subject of his thoughts.

Lewis Payne was the observed of all observers, as he sat motionless and imperturbed, defiantly returning each gaze at his remarkable face and person. He was very tall, with an athletic, gladiatorial frame ; the tight knit shirt which was his only upper garment disclosing the massive robustness of animal manhood in its most stalwart type. Neither intellect nor intelligence was discernible in his unflinching dark gray eyes, low forehead, massive jaws, compressed full lips, small nose with large nostrils, and stolid, remorseless expression. His dark hair hung over his forehead, his face was beardless, and his hands were not those of a man who had been accustomed to labor. Report said that ho was a Kentuckian by birth, and one of a family of notorious desperadoes ; one of his brothers having been such a depraved criminal, that the rebels hung him. But, for weeks after the trial commenced, all that was certainly known of him was, that he was the ruffian who made the ferocious series of assaults on Secretary Seward and his family.

David E. Herold was a doltish, insignificant-looking young man, not much over one and twenty years of age, with a slender frame, and irresolute, cowardly appearance. He had a narrow forehead, a somewhat Israelitish nose, small dark hazel eyes, thick black hair, and an incipient mustache which occupied much of his attention. Few would imagine that any villain would select such a contemptible-looking fellow as an accomplice.

Mrs. Mary E. Surratt, who was a belle in her youth, has borne her five and forty years or more bravely ; and, when she raised her veil in court that some witness might identify her, she exposed rather pleasing features, with dark gray eyes and brown hair. While some of the spectators could see upon her face a haunting revelation of some tragic sorrow resembling that which Guido's art has stamped upon the features of Beatrice Cenci, others declared that she was evidently the devoted mother of an attached family, of pious sentiments, and evidently deserving the recommendations so lavishly given of her by her religious advisers. Whether she was guilty or innocent, it was easy to perceive that she desired to make a favorable impression upon the court, and to inspire feelings of pity. Those who had hunted up her antecedents ascertained that she received a good education, and was married to Surratt about the year 1835 ; the young couple settling on a farm near Washington, which he had inherited. After they had lived there, their house was set on fire by one of their slaves, who seemed to have been infuriated by the cruel treatment to which he had been subjected. Surratt afterwards made some money as a contractor on a Virginia railroad, and, on his return to Maryland, purchased the place afterwards known as Surratt's, where he established a tavern, and was appointed postmaster. He sympathized with secession ; and, before his death, one of his sons, Isaac, went South, and joined the rebel army. After Surratt's death, his widow removed to Washington, where she opened a boarding-house ;

her younger son, John, spending his time in idleness. Her other child, an intelligent young lady, was one of her mother's witnesses.

President Johnson's special order convening the Commission having been read in the hearing of the prisoners, they were asked if they had any objection to any member of the Commission; to which they all severally replied, they had not.

The Commission, the Judge Advocate General and his associates, and the reporters, having been duly sworn, the prisoners — Samuel Arnold, Samuel A. Mudd, Edward Spangler, Michael O'Laughlin, George B. Atzerodt, Lewis Payne, David E. Herold, and Mary E. Surratt — were arraigned on the following charges and specifications.

CHARGE I. — For maliciously, unlawfully, and traitorously, and in aid of the existing armed Rebellion against the United States of America, on or before the 6th day of March, A.D. 1865, combining, confederating, and conspiring, together with one John H. Surratt, John Wilkes Booth, Jefferson Davis, George N. Sanders, Beverly Tucker, Jacob Thompson, William C. Cleary, Clement C. Clay, George Harper, George Young, and others unknown, to kill and murder, within the Military Department of Washington, and within the fortified and intrenched lines thereof, Abraham Lincoln, late, and at the time of said combining, confederating, and conspiring, President of the United States of America, and Commander-in-Chief of the army and navy thereof; Andrew Johnson, then Vice-President of the United States aforesaid; William H. Seward, Secretary of State of the United States aforesaid, and Ulysses S. Grant, Lieutenant-General of the army of the United States aforesaid, then in command of the armies of the United States under the direction of the said Abraham Lincoln; and in pursuance of and in prosecuting said malicious, unlawful, and traitorous conspiracy aforesaid, and in aid of said Rebellion, afterwards, — to wit, on the 14th day of April, A.D. 1865, — within the Military Department of Washington aforesaid, and within the fortified and intrenched lines of the said Military Department, together with said John Wilkes Booth and John H. Surratt, maliciously, unlawfully, and traitorously assaulting, with intent to kill and murder, the said William H. Seward, then Secretary of State of the United States as aforesaid, and lying in wait with intent maliciously, unlawfully, and traitorously to kill and murder the said Andrew Johnson, then being Vice-President of the United States, and the said Ulysses S. Grant, then being Lieutenant-General, and in command of the armies of the United States as aforesaid.

Specification 1. — In this, that they, the said David E. Herold, Edward Spangler, Lewis Payne, John H. Surratt, Michael O'Laughlin, Samuel Arnold, Mary E. Surratt, George A. Atzerodt, and Samuel A. Mudd, incited and encouraged thereunto by Jefferson Davis, George N. Sanders, Beverly Tucker, Jacob Thompson, William C. Cleary, Clement C. Clay, George Harper, George Young, and others, unknown, citizens of the United States aforesaid, and who were then engaged in armed rebellion against the United States of America, within the limits thereof, did, in aid of said armed rebellion, on or before the 6th day of March, A.D. 1865, and on divers days and times between that day and the 15th day of April, A.D. 1865, combine, confederate, and conspire together at Washington City, within the Military Department of Washington, and within the intrenched fortifications and military lines of the said United States, there being, unlawfully, and maliciously, and traitorously to kill and murder Abraham Lincoln, then President of the United States aforesaid, and Commander-in-Chief of the army and navy thereof; and unlawfully, maliciously, and traitorously to kill and murder Andrew Johnson, then Vice-President of the said United States, upon whom, on the death of said Abraham Lincoln, after the 4th day of March, A.D. 1865, the office of President of the said United States, and Commander-in-Chief of the army and navy thereof, would devolve; and to unlawfully, maliciously, and traitorously kill and murder Ulysses S. Grant, then Lieutenant-General, and under the direction of the said Abraham Lincoln, in command of the armies of the United States aforesaid; and unlawfully, maliciously, and traitorously to kill and murder William H. Seward, then Secretary of State of the United States aforesaid, whose duty it was by law, upon the death of said President and Vice-President of the United States aforesaid, to cause an election to be held for electors of President of the United States, — the conspirators aforesaid designing and intending by the killing and murder of the said Abraham Lincoln, Andrew Johnson, Ulysses S. Grant, and William

H. Seward, as aforesaid, to deprive the army and navy of the said United States of a constitutional commander-in-chief, and to deprive the armies of the United States of their lawful commander, and to prevent a lawful election of President and Vice-President of the United States aforesaid, and by the means aforesaid to aid and comfort the insurgents engaged in armed rebellion against the said United States as aforesaid, and thereby to aid in the subversion and overthrow of the Constitution and laws of the said United States ; and being so combined, confederated, and conspiring together in the prosecution of said unlawful and traitorous conspiracy, on the night of the 14th day of April, A.D. 1865, at the hour of about ten o'clock and fifteen minutes P.M., at Ford's Theatre, on Tenth Street, in the city of Washington, and within the Military Department and military lines aforesaid, John Wilkes Booth, one of the conspirators aforesaid, in pursuance of said unlawful and traitorous conspiracy, did, then and there, unlawfully, maliciously, and traitorously, and with intent to kill and murder the said Abraham Lincoln, discharge a pistol then held in the hands of him, the said Booth, the same being then loaded with powder and a leaden ball, against and upon the left and posterior side of the head of the said Abraham Lincoln ; and did thereby, then and there, inflict upon him, the said Abraham Lincoln, then President of the said United States, and Commander-in-Chief of the army and navy thereof, a mortal wound, whereof afterwards, to wit, on the 15th day of April, A.D. 1865, at Washington City aforesaid, the said Abraham Lincoln died ; and thereby, then and there, and in pursuance of said conspiracy, the said defendants, and the said John Wilkes Booth, did, unlawfully, traitorously, and maliciously, and with the intent to aid the Rebellion as aforesaid, kill and murder the said Abraham Lincoln, President of the United States as aforesaid.

And in further prosecution of the unlawful and traitorous conspiracy aforesaid, and of the murderous and traitorous intent of said conspiracy, the said Edward Spangler, on the 14th day of April, A.D. 1865, at about the same hour of that day, as aforesaid, in this said Military Department, and the military lines aforesaid, did aid and assist the said John Wilkes Booth to obtain entrance to the box in said theatre, in which said Abraham Lincoln was sitting at the time he was assaulted and shot, as aforesaid, by John Wilkes Booth ; and also did then and there aid said Booth in barring and obstructing the door of the box of the theatre, so as to hinder and prevent any assistance to or rescue of the said Abraham Lincoln against the murderous assault of the said John Wilkes Booth, and did aid and abet him in making his escape after the said Abraham Lincoln had been murdered in manner aforesaid.

And in further prosecution of said unlawful, murderous, and traitorous conspiracy, and in pursuance thereof, and with the intent as aforesaid, the said David E. Herold did, on the night of the 14th of April, A.D. 1865, within the Military Department and military lines aforesaid, aid, abet, and assist the said John Wilkes Booth in the killing and murder of the said Abraham Lincoln, and did then and there aid and abet and assist him, the said John Wilkes Booth, in attempting to escape through the military lines aforesaid, and did accompany and assist the said John Wilkes Booth in attempting to conceal himself and escape from justice, after killing and murdering said Abraham Lincoln as aforesaid.

And in further prosecution of said unlawful and traitorous conspiracy, and of the intent thereof as aforesaid, the said Lewis Payne did, on the same night of the 14th day of April, A.D. 1865, about the same hour of ten o'clock fifteen minutes P.M., at the city of Washington, and within the Military Department and the military lines aforesaid, unlawfully and maliciously make an assault upon the said William H. Seward, Secretary of State, as aforesaid, in the dwelling-house and bed-chamber of him, the said William H. Seward ; and the said Payne did then and there, with a large knife held in his hand, unlawfully, traitorously, and in pursuance of said conspiracy, strike, stab, cut, and attempt to kill and murder the said William H. Seward, and did thereby, then and there, and with the intent aforesaid, with said knife, inflict upon the face and throat of the said William H. Seward divers grievous wounds.   And the said Lewis Payne, in further prosecution of said conspiracy, at the same time and place last aforesaid, did attempt with the knife aforesaid, and a pistol held in his hand, to kill and murder Frederick W. Seward, Augustus H. Seward, Emrick W. Hansell, and George F. Robinson, who were then striving to protect and rescue the said

2*

William II. Seward from murder by the said Lewis Payne ; and did then and there, with the said knife and pistol held in his hands, inflict upon the head of said Frederick W. Seward, and upon the persons of said Augustus II Seward, Emrick W. Hansell, and George F. Robinson, divers grievous and dangerous wounds, with intent then and there to kill and murder the said Frederick W. Seward, Augustus II. Seward, Emrick W. Hansell, and George F. Robinson.

And in further prosecution of the said conspiracy and its traitorous and murderous designs, the said George A. Atzerodt did, on the night of the 14th of April, A.D. 1865, and about the same hour of the night aforesaid, within the Military Department and military lines aforesaid, lie in wait for Andrew Johnson, then Vice-President of the United States aforesaid, with the intent unlawfully and maliciously to kill and murder him, the said Andrew Johnson.

And in further prosecution of the conspiracy aforesaid, and of its murderous designs and treasonable purposes aforesaid, on the nights of the 13th and 14th of April, A.D. 1865, at Washington City, and within the Military Department and military lines aforesaid, the said Michael O'Laughlin did then and there lie in wait for Ulysses S. Grant, then Lieutenant-General and Commander of the armies of the United States aforesaid, with intent then and there to kill and murder the said Ulysses S. Grant.

And, in further prosecution of said conspiracy, the said Samuel Arnold did, within the military lines aforesaid, on or before the 6th day of March, A.D. 1865, combine, conspire with, and aid, counsel, abet, comfort, and support, the said John Wilkes Booth, Lewis Payne, George A. Atzerodt, Michael O'Laughlin, and their confederates in said unlawful, murderous, and traitorous conspiracy, and in the execution thereof as aforesaid.

And, in further prosecution of the said conspiracy, Mary E. Surratt did at Washington City, and within the Military Department and military lines aforesaid, on or before the 6th day of March, A.D. 1865, and on divers other days and times between that day and the 20th day of April, A.D. 1865, receive, entertain, harbor and conceal, aid and assist, the said John Wilkes Booth, David E. Herold, Lewis Payne, John II. Surratt, Michael O'Laughlin, George A. Atzerodt, Samuel Arnold, and their confederates, with knowledge of the murderous and traitorous conspiracy aforesaid, and with intent to aid, abet, and assist them in the execution thereof, and in escaping from justice after the murder of the said Abraham Lincoln as aforesaid.

And, in further prosecution of said conspiracy, the said Samuel A. Mudd did, at Washington City, and within the Military Department and military lines aforesaid, on or before the 6th day of March, A.D. 1865, and on divers other days and times between that day and the 20th day of April, A.D. 1865, advise, encourage, receive, entertain, harbor and conceal, aid and assist, the said John Wilkes Booth, David E. Herold, Lewis Payne, John H. Surratt, Michael O'Laughlin, George A. Atzerodt, Mary E. Surratt, and Samuel Arnold, and their confederates aforesaid, with knowledge of the murderous and traitorous conspiracy aforesaid, and with intent to aid, abet, and assist them in the execution thereof, and in escaping from justice after the murder of the said Abraham Lincoln, in pursuance of said conspiracy in manner aforesaid.

By order of the President of the United States.

J. HOLT,
Judge Advocate General.

Each of the prisoners pleaded " Not guilty " to the charges and specifications. They were then permitted to designate such counsel as they desired to employ.

Before adjourning, the Commission agreed upon the rules by which it would be governed. It was determined on to exclude all persons except those officially engaged in the trials, and to swear them to secrecy. The testimony, when written out by the phonographers, was to be placed in the hands of the Judge Advocate General, who was to designate such portions of it as he might think could be published without injury to the interests of the Government. This action of secrecy was based upon the fact that the developments of the trial would implicate many parties not under arrest, who might escape should publicity be given to the proceedings. It was also asserted that several witnesses were in great trepidation, fearing that they might be assassinated should their testimony be made public.

Several of the gentlemen designated by the prisoners as their counsel appeared, and were permitted to converse with them. Hon. Reverdy Johnson, who had been solicited to appear in behalf of Mrs. Surratt, was not present; but she conferred with Mr. Frederic A. Aiken, a native of Massachusetts, who was admitted to the bar in Vermont, and afterwards came to Washington to enter into practice. Mr. Thomas Ewing, jun., appeared as counsel for Arnold and Dr. Mudd, and was the leading spirit of the defence. He is a tall, fine-looking gentleman, of pleasing address, and well versed in the law. Mr. W. E. Doster appeared for Payne and Atzerodt, Mr. Frederic Stone for Dr. Mudd, and Mr. Walter E. Cox for O'Laughlin. The counsel were furnished with printed copies of the charges and specifications, which they pledged themselves to regard as confidential.

FRIDAY, May 12.

The session of the Commission was not public; but subsequently the injunction of secrecy was removed from the following portions of the evidence taken.

HENRY VAN STEINACKER,

a witness called for the prosecution, being duly sworn, testified as follows: —

By Judge Advocate HOLT:

Q. Have you or not for several years been in the military service of the so-called Confederate States?

A. Yes, sir: I have been.

Q. In what capacity?

A. I was employed in the Topographical Department, ranking as engineer-officer, with the pay of an engineer-officer.

Q. On whose staff?

A. The staff of General Edward Johnson.

Q. Were you or not in the State of Virginia in the summer of 1863? and at what point?

A. When we came back from Pennsylvania, after the battle of

Gettysburg, I was ordered with another engineer-lieutenant, who was very sick, to convey him to his home at Staunton, in the Valley of Virginia; and from there I took my way back to find the army again; and near Harrisonburg, twenty-five miles from Staunton, at Swift Run Gap, I was overtaken by three citizens, with whom I got better acquainted after having ridden a while with them; and I found them out to belong to Maryland. The name of one was Booth, and the other one's name was Shepherd.

Q. Do you remember the features of Booth?

A. I do not remember the features of all of them.

Q. Look at that photograph. [Handing to the witness a photograph of J. Wilkes Booth.]

A. There is a resemblance; but the face was fuller.

Q. You think it is the same person, but he had a fuller face than this?

A. I believe it is.

Q. Did you learn at that time that it was John Wilkes Booth, the actor?

A. I heard the other gentlemen call him Booth. I thought first it was a nickname; but afterwards I found out that it was Booth.

Q. How far did you ride with those persons?

A. We staid at the tavern at the foot of the mountain until the next day. There I got better acquainted with them.

Q. How long were you together? How many hours do you suppose?

A. Eighteen or twenty hours.

Q. Did you have any free conversations in regard to public affairs while you were with him?

A. Yes, sir.

Q. Will you state what Booth said to you in regard to any contemplated purpose of attack upon the President of the United States? State all that he said.

A. I was asked by Booth, and by those others too, what I thought of the probable success of the Confederacy; and I told them, that, after such a chase as we had then got from Gettysburg, I believed it looked rather *gloomy*. And then Booth told me, "That

is nonsense : if we only act our part right, the Confederacy will
gain their independence ; old Abe Lincoln must go up the spout,
and the Confederacy will gain their independence anyhow." That
was the expression at the time.

Q. What did you understand by the expression, he "must go
up the spout," from all that Booth said ?

A. It was a common expression, meaning he must be killed.
That I understood always.

Q. Did he state under what circumstances that would become
necessary ?

A. He said so soon as the Confederacy was near giving out, so
soon as they were nearly whipped, that must be done ; that would
be the final resource to gain the independence of the Confederacy.

Q. Did the citizens who were with him engage in conversation ?

A. Yes, sir.

Q. Did they seem to assent to his sentiments ?

A. Certainly.

Q. Did not Booth know that you were a Confederate soldier ?

A. Yes, sir. They asked, when they overtook me on the road,
where I was going to. I told them I belonged to General Edward
Johnson's staff, and was going to the army, coming from Staunton.

Q. At what point did you arrive together ?

A. I do not know the name of the place : it is near the foot of
the Swift Run Gap.

Q. Did you meet there a number of Confederate officers — I
speak of the end of your ride — with the Stonewall Brigade ?

A. Yes, sir. That was about three or four days afterwards.
They went from me the next day. My horse could not keep up
with the other horses : they were splendidly mounted, and my
horse was nearly broken down ; so they went on. Three or four
days afterwards, I was called to some of the regimental camps, and
told that some strangers, friends of mine, wanted to see me. I
did not know who it was. When I came to camp, I found those
three citizens, and was introduced by Captain Randolph personally,
formally to Booth and Stephens.

Q. Was that the Stonewall Brigade ?

A. It was the camp of the Second Virginia Regiment.

Q. Do you or do you not know whether there was a secret meeting of rebel officers on that occasion?

A. That evening there was a secret meeting, where I was not admitted.

Q. Did they state to you the purpose of that meeting, and what conclusion they reached?

A. Some officer afterwards, who was about the meeting, stated to me what was the purpose of it.

Q. Was Booth in that meeting?

A. I believe so. They were all in together.

Q. What did he state to you was the determination and purpose of that meeting?

A. The purpose of the meeting was, as I was informed afterwards, to send certain officers on detached service to Canada and the borders, and to deliver prisoners, to lay Northern cities in ashes, and finally to get after the members of the Cabinet, and kill the President. That was the main purpose. I heard that more than a thousand times, but never so much as at the time when I was informed it was the purpose of the meeting. I always considered it common braggadocio before.

Q. What was the name of the officer who gave you this account of the proceedings of the meeting?

A. Lieutenant Cockerill.

Q. To what portion of the service did he belong, do you know?

A. To the Second Virginia Regiment, I believe, and the same company that Captain Beall belonged to, — the captain who was executed at Governor's Island.

Q. Was any thing said as to what part Captain Beall — the one afterwards executed — was to play in these movements at the North?

A. Cockerill told me Beall was on detached service, and we would hear of him.

Q. Cockerill was a member of that meeting, I understood you to say?

A. Yes, sir.

Q. Did you, while there, see Booth and Cockerill associated together?

A. I did not see them particularly. I saw them all in a crowd together.

Q. Was Booth associating with all the officers?

A. He was associating with a great many of them.

Q. Did you know of any other secret association or meeting, having similar objects, at any time in the service with which you have been connected?

A. I heard of the existence of secret orders for certain purposes to assist the Confederacy. I heard one name very frequently called, the name of one order, the "Golden Circle;" and several times I heard the name of the "Sons of Liberty."

Q. How many years do you state you were in the Confederate service?

A. Not quite three years.

Q. State whether, during the last year or two, since the reverses of the Confederacy have commenced, it has not been freely and frequently spoken of in the rebel service as an object finally to be accomplished, — the assassination of the President of the United States?

A. Yes, sir: I heard that very often.

Q. Have you not heard it spoken of freely in the streets of Richmond, among those connected with the Rebel Government?

A. Yes, sir.

Q. About what time? When is the latest you can now recall having heard declarations of that sort at Richmond?

A. At the time after the battle of Chancellorsville, when I do not know what general it was, but believe it was General Kilpatrick, who was on a raid near Richmond, — at that time I heard it. I was in Richmond on a furlough at the same time.

Q. Whenever and wherever spoken of, do I understand you to say that this sentiment of the necessity of the assassination of the President of the United States was generally assented to in the service?

A. Yes, sir.

Q. The "detached service" of which you speak, on which these parties were to be sent, you say related to Canada and the destruction of the Northern cities along the Canada frontier?

A. It was outside of the Confederate lines, — either here in the Northern cities or in Canada.

Q. Did you understand that the "detached service" was to be performed in that direction along the Canada frontier and in our Northern cities?

A. This "detached service" was a nickname in the Confederate army for such purposes.

Q. It meant that sort of warfare?

A. Yes, sir.

Q. You spoke of laying the Northern cities in ashes. Did you understand that that was the mode in which that warfare was to be conducted, by firing our cities?

A. Yes, sir : by firing the cities down and getting the people dissatisfied with the war, and by that means to bring forward a revolution amongst the people in the North. That was the purpose.

No cross-examination.

The Judge Advocate offered in evidence, without objection, the photograph of J. Wilkes Booth, shown to the witness Van Steinacker. It is attached to this record, and marked Exhibit No. 1.

Mrs. Mary Hodspeth,

a witness called for the prosecution, being duly sworn, testified as follows : —

By the Judge Advocate :

Q. Where do you reside?

A. At Harlem, N.Y.

Q. Will you state whether or not in the month of November last you were riding in the railroad cars of New-York City, the Third-Avenue cars, and whether you observed that there were two men in the cars that attracted your attention, one of whom, on leaving the cars, dropped a letter which you picked up?

A. I was going down to the city. There were two gentlemen in the car. Whether they were in or not when I got in I am not confident. I overheard their conversation : they were talking most earnestly. One of them said he would leave for Washington the day after to-morrow ; and the other was going to Newburg, or Newbern, that night. They left the car: the man that was sitting near me pushed his hat forward, and with that pushed his whiskers at the same time; they were false whiskers. The front-face was much darker than it was under the whiskers.

Q. Was he a young man?

A. He was young.

Q. Do you think you would recognize his features again?

A. I think I should.

Q. [Exhibiting to the witness the photograph of Booth, Exhibit No. 1.] Look at that, and say whether it recalls him to you.

A. The face is the same: he had a scar on his right cheek.

Q. Was it on the cheek, or neck?

A. It was something like a bite, near the jawbone.

Q. Did you judge from his conversation that he was a man of education and culture?

A. He was a man of education, and the other was not. The other's name was Johnson.

Q. Did you observe his hands? Did he seem to have been a man who had led a life of ease or not?

A. The hand that was ungloved was very beautiful: the other hand had a gauntlet on. They exchanged letters in the cars. The one who had false whiskers put back the letters in his pocket; and I saw a pistol in his belt.

Q. Did any of the conversation fall on your ears? Were you able to hear it?

A. I overheard him say he would leave for Washington the day after to-morrow.

Q. That is the one who had the ungloved hand and false whiskers?

A. Yes; and the other was very angry because it had not fallen on him to go to Washington: he had been sent for to some place by a messenger.

Q. You say he seemed very angry because it had not fallen to his lot to go to Washington instead of the other?

A. Yes, sir. I had letters of my own to post at the Nassau-street post-office. One of them left about Twenty-sixth or Twenty-seventh Street; and, as he left, I moved up into his place: the car was crowded. My daughter said that I had dropped one of my letters. She picked something up, and gave it to me. When I went down to the broker's, where I was going with some gold, I went to take out my pocket-book, and I saw an envelope with two letters in it. I thought it of importance because of the conversation.

Q. Are you certain it is the envelope with the letters dropped by one of these men ?

A. It must have been, because I saw them exchange letters, and there was no one else at that seat.

Q. Was it picked up at the point where they were sitting ?

A. Yes, just at the end of my dress.

Q. Would you recognize the envelope if you were to see it ?

A. Yes, sir.

Q. [Exhibiting an envelope with two letters.] Look at that, and see if it is the same envelope and letter.

A. It is the same.

Q. Were both letters in that envelope as you now have them ?

A. Yes, sir.

The letters were then presented and read to the Commission, as follows : —

DEAR LOUIS, — The time has at last come that we have all so wished for, and upon you every thing depends. As it was decided before you left, we were to cast lots. Accordingly, we did so ; and you are to be the Charlotte Corday of the nineteenth century. When you remember the fearful, solemn vow that was taken by us, you will feel there is no drawback. *Abe* must *die*, and *now*. You can choose your weapons, — the *cup*, the *knife*, the *bullet*. The cup failed us once, and might again. Johnson, who will give *this*, has been like an enraged demon since the meeting, because it has not fallen upon him to rid the world of the monster. He says the blood of his gray-haired father and his noble brother call upon him for revenge, and revenge he will have : if he cannot wreak it upon the fountain-head, he will upon some of the blood-thirsty generals. Butler would suit him. As our plans were all concocted and well arranged, we separated ; and as I am writing, on my way to Detroit, I will only say that all rests upon you. You know where to find your friends. Your disguises are so perfect and complete, that, without *one* knew *your face*, no police telegraphic despatch would catch you. The English gentleman, *Harcourt*, must not act hastily. Remember, he has ten days. Strike for your home, strike for your country; bide your time, but strike sure! Get introduced, congratulate him, listen to his stories: not many more will the bruto tell to earthly friends. Do any thing but fail; and meet us at the appointed place within the fortnight. Enclose this note together with one of poor Leenea. I will give the reason for this when we meet. Return by Johnson. I wish I could go to you; but duty calls me to the *West:* you will probably hear from me in Washington. Saunders is doing us no good in Canada.

Believe me, your brother in love,

CHARLES SELBY.

[The original of the foregoing is attached to this record, and marked Exhibit No. 1.]

ST. LOUIS, Oct. 21, 1864.

DEAREST HUSBAND,—Why do you not come home? You left me for ten days only, and you now have been from home more than two weeks. In that long time, only sent me one short note, a few cold words, and a check for money, which I did not require. What has come over you? Have you forgotten your wife and child? Baby calls for papa until my heart aches. *We are so lonely* without you! I have written to you again and again; and, as a last resource, yesterday wrote to Charlie, begging him to see you, and tell you to come home. I am so ill, not able to leave my room: if I was, I would go to you wherever you were, if in *this world.* Mamma says I must not write any more, as I am too weak. Louis, darling, do not stay away any longer from your heart-broken wife.

LEENEA.

[The original of the foregoing is annexed to this record, and marked Exhibit No. 3.]

Q. At what time in November did you pick up this envelope and these letters?

A. The day General Butler left New York. I cannot tell the precise date; but General Scott told me he had left that morning.

Q. Was that after the Presidential election in November?

A. Yes, sir.

Q. What did you do with these letters after you examined them, and found their character?

A. I took them to General Scott, who asked me to read them to him. He said he thought it was of great importance, and asked me to take it to General Dix. I did so, and gave it to General Dix.

Q. You say the men exchanged letters. Which was giving letters to the other, the large or the small man?

A. They exchanged twice: the larger one gave them to the one next to him, and he handed them back; and they were exchanged again.

Q. Did you see more than one?

A. Yes, sir.

Q. The smaller one, or educated one, said he would leave for Washington the second day after?

A. Yes: "The day after to-morrow."

No cross-examination.

G. W. BUNKER,

a witness called for the prosecution, being duly sworn, testified as follows : —

By the JUDGE ADVOCATE:

Q. Will you please state whether you were during the last fall, and still are, clerk at the National Hotel in this city?

A. I have been connected with the National Hotel nearly five years.

Q. Did you know John Wilkes Booth?

A. I did.

Q. Was he in the habit of stopping at that hotel when he came to the city?

A. I think he made that his home when in the city.

Q. Have you the hotel-books here for November last?

A. Three of them are here.

Q. I wish you to examine them, and state whether it appears or not that John Wilkes Booth was a guest at the National Hotel, and

3*

was in the hotel in the month of November; and, if so, at what time, and at what time he left.

A. He arrived at the National Hotel Wednesday, Nov. 9, in the evening.

Q. When did he leave?

A. The memorandum states that he left on the morning of the 11th. I see that one cash-book, which I supposed was here, is not: but the memorandum is correct, as it was made out in the hotel, and receipted; but I have not the book to refer to.

Q. When does it appear that he returned again?

A. He returned Nov. 14, in the early part of the evening, and left again on the 16th.

Q. Does it appear at what time he left on the 16th?

A. I have not the book that I could refer to for that: as it is not here, I am not able to state.

Q. Was he there during the month of October.

A. His name does not appear on the books for October, I believe: I have not looked that book through fully, as I was not so requested by the parties who came to the hotel.

Q. Have you taken from the books memoranda to enable you to state as to his subsequent arrivals and departures during the following months?

A. They are all contained in this memorandum from Nov. 9.

Q. When was his next return after leaving on Nov. 16?

A. They are all included in this memorandum from Nov. 9, 1864, to April 8, 1865.

Q. That paper, then, as you hold it in your hand, you state to be an accurate transcript from the books?

A. Yes, sir; from our books at the hotel.

Q. Do you know who were his associates in the hotel generally when he was there, — his room-mates?

A. His most intimate friends? One was John McCullough, an actor.

Q. Was he his room-mate?

A. He roomed with him a portion of the time.

Q. Could you name any other of his room-mates during that time?

A. John P. Wentworth, of California. He also roomed with Mr. McArdle, agent of Edwin Forrest, while he was rooming with Mr. McCullough. The three occupied the same room.

Q. That memorandum which you have brings him down to the 8th of April, you say?

A. Yes, sir.

Q. Did he leave on that day?

A. That was his last arrival at the hotel.

Q. He remained there until the assassination of the President?

A. Yes, sir.

Q. Had he a room there at the time the President was assassinated?

A. He had.

Q. Were you present when his trunk was opened by the officers?

A. I was not. I packed his baggage the next day, and had it removed to our baggage-room.

Q. Do you know John H. Surratt, of this city?

A. I do not by name. Booth had a great many callers that I knew by sight, but did not know their names.

Q. Have you seen any of these prisoners before?

A. I know this small one with black whiskers and imperial. I do not know his name, but know him by sight. [Pointing to Michael O'Laughlin.]

Q. Did you see him at the hotel?

A. Very often. He frequently called on Booth.

Q. Look at all the rest, and see if you recollect any of the others.

A. No, sir [after looking at the various accused].

Q. You say he called frequently. Would he remain with Booth in his room? Did he remain at night at any time?

A. We were so busy during the winter, that I never paid much attention to these things.

Q. Do you know how long these calls were continued, whether they were up to the last moments of Booth's stay?

A. I do not think I saw him the last few days of Booth's remaining there. I do not recollect that he called then.

No cross-examination.

The Judge Advocate offered in evidence, without objection, the following portions of the memorandum spoken of by the witness Bunker : —

J. Wilkes Booth was not at the National Hotel during the month of October, 1864.

He arrived there Nov. 9; occupied room 20; left on early train, morning of 11th.

Arrived again Nov. 14, and left on the 16th.

His next arrival was Dec. 12; left Dec. 17, morning train.

Arrived again Dec. 22; left 24th, 11.15 A.M. train.

Arrived again Dec. 31; left Jan. 10, 1865, 7.30 P.M.

Arrived again Jan. 12; left 28th, 7.30 P.M. train; occupied room 50½.

Arrived again Feb. 22; occupied room 231, in company with John P. H. Wentworth and John McCullough. Wentworth went into this room at the suggestion of Mr. Merrick, clerk, as they were short of rooms. Booth left Feb. 18, 8.15 A.M. train, closing his account to date, inclusive. His name does not appear on the register, but another room is assigned him; and his account commences March 1, without any entry upon the register of that date. 2d, 3d, and 4th, he is called at 8 A.M. 21st March, pays $50 on account, and left on 7.30 P.M. train.

Arrived March 25; room 231; to tea; and left April 1, on an afternoon train.

Arrived again April 8; room 228. Directly below Booth is registered, of that date, the name of A. Cox; residence not known : it was cut out by some one who cut out the name of Booth.

[The original memorandum is annexed to this record, marked Exhibit No. 4.]

WILLIAM E. WHEELER,

a witness called for the prosecution, being duly sworn, testified as follows : —

By the JUDGE ADVOCATE :

Q. Where do you reside ?

A. My home is in Chicopee, Mass.

Q. Were you in Canada during the last autumn ?

A. Yes, sir.

Q. At what point in Canada?

A. Montreal.

Q. Did you meet there citizens of the United States from the Southern States?

A. I met some.

Q. Will you mention some whom you met there, and when?

A. The only one there that I knew the name to swear to was Mr. Booth.

Q. Do you mean John Wilkes Booth, the actor?

A. Yes, sir.

Q. Where did you meet him?

A. I was standing in front of the St. Lawrence Hall, Montreal, and saw him go across from a broker's office on the opposite side.

Q. What time was that?

A. I cannot say the day exactly; but it was in October or November last.

Q. Did you see any others who were pointed out to you by name?

A. There was another man who came across with him. Who he was I do not know, and never heard his name. I spoke to Mr. Booth when he came across, and asked him if he was going to open the theatre there. He said no, he was not, and left me directly, and entered into conversation with a third man who was there; and some time after that, as I was walking along with a gentleman, he pointed him out to me as George Sanders.

Q. You saw Sanders and Booth in conversation together?

A. Yes, sir.

Q. You did not see Clement C. Clay or Jacob Thompson?

A. No, sir, not to know them.

Q. You had met Booth before, and knew him?

A. I had seen him play on the stage in Springfield, Mass.

No cross-examination.

JOHN DEVENEY,

a witness called for the prosecution, being duly sworn, testified as follows : —

By the JUDGE ADVOCATE :

Q. Where do you reside?

A. I am living in Washington at present: my home is in Philadelphia; at least, my father lives there.

Q. Were you, during the past autumn or winter, in Canada?

A. I was.

Q. At what point?

A. At Montreal.

Q. In what month were you there?

A. I went over there in July, and left there on the 3d or 4th of February; I forget which.

Q. Were you or not acquainted with John Wilkes Booth?

A. Very well.

Q. Did you meet him there?

A. I did.

Q. In company with whom did you see him there?

A. The first time I saw him in Canada, I saw him standing in the St. Lawrence Hotel, Montreal, talking with George N. Sanders.

Q. Can you tell about what time that was?

A. I cannot tell you the month; but, from what I have seen in the papers, I am constrained to believe it was in October; but I am not willing to swear it was that month.

Q. Did they or not seem to be intimate?

A. They seemed to be talking very confidentially.

Q. Were they drinking together?

A. Yes. I saw them go into Dowley's, and have a drink together.

Q. You mean George N. Sanders?

A. Yes: George N. Sanders, who used to be navy-agent at New York.

Q. Did you see in Canada, at the same time, Jacob Thompson of Mississippi, who was Secretary of the Interior under the Administration of President Buchanan?

A. I saw Mr. Thompson, Mr. Clay, Mr. Tucker, and several others. They were pointed out to me; but I was not acquainted with those gentlemen.

Q. You mean Clement C. Clay of Alabama, formerly United-States senator?

A. That was the man. I mean him. I presume he was the man. He was pointed out to me as that person.

Q. Did you have conversations with Booth?

A. Yes: I spoke to him. I asked him what he was doing there. I asked him, "Are you going to play here?" knowing that he was an actor. He said, "No, he was not." Said I, "What are you going to do?" Said he, "I just came here on a visit, a pleasure-trip. I saw in the papers afterwards that he had been trying to make an engagement with Buckland, of the Theatre Royal there; but I do not believe it.

Q. You say you saw him talking to Clay, Sanders, Holcomb, and Thompson?

A. I believe I did. I am not very positive that I saw him talking to those parties; but I did see him talk to Sanders. That I can swear to, because I was standing up against a pillar in the hotel; and it was right in the hotel. Sanders was leaning against a pillar, and Booth standing in front of him.

Q. You say you have seen the others with Sanders?

A. Yes, sir. I do not know that I saw them there standing talking to Sanders that day; but I have seen those other men with Sanders at different times talking to him.

Q. And with Booth?

A. I will not say that. I saw Booth talking to Sanders, though. Of that I am positive, because those two were standing together when I came up. I just came from the post-office, which is opposite the hotel. I came over, and saw them talking there. I was surprised to see him; and that is what made me take particular notice of it. I thought, as a matter of course, he came there to play.

Q. When was the next time you saw Booth?

A. The next time I saw Booth was on the steps of the Kirkwood House, in this city, the night of the 14th of April, a few minutes before five, or between five and six o'clock.

Q. What occurred then?

A. He was going into the hotel. I was standing talking to a young man named Callan, I think, who works in one of the departments : he was formerly a sergeant of cavalry, I think. I said to Callan, " I would like to go up to Willard's Hotel, and see if we can see General Grant." I had never seen him. Said I, " Will you come, and go along?" He said, " No : I have got an engagement to be here at five o'clock to meet some person." So I did not go, but went into the hotel, saying, " I wonder what time it is now : it must be time for your friend to come, if he is coming." I went in, and found it was five, or a few minutes of it ; and said I, " I guess you can go now : that engagement is up." He said, " No : I will wait a little longer." Just then, Booth passed me, going into the hotel, and turned round and spoke to me. I asked him when he came from Canada ; for I did not know he had left there. He said he had been back some time, and was going to stay here some time, and would see me again. I asked, " Are you going to play here again?" Said he, " No : I am not going to play again : I am in the oil business." I laughed and joked at that ; it being a common joke to talk about the oil business. A few minutes afterwards, I saw him coming down street on horseback, on a bay horse. I took particular notice what kind of a looking rig he had on the horse. I do not know what made me do it. The next I saw of him I heard the speech, and saw him jump out of the box at the theatre ; and, when he fell, he fell on one hand and one knee, and I recognized him. He fell with his face towards the audience. I said, " He is John Wilkes Booth, and he has shot the President!" I made that remark right there. That is the last ever I saw of him, when he was running across the stage.

Q. You say you are certain you saw him and Sanders drinking together, as well as talking?

A. Yes, sir, I did : I am sure of it. Sanders says he never saw him ; but Sanders tells a lie, because he did see him. I saw him talking to him.

Cross-examined by MR. AIKEN :

Q. How long have you resided in this city?

A. I have been off and on here for a year or two. I was formerly an officer in the army, Fourth Maryland Regiment, as lieutenant in Company E. I was in the employ of Adams's Express Company a great many years, and worked with them in Washington for some time.

Q. Are you acquainted with any of the prisoners?

A. Not that I know of.

Q. You are not acquainted with John H. Surratt?

A. No, sir: I never saw him in my life, to my knowledge.

By the COURT:

Q. Why did you say it was John Wilkes Booth, and that he had shot the President?

A. I did not know Mr. Lincoln had been shot; but it flashed on my mind, when Booth jumped out of that box, that he had done such a thing, because I knew the President was in the box: I saw him go in, and I heard the pistol-shot, and the words, " *Sic semper tyrannis;*" and I knew from my schoolboy knowledge that was the motto of the State of Virginia.

By the JUDGE ADVOCATE:

Q. You say Booth shouted, " *Sic semper tyrannis* "?

A. I heard the words in the box. I think it was Booth said that. I heard the words before I saw the man.

Q. Had he his knife in his hand as he went across the stage?

A. He had.

Q. Did he make any remark as he crossed the stage?

A. It is said he did; but I did not notice it. The excitement was so great, that I did not notice it. I can safely swear that I did not hear any remark; at least, I cannot call to mind that I did.

Lieutenant-General ULYSSES S. GRANT,

a witness called for the prosecution, being duly sworn, testified as follows:—

By the JUDGE ADVOCATE:

Q. Will you state whether you are acquainted with Jacob Thompson, formerly Secretary of the Interior under President Buchanan's Administration?

A. I met him once: that was when the army was lying opposite Vicksburg, at what is called Milliken's Bend and Young's Point. A little boat was discovered coming up on the opposite shore, apparently surreptitiously, trying to avoid detection; and a little tug was sent out from the navy to pick it up. When they got to it, they found a little white flag sticking out of the stern of the row-boat, and Jacob Thompson in it. They brought him to Admiral Porter's flag-ship; and I was sent for, and met him. I do not recollect now the ostensible business he had. There seemed to be nothing important at all in the visit; but he pretended to be under a flag of truce, and therefore he had to be allowed to go back again.

Q. When was that?

A. I cannot say whether it was in January or February, 1863. It was the first flag of truce we had, though.

Q. Did he profess to be, and seem to be, in the military service of the rebels?

A. He said he had been offered a commission, — any thing that he wanted; but, knowing that he was not a military man, he preferred having something more like a civil appointment, and he had taken the place of an inspector-general in the rebel service.

Q. Did he then hold that position?

A. That was what he said; that he was an inspector-general, or assistant inspector-general, with the rank of lieutenant-colonel, I think he said.

Q. The Military Department of Washington, as it is spoken of in military parlance, embraces the city of Washington, does it not? and did it not during the past year?

A. Yes, sir.

Q. And all the defences of the city?

A. Yes, sir; and on the other side of the river, and Alexandria.

Q. It embraces all the fortifications on both sides?

A. Yes, sir.

Q. I have in my hand a copy of your commission as lieutenant-general of the armies of the United States, bearing date the 4th day of March, 1864. Will you state whether or not, since that time, you have continued to be in command, under that commission, of the armies of the United States?

A. I have.

[The Judge Advocate offered in evidence, without objection, the commission of Lieutenant-General Grant, dated March 4, 1864, accompanied by General Orders No. 98, March, which are appended to the record, marked Exhibit No. 6.]

Cross-examined by Mr. Aiken :

Q. Are you aware that the civil courts are in operation in this city, all of them ?

A. Yes, sir.

Q. How far towards Baltimore does the Department of Washington extend ?

A. I could not say exactly to what point. Any troops that belong to General Augur's command, however, that he sends out to any point, would necessarily remain under his command. He commands the Department of Washington.

Q. Is any portion of the State of Maryland in the Department of Washington ?

A. Oh, yes, sir! Martial law, I believe, extends to all the territory south of the railroad that runs across from Annapolis, running south to the Potomac and the Chesapeake.

Cross-examined by Mr. Ewing :

Q. By virtue of what order does martial law extend south of Annapolis ?

A. I never saw the order. It is just simply an understanding.

Q. It is just an understanding ?

A. Yes, sir; just an understanding that it does exist.

Q. You have never seen any order ?

A. No, sir.

Q. And do not know that such an order exists ?

A. No, sir : I have never seen the order.

Joseph H. Simonds,

a witness called for the prosecution, being duly sworn, testified as follows : —

By the Judge Advocate :

Q. Were you acquainted with J. Wilkes Booth in his lifetime ?

A. I was.

Q. What relation did you sustain to him? Were you his agent?

A. I was his business agent, really.

Q. In what region of country, and in connection with what business?

A. I was principally in the oil region. I did some little business for him in the city of Boston, but very little, which was entirely closed up before I left there.

Q. What was the character of his interest there in the oil region?

A. He owned a third undivided interest, at first, in a lease of three and a half acres on the Alleghany River, near Franklin.

Q. For which he paid how much?

A. It was bought by means of contracting to pay off the old debts of that lease, and carry on the work. Afterward the land interest was bought, he furnishing one-half of the purchase-money of the land-interest, and owning one undivided third as before stated.

Q. How much did he pay?

A. The land-interest cost $4,000. He paid $2,000, — one-half of it.

Q. Did he make any other investments on which he paid money?

A. Yes, sir.

Q. What was the total amount of them?

A. He purchased, for $1,000, an interest in an association there owning an undivided thirtieth of a tract.

Q. What other purchases did he make?

A. That is all that he ever absolutely purchased. There was money spent in carrying on the expenses of this lease previous to his purchase of the land-interest. At the time of the purchase of the land-interest, the work was stopped, and there were no more expenses.

Q. These interests of which you speak were all that he possessed in the oil region?

A. Yes, sir: all that he ever possessed in Venango, to my knowledge.

Q. Did he ever realize any thing from them?

A. Not a dollar.

Q. They were a total loss?

A. Yes, as far as he was concerned.

Q. When did this occur? In what year?

A. The first interest he acquired in any way was either in December, 1863, or January, 1864 : I cannot say as to the date. It was only from his report to me that I knew of it. My first knowledge of it was in May, 1864. I accompanied him to the oil regions in June, 1864, for the purpose of taking charge of his business there.

Q. Have you given the total amount of the investment that Booth made? What do you consider the total amount?

A. The whole amount invested by him in this Alleghany-River property, in every way, was about $5,000. I cannot give the exact figures in dollars and cents.

Q. And the other investment was about $1,000?

A. Yes, sir.

Q. Making $6,000 in all?

A. Yes, sir.

Q. And that you know to have been a total loss to him?

A. Yes, sir ; that is, it was transferred. His business was entirely closed out there in the latter part of September, 1864 : I think, on the 27th of September.

Q. Was it placed in your hands as trustee? or to whom was it transferred?

A. There were three owners, as I have told you. He held an undivided third. The three owners all decided to place the property in my hands as trustee to hold for them. It was so mentioned in the deed, and their several names were mentioned in the deed. Immediately upon the execution of that deed, he asked me to make a deed conveying his interest away, which I did in accordance with his instructions. Those deeds were properly executed, conveying his whole interest away in that way. At the same time, this other interest in a different portion of the county, on a different stream, for which he had paid $1,000, he also transferred, which was done by a different process, by assignment on the receipt which he held for his interest.

Q. This was all done last fall?

4*

A. It was done in September: I think, the 27th or 28th of the month. I cannot be exact as to the date. It was done the day he left Franklin, the last time I ever saw him.

Q. Were the conveyances without compensation or voluntary gifts?

A. One was made to his brother, Junius Brutus Booth, which was without compensation; but a consideration was mentioned in the deed.

Q. But there was none in fact?

A. No, sir; none in fact. The other was to me, and the same consideration was mentioned; but it was done in consideration of my services, for which I have never received any other pay.

Q. There was nothing paid him at all on either of them?

A. No, sir; not a dollar: and he paid all the expenses of the transfer and the conveyances.

SAMUEL P. JONES (blind),

a witness called for the prosecution, being duly sworn, testified as follows: —

By the JUDGE ADVOCATE:

Q. Have you resided in Richmond at any time during the war?
A. I have.

Q. State any conversations you may have heard there, to which officers of the Rebel Government were parties, in regard to the contemplated assassination of the President of the United States.

A. The nearest I know any thing to that point among the officers there is their common conversation in camp, as I would go about amongst them; and their conversations would be of this nature: That all suspicious persons, or those kind of people they were not certain were of their way of thinking, they would hush up as soon as they came near them. But, after I found out what I could learn in reference to these things, they were desperately anxious that any such as this should be accomplished.

Q. Will you state any particular occasion?

A. In a general way, I have heard sums offered, to be paid with a Confederate sum, for any person or persons to go North and assassinate the President.

Q. Do you remember any occasion when any such offers were made, or any amount named, and by what kind of officers?

A. At this moment, I cannot tell you the particular names of shoulder-straps, &c.

Q. Do you remember any occasion, — some dinner occasion?

A. I can tell you this. I heard a citizen make the remark once, that he would give from his private purse $10,000, in addition to the Confederate amount, to have the President assassinated, — to bring him to Richmond, dead or alive, for proof.

Q. What was meant by that phrase, "In addition to the Confederate amount"?

A. I know nothing about that, any more than the way they would express it. I should judge, from drawing an inference, that there was any amount offered by the Government, in that trashy paper, to assassinate any officials that were hindering their cause; and even I have heard it down as low as a private or citizen. For instance, if it is not digressing from the purpose, I know of a Kentuckian, but cannot tell you the name now, that was putting up at the Exchange Hotel, or otherwise Ballard House (they belong to the same property, and are connected by a bridge over Franklin Street). He was arrested under suspicion of being a spy. I can tell you the name now: his name was Webster, if I remember rightly. I always supposed, from what I understood, that he came down to buy goods; but they took him as a spy, and hung him. Whether it was in reference to this assassination, I cannot say.

Q. I understood you to say that it was a subject of general conversation among the rebel officers?

A. It was. The rebel officers, as they would be sitting around their tent-doors, would be conversing on such a subject a great deal. They would be saying they would like to see his head brought there, dead or alive, and they should think it could be done; and I have heard such things stated as that they had certain persons undertaking it.

SAMUEL KNAPP CHESTER,

a witness called for the prosecution, being duly sworn, testified as follows:—

By the JUDGE ADVOCATE :

Q. Your profession is that of an actor?

A. Yes, sir.

Q. Have you known J. Wilkes Booth a good many years?

A. I have known him about ten or eleven years,— since I first met him.

Q. Quite intimately, I suppose?

A. For about six or seven years, intimately.

Q. Can you recall a conversation which you are supposed to have had with him, in November last, in New York?

A. Yes, sir.

Q. What time in the month was it?

A. I think it was in November that I had a conversation with him.

Q. What time in November? State about the period of time.

A. I cannot think of the exact date ; but it was in the early portion of November. One day we were in conversation, and I asked him why he was not acting; and he told me that he did not intend to act in this portion of the country again ; that he had taken his wardrobe to Canada, and intended to run the blockade.

Q. Did you meet him after that, and have some conversation with him in regard to oil speculations? or was it at the same time?

A. No, sir. The next time I met him was about the time we were to play "Julius Cæsar," which we did play on the 25th of November ; and it was either on the 24th or 25th that he asked me to take a walk with him, or asked if I knew some costumers where he might get some dresses for his character in that play ; and I asked him where his own wardrobe was.

Q. Was that in the city of New York?

A. Yes. I never had any conversation with him relative to this affair out of New York. He said it was still in Canada, in charge of a friend, I think he said, named Martin. I will not be positive ; but I think he said it was in Montreal. He did not say any thing to me at all about the oil business then, that I remember,

Q. Did he not ask you how you would like to go into the oil business with him?

A. Not in the oil business. He never mentioned that.

Q. He told you he had a big speculation on hand?

A. Yes, sir.

Q. Did he ask you to go in with him?

A. Yes, sir. I met him, and he was talking with some friends, and they were joking with him about the affair. I met him on Broadway. After he left them, he said he had a better speculation than that on hand, and one they would not laugh at. Some time after that, I met him again, and he again talked of this speculation, and asked me how I would like to go in with him. I told him I was without means; that I could not : and he said it did not matter; he always liked me, and would furnish the means. The next time I heard from him, he was in Washington.

Q. State the whole of the conversation in which he urged you to go into this speculation in New York.

A. As well as I can remember, I will tell you from beginning to end. He left me then in New York; and I received several letters from him from Washington, telling me he was speculating in farms in Lower Maryland and Virginia, and still telling me that I must join him; that it was sure to coin money; that I must go in with him. I paid very little attention to it. Then, about the latter part of December or early in January, — I will not be positive which it was, but late in December or early in January, — he came to New York, and came to my house. I then lived at No. 45, Grove Street. He asked me to take a walk with him. I did so. We went out, and went to a saloon known as the House of Lords, on Houston Street. We remained there a considerable time — I suppose an hour — eating and drinking. He had often mentioned this affair, that is, his speculation, but would never say what it was. If I would ask him what it was, he would say he would tell me by and by. We left there, and went to another saloon, under the Revere House, and ate some oysters. We then started up Broadway. I thought it was time to go home, and my way was down Bleeker Street, — that is, up Broadway from the corner of Houston; and I had to turn down Bleeker Street to get to Grove Street. I bade him good-night. He asked me to walk a piece farther up the street with him, and I did so. I walked a square; that is, to Fourth Street, or next street. He asked me to walk up there with him, and I did so. He asked me to walk up Fourth Street because Broadway was crowded : he said Fourth Street was not so full of people as Broadway, and he wanted to tell me about that speculation. I walked up there with him ; and, when we got into an unfrequented portion of the street, he stopped, and told me then that he was in a large conspiracy to capture the heads of the Government (including the President), and take them to Richmond. I asked him if that was what he wished me to go in. He said it was. I told him I could not do it ; that it was an impossibility ; only to think of my family. He said he had two or three thousand dollars that he could leave them. I still said I could not do it. He urged it, and talked with me for, I suppose, twenty minutes or half an hour ; and I still refused. He then told me that at least I would not betray him, and said I dare not. He said he could implicate me in the affair, anyhow. He said that the party were sworn together, and that, if I attempted to betray them, I would be hunted down through life ; and talked some more about the affair. I cannot remember it now ; but still urging me, saying I had better go in. I told him no, and bade him good-night ; and I went home.

Q. Did he indicate to you what part he wished you to play in carrying out this conspiracy ?

A. Yes, sir.

Q. What did he say ?

A. That I was to open the back door of the theatre at a signal.

Q. Did he indicate at what theatre this was to occur ?

A. Yes : he told me Ford's Theatre ; because it must be some one acquainted or connected with the theatre who could take part in it.

Q. Ford's Theatre in Washington ?

A. Yes, sir.

Q. Did he urge you upon the ground that it was an easy affair, and that you would have very little to do ?

A. Yes : he said that. That was all I would have to do, he said. He said the thing was sure to succeed.

Q. What preparations did he say, if any, had been made toward the conspiracy ?

A. He told me that every thing was in readiness ; that it was

sure to succeed, for there were parties on the other side ready to co-
operate with them.

Q. Did you understand from him that the Rebel Government was
sanctioning what he was doing?

A. He never told me that.

Q. What do you mean by parties on the other side?

A. I imagined that they were on the other side; but he did not
say who they were. I mean they were those people. He said on
the other side.

Q. Did he mention the probable number of persons engaged in
the conspiracy?

A. He said there were from fifty to a hundred: he said that when
he first mentioned the affair to me.

Q. Did he write to you?

A. He wrote about this speculation, and then he wrote to me
again: that must have been in January.

Q. Have you those letters?

A. I never kept my letters. Every Sunday I devote to answering my correspondents, and generally destroy their letters then.

Q. Did he or not make you any remittance with a view of enabling
you to come to Washington?

A. Oh, yes, sir! After I had declined going, — had refused him,
— I got a letter from him stating that I must come. This was the
letter in which he told me it was sure to succeed. I wrote back
that it was impossible; I would not come. Then, by return mail,
I think, I got another letter, with fifty dollars enclosed, saying I
must come, and must be sure to be there by Saturday night. I did
not go. I had not been out of New York since last summer.

Q. Can you remember the time you received the last letter, with
the fifty dollars in it?

A. That was in January, I think.

Q. You say he said he had one thousand dollars to leave to your
family?

A. That was before, at the first interview.

Q. Did he, at the time he sent you the first fifty dollars, mention
any more?

A. In the letter, he did not.

Q. Did he speak of having plenty of funds for the purpose?

A. Not in his letter.

Q. Did he in his conversation?

A. In his conversation after he came to New York again.

Q. What did he say then?

A. When he came to New York he called on me again, and asked me to take a walk with him; and I did so. He told me that he had been trying to get another party to join him, named John Matthews; and when he told him what he wanted to do, that the man was very much frightened, indeed, and would not join him; and he said he would not have cared if he had sacrificed him. I told him I did not think it was right to speak in that manner. He said no: he was a coward, and was not fit to live. He then asked me again to join him: he told me I must do so. He said that there was plenty of money in the affair; that, if I would do it, I would never want again as long as I lived; that I would never want for money. He said that the President and some of the heads of the Government came to the theatre very frequently during Mr. Forrest's engagements. I still urged him not to mention the affair to me; to think of my poor family. He said he would provide for my going with him. I still refused. He said he would ruin me in the profession if I did not go. I told him I could not help that, and begged of him not to mention the affair to me. When he found I would not go, he said he honored my mother, and respected my wife, and he was sorry he had mentioned this affair to me, and told me to make my mind easy; he would trouble me about it no more. I then returned him the money he sent me. He said he would not allow me to do so; but that he was very short of funds, — so very short, that either himself or some of the party must go to Richmond to obtain means to carry out their designs.

Q. He said, however, that there was plenty of money in the enterprise?

A. Yes, sir.

Q. When did this last conversation occur?

A. That, I think, was in February.

Q. Did he have any conversation with you at a later period,

after the inauguration, as to the opportunity which he had for the assassination of the President? Did he speak of that?

A. Yes, sir. On Friday, one week previous to the assassination, he was in New York.

Q. What did he say then?

A. We were in the House of Lords at the time, sitting at a table; and had not been there long before he exclaimed, striking the table, "What an excellent chance I had to kill the President, if I had wished, on inauguration-day!" That was all he said relative to that.

Q. Did he explain what the chance was?

A. No. He said he was as near the President on that day as he was to me. That is all he said.

Q. Can you tell at what time in February he said it would be necessary to send to Richmond for money?

A. No, sir. I cannot tell positively.

Cross-examined by Mr. CLAMPITT:

Q. Did he mention any names of those who were connected with him in his plan as communicated to you in reference to the assassination of Mr. Lincoln?

A. No, sir; not that I am aware of.

Q. You never heard him mention any names?

A. I never did.

Cross-examined by Mr. EWING:

Q. Do I understand you to say that he spoke to you of a plan to assassinate the President, and to capture him?

A. To capture him.

Q. Did he say any thing to you as to how he would get him off?

A. No.

Q. As to where he would take him?

A. To Richmond.

Q. By what route?

A. He did not say.

Q. He spoke of there being persons on "the other side"?

A. Yes, sir.

Q. Did he use just simply that expression ? or did he explain what he meant by the " other side " ? What did you understand him to mean ? "

A. He did not explain it at all ; but I supposed it was in the South.

Q. Across the lines ?

A. Yes, sir.

Q. Across the river ?

A. Across the Potomac.

Q. Did he say nothing to you as to the means he had provided, or proposed to provide, for conducting the President after he should be seized ?

A. No, sir. On one occasion, he told me that he was selling off horses, after he had told me that he had given up this project.

Q. When did he say to you that he had abandoned the idea of capturing the President ?

A. In February, I think.

Q. Did he say why he had abandoned it ?

A. He said the affair had fallen through, owing to some of the parties backing out.

Q. On what day was it that he said to you what an excellent chance he had for killing the President ?

A. That was on a Friday, one week previous to the assassination.

Q. On what day of April was that ?

A. The 7th.

Q. Did he say any thing to you as to his then entertaining, or having before that entertained, the purpose to assassinate the President ?

A. No, sir.

Q. Did he say any thing to you then as to why he did not assassinate the President ?

A. No, sir. That was the only exclamation he made use of relative to it.

Q. State his exact words, if you can.

A. He said, " What an excellent chance I had, if I wished, to kill the President on inauguration-day ! I was on the stand, as close to him nearly as I am to you." That is as near his language as I can give.

Q. State how far he explained to you his project for capturing the President in the theatre.

A. I believe I have stated as far as I know.

Q. Did he ever indicate how he expected to get him from the box to the stage without being caught?

A. No, sir.

Q. Did he say how many were to help him in seizing the President?

A. No, sir.

Q. Did he name any other officials who were to be seized besides the President?

A. No. The only time he told me, he said, " The heads of the Government, including the President."

By the JUDGE ADVOCATE:

Q. I understood you to say that he stated that the particular enterprise of capturing the President and heads of the Government had been given up; and that, in consequence, he was selling off the horses he had bought for the purpose?

A. Yes, sir.

Q. He did not state to you what mode of proceeding had been substituted for that, but simply that that one had been given up?

A. He told me they had given up the affair.

Q. That it had fallen through?

A. Yes, sir.

The Commission then adjourned until to-morrow, Saturday morning, May 13, at ten o'clock.

SATURDAY, May 13.

Spectators were admitted into the court-room, and permission was given to reporters for the public press to publish the testimony. The report made for the Washington " National Intelligencer " by the corps of phonographers who report the proceedings of the United States Senate for official publication is so correct and complete that it is given here as a reliable record of this important trial.

The Court having heard the records of the preceding day read, proceeded as follows:—

The JUDGE ADVOCATE. It is proper that the names of all gentlemen who appear as counsel should be entered on the record. Do I understand Mr. Johnson as appearing for any of these prisoners?

MR. JOHNSON. I do not know whether I shall be able to appear or not. I have taken no part in the case thus far, except to speak to the counsel. Whether I shall appear or not will depend on whether I can find that I can stay as long as may be necessary. I have no objection to appearing if the Court will permit me to leave it at any time.

The PRESIDENT of the Commission (General Hunter). In relation to Mr. Johnson appearing here as counsel for Mrs. Surratt, or either of the prisoners, I have a note from one of the members of the Court: —

"*Mr. President,* — I feel it to be my duty to object to the admission of Mr. Reverdy Johnson as a counsel before this Court, on the ground that he does not recognize the moral obligation of an oath that is designed as a test of loyalty, or to enforce the obligation of loyalty to the Government of the United States; and, in support of this objection, have the honor to refer the members of the Court to his opinions on this subject, published in a letter over his signature, pending the adoption of the new constitution of Maryland, in 1864."

MR. JOHNSON. May I ask who the member of the Court is that makes that objection?

The PRESIDENT. Yes, sir: it is General Harris; and, if he had not made it, I should have made it myself.

MR. JOHNSON. I do not object to it at all. The Court will decide if I am to be tried.

The PRESIDENT. The Court will be cleared.

MR. JOHNSON. I hope I shall be heard.

GEN. EKIN. I think it can be decided without clearing the Court.

GEN. WALLACE. I move that Mr. Johnson be heard.

The PRESIDENT and others. Certainly.

MR. JOHNSON. Is the opinion here to which the objection refers?

The PRESIDENT. I believe it is not.

MR. JOHNSON. *Mr. President and Gentlemen,* — It is difficult to speak of this objection, and speak as I feel, without having the opinion before me. That opinion cannot be tortured by any reasonable man into any such conclusion. It is an utter misapprehension of my meaning, and an utter misapprehension of the terms of that opinion. There is no member of this Court, including the President, and the member that objects, who recognizes the obligation of an oath more absolutely than I do; and there is nothing in my life, from its commencement to the present time, which would induce me for a moment to avoid a comparison in all moral respects between myself and any member of this Court. In this Rebellion, which has broken down so many moral principles, it has been my pride to stand by the Government from the beginning to the present moment, to take every obligation which the Government has thought it necessary to impose, and to do my duty faithfully in every department of the public service, as well as in my individual capacity. If such an objection was made in the Senate of the United States, where I am known, I forbear to say how it would be treated, because I know the terms in which it would be decided. I have lived too long, gone through too many trials, rendered the country such services as my abilities enabled me, and the confidence of the people in whose midst I am has given me the opportunity, to tolerate for a moment — come from whom it may — such an aspersion upon my moral character. I am glad it is made now, when I have arrived at that period of life when it would be unfit to notice it in any other way.

But I repeat, there is not one word of truth in the construction which has been given to that opinion. I have it not by me; but I recollect substantially what it is. The convention called to frame a new constitution for the State was called under the authority of an act of the Legislature of Maryland, and under that alone. By that legislation, their proceedings were to be submitted to the then legal voters of the State. The convention thought that they were authorized themselves, not only to impose, as an authority to vote, what was not imposed by the then existing constitution and laws, but to admit to vote those who were prohibited from voting by such constitution and laws; and I said, in common with the whole bar of the State (and with what the bar throughout the Union would have said if they had been consulted), that, to that extent, they had usurped the authority under which alone they were authorized to

5*

meet; and that, so far, the proceeding was a nullity. They had prescribed this oath; and all that the opinion said, or was intended to say, was, that to take the oath voluntarily was not a craven submission to usurped authority, but was necessary, in order to enable the citizen to protect his rights under the then constitution; and that there was no moral harm in taking an oath which the convention had no authority to impose. I mean it as no reflection to any member of this Court when I say, that, upon a question of that description, I feel myself at least as able to form a correct opinion as any one of the gentlemen around this table.

I am here at the instance of that lady [pointing to Mrs. Surratt], whom I never saw until yesterday, and never heard of, she being a Maryland lady; and thinking that I could be of service to her, and protesting, as she has done, her innocence to me, — of the facts I know nothing, — because I deemed it right, I deemed it due to the character of the profession to which I belong, and which is not inferior to the noble profession of which you are members, that she should not go undefended. I knew I was to do it voluntarily, without compensation: the law prohibits me from receiving compensation; but if it did not, understanding her condition, I should never have dreamed of refusing upon the ground of her inability to make compensation.

I am here no volunteer, gentlemen. I am here to do whatever the evidence will justify me in doing in protecting this lady from the charge upon which she is now being tried for her life. I am here detesting from the very bottom of my heart every one concerned in this nefarious plot, carried out with such fiendish malice, as much as any member of this Court; and I am not here to protect any one whom, when the evidence is offered, I shall deem to have been guilty, even her.

The Court, therefore, or the honorable member of the Court who thinks proper, or thinks it his duty, to make this objection, and the President who said that he should have thought it his duty to make the objection if no member of the Court had done it, are to understand that I am not pleading here for any thing personal to myself. I stand too firmly settled in my own conviction of honor, and in my own sense of duty, public and private, to be alarmed at all at any individual opinion that may be expressed : but I ask the Court to decide; and I have no right to suppose they will not decide as they shall see to be best. If it shall be such a decision as the President seems himself to be disposed to make, I can take care of myself in the future.

GEN. HARRIS. *Mr. President and Gentlemen of the Commission,* — I trust it is not necessary that I should assure you, or the gentleman to whom I felt it my duty to object as a counsellor before this Court, that I desire above all things not to do injustice to any man. Neither, I hope, need I assure you, that, in doing what I felt it to be my duty to do, I have not been influenced by any personal considerations. Although I have never had the pleasure of the personal acquaintance of the gentleman to whom I objected, I have known him long as an eminent public man of our country; and I must say that my impressions of him have been of a very favorable character. But in regard to the matter of the objection, if my recollection serves me aright, I must contend that it is well founded. It is due to the gentleman and to the members of the Court, however, that I should say that I have made this objection simply from a recollection of the letter alluded to, which I read, perhaps, near a year ago, and of the effects of that letter upon the vote of his State.

Now, if I understand the remarks of the gentleman in explanation, I cannot see that they remove the difficulty : they do not from my mind at least. I understand him to say that the doctrine which he taught to the people of his State was, that because the convention had framed an oath, and required the taking of that oath as a qualification for the right of suffrage, which oath was unconstitutional and illegal in his opinion, therefore it had no moral binding force, and that people might take it, and then go and vote without any regard to the subject-matter of that oath.

MR. JOHNSON. If you suppose I have said so, general, you are under a misapprehension. I have not said any such thing.

GEN. HARRIS. That is my understanding of the gentleman's remarks this morning; but, as I said at the outset, I should be very sorry indeed to do injustice to any man whatever.

The PRESIDENT. Permit me to interrupt you one moment, General Harris. We should like to have the remarks read from the record, so that it may be shown whether you are right or wrong.

Mr. D. F. Murphy, one of the official reporters of the Commission, then read from his short-hand notes that portion of Mr. Johnson's remarks relative to the action of the Maryland Convention, and the opinion given by him as to the oath prescribed by it.

Mr. Johnson (to the reporter). That is right.

Gen. Harris. *Mr. President and Gentlemen of the Court,* — If that language does not justify my conclusion, I confess I am unable to understand the English language. I wish the gentleman to understand, that, in regard to his ability to determine a legal question, I do not intend to enter into any controversy. He remarked to the Court, rather boastingly, that he, perhaps, was as able as any other man, or considered himself so, to judge in regard to a legal point. That is not the matter in question. It is a question of ethics; it is the morality of the thing; the moral obligation of an oath voluntarily taken, which, if I understand that language, he taught his people might be set aside, and considered as having no force or binding obligation on them. He taught them that the convention had transcended its authority, had done something that it had no right to do, was requiring as a qualification for the exercise of the right of suffrage something that it had no right to require, and that, consequently, they might voluntarily take this oath in order simply to entitle them to vote, without considering it as having any moral binding force in it ; and I am much mistaken in my recollection of the history of the times and the effect of that opinion on the vote of his State if it was not so considered, and if a large number of the people of his State did not cast their suffrage under that ethical doctrine taught to them by the gentleman to whom I have objected. But, as I was about to remark a while ago, I should be very sorry indeed to do injustice to the gentleman or to any other man ; and, having made my objection simply from my recollection of this letter, it is perhaps due to the gentleman and to the members of the Court that the letter should be submitted to the scrutiny of the Court before making their decision. I may be wrong : if so, none will be more ready than myself to acknowledge that fact.

Mr. Johnson. *Mr. President,* — I do not propose to make an extended reply to the honorable member's construction of my remarks, but only to say a word or two. As to my " boasting," in a boasting manner asserting my competence to decide a question of law as well as any man, the honorable member is mistaken. I said that I thought I was as capable of deciding questions of that sort as any member of this Court; they not being lawyers, as I presume.

Now, the honorable member seems to suppose, that because in that opinion to which reference is made, according to my recollection of it, I said there was no harm in taking an oath, that meant to tell the people of Maryland that there would be no harm in breaking it after it was taken. We learn something every day; and, if that is the correct interpretation of the words, I am better informed now than I was when I used them. I said to the Court, and I repeat it, that I had no idea of using them for any such purpose; that, according to my interpretation of them, they admit of no such construction; and that ought to be sufficient. When gentlemen are dealing with gentlemen, even if the words were liable, by any thing but what I must be permitted to call hypercriticism, to such interpretations as the honorable member has thought proper to give, I submit, that, amongst gentlemen (and I hope I may not be considered as boasting when I say that in that capacity I am the equal of every member of this Court), when I say that the words were not used for any such design, a gentleman to whom the explanation is given would not be disposed to hold that they were, in point of fact, used with that design.

Now, as to the effect upon the people of Maryland. I do not know where the honorable member is from. He is not a citizen of our State, I suppose.

Gen. Harris. I am a citizen of West Virginia, sir.

Mr. Johnson. Very well: that is not a citizen of Maryland.

Gen. Harris. No, sir.

Mr. Johnson. I was about to say that, whoever supposes — and I hope that he will sooner or later, if he is under that impression, come to a different conclusion hereafter — that the people of Maryland can be induced by an individual opinion to take an oath

with a view to violate it, is under a great misapprehension, — a very
great misapprehension. We had in this controversy, much to my
regret, hundreds and hundreds of our citizens who left our borders
and participated in this Rebellion; but hundreds and hundreds of
those who remain have proved true to their flag, and evidenced
their loyalty upon the battle-field with their blood and their lives;
and in the relation in which I stand to the people of Maryland,
who are supposed to be capable of being influenced to do an im-
moral act by the opinion of any one man, I may be permitted to
say, that they are the equals patriotically of the people of Western Virginia.

There were other topics involved in the constitution which influenced the vote of those who voted against it, to which it is
unnecessary and useless here to refer; but I deny, and deny expli-
citly, that there was a single man who voted because of that
opinion, taking the oath with a view to vote, intending thereafter
to violate that obligation.

But, as a legal question, it is something new to me that the
objection, if it was well founded in fact, is well founded in law. Are
the members of the Court to measure the moral character of every
counsel who may appear before them? Is that their function?
What if it is bad? What if it is known to be bad? I mention it
only by way of supposition; for I scorn it as applying to myself.
What if it is bad? What influence has that upon the Court, by
which their judgments could be led astray? His client may suffer
from the possible prejudice which the fact may create in the
minds of the Court; but how can the Court suffer? Who gives
to the Court the jurisdiction to decide upon the moral character of
the counsel who may appear before them? Who makes them the
arbiters of the public morality and professional morality? What
authority have they, under their commission, to rule me out, or to
rule any other counsel out, upon the ground, above all, that he
does not recognize the validity of an oath, even if they believed it?

But I put myself upon no such ground as that, Mr. President
and gentlemen. I claim again, and in no boasting spirit, but as
due to a reputation won through a long life of arduous labor and
patriotic service, — I claim, in all moral respects, to be the equal

of every member of this tribunal. They may dispose of the question as they please : it will not touch me.

GEN. HARRIS. *Mr. President and Gentlemen of the Court,* — I will beg your indulgence but for a moment. I am sure the Court did not understand me as intending to cast any reflection upon the people of Maryland, either in regard to loyalty or morality, nor in regard to patriotism; for I know, and am proud to say, that the State of Maryland has a good record in this great contest through which our country has just passed. But whilst that is true, as it is true of my State (and I am proud to make the assertion), it is equally true of Maryland as it is of my own State (and I am sorry to say it is true), that a portion of the people stand in a very different attitude, and have made for themselves a terrible record.

And the circumstances of this case were rather peculiar. They were about to vote on an alteration in the fundamental law of the State, on the adoption of a new constitution which made some radical changes in regard to the social *status* or condition of the people of Maryland : the institution of slavery was about to be blotted out from the fundamental law of the land. That was the proposition; and it was an unfortunate fact, that that portion of the citizens of Maryland who were immediately interested in that proposed change were, as a general thing, the disloyal portion; and it was in reference to the effect which the opinion expressed by the honorable gentleman in the letter referred to had upon that vote, upon the action of that portion of the people, that my objection was in part founded : for it did seem that they understood it, as I understood it, as ignoring the moral obligation of that oath.

Now, one word in regard to the question of the right of this Court to inquire into the moral character of counsel. As an abstract question, we do not propose to do any such thing : we have no such right. I do not know whether the honorable gentleman is aware of the fact, that the order constituting this commission gives it power to make rules and regulations for its proceedings; and one of the rules thus made allows the accused to have counsel; and one of the provisions in regard to that matter is, that gentlemen appearing as counsel shall submit to the Court a certificate of having taken the oath of loyalty, or, in default of that, must take the oath in the presence of the Court.

This, then, is a qualification which puts it entirely in the power of the Court, and makes it competent to decide this question, because that oath brings up the very question of loyalty and the obligation of an oath; and here is a special question in reference to the opinions of a man, a gentleman of the bar, who may be proposed as counsel. If it appears that he ignores the moral obligation of an oath of that character, we defeat the very provision of the order by admitting such a man as counsel. It defeats the very end in view. I contend, therefore, that it is competent to the Court, and proper for me as a member of the Court, to make an objection of that character. Then the only question is, whether, in point of fact, the objection is well founded.

The gentleman disclaims any intention to inculcate such a doctrine as that to which I have taken exception; and I am glad to give him the benefit of that disclaimer. It is a tacit admission that the language of that letter may have been unguarded; that it may have had an effect that it was not intended to have, and that effect was an injurious one; and, if so, it was not in accordance with the intention of his mind in writing the letter. That, of course, is an explanation that ought to be satisfactory in regard to the moral question; but it was a very unfortunate thing if the gentleman wrote a letter of such a character that it was so terribly misconstrued by the people of his State. If that was not the intention of the writer, then, as a question of ethics, we must exonerate him. We are bound to take his present explanation. He disavows having had any such intention, and claims for himself a moral character which he is not ashamed to put up in comparison with that of any member of the Court. It was not my purpose to measure characters at all; but it was simply my purpose to bring forward, which I did conscientiously, — I felt it to be my duty, — I could not do any thing else, — an objection founded on the understanding that I had of the letter referred to. I was sorry to have to do it. I did it in no spirit of personal ill-will or bad feeling. I was sorry that I felt it to be my duty to do such a thing; but I could not do any thing else with the impressions I had on my mind.

The gentleman, as an honorable gentleman, will understand what I mean by this. He understands, according to his own estimation of his own character, what the force of conscientious convictions must be; and that if a man acts from principle in every act of his life, if he intends to be governed by moral principle, it will occasionally impose upon him some unpleasant duties, as it has upon me in the present case. The disavowal by the gentleman of any such intention I am bound to take. I know nothing of the history of the gentleman that would for a moment incline me not to take his explanation and his disavowal. It is satisfactory to me; but it is, I must insist, a tacit admission that there was some ground for the view upon which my objection was founded.

Mr. Johnson. Mr. President, a word more. The admission I made was certainly not intended to imply at all that the honorable member himself, except upon grounds that he supposed to be sufficient, had made the objection. He has not seen the opinion, as he says, for a good while, or perhaps never saw it; but, if he understood me as admitting that the people of Maryland so construed it, he has misunderstood me. I have no idea that they did so construe it; but, as he is satisfied with my statement that it was not my purpose to inculcate any such doctrine, that ends it.

All that I propose to say, if he will not conclude it in that way, is, that the order under which you are assembled gives you, in my case, no authority to refuse me admission, because you have no authority to administer the oath to me. I have taken the oath in the Senate of the United States, — the very oath that you are administering; I have taken it in the Circuit Court of the United States; I have taken it in the Supreme Court of the United States; and I am a practitioner in all the courts of the United States in nearly all the States; and it would be a little singular if one who has a right to appear before the supreme judicial tribunal of the land, and who has a right to appear before one of the legislative departments of the Government, whose law creates armies, and creates judges and courts-martial, should not have a right to appear before a court-martial. I have said all that I propose to say.

The President. Mr. Johnson has made an intimation in regard

to holding members of this Court personally responsible for their action.

Mr. Johnson. I made no such intimation : did not intend it.

The President. Then I shall say nothing more, sir.

Mr. Johnson. I had no idea of it. I said I was too old to feel such things, if I ever would.

The President. I was going to say that I hoped the day had passed when free men from the North were to be bullied and insulted by the humbug chivalry; and that, for my own part, I hold myself personally responsible for every thing I do here. The Court will be cleared.

The Commission was thereupon cleared for deliberation ; and, on re-opening, the Judge Advocate read the following paper : —

"Mr. President, — I desire to withdraw my objection to the admission of Mr. Reverdy Johnson as counsel before this Court, on the ground that his disclaimer of any intention to inculcate the doctrine that the moral obligation of an oath might, under certain circumstances, be disregarded, or under any circumstances, is, to my mind, a satisfactory removal of the grounds of the objection.

"T. M. Harris, Brigadier-General."

Mr. Johnson. I have not brought with me my certificate of having taken this oath ; but I will take the oath prescribed.

Gen. Wallace. I suppose it is within the knowledge of every member of the Commission that Mr. Senator Johnson has taken this oath in the Senate of the United States. I therefore suggest that the requirement of his taking the oath here be dispensed with.

The suggestion was acquiesced in *nem. con.*

Mr. Johnson. I appear, then, as counsel for Mrs. Surratt.

The Judge Advocate then proceeded to continue the calling of witnesses on the part of the Government.

John Lee,

a witness for the prosecution, being duly sworn, testified as follows : —

By the Judge Advocate :

Q. Do you belong to the military police force of this city?

A. Yes, sir.

Q. Will you state whether at any time you examined in the Kirkwood House the room of the prisoner, Atzerodt?

A. I was ordered there by Major O'Beirne, with the rest of his force. I was chief of his force. He told me to go to the top part of the building, and see how the house was situated, whether any person could get in there or not. I went and made the examination, and told him the house could very easily be got into from the roof and from a stairway that went up from the back-yard to the top of the building, which would leave you to go anywhere you wanted in the building. I told the major of these circumstances: he was in quite a hurry at that time; in fact, everybody was in a great deal of hurry.

Q. When was that?

A. On the night of the 15th of April. I then went out into the bar-room; and, while I was there, a friend came up to me,—I say a friend, because it was a man whom I see about the streets every day. He said there was rather a suspicious-looking man there who had taken a room the day previous, and that I had better go and look at the book. I went, and found the name, as near as I could make it out,—it was written very badly,—G. A. Atzerodt. It was written very badly: in fact, nobody could make it out until I went to the book. The proprietor of the house could not make it out.

Q. Did you go to the room which it was indicated on the register he had taken?

A. I then went up stairs to the room. I saw one of the clerks or men attached to the house, and asked him to go up to the room with me, saying that I should like to go and see it. I went up stairs to the room. The door was locked. The man said that he thought the party who had taken the room had carried the key away with him. I did not altogether like the appearance of things; so I went down to one of the proprietors, and asked him if he had any objections to going up to the room, and if he could get a key to fit the door. He said he had not one that would. I went up stairs again to the room, tried all the keys, and could not get one

to fit.   I then asked him if I had his permission to burst the door.
He said he had no objection ; and I burst open the door, and went
into the room.   There was a coat hanging on the wall.

Q. [Exhibiting a black coat marked No. 9.]   Is this it?

A. This black coat was hanging up on the wall, on the left-hand
side as you go in the door.   This is the coat.

[The coat was offered in evidence without objection.]

The witness proceeded : The coat was hanging on the wall, and
right opposite was the bedstead.   I went towards the bed, and, underneath the pillow or bolster, found a pistol all loaded and capped.

Q. [Exhibiting to the witness a pistol, loaded and capped, marked
No. 2.] Is that it?

A. It is.

[The pistol was offered in evidence without objection.]

Q. Did you find any thing else in the room?

A. Yes, sir.   I then went down stairs and tried to find Major
O'Beirne, my superior, the Provost Marshal of the Board of Enrolment : I saw him, and came up stairs again with him ; but it was
dark, and we came down again, and he went off, leaving me to in-
vestigate the matter.   I then went to the proprietor, who gave me
the number of the room, and we went up together.   I then took
the coat down.   I found in the pocket of the coat two books, which
are numbered No. 4 and No. 6.   The numbers on these articles
were affixed by me.   One book shows an account with the Ontario
Bank for $455.

[The book was offered in evidence without objection.]

[The other book, containing a map, was also received in evidence.]

I then put my hand in the pocket again, and took out a white
handkerchief with " Mary R. E. Booth " on it.   It is numbered 7.

[The hankerchief was offered in evidence without objection.]

I then pulled out the white handkerchief marked No. 9, and had
a good deal of difficulty in trying to make out the name on it ; but
I think it is F. M. or F. A. Nelson.

[The handkerchief was offered in evidence without objection.]

There was also a white handkerchief, with the letter H in the
corner.

[The handkerchief was offered in evidence.]

There was in the bank-book. an envelope, with the frank of the Hon. John Conness. There was a pair of new gauntlets, marked No. 20.

[The gauntlets were offered in evidence without objection.]

There was also a colored handkerchief, numbered 10.

[The handkerchief was offered in evidence without objection.]

There was also three boxes of Colt's cartridges, numbered 11, 12, and 13.

[The boxes of cartridges were offered in evidence without objection.]

I found also a piece of licorice and a tooth-brush.

[These articles were offered in evidence without objection.]

Q. Is the writing on the cover of the bank-book just as you found it?

A. Yes, sir: "J. W. Booth, 53;" and on the inside of the book was written: —

"Mr. J. Wilkes Booth, in account with the Ontario Bank,
Canada.

Dr.	1864.	Cr.
———	Oct. 27. By Dep.	$455."

I then got also this spur, No. 5.

[The spur was offered in evidence without objection.]

Also a pair of socks, No. 14; two collars, Nos. 16 and 17.

[These articles were offered in evidence without objection.]

Q. Do you remember the number of the room?

A. Yes, sir: No. 126, the next floor above where Vice-President Johnson was at the time.

Q. Was he right over Vice-President Johnson's room?

A. On the next floor above, going up, and through an entry, and then a little off on one side. I then went round the room, took up the carpet, examined under the carpet, wash-stand, and bureau, and in the stove: I got out all the cinders and ashes; and I made a thorough search of every thing in the room. I then went to the bed, took up the covering piece by piece, and felt all through it to see if there was any thing in the quilt. After I got down un-

6*

derneath the sheets, between the sheets and the mattress, I got the bowie-knife, marked No. 3.

[The knife was offered in evidence without objection.]

Q. You did not yourself see the occupant of the room?

A. I did not.

Q. He had come there the day before, you understood?

A. Yes, sir: the clerk employed in the house says he would recognize the man who was there if he saw him.

Q. What is his name?.

A. I do not know.

Cross-examined by MR. DOSTER:

Q. What is your business?

A. I am chief of the detective force of the Board of Enrolment of the District of Columbia. Major O'Beirne is the Provost Marshal of the Board.

Q. How long have you followed the business?

A. I have been in the secret service ever since I left New York, at the commencement of the war, in the Ninety-fifth New-York Volunteers.

Q. How long have you been a detective here in Washington?

A. Ever since the burning of Aquia-Creek Village. I left Aquia Creek and came here, and was then detailed from my regiment to Colonel Baker's force, and staid with him until the Secretary of War gave me a discharge; and I then went from that to the Provost Marshal's office of the District of Columbia, and have been there to the present time.

Q. You have been discharged as detective already by the Secretary of War, you say?

A. Not as detective, but as a volunteer in the Ninety-fifth New-York Volunteers.

Q. You mentioned a conversation with some one in reference to a suspicious person at the Kirkwood House?

A. Yes, sir.

Q. Do you know who the person was?

A. He was employed in that house; but I cannot tell you his name.

Q. Where did you see him in the house?

A. On the first floor of the house, in the front of the building.

Q. Was he a clerk?

A. I do not know whether he was a night watchman or clerk; either one or the other, I think.

Q. What was his precise language to you?

A. He said to me that there was a very suspicious, bad-looking, villanous-looking fellow came into the place there, and took a room in the house, and he did not like the appearance of him; that I had better look after him. I think that was it.

Q. When did he say the person had come into the house and taken a room?

A. I think it was the day before.

Q. You are not positive: you cannot say for certain?

A. No, sir: I cannot say for certain. I could not be positive about it; but I think, to the best of my knowledge, it was the day before.

Q. Did he describe to you the appearance of this suspicious-looking person?

A. He did.

Q. Will you repeat the description?

A. I do not think I could describe it as he described it to me. I do not recollect. I think, though, that he said he had a gray coat on.

Q. Have you ever, to your knowledge, seen this Atzerodt?

A. I do not know that I ever have. I have seen almost everybody that has been about Washington knocking around.

Q. But you have never seen him?

A. I do not know that I ever saw him to know him by name. I do not say that I have not or that I have. I do not know.

Q. What first brought you to the Kirkwood House to speak with this clerk?

A. I was home, eating my supper; and one of my men, Mr. Cunningham, came over to me. I came out of my house just after eating my supper, and met him half-way on the block. He said, "You are wanted immediately down at the Kirkwood House." I went down to the Kirkwood House, and there met Major O'Beirne; and I found that the men were detailed there — they were just making the arrangements — to protect the person of the Vice-President at the time.

Q. Now describe the appearance of the man who gave you the information that there was a suspicious person there.

A. A man about your build, as near as I know of.

Q. Does he look like I do?

A. Yes: he may be a little heavier than you. I think he is near about your height.

Q. How old does he look about to be?

A. Somewheres in the neighborhood of your age.

Q. What is my age?

A. I should take you to be about thirty.

Q. You do not know his name?

A. I do not.

Q. Describe accurately the relative position of Mr. Johnson's room, if you know, and the room where you say you found this coat.

A. In the Kirkwood House, you go right up the main entrance into the office, and the stairway goes right up. As you turn the stairway, you go right up straight half-way till you get to the second story, and you file left, and then go on up the stairs and to the right hand: after you get up, you face the parlors. Mr. Johnson's room was right opposite the parlors; but you cannot go into them by being directly opposite them there. You go up a little farther to reach the parlor doors on the same passage; then there is a little recess that runs into a window that looks out on Twelfth Street.

Q. How many doors is it from Mr. Johnson's door to the door of the room where you found these things?

A. I do not know. It is on the floor above. You face Mr. Johnson's room door as you go in, and come to a stairs leading to the floor above. When you get to the next floor, you meet an entry. You go along that entry till you come to a passage-way, and then file right; and the room where I found these things is in a corner there, facing, I think, in the direction of Pennsylvania Avenue. It is rather a peculiarly constructed house up-stairs; and it is impossible for me to describe it exactly. To give an exact idea of it, a draught of it should be taken.

Q. Did you find the signature of Atzerodt on any thing in the room?

A. I did not.

Q. Did you find his name there?

A. I did not.

Q. What made you believe it was his room?

A. Because it said so on the register.

Q. What said so on the register?

A. His signature was there, and the number of the room opposite, No. 126.

Q. Had you any other evidence that that was his room, except the register?

A. I do not know that I had any other evidence of it.

By the JUDGE ADVOCATE:

Q. In coming down from room No. 126 to reach the office of the hotel, would a person pass the room then occupied by Vice-President Johnson?

A. Yes, sir. When I came down, there was a soldier at the door at the time this search was made. A man of any courage coming right down the stairs could throw a handful of snuff in the soldier's eyes, and get right into Mr. Johnson's room.

LOUIS J. WEICHMANN,

a witness for the prosecution, being duly sworn, testified as follows : —

By the JUDGE ADVOCATE:

Q. Will you state whether you know John H. Surratt?

A. I do.

Q. When did you first make his acquaintance?

A. My acquaintance with John H. Surratt commenced in the fall of 1859, at St. Charles's College, Md.

Q. How long were you together?

A. We left college in the summer of 1862, in July, together.

Q. When did you renew your acquaintance with him here in this city?

A. I renewed my acquaintance with him in 1863, in January, in this city.

Q. When did you begin to board at the house of his mother, Mrs. Surratt, a prisoner here ?

A. The 1st of November, 1864.

Q. In this city ?

A. Yes, sir.

Q. In what part of the city ?

A. H Street, between Sixth and Seventh, No. 541.

Q. You speak of Mrs. Surratt, who is sitting near you there ?

A. Yes, sir : she is the lady.

Q. State when you first made the acquaintance of the prisoner, Dr. Samuel A. Mudd ?

A. It was about the 15th of January, 1865.

Q. State under what circumstances.

A. I was passing down Seventh Street, in company with Mr. Surratt ; and, when opposite Odd Fellows' Hall, some one called, " Surratt, Surratt ! " and, turning round, Mr. Surratt recognized an old acquaintance of his, Dr. Samuel A. Mudd, of Charles County, Md.

Q. The prisoner at the bar?

A. Yes, sir : that is the gentleman there (pointing to Samuel A. Mudd). Mr. Surratt introduced Dr. Mudd to me ; and Dr. Mudd introduced Mr. Booth, who was in company with him, to both of us.

Q. He and Booth were walking together in the street ?

A. Yes, sir. They were coming up Seventh Street, and we were going down.

Q. You mean J. Wilkes Booth ?

A. Yes, sir : J. Wilkes Booth.

Q. Where did you go to from that, when you went ?

A. Booth then invited us to his room at the National Hotel.

Q. What occurred there ?

A. Booth told us to be seated ; and he ordered cigars and wines to the room for four. Dr. Mudd then went out into the passage, and called Booth out, and had a private conversation with him. Booth and Dr. Mudd came in, and they then called Surratt out.

Q. Both of them called him out ?

A. No, sir : Booth went out with Surratt ; and then they came in, and all three went out together, and had a private conversation in the passage, leaving me alone.

Q. How long did that conversation last?

A. It must have been about fifteen or twenty minutes.

Q. You did not hear what it was?

A. No, sir: I do not know the nature of the conversation. I was seated on a lounge at the time, near the window. On returning to the room the last time, Dr. Mudd came to me, and seated himself by my side on the settee; and he apologized for his private conversation, stating that Booth and he had some private business; that Booth wished to purchase his farm.

Q. Did you see any maps or papers of that sort used?

A. No, sir. Booth at one time took out the back of an envelope, and made marks on it with a pencil. I should not consider it writing, but more in the direction of roads or lines. Surratt and Booth and Dr. Mudd were at that time seated round the table, — a centre-table, — in the centre of the room.

Q. Did you see the marks?

A. No, sir: I just saw the motion of the pencil. Booth also came to me, and stated that he wished to purchase Dr. Mudd's farm. Dr. Mudd had previously stated to me that he did not care about selling his farm to Booth, because Booth was not going to give him enough.

Q. But you did not hear a word spoken yourself in regard to the farm in their conference?

A. No, sir: I do not know the nature of the conversation they had at all.

Q. I understood you to say you did not hear any of their private conversation?

A. No, sir: I did not.

Q. You only saw the motion of the pencil as they were marking?

A. No, sir. What their conversation was I do not know.

Q. You continued to board at the house of Mrs. Surratt, the prisoner?

A. I boarded at Mrs. Surratt's house up to the time of the assassination.

Q. After this interview at the National Hotel, will you state whether Booth called frequently at Mrs. Surratt's?

A. He called there frequently.

Q. Whom did he call to see?

A. He generally called for Mr. Surratt,—John H. Surratt; and, in the absence of John H. Surratt, he would call for Mrs. Surratt.

Q. Were their interviews always apart from other persons, or in the presence of other persons?

A. They were always apart. I have been in the company of Booth in the parlor; but Booth has taken Surratt out of the room and taken him up-stairs, and engaged in private conversation in rooms up-stairs. Booth would sometimes, when there, engage in a general sort of conversation, and would then say, "John, can you go up-stairs, and spare me a word?" They would go up-stairs, and engage in private conversation, which would sometimes last two or three hours.

Q. Did the same thing ever occur with Mrs. Surratt?

A. Yes, sir.

Q. Have you ever seen the prisoner, Atzerodt?

A. I have.

Q. Do you recognize him here?

A. Yes, sir.

Q. Have you seen him at Mrs. Surratt's?

A. He came to Mrs. Surratt's house, as near as I can remember, about three weeks after I formed the acquaintance of Booth.

Q. For whom did he inquire?

A. He inquired for John H. Surratt or Mrs. Surratt, as he said.

Q. Did you ever see him with Booth there, or only with Surratt?

A. I have never seen him in the house with Booth.

Q. How often did he call?

A. He must have been at the house ten or fifteen times.

Q. What was the name by which he was known to the ladies of the house?

A. The young ladies of the house could not comprehend the

name that he gave. They understood that he came from Port Tobacco, the lower portion of Maryland; and, instead of calling him by his proper name, they gave him the nickname of "Port Tobacco."

Q. Did you ever meet him on the street, and go with him — you and Mrs. Surratt — to the theatre? and under what circumstances?

A. Yes, sir. I met him at the corner of Seventh Street and Pennsylvania Avenue about the time that Booth played the part of Pescara, in "The Apostate." Booth had given Surratt two complimentary tickets on that occasion; and we went down, and met Atzerodt at the corner of Seventh Street and Pennsylvania Avenue, and told him that we were going. He said he was going along too; and at the theatre we met David E. Herold.

Q. Do you see him, sir?

A. Yes, sir: there he is [pointing out David E. Herold, who smiled and nodded in recognition of the witness]. There was also another gentleman there, who boarded in the house, — Mr. Holahan: we met him.

Q. Where did you meet him?

A. At the theatre. We remained in the theatre till the play was over; and, on leaving the theatre, the five of us left together, — Mr. Surratt, Mr. Holahan, and myself in company; and we went as far as the corner of Tenth and E Streets; and, on turning round, Surratt noticed that Atzerodt and Herold did not follow him, and told me to go back. I went back, and found Atzerodt and Herold in a restaurant adjoining the theatre, talking very confidentially with Booth; and, on my approaching them, they separated, and Booth said, "Mr. Weichmann, will you not come and take a drink?" And we approached the counter, and took a drink; and Booth introduced me to a gentleman there whose name I do not remember, but whose face I have seen very frequently around town here. We left the restaurant, and joined the other two gentlemen on E Street, and then went to Kloman's and had some oysters. We there separated; Mr. John H. Surratt and myself and Mr. Holahan going home, and the others going down Seventh Street.

Q. You say, that to this conversation at the National, which was stated to be about buying a farm, John H. Surratt was a party?

A. Yes, sir.

Q. They did not explain to you what he had to do with the buying of Dr. Mudd's farm by Booth?

A. No, sir: they did not.

Q. Do you know where John H. Surratt kept his horse in this city?

A. John H Surratt stated to me that he had two horses, and that he kept them at Howard's stable, on G Street, between Sixth and Seventh.

Q. Did you ever see the prisoner, Atzerodt, there?

A. Yes, sir. I saw him there the day of the assassination.

Q. What time in the day?

A. At about half-past two o'clock.

Q. What did he seem to be doing there?

A. He wished to hire a horse. I had been sent there by Mrs. Surratt for the purpose of hiring a buggy; and, when I went to the stable, I saw Atzerodt there, and asked him what he wanted. He said he was going to hire a horse; and he asked Mr. Brooks in my presence [that is the name by which the stable-keeper is known to me] if he could have a horse, and Mr. Brooks told him he could not. Then we both left, and went as far as the post-office. I had a letter to drop in the post-office; and we went down F Street towards Tenth. Since that time I have never seen him.

Q. Were those horses that were kept there Surratt's or Booth's?

A. I would state, that, on the Tuesday previous to the Friday of the assassination, I was also sent by Mrs. Surratt to the National Hotel to see Booth for the purpose of getting his buggy. She wished me to drive her into the country on that day; and Booth said that he had sold the buggy, but that he would give me ten dollars instead, and I should hire a buggy. He spoke about the horses that he had kept at Brooks's stable; and I remarked to him, "Why, I thought they were Surratt's horses!" Said he, "No: they are mine."

Q. I understand you to say that Booth did give you the ten dollars?

A. Yes, sir : he gave me the ten dollars.

Q. Did you drive Mrs. Surratt out on that day?

A. I did.

Q. To what point in the country?

A. We left the city about nine o'clock, and reached Surrattsville at about half-past twelve o'clock on Tuesday, the 11th of April.

Q. Did you return that day?

A. Yes, sir. We remained at Surrattsville about half an hour, —probably not that long; and Mrs. Surratt stated that she went there for the purpose of seeing Mr. Nothe, who owed her some money.

Q. Will you state whether, on the following Friday, that is, the day of the assassination, you drove Mrs. Surratt to the country?

A. Yes, sir. We left about half-past two o'clock in the afternoon. She herself gave me the money on that occasion, — a ten-dollar note; and I paid six dollars for the buggy.

Q. Where did you drive her to?

A. To Surrattsville; arriving there about half-past four.

Q. Did you stop at the house of Mr. Lloyd, who keeps tavern there?

A. Yes, sir. Mrs. Surratt went into the parlor, and I remained outside a portion of the time; and a portion of the time I went into the bar-room, until Mrs. Surratt sent for me.

Q. What time did you leave on your return?

A. About half-past six o'clock.

Q. Is it about two hours' drive?

A. Yes, sir : a person can get down there very easily in two hours when the roads are good.

Q. Will you state whether you remember, some time in the month of March, of a man calling at Mrs. Surratt's, where you were boarding, and giving himself the name of Wood, and inquiring for John H. Surratt?

A. Yes, sir : I myself went to open the door; and he inquired for Mr. Surratt. I told him Mr. Surratt was not at home; but I would introduce him to the family if he desired it. He thereupon expressed a desire to see Mrs. Surratt; and I accordingly introduced him, having first asked his name. He gave the name of Wood.

Q. Do you recognize him among these prisoners?

A. That is the man (pointing to Lewis Payne, one of the accused).

Q. He called himself Wood?

A. Yes, sir.

Q. How long did he remain with Mrs. Surratt?

A. That evening, he stopped in the house all night. He had supper served up to him in my own room. I brought him supper from the kitchen.

Q. When was that?

A. As near as I can remember, it must have been about eight weeks previous to the assassination. I have no exact knowledge of the date.

Q. Did he bring any baggage with him to the house?

A. No, sir. He had a black overcoat on, and a black frock-coat, with gray pants, at that time.

Q. You say he remained until the next day?

A. He remained until the next morning, leaving in the earliest train for Baltimore.

Q. Do you remember whether, some weeks after this, the same man called again?

A. I should think it was about three weeks afterwards that he called again; and I again went to the door, and again ushered him into the parlor: and, in the mean time, I had forgotten his name, and I asked him his name. That time he gave the name of Payne.

Q. Was it the same man?

A. Yes, sir.

Q. Did he have an interview then with Mrs. Surratt?

A. He was ushered into the parlor. Mrs. Surratt, Miss Surratt, and Miss Honora Fitzpatrick, were present.

Q. How long did he remain?

A. He remained about three days at that time. He represented himself as a Baptist preacher: he also said that he had been in prison in Baltimore for about a week, and that he had taken the oath of allegiance, and was going to become a good and loyal citizen.

Q. Are not the family of Mrs. Surratt and Mrs. Surratt herself Catholics?

A. Yes, sir. Mr. Surratt is himself a Catholic, and was a student of divinity at the same college.

Q. Did you hear any explanation made why a Baptist preacher should go there seeking hospitality?

A. No, sir. They only looked upon it as odd, and laughed at it. Mrs. Surratt herself remarked that he was a great looking Baptist preacher.

Q. Did they not seem to recognize him as the "Wood" of former days who had been there?

A. Yes, sir. In the course of conversation, one of the young ladies called him Wood; and then I recollected, that, on his first visit, he had given the name of Wood.

Q. How was he dressed on the last occasion?

A. He was dressed in gray, — a complete suit of gray.

Q. Did he have any baggage with him on the last occasion?

A. Yes, sir. He had a linen coat, and two linen shirts.

Q. Did you observe any traces of disguise about him, or attempted preparations for disguise?

A. I would say, that one day, returning from my office, I found a false mustache on the table in my room. I took the mustache, and threw it into a little toilet-box I had on the table. This man Payne searched around the table, and inquired for his mustache. I was sitting on the chair, and did not say any thing. I have retained the mustache since, and it was found in my baggage: it was among a box of paints that I had in my trunk.

Q. Did you ever see Payne during that visit, and John H. Surratt, together in their room by themselves?

A. Yes, sir.

Q. What were they occupied with doing?

A. It was on the same day. On returning from my office, I went up stairs to the third story; and I found John H. Surratt and this man Payne seated on a bed, playing with bowie-knives. It was the occasion of Payne's last visit.

7*

Q. Were there any other weapons about them?

A. Two revolvers, and four sets of new spurs.

Q. [Exhibiting the spur identified by the last witness as found in the room in the Kirkwood House.] Were the spurs like this?

A. They were. That is one of the spurs.

Q. [Exhibiting the bowie-knife identified by the last witness as found in the room in the Kirkwood House.] Is that the bowie-knife?

A. I do not recognize that as the bowie-knife. It was a smaller one.

Q. But you know the spur? You are satisfied as to that?

A. Yes, sir: there were three spurs similar to this in a closet in my room when I was last there; and those three I am sure belonged to the eight that had been purchased by Surratt.

Q. Did you say there was a brace of pistols?

A. Two long navy revolvers.

Q. [Exhibiting the revolver identified by the last witness as found in the room at the Kirkwood House.] Is that the pistol?

A. That looks like it.

Q. Was it a round barrel like that, or octangular?

A. The barrel was not round: it was octangular. It was about the same size, though.

Q. Do you remember having gone with John H. Surratt to the Herndon House for the purpose of renting a room?

A. Yes, sir.

Q. What time was that?

A. It must have been on or about the 19th of March.

Q. For whom did he wish to rent this room?

A. He went to the door, and inquired for Mrs. Mary Murray; and, when Mrs. Mary Murray came, he stated that he wished to have a private interview with her. She did not seem to comprehend; and said he, "Perhaps Miss Anna Ward has spoken to you about this room. Did she not speak to you about engaging a room for a delicate gentleman, who was to have his meals sent up to his room?" Then Mrs. Murray recollected: and Mr. Surratt said that he would like to have the room for the following Monday; that the gentleman would take possession of it on Monday. It was the Monday previous to the 31st of April. I think it was the 27th of March that the room was to have been taken possession of.

Q. The name of the person was given?

A. No, sir: there was no name mentioned.

Q. Did you afterwards learn that the prisoner, Payne, was at that house, — the Herndon House?

A. Yes, sir. I met this man, Atzerodt, one day on the street; and I asked him where he was going, and he said that he was going to see Payne; and then I asked him, "Is it Payne who is at the Herndon House?" and he said, "Yes."

Q. That was after the visit John H. Surratt made there to engage the room?

A. Yes, sir.

Q. Have you ever met the prisoner, Herold, at Mrs. Surratt's?

A. I met him there once.

Q. Where else have you met him?

A. I met him on the occasion of the visit to the theatre when Booth played Pescara. I also met Herold at Mrs. Surratt's, in the country, in the spring of 1863, when I first made Mrs. Surratt's acquaintance. He was there at that time with a party of musicians, who were serenading some county officers who had been elected; and then again I met him in the summer of 1864, at a church in the country, — the Piscataway Church; and then in the theatre, and once at Mrs. Surratt's house. These are the only times, to my recollection, that I have met him.

Q. Do you know either of the prisoners, Arnold or O'Laughlin?

A. No, sir.

Q. What knowledge have you, if any, of John H. Surratt having gone to Richmond?

A. About the 17th of March, 1865, a woman by the name of Mrs. Slater came to the house, and stopped there one night. This lady went to Canada and Richmond. On Saturday, the 23d of March, Mr. Surratt drove her into the country about eight o'clock in the morning: he had hired a two-horse team, white horses, at Brooks's. He left in company with Mrs. Slater; and Mrs. Surratt was also in the buggy.

Q. It was understood that John H. Surratt went to Richmond?

A. Yes, sir. On returning, Mrs. Surratt told me that he had gone to Richmond with Mrs. Slater. This Mrs. Slater, to the best of my knowledge, was to have met a man by the name of Howe there, a blockade-runner. This Howe was captured on the 24th of March, and could not take her back to Richmond; so Surratt took her back.

Q. Was Mrs. Slater a blockade-runner herself?

A. I believe she was either a blockade-runner or a bearer of despatches.

Q. Did Mrs. Surratt tell you so?

A. Yes, sir.

Q. Do you know when John Surratt returned from Richmond?

A. He returned from Richmond on the occasion of the fall of Richmond, — the 3d of April.

Q. Do you know of his having brought gold with him?

A. He had about nine or eleven twenty-dollar gold-pieces in his possession.

Q. You saw that money in his possession when he came back?

A. Yes, sir.

Q. That was all you saw? You do not know whether he had more or not?

A. He had some greenbacks. He had about fifty dollars in greenbacks. He gave forty dollars of this gold to Mr. Holahan, and Mr. Holahan gave him sixty dollars in greenbacks for it.

Q. Did he leave the city immediately on his arrival here?

A. He remained in the house about an hour; and he told me that he was going to Montreal, and asked me to walk down the street with him to take some oysters. We went down Seventh Street and along Pennsylvania Avenue, and took some oysters.

Q. And he left immediately, did he?

A. Yes, sir: he left me that evening.

Q. Saying that he was going to Canada?

A. He said he was going to Montreal. I have not seen him since.

Q. Have you seen a letter from him?

A. Yes, sir: I saw a letter from him dated St. Lawrence Hall, Montreal, Can., April 12. It was received here on the 14th of

April. I also saw another letter, written to a Miss Ward : the date
I do not remember ; but the receipt of that letter was prior to the receipt of the letter to his mother.

Q. Did you have any conversation with him, as he passed through,
about the fall of Richmond ?

A. Yes, sir. He told me he did not believe it ; that he had seen
Benjamin and Davis, and they had told him that Richmond would
not be evacuated.

Q. He said that they had told him so while he was in Richmond ?

A. Yes, sir.

Q. On his arriving here, the intelligence of its fall was received,
and you communicated it to him ?

A. Yes, sir : I communicated it to him, and he seemed to be in-
credulous.

Q. Have you been to Canada yourself since ?

A. Yes, sir.

Q. What did you learn of his whereabouts and movements there ?

A. I learned that he had arrived in Montreal on the 6th of April,
and left there on the 12th for the States ; returning on the 18th,
and engaging rooms at St. Lawrence Hall, Montreal. He left St.
Lawrence Hall that night,—the night of the 18th ; and he was
seen to leave the house of a Mr. Porterfield in company with three
others in a wagon. I did not see him there myself ; but my knowledge was obtained from the register at St. Lawrence Hall. I did
not arrive at Montreal until the 19th.

Q. Do you remember, early in the month of April, of Mrs. Surratt's having sent for you, and asking you to give Mr. Booth notice
that she wished to see him ?

A. Yes, sir.

Q. What was the message which she desired to be communicated
to him ?

A. She merely stated that she would like to see him, and for
him to come to the house.

Q. Did she state that she wished to see him on private business,
or use any expression of that kind ?

A. Yes, sir : she said, "Private business."

Q. What did Booth say when you communicated the message to him?

A. He said he would come to the house in the evening, as soon as he could.

Q. Did you say that was in April?

A. Some time in April: early in April.

Q. Before the assassination?

A. Yes, sir. It was on the 2d of April when Mrs. Surratt sent me to the hotel; and I at that time found in Booth's room Mr. John McCullough, the actor; and I communicated my message to Booth. I told him that Mrs. Surratt would like to see him, and he said he would come in the evening; and he did come on the evening of the 2d of April.

Q. Will you state whether, on the afternoon of the 14th of April, the day of the assassination, Mr. Booth did not call and have a private interview with Mrs. Surratt at her house?

A. I will state, that about half-past two o'clock, when I was going to the door, I saw Mr. Booth. He was in the parlor, and Mrs. Surratt was speaking with him.

Q. Were they alone?

A. Yes, sir: they were alone in the parlor.

Q. How long was it after that before you drove to the country with Mrs. Surratt?

A. He did not remain in the parlor more than three or four minutes.

Q. And was it immediately after that you and Mrs. Surratt set out for the country?

A. Yes, sir.

Cross-examined by Mr. Johnson:

Q. How long did you live at Mrs. Surratt's house?

A. I have been living at the house since the 1st of November, 1864. Mrs. Surratt at that time removed to the city from the country. She had rented her farm to Mr. Boyd.

Q. Had you lived with her in the country?

A. No, sir: I had visited her several times during the year 1863–4 in the country.

Q. You knew her very well at that time?

A. No, sir: not very well. I had made her acquaintance through her son. Her son was a schoolmate of mine. He had been at college with me for three years; and, when I went there, it was to exchange the usual civilities, and I always experienced the utmost kindness and courtesy.

Q. What sort of a house had she in the city, — a large or a small one? How many rooms?

A. Eight rooms, — six large rooms and two small ones.

Q. Was she in the habit of renting her rooms out?

A. Yes, sir: she has been since I have been there.

Q. Did she furnish board as well as rooms?

A. Yes, sir.

Q. You say young Surratt told you some time in April that he was going to Montreal. Did you ever know him to go to Montreal before that time?

A. No, sir.

Q. Had he been here through the winter of 1864-5, at his mother's house?

A. Sometimes he was at home, and sometimes he was not. During the winter of 1864, especially in the month of November, he was down in the country almost all the time. His stay at home has not been permanent at all, because he would sometimes remain at home half a week, and go into the country the other half; and sometimes he would be three or four weeks at a time in the country:

Q. During that winter of 1864-5, was he away any time so long as that he could have gone to Canada and returned without your knowing it?

A. Yes, sir. He could have gone to Canada without my knowledge; but he could not have returned to the house without my knowledge.

Q. Have you any reason to believe, from your own knowledge, that he was in Canada in the winter of 1864-5?

A. No, sir.

Q. Were you upon intimate terms with him?

A. Very intimate, indeed.

Q. Did he ever intimate to you or anybody else, to your knowledge, that there was a purpose to assassinate the President?

A. No, sir. He stated to me in the presence of his sister, shortly after he made the acquaintance of Booth, that he was going to Europe on a cotton speculation ; that three thousand dollars had been advanced to him by an elderly gentleman residing somewhere in his neighborhood,— the name of that elderly gentleman he never mentioned to me ; and he stated that he was going to Europe, to Liverpool, and would probably remain there only two weeks to transact his business : from Liverpool he would go to Nassau ; from Nassau to Matamoras, Mexico, to find his brother Isaac, who was in the rebel army.

Q. His brother ?

A. Yes, sir : his brother is in Magruder's army, in Texas, and has been there since 1861.

Q. Did not his brother go to Texas before the Rebellion ? or do you know ?

A. I do not know.

Q. You have never seen the brother ?

A. I never saw the brother.

Q. Were you in the habit of seeing John H. Surratt almost every day when he was at home, at his mother's ?

A. Yes, sir : he would be seated at the same table.

Q. Was he frequently in your room, and you in his ?

A. He partook of the same room, shared my bed with me, slept with me.

Q. And during the whole of that period you never heard him intimate that it was his purpose, or that there was a purpose, to assassinate the President ?

A. Never, sir.

Q. You never heard him say any thing on the subject, or anybody else, during the whole period from November until the assassination ?

A. No, sir. At one time he mentioned to me that he was going on the stage with Booth ; that he was going to be an actor ; and that they were going to play in Richmond.

Q. You say that he had been educated at what college ?

A. At St. Charles's College, Maryland.

Q. A Catholic college ?

A. Yes, sir. He was a student of divinity for three years.

Q. Were you a student of divinity with him?

A. Yes, sir. I was there a year longer than he was.

Q. During the whole of that period, what was his character?

A. His character was excellent. On leaving college, he shed tears; and the president approached him, and told him not to weep; that his conduct had been so excellent during the three years he had been there, that he would always be remembered by those who had charge of the institution.

Q. When was the first of the two occasions on which, you say, you drove Mrs. Surratt to Surrattsville?

A. The first occasion was on Tuesday, the 11th of April.

Q. Did she tell you what her object in going was?

A. She told me she had some business with a man by the name of Nothe. This man Nothe, she told me, owed her a sum of money, about four hundred and seventy-nine dollars, and the interest on it for thirteen years, as near as I can remember.

Q. Was there such a man there?

A. Yes, sir: there is a man resides in that portion of the country by the name of Nothe.

Q. Do you know whether she saw him when she went on that occasion?

A. We arrived at the village about half-past twelve o'clock; but Mr. Nothe was not there. She told Mr. Nott, the bar-keeper, to send a messenger for him; and he immediately sent a mounted messenger to Mr. Nothe. In the mean time, Mrs. Surratt, and myself went to Captain Gwynn's place, about three miles lower down, and remained there about two hours, taking dinner. Mrs. Surratt stated that she would like to have Captain Gwynn return with her; and Captain Gwynn did return with us.

Q. To Surrattsville?

A. Yes, sir; and, on returning, Mrs. Surratt and Captain Gwynn found Mr. Nothe in the parlor, and there they transacted their business. I was not a witness to it.

Q. There was such a man living there, and she did see him?

A. Yes, sir: she saw him on that day,—she so stated.

Q. You knew the man when you saw him?

A. No, sir,

Q. Was he not pointed out to you?

A. No, sir: I have never seen him.

Q. I thought you said he was at Surrattsville?

A. Mr. Nott said he was in the parlor.

Q. You did not go in?

A. No, sir: I did not go in.

Q. Did she state to you what her purpose was in making the second visit?

A. She said, when she rapped at my room on that afternoon, that she had received a letter from Charles Calvert with regard to this money that was due her by Mr. Nothe.

Q. The same debt?

A. Yes, sir; and she stated that she was again compelled to go to the country, and she asked me to bring her down; and, of course, I consented.

Q. Did she tell you that the letter was from Calvert?

A. No, sir.

Q. Did you see it?

A. No, sir: I did not see the letter.

Q. She said she had received a letter from Mr. Charles Calvert?

A. Yes, sir; and that it was concerning this man Nothe.

Q. That required her, as she thought, to go to Surrattsville?

A. Yes, sir. That is all I know about the letter.

Q. Did you go in a buggy?

A. Yes, sir.

Q. Nobody but yourself and Mrs. Surratt?

A. No one but ourselves.

Q. Did you take any thing with you, — any weapons of any sort?

A. No weapons. She took two packages. One was a package of papers about her property at Surrattsville; and then another was a package which was done up in paper, about six inches, I should think, in diameter, It looked to me like a saucer or two, or two or three saucers, wrapped in paper. That was deposited in the bottom of the buggy, and taken out by Mrs. Surratt when we arrived at Surrattsville.

Q. That is all, you say?

A. That is all I know of.

Q. How long did you remain there ?

A. We remained there until half-past six o'clock.

Q. It was not dark at that time ?

A. No, sir : it was not dark.

Q. At what time did you reach here?

A. We reached here at about half-past eight or nine o'clock.

Q. When did you hear, or did you hear, of the assassination of the President, and the attack on Secretary Seward, that evening?

A. I heard of the assassination of President Lincoln and the attack on Secretary Seward at three o'clock on Saturday morning, when the detectives came to the house and informed us of it.

Q. And not until that ?

A. Not until that time.

Q. Who came to the house between the period of your return and three o'clock on Saturday morning when the detectives came ? Anybody?

A. There was some one that rang the bell ; but who the person was I do not know.

Q. Was the bell answered ?

A. Yes, sir.

Q. By whom ?

A. It was answered by Mrs. Surratt.

Q. Was there any one at the door ?

A. Yes, sir : I heard steps going into the parlor, and immediately going out, going down the steps.

Q. How long was that after you had got back from Surrattsville ?

A. It must have been about ten minutes. I was taking supper at the time.

Q. That was before ten o'clock, was it not ?

A. Yes, sir : it was before ten o'clock.

Q. Before what is understood to have been the time of the assassination ?

A. Yes, sir. The assassination is said to have taken place at half-past ten. It was before that time.

Q. Have persons been in the habit of going there for rooms, and staying a day or two ?

A. Persons have been in the habit of coming from the country and stopping at the house. Mrs. Surratt had a great many acquaintances, and was always very hospitable; and they could remain just as long as they chose.

Q. The man who took the room, you say, was Atzerodt?

A. Atzerodt, to my knowledge, stopped in the house only one night.

Q. Did he take a room?

A. Not that I know of.

Q. Did he sleep there one night?

A. Yes, sir.

Q. What room did he sleep in?

A. A room in the third story, — a back room.

Q. Was there anybody there with him in that room?

A. No, sir: there was no one in that room.

Q. Then he had a room there that night?

A. Yes, sir: he had a room that night.

Q. Did he leave there the next day?

A. Yes, sir.

Q. You saw Payne yourself when he came there?

A. The first time I saw that man, he gave the name of Wood. I saw Payne myself. I went to the door, and opened the door; and he said he would like to see Mrs. Surratt.

Q. As he was dressed at that time, was his appearance genteel?

A. Yes, sir. He had a long black coat on; and, when he went into the parlor, he acted very politely. He asked Mrs. Surratt to play on the piano; and he raised the piano-cover, and did every thing which indicated a person of breeding.

Q. Do you know why Atzerodt left the house?

A. No, sir.

Q. Had he been with any one drinking in the room he got, or either of the rooms up stairs?

A. Yes, sir. The time he stopped in the house was about the beginning of February; and at that time there was a man there by the name of Howell. Mr. John Surratt had been in the country, and he returned from the country that evening; and John Surratt slept that night with Howell.

Q. What I asked was, whether there was any drinking in the room?

A. Yes, sir.

Q. Was that the room occupied by Atzerodt?

A. Yes, sir.

Q. Were they noisy at all?

A. No, sir; not noisy.

Q. Have you any knowledge that he was told he could not stay there any longer?

A. No, sir.

Q. You did not hear that from any of the family?

A. No, sir.

Q. But he did leave there the next day?

A. Yes, sir: he left the next day. His leaving was owing to the arrival of Mr. Surratt at that time, as near as I could judge. He said he wanted to see John; and, as soon as he saw John, he left.

Q. You did not hear from Mrs. Surratt, or any of the family, that she had told John he could not stay there?

A. No, sir; not at that time. I heard Miss Anna and Mrs. Surratt afterwards say, that they did not care about having him brought to the house.

Q. Was that before the assassination?

A. Yes, sir.

Q. What reason did they give for not wishing him brought to the house?

A. The way Miss Anna Surratt expressed it, she said she did not care about having such sticks brought to the house; that they were not company for her.

Q. He never did go there afterwards, that you know of?

A. He has not been to the house, to the best of my knowledge, since the 2d of April.

Q. You say you found upon your own table a false mustache. What was the color of the hair?

A. It was black.

Q. Was it a large or diminutive mustache?

8*

A. It was about a medium-sized mustache. It was not a very small one, nor was it what I would call a very large one.

Q. Was it so large that it would entirely change the appearance of the wearer?

A. Yes, sir.

Q. You think it was?

A. I think so.

Q. You took that off the table where you found it; and you put it in your own box, where you had your paints?

A. Yes, sir: I put it first in my toilet-box, a box standing on the table; and afterwards removed it from that box, and put it in a box of paints which was in my trunk.

Q. And you have kept it ever since?

A. Yes, sir.

Q. When he came home, as I understood you, he seemed to be feeling for something; said he had lost something. Did he not ask for the mustache?

A. Yes, sir: he said, " Where is my mustache?"

Q. Why did you not give it to him? It was not yours.

A. No, sir: it was not mine.

Q. Why did you not give it to him? Did you suspect him at that time of intending any thing wrong?

A. I thought it rather queer that a Baptist preacher should use a mustache; and I did not care about having false mustaches lying around on my table.

Q. But you locked it up?

A. I know I locked it up.

Q. What did you intend to do with it?

A. I did not intend to do any thing with it. I took it, and exhibited it to some of the clerks in the office the day afterwards, and was fooling with it. I put on a pair of spectacles and the mustache, and was making fun of it.

Q. Your only reason for not giving it to him, when he said it was his, was, that you thought it was singular that a Baptist preacher should be fooling with a mustache?

A. Yes, sir; and I did not want a false mustache about my room.

Q. It would not have been about your room if you had given it to him, would it?

A. No, sir.

Q. That would have taken it out of your room; but, to keep it out of your room, you locked it up in a box, and kept the box with you?

A. Then, again, I thought no honest person had any reason to wear a false mustache.

Q. Can you describe to the Court young Surratt, his height and general appearance?

A. He is about six feet high, with a very prominent forehead, a very large nose, with his eyes sunken. He has a goatee, and very long hair of a light color.

Q. Do you recollect how he was dressed the day he told you he was going to Montreal?

A. He had on cream-colored pants, a gray coat.

Q. An overcoat?

A. No, sir, a frock coat; a gray vest; and then he had a shawl thrown over it.

Q. A Scotch shawl, or plaid shawl?

A. One of these plaid shawls.

Q. He went to Richmond, you say, some time towards the latter part of March; and, when he got back here, the fact of the fall of Richmond had reached here, and you saw in his possession some twenty-dollar pieces?

A. I saw nine or eleven twenty-dollar gold-pieces.

Q. Did he tell you from whom he got them?

A. No, sir: I did not make any inquiries.

Q. He told you, however, that he had seen Jefferson Davis and Benjamin. Did you understand Benjamin to be the man who was acting as Secretary of State there? Did he refer to him as an official of the Rebel Government?

A. He merely said he had seen Benjamin and Davis, and they had told him that Richmond would not be evacuated. That is the exact language he used at the time.

Q. Did he tell you he had any communication with them at all on business?

A. No, sir: he said nothing further than that.

Q. You did not ask him, and he did not volunteer to tell you, how he got that money?

A. No, sir.

Q. Do you know, or not, that he had not the gold when he left here?

A. I know he had no gold about him when he left here.

Q. And he came back with ten or eleven twenty-dollar gold-pieces?

A. Yes, sir. He gave two of them — forty dollars — to Mr. Holahan, who had a room adjoining; and Mr. Holahan gave him sixty dollars in greenbacks for them. Mr. Holahan also saw the gold.

Q. What is the date, or did you give the date, of the letter which his mother has received from him since he went to Canada?

A. Yes, sir: the letter was dated "St. Lawrence Hall, Montreal, C. E., April 12," and was received here April 14.

Q. The day of the assassination?

A. Yes, sir. The evening of the assassination it was shown to me.

Q. Did you become acquainted with the date of the letter from a memorandum on the envelope, or from the letter being opened?

A. I saw the heading in the letter. Mrs. Surratt permitted me to read the letter.

Q. State what the letter contained.

A. The letter was written in general terms. He stated that he was much pleased with the city of Montreal; that he was much pleased with the French cathedral there; that he had bought a French pea-jacket, for which he paid ten dollars in silver; that board was too high at St. Lawrence Hall, — two dollars and a half a day in gold; that he would probably go to some private boarding-house, or that he would soon go to Toronto.

Q. There was nothing in that letter which indicated any purpose of his, or anybody else, to commit murder?

A. No, sir: the letter was signed John Harrison, — not his whole name.

Q. Is that his name in part?

A. His name is John Harrison Surratt.

Q. Was he not called by his Christian name by his mother?

A. Yes, sir.

Q. Did you understand that the letter to Miss Ward, before referred to by you, went direct to her, and did not go to her through his mother? Was it directed to her?

A. It was directed to Miss Anna Ward.

Q. And received in the usual course, as you supposed?

A. Yes, sir.

Q. Do you know what that letter was about?

A. No, sir.

Q. You never saw, and never heard from Mrs. Surratt, what it was?

A. I merely heard Mrs. Surratt say that Miss Anna Ward had received a letter from John.

Q. What it was you do not know?

A. What it was I do not know.

Q. You have known Mrs. Surratt ever since November, and before that?

A. I have known her since 1863.

Q. You have been living at her house since November?

A. Since November.

Q. During the whole of that time, as far as you could judge, was her character apparently good and amiable?

A. Her character was exemplary and ladylike in every particular.

Q. Was she a member of the church?

A. Yes, sir.

Q. A regular attendant?

A. Yes, sir.

Q. Of the Catholic Church?

A. Yes, sir.

Q. Are you a Catholic?

A. Yes, sir: I am a Catholic.

Q. Have you been to church with her?

A. I generally accompanied her to church every Sunday.

Q. As far, then, as you could judge, her conduct, in a religious and in a moral sense, was altogether exemplary ?

A. Yes, sir. She went to her religious duties at least every two weeks.

Q. Did she go early in the morning ?

A. Sometimes early in the morning, and sometimes at late mass.

Q. Was that the case during the whole period up to the assassination ?

A. Yes, sir.

Q. Then, if I understand you, from November up to the 14th of April, whenever she was here, she was regular in her attendance at her own church, and apparently, as far as you could judge, doing all her duties to God and to man ?

A. Yes, sir.

Cross-examined by MR. EWING :

Q. What time was it that you said Dr. Mudd introduced Booth to yourself and Surratt ?

A. It was on or about the 15th of January, as near as I can remember.

Q. Have you any means of fixing the exact date ?

A. Yes, sir : I could fix the exact date if reference could be had to the register of the Pennsylvania House, where Dr. Mudd had a room at that time.

Q. Are you sure that it was before the 1st of February ?

A. Yes, sir : I am sure.

Q. Are you sure it was after the 1st of January ?

A. Yes, sir.

Q. Why are you sure ?

A. From a letter that I received at that time, that I had received about the 16th of January, and from a visit I had made to Baltimore, and circumstances which took place about that time ; and then, again, it was immediately after the recess of Congress. The room that was occupied by Booth at the hotel had been previously occupied by a Congressman. He walked around the room, put his hand on the shelf, and pulled out some Congressional documents ; and he made the remark, " What a good read I shall have when I am left to myself ! "

Q. You are certain that it was after the Congressional holiday vacation?

A. Yes, sir.

Q. Have you any other means of knowing that it was after the 1st of January?

A. No, sir.

Q. Have you any means of knowing that it was after Christmas?

A. Merely by the fact of its being after the Congressional holidays, and this member had not returned. The other Congressmen had nearly all returned; and ho was one whose return had been delayed for some time, it appears.

Q. How do you know that?

A. As near as I can understand, the Congressional holidays last for about a week, or perhaps two weeks.

Q. Who said any thing about the member not having returned?

A. Mr. Booth.

Q. Do you know who the member was?

A. No, sir: I do not. There were the books lying on the table, — Congressional documents; and tho room had been previously occupied, so Booth said, by a member of Congress.

Q. How do you know that the members had pretty much all returned?

A. Because Congress was in session at the time.

Q. How do you happen to recollect that it was in session at the time of this interview?

A. I have no particular way of recollecting it, except according to my memory. I do not recollect it by any external facts.

Q. How does the interview connect itself in your mind with the session of Congress, so that you are able to say that Congress was in session at the time?

A. Merely because Mr. Booth got out of his chair, and went to this table; and he took some documents off the top of the desk, and said he, "Congressional documents! What a good read I shall have when I am left to myself!" Booth said the room had been previously occupied by a member of Congress. It was the very first day of Booth's arrival in the city, and of his taking possession of that room.

Q. It was the first day of his arrival in the city?

A. So I understood.

Q. And the first day he had taken possession of that room?

A. Yes, sir : so I understood from him.

Q. Did Booth say any thing about the member of Congress being absent from the city on vacation?

A. No, sir.

Q. Do you recollect that it was after the Congressional holiday as distinctly as you recollect any part of the conversation?

A. I do not recollect that fact as distinctly as I do recollect the conversation about the purchase of the farm.

Q. Have you no memorandum of your own that would enable you to fix the date?

A. No, sir. The date could be probably fixed by a reference to the register at the Pennsylvania House. Dr. Mudd had rooms at the Pennsylvania House at that time.

Q. On what street was it that you met Dr. Mudd?

A. I met him on Seventh Street, directly opposite Odd Fellows' Hall.

Q. What did Dr. Mudd say in explanation of the introduction? Any thing?

A. Nothing that I can remember. Mr. Surratt introduced him to me, and he introduced Booth to both of us; and then Booth invited us down to the National Hotel.

Q. Which introduction came first?

A. The introduction of Dr. Mudd by Mr. Surratt to me came first.

Q. And did Booth immediately invite you all to his room?

A. Yes, sir.

Q. What was said by Booth, if any thing, why you should go to his room?

A. Nothing that I remember.

Q. He did not give any reason for wishing you to go?

A. No, sir : he did not give any reason to me. In going down

Seventh Street, Mr. Surratt took Dr. Mudd's arm, and I walked with Booth.

Q. You went directly to Booth's room?

A. Yes, sir.

Q. How long, in all, did you stay there?

A. That I cannot say exactly. I suppose the conversation must have lasted about three-quarters of an hour.

Q. You say that Dr. Mudd wrote something on a piece of paper?

A. I say that Booth took an envelope out of his pocket, and took a pencil; and he drew, as it were, lines on the back of this envelope; and Mr. Surratt and Dr. Mudd were looking at him whilst he was doing it; and they were engaged in deep conversation, — private conversation: it was scarcely audible.

Q. You were in the room at the time?

A. Yes, sir.

Q. How close were you to them?

A. I was as close to them as that gentleman sitting at the far window is to me. [Pointing to Judge Advocate General Holt, — a distance of about eight feet.]

Q. What was the conversation about?

A. That I do not know.

Q. You said it was " scarcely audible : " was it not, in part, audible?

A. It was an indistinct murmur.

Q. You heard none of it?

A. No, sir. I heard none of the conversation.

Q. Which one went out with Dr. Mudd first?

A. Booth.

Q. Are you sure?

A. Yes, sir.

Q. How long were they out together?

A. As near as I can judge, not more than five or eight minutes.

Q. Where did they go?

A. They went into a passage right along the room, — a dark passage, — a passage that leads to the front of the room there.

Q. Do you know that they stopped there?

A. That I do not know, because the door closed after them.

Q. You mean simply that the door opened on to this passage?

A. The door opened on to this passage; and, from their movements, I should judge that they remained outside.

Q. What makes you think so?

A. Because I did not hear any retreating footsteps.

Q. Did you listen to hear retreating footsteps?

A. Yes, sir: I listened. If they had gone down stairs, a person would have naturally supposed that a noise would have been made with their feet; and then, again, they did not take their hats.

Q. How far were they from the stairs?

A. That I do not know.

Q. After they returned, how long was it before Surratt went out?

A. Surratt went out almost immediately after their return.

Q. How long did the three stay out then together?

A. They must have staid out about the same length of time as at the first interview.

Q. Are you sure that Booth was with them when they went out the second time?

A. Yes, sir.

Q. Did Dr. Mudd say nothing as to how he came to introduce Booth to Surratt?

A. No, sir.

Q. Which one of them was it that said the business between Booth and Mudd was, that Booth wanted to buy Mudd's farm?

A. Dr. Mudd came and apologized to me for his private interview; and he himself said that the business was, that Mr. Booth wanted to purchase his farm, and that Booth was not willing to offer him a sufficiently high price, and that he did not care about selling it.

Q. You had never seen Mudd before?

A. No, sir: I had never seen him.

Q. Had you heard him spoken of in Mrs. Surratt's house?

A. I had heard the name Mudd mentioned; but whether it was this Dr. Samuel Mudd, I cannot say.

Q. Did you hear it mentioned in connection with any visit to the house?

A. No, sir.

Q. Do you know whether, in fact, he did visit the house, have you any reason to suppose that he did, during the time you were there?

A. No, sir.

Q. Where did Mrs. Surratt formerly live?

A. She lived at Surrattsville.

Q. Is that on the road to Bryantown?

A. I cannot say whether it is on the road to Bryantown or not, because I have never been at Bryantown, and I am not sufficiently acquainted with roads in the country there to give the information. I have never been any farther than Piscataway.

Q. Do you know whether it is on the road to the place where Dr. Mudd lives?

A. There are several ways of arriving at Dr. Mudd's place. You can take one road that I am acquainted with, that leads to Piscataway, called the Port Tobacco Road; and that would lead to his house.

Q. How far is Dr. Mudd's house from this city?

A. That I do not know. I have never been at his house. All I know of his house is, that he lived in Charles County, Md.

Q. How far is Surrattsville from the city?

A. It is about ten miles from the Navy-yard Bridge.

Q. Did you ever hear Dr. Mudd spoken of as being in the city?

A. No, sir.

Q. You heard the name of Mudd mentioned in the family?

A. Yes, sir. I have heard the name of Mudd, — Dr. George Mudd and Dr. Samuel Mudd. I have met Dr. Samuel Mudd only once, and that was the occasion referred to of meeting Booth.

Q. After Booth and Surratt and Mudd returned from the passage outside, or from outside, how long did you remain in the room together then?

A. That I do not know.

Q. About how long?

A. Probably twenty minutes.

Q. And then where did you go?

A. Then we left the National Hotel, and went to the Pennsylvania House, where Dr. Mudd had rooms. We all went into the sitting-room; and Dr. Mudd came and sat down with me, and we talked about the war. He expressed the opinion that the war would soon come to an end, and spoke like a Union man. Booth was speaking to Surratt. Booth then bade us good-night, and went out; and then Surratt and I bade Dr. Mudd good-night, and he remained there, and left the next morning.

Q. He left the next morning?

A. He said he was going to leave the next morning. Whether he left or not, I do not know.

Q. At what time was it that you separated?

A. It must have been about half-past ten o'clock in the evening.

Q. Was Booth talking when he was drawing those lines that you speak of?

A. Yes, sir.

Q. He was in conversation?

A. Yes, sir.

Q. And Mudd and Surratt were attending?

A. Yes, sir: they were all three sitting around the table; and they were looking at what Booth was marking with his pencil, and talking.

Q. Are you sure they were looking at what Booth was marking with his pencil? or were they simply attending to what Booth was saying, their eyes resting on the paper? Did you observe it close enough to swear as to that?

A. They looked at the envelope, and they looked at the motions of the pencil: I could swear to that.

Q. Their eyes were on the envelope?

A. Yes, sir: their eyes were on the envelope.

Q. And Booth was talking at the same time?

A. Yes, sir.

Q. How close were you to them?

A. As I have stated, I was about as close to them as I am to that gentleman over there. [Pointing to Judge Advocate General Holt.]

Q. What distance in feet?

A. Perhaps eight feet.

Q. Did they watch you?

A. No, sir.

Q. How large was the room?

A. I have no means of arriving at that.

Q. About how large?

A. I should think the room was about half the size of this one. By running a partition across this room, you would about get the size of that room.

Q. Do you mean half as large as this whole room?

A. Yes, sir. By drawing a partition across the room here, near the middle pillar, you might get an idea of the true proportion of it, so as to give an idea of the size of the room.

Q. In what part of the room was the table?

A. The table was in the centre.

Cross-examined by MR. STONE:

Q. You say that you saw Mr. Herold in the summer of 1863 down at Mrs. Surratt's, at Surrattsville?

A. Yes, sir.

Q. At a sort of serenade there, — a musical party?

A. It was at the time of the election of the county officers. There was a band that had gone down from the city to serenade the officers who had been elected; and this band stopped during the night at Mrs. Surratt's on going down, and serenaded us, and, on returning in the morning, again stopped at the door and serenaded us; and it was on that occasion that John Surratt introduced Herold to me. Herold was with this party.

Q. You saw him, you say, once in Mrs. Surratt's house after she moved to the city?

A. Yes, sir.

Q. And only once?

A. Only once.

Q. The third time you saw him was at the theatre?

A. Yes, sir: I saw him at the theatre. I also saw him once, in July, at a church in the country, the Piscataway Church. He had been to church there; and, when he came out, he got on his horse, and rode off.

Q. When you left the theatre that night, you all walked down the street together a portion of the way, as I understood you?

A. There were five of us left the theatre together, — Mr. Surratt, Mr. Holahan, and I in company, and Atzerodt and Herold behind. When Surratt, Holahan, and I arrived at the corner of Tenth and E Streets, Surratt turned round, and saw that the other two were not following; and he told me to go back and find them. I went back, and found them in the restaurant, engaged in close conversation with Booth.

Q. They had met Booth in the restaurant?

A. Yes, sir. On my approaching them, Booth asked me to go and take a drink with them; and the four of us approached the counter, and Mr. Booth introduced a man to me, whose name I do not remember, but whose face is familiar to me. I have seen him frequently about the town.

Q. You did take a drink?

A. Yes, sir.

Q. When you went into the restaurant, you say, they were standing in close conversation. Do you mean standing close together?

A. Yes, sir: the three of them were standing together; and they were conversing, as it were, very privately.

Q. Were they standing near the door?

A. No, sir: they were standing near the stove.

Q. Was it a cool evening?

A. No, sir: no fire had been kindled in the stove. It was a very pleasant evening.

Q. Booth did not leave the theatre with you?

A. No, sir.

Q. You do not know whether Herold and Atzerodt had taken a drink with Booth before you came in?

A. No, sir: I am not aware of that.

Q. When you left the restaurant, did you all leave together?

A. Herold, Atzerodt, and I left together; and we overtook Mr. Holahan and Mr. Surratt on E Street. Then we went to Kloman's, on Seventh Street; and Mr. Holahan invited us to take some oysters, and we took oysters there. Then Holahan, Surratt, and myself went home, and Atzerodt and Herold went down Seventh Street.

Q. Do you know where Mr. Herold lived?

A. I was at his house only once. I knew that he lived at the Navy Yard; but the precise spot I did not know. I was at his house on Saturday, the 15th of April, with a detective officer by the name of McDevitt; and he, at that time, procured Herold's photograph.

Cross-examined by Mr. Clampitt:

Q. You remarked, that one evening, in company with Mr. Booth, you went to the National Hotel?

A. Yes, sir.

Q. Was Booth called out, on that occasion, by Surratt or by Dr. Mudd?

A. Booth was called out by Dr. Mudd, as near as I can remember.

Q. Did you not say that he was also called out by Surratt?

A. The three of them then went out together.

Q. Was Surratt in company with you at the time that you went to the National Hotel?

A. He was.

Q. Was Dr. Mudd in company with you?

A. Dr. Mudd, Mr. Booth, Surratt, and myself were all in company. In going down Seventh Street, Surratt joined Dr. Mudd, and I went with Booth. We went down together, and entered the room.

Q. Then, if I understand you correctly, Dr. Mudd, immediately after you entered the hotel, called Mr. Booth out?

A. I could not say that it was immediately after.

Q. Well, within a few minutes, or a short time, — half an hour?

A. I have said that wines and cigars were first ordered.

Q. You were then all in the room together, at one time?

A. Yes, sir.

Q. And then Dr. Mudd walked out, and called Booth out?

A. Yes, sir.

Q. And then Surratt called him out?

A. I did not say that Surratt called him out. Surratt was called out. They came in, and Surratt was called out.

Q. And you were left alone?

A. Yes, sir.

Q. After their return to the room, was any thing else remarked to you, with the exception of the apology of Dr. Mudd, about their meeting outside?

A. Booth offered an apology to me also, stating that he wished to buy Dr. Mudd's farm. Apologies were offered to me both by Dr. Mudd and Booth.

Q. There was nothing said that led you to believe that there was any thing like a conspiracy going on between them?

A. No, sir.

Q. You remarked that sometimes you were in company with Mrs. Surratt at the time these parties would call to see her. Do you ever remember of Mrs. Surratt seeking an opportunity to have a private conversation with Booth or any of his accomplices?

A. On the 2d of April, she sent me to the hotel, and told me to tell Mr. Booth she would like to see him on some private business; and Mr. Booth called at her house that evening, which was Sunday.

Q. In reference to the ten dollars that was offered to you to hire a buggy with by Booth, did you accept it?

A. Yes, sir.

Q. Did you suppose it was any thing more or less than an act of kindness or friendship?

A. I thought it was an act of friendship at the time. I had been told that Booth was in the habit of keeping a buggy at Brooks's stable; and, on going to the hotel that morning, I said to Booth, "I am come with an order for that buggy that Mrs. Surratt asked you for last evening." Said he, "I have sold my buggy; but here is ten dollars, and you can go and hire one." I never told Mrs. Surratt that.

Q. At what time did you go to Montreal?

A. We went to Montreal on the 18th of April, the Monday after the assassination.

Q. What business had you there?

A. We went there for the purpose of seeking John Surratt.

Q. Did you find him?

A. No, sir: we did not find him.

Q. Did you ever see Mrs. Surratt leaving the parlor to have a private interview with Booth?

A. I have heard Booth ask Mrs. Surratt to spare him a word; and Mrs. Surratt would go into the passage, and talk with Booth.

Q. How much time would those conversations occupy?

A. Generally, not more than five or eight minutes.

Cross-examined by MR. AIKEN:

Q. At the time you went to Surrattsville, on the 14th of April last, did you transact any business for Mrs. Surratt while there?

A. I wrote one letter to this man Nothe.

Q. What was in it?

A. Only, "Mr. Nothe. Sir,—Unless you come forward and pay that bill at once, I will bring suit against you immediately."

Q. Did you do any thing else for her?

A. No, sir.

Q. Did you make up a sum in interest?

A. Yes, sir: I figured up a sum in interest,—the interest on the sum of four hundred and seventy-nine dollars for thirteen years.

Cross-examined by MR. DOSTER:

Q. You have mentioned an interview at the theatre between Atzerodt and Booth, and, as I understood you, with Surratt and Payne at the same time.

A. It was not Payne. It was Booth and Herold and Atzerodt. Payne was not there.

Q. Was that at the theatre?

A. It was in the restaurant adjoining the theatre.

Q. Do you know what passed at that interview?

A. No, sir.

Q. It was entirely outside of your hearing?

A. Yes, sir. When I approached them, they separated, and asked me to take a drink.

Q. Were you present at any other interview between Atzerodt and Booth?

A. Yes, sir.

Q. Can you tell us what passed there?

A. No, sir.

Q. You do not know any thing about it?

A. No, sir.

Q. Can you tell us of any interview Atzerodt had with Surratt?

A. Atzerodt has been to the house frequently, and had interviews with Surratt in the parlor.

Q. Do you know what passed there?

A. No, sir.

Q. You do not know any thing about it?

A. No, sir: I do not know any thing about it?

Q. Did you know of any interviews between Payne and Atzerodt?

A. Yes, sir.

Q. State where they were.

A. It was on the occasion of Payne's last visit to the house. Atzerodt came to see Surratt once; and they were in my room, and they were talking there.

Q. What did they say?

A. That I do not know.

Q. You do not know of any conversation that passed between Atzerodt and Booth, or between Atzerodt and Payne, having reference to a conspiracy?

A. No, sir. Surratt was continually speaking about cotton speculations, and of going to Europe; and I heard Atzerodt once remark that he was also going to Europe, but he was going there on horseback. From that remark, I concluded that he was going South.

Q. Have you ever heard, in conversation, any reference to the assignment of Atzerodt to the assassination of Vice-President Johnson?

A. No, sir.

Q. Have you ever heard any conversation having reference to Payne's assignment to the assassination of the Secretary of State?

A. No, sir.

Q. You say, that, at half-past two o'clock on the afternoon of the 14th, you saw Atzerodt at the livery-stable trying to get a horse ?

A. Yes, sir.

Q. Did he say what he was going to do with the horse ?

A. He said he was going to ride out into the country.

Q. You stated that he did not get any horse then.

A. The stable-keeper, in my presence, refused to let him have one.

Q. Do you know whether he succeeded in getting any horse that same day ?

A. That I do not know. I know he did not succeed in getting a horse at that particular stable.

Q. When did you part with him ? — how soon after that ?

A. I parted with him immediately.

Q. At the stable ?

A. At the post-office. I dropped a letter in the post-office, and I came back.

Q. Was that the last interview you had with him before the assassination ?

A. Yes, sir : that was the last interview.

Q. When did you see him again ?

A. In the dock here, to-day.

Q. You say you recognize the spur that was exhibited to you, as having been seen on the bed in the room of Payne, at the house of Mrs. Surratt ?

A. Yes, sir.

Q. What makes you recognize that spur ? What marks are there on it that distinguish it from spurs in general ?

A. No particular marks. The spur is familiar to me.

Q. How far were you from the spurs when you saw it ?

A. I had them in my hand.

Q. And the knife also ?

A. No, sir : I did not have that in my hand. I took up a sword Mr. Surratt had on the mantle-piece, and commenced fencing with him.

Q. I understood you to swear that you had seen that knife before in the room of Mr. Payne ?

A. No, sir: I saw two bowie-knives; and, when I returned from my office at four o'clock, and went up in the room, I found Surratt and Payne playing on the bed with these bowie-knives, and with two revolvers, and four sets of spurs.

Q. Do you know that that was one of them? [Exhibiting to the witness the knife identified by John Lee.]

A. I cannot say: I did not say that I recognized that as one of the knives.

Q. Do you say that the pistol shown to you was the identical pistol that was on the bed that day?

A. No, sir.

Q. Do you know where Payne was stopping on the 14th of April? Do you know any thing about Payne on that day?

A. Yes, sir. I remember that I asked Atzerodt where he was going, and he said he was going to ride in the country; and he said he was going to get a horse, and send for Payne.

Q. I want to know where Payne was on that day.

A. I do not know any thing about it. I do not know where he was. I have seen this man Payne only on two occasions.

Q. Where was Atzerodt stopping on that day? Did he tell you, when you saw him at the livery-stable?

A. No, sir.

Q. He did not speak of the place where he was stopping?

A. No, sir.

Q. Do you know of his having stopped at the Herndon House; and, if so, how long?

A. I know of his having stopped at the Herndon House, because this man Atzerodt told me so. I stated that I met Atzerodt one day in Seventh Street, and I asked him where he was going. He said he was going to see Payne. I asked him, "Was it Payne who was at the Herndon House?" He said, "Yes."

Q. You say that Payne paid a visit to the Surratts, and stopped only over night during his first visit?

A. Yes, sir.

Q. With whom did he seem to have business?

A. He inquired for Mr. Surratt. His business appeared to be

with Mr. Surratt. On the occasion of his first visit, I was in the parlor during the whole time.

Q. He did not appear to have any thing to say to Mrs. Surratt?

A. He asked Mrs. Surratt to play on the piano for him; and he raised the piano-cover.

Q. Did he have, besides that false mustache you speak of, any other disguise going to show that he wanted to conceal himself?

A. No, sir.

Q. Nothing that you saw?

A. Nothing.

Q. Did you see Payne after the assassination until to-day?

A. I did not.

Q. Was he treated by Mr. Surratt as an intimate friend?

A. He appeared to be treated kindly by Mr. Surratt, as if he was an old acquaintance. On the occasion of his second visit to the house, Mr. Surratt, when meeting him, recognized him as though he had known him.

Q. You say he represented himself to be a Baptist minister. Did the family regard him as a man in disguise? or did they regard him as a Baptist minister?

A. That I do not know. One of the young ladies looked at him, and remarked that he was a queer-looking Baptist preacher; that he would not convert many souls.

Q. Did you ever see Payne and Atzerodt in company?

A. Yes, sir. Atzerodt was at the house on the occasion of Payne's last visit?

Q. Did they have any communication, to your knowledge?

A. I saw them talking in my own room.

Q. But you do not know any thing of their conversation?

A. I do not.

By the JUDGE ADVOCATE:

Q. How long did you say the interview between Payne and Atzerodt lasted?

A. I did not give any time.

Q. Will you state now how long they were together?

A. I suppose Atzerodt must have been in the house about an

hour : it was on the occasion of Payne's last visit. To my recollection, he was in the house only twice. Atzerodt came into the house one evening, had a talk with Payne and Surratt, and stopped about an hour.

Q. Were they together in their room, or in the parlor, or where ?

A. They were together in their room.

Q. Were you, or not, at Mrs. Surratt's when Payne was arrested for the assassination ?

A. No, sir : I was not. I was out of the city at that time.

Q. You were there when the officers came and took possession of Mrs. Surratt's house, were you not ?

A. I was not. When the city officers came at three o'clock on Saturday morning, I was there. I thought you had reference to the Government officers, Colonel Foster and others.

Q. Payne was not there then ?

A. He was not.

By the COURT :

Q. You spoke of your "office :" what profession or business do you follow ?

A. I was a clerk in the office of the Commissary General of Prisoners, General Hoffman ; and had been since Jan. 9, 1864.

ROBERT R. JONES,

a witness for the prosecution, being duly sworn, testified as follows : —

By the JUDGE ADVOCATE :

Q. Are you a clerk at the Kirkwood House in this city ?

A. I am.

Q. [Exhibiting to the witness a leaf of paper headed "Kirkwood House," and containing entries of names.] Look at that paper, and see if it is a leaf taken from the register of that hotel.

A. It is.

Q. Is the name of Atzerodt there ?

A. It is : "G. A. Atzerodt, Charles County."

[The sheet or leaf taken from the hotel register was offered in evidence without objection. It is marked Exhibit No. 24.]

Q. From that register, does it appear that Atzerodt took a room there? and on what day, and what hour of the day?

A. He took a room there, by the register, on the 14th of April last; I should think, in the morning, before eight o'clock.

Q. What was the number of the room?

A. No. 126.

Q. Have you any recollection of the man?

A. I saw him that day.

Q. Would you recognize him here among these prisoners?

A. That looks like the man.

Q. Look at him well, and see if you can determine the question.

A. That is the man, I think.

Q. Do you remember what became of him after taking the room? Did he appear there again that day?

A. Not that I know of. I did not see him again myself. It was between twelve and one o'clock that day when I saw him.

Q. Do you know any thing about J. Wilkes Booth having called that day, and inquired the number of Vice-President Johnson's room?

A. I do not know that he inquired about the room. I gave a card of J. Wilkes Booth to Colonel Browning, Mr. Johnson's secretary: it was put in the box. I gave him that card, and it was left for Colonel Browning.

Q. Did you receive it yourself from Booth?

A. I have no positive recollection of having received it, although I may have done so.

Q. You have not seen the prisoner Atzerodt since till now?

A. No, sir.

Q. Were you present when the room was opened, and certain articles taken out of it?

A. I was not there when the room was opened. I went up with Mr. Lee after the room had been opened. When he took the things from the room, I was there with him.

Q. Did you see anybody there, at any time during that day, with Atzerodt?

A. A young man spoke to him when he stood at the office counter when I saw him.

Q. But after that you saw nobody in the room with him or about with him?

A. No, sir.

Q. Do you know the name of that young man?

A. I do not.

Q. Would you know J. Wilkes Booth?

A. I do not think I should. I saw him at the house some time before the occurrence; but I do not think I should recollect him.

Q. [Exhibiting the bowie-knife identified by the witness John Lee.] Were you, or not, present when that bowie-knife was taken from under the bed?

A. I was present when a knife similar to that was taken from under the sheet of that bed.

Q. It was under the sheet?

A. Yes, sir; between the sheet and the mattress.

Q. What day or night was that?

A. The evening after the murder of the President.

Q. Did the bed appear to have been occupied, or not?

A. The bed had not been occupied: the chambermaid had not been in there.

Q. Did you see Atzerodt at all on the night of the assassination?

A. No, sir; not that I know of. It was between twelve and one o'clock on the day of the 14th when I saw him; and he then asked me if any one had inquired for him within a short time.

Q. Did he pay something in advance for his room?

A. Yes, sir; he paid one day in advance: it so appears on the books.

Q. Had he ever been to the hotel before, to your knowledge?

A. I had never seen him there before.

Cross-examined by Mr. DOSTER:

Q. Were you the clerk at the desk on the day when Atzerodt registered his name in the register?

A. I was there after twelve o'clock.

Q. Were you at the desk the day Atzerodt registered his name in the register?

A. I went in the office at twelve o'clock that day.

Q. Did you see him register his name?

A. No, sir.

Q. What reason have you for supposing that the person you have just now identified was the person who wrote his name in this place on the register? You did not see him write it?

A. He came to the counter, and pointed to his name on the register, and asked me if any one had called to see him.

Q. When was that?

A. On Friday, between twelve and one o'clock.

Q. What did you answer?

A. I told him, "Not to my knowledge."

Q. Did you see him after that again in the house?

A. No, sir; not after he left the counter.

Q. Did you see whether he had any baggage when he arrived?

A. I was not there when he arrived.

Q. Did you go to his room during the time he was there?

A. I did not go to his room until the next evening. I think it was between six and seven o'clock.

Q. Do you know whether he slept there that night?

A. I do not think he did. I called the chambermaid, and asked if she had been in the room. She said she had not been in there that day: she had been unable to get in, because she could not find the key.

Q. Have you ever obtained that key?

A. I have never seen it since.

Q. Did you have any conversation with a detective, in the course of the evening of the 15th, in reference to a suspicious person at the Kirkwood House?

A. That was the day after the murder. I think probably I had; but I do not recollect any particular conversation in regard to it. We were talking of it pretty nearly all the time, though.

Q. Do you remember going with a detective to the room?

A. Yes: I went to the room with Mr. Lee.

Q. Do you know whether Atzerodt had expressed any predilection in the choice of rooms, or for the particular No. 126?

10*

A. I was not there when he was roomed, and cannot say any thing about that.

Q. Did you inspect with the detective the different articles that were in the pockets of the coat?

A. Yes, sir: I saw them as Mr. Lee took them out.

Q. Are you prepared to identify the pistol that you saw on that occasion?

A. I do not think I could identify the particular one. It was quite a large pistol.

Q. Can you describe it? Was it a Derringer or revolver?

A. It was a large pistol, such as cavalry officers wear.

Q. Was it loaded or not?

A. It was loaded and capped.

Q. How were the barrels, rectangular or round on the inside?

A. I think it was round, — single-barrelled, with chambers.

Q. Would you be able to recognize the books that were found in that room?

A. I think I could recognize the book that had the name of J. Wilkes Booth on the inside.

Q. Could you describe the knife you saw there?

A. It was a sheath-knife, similar to the one lying on the table. [Pointing to the bowie-knife identified by the witness, John Lee.]

Q. You cannot swear as to the identity of it?

A. I cannot.

The JUDGE ADVOCATE then called John M. Lloyd as a witness.

MR. AIKEN applied to the Commission to postpone the examination of John M. Lloyd until Monday next, when Mr. Johnson, the senior counsel for Mrs. Mary E. Surratt, one of the accused, would be present, he having left the court-room to-day; as the testimony of the witness now called would be of the gravest importance as affecting Mary E. Surratt.

The JUDGE ADVOCATE objected to the application for delay. Mrs. Surratt had now two counsels present.

The Commission overruled the application.

John M. Lloyd,

a witness called for the prosecution, being duly sworn, testified as
follows : —

By the Judge Advocate:

Q. Where do you reside ?

A. I have been residing at Mrs. Surratt's tavern, Surrattsville.

Q. In what business are you engaged there ?

A. Hotel-keeping and farming.

Q. Were you acquainted with John H. Surratt.

A. I have had a very small acquaintance with him since about
the 1st of December last ; not much previous to that.

Q. Do you know the prisoner Herold ?

A. I know Herold. He has been in my house several times.

Q. Do you know the prisoner Atzerodt ?

A. Yes, sir.

Q. Will you state whether or not, some five or six weeks before
the assassination of the President, any or all of these men about
whom I have inquired came to your house ?

A. They were there.

Q. All three together ?

A. Yes : John H. Surratt, Herold, and Atzerodt were there together.

Q. What did they bring to your house ? and what did they do
there ?

A. When they drove up there in the morning, John H. Surratt
and Atzerodt came first : they went from my house, and went towards
T. B., — a post-office kept about five miles below there. They had
not been gone more than half an hour when they returned with
Herold : then the three were together, — Herold, Surratt, and Atzerodt.

Q. What did they bring to your house ?

A. I saw nothing until they all three came into the bar-room. I
noticed one of the buggies — the one I supposed Herold was driving
or went down in — standing at the front gate. All three of them,
when they came into the bar-room, drank, I think ; and then John
Surratt called me into the front parlor, and on the sofa were two

carbines with ammunition. I think he told me they were carbines.

Q. Any thing besides the carbines and ammunition ?

A. There was a rope, and also a monkey-wrench.

Q. How long a rope ?

A. I cannot tell. It was in a coil, — a right smart bundle, — probably sixteen or twenty feet.

Q. Were those articles left at your house ?

A. Yes, sir. Surratt asked me to take care of them, to conceal the carbines. I told him there was no place there to conceal them, and I did not wish to keep such things in the house.

Q. You say that he asked you to conceal those articles for him ?

A. Yes, sir : he asked me to conceal them. I told him there was no place to conceal them. He then carried me into a room that I had never been in, which was just immediately above the storeroom, as it were in the back building of the house. I had never been in that room previous to that time. He showed me where I could put them underneath the joists of the house, — the joists of the second floor of the main building. This little unfinished room will admit of any thing between the joists.

Q. Were they put in that place ?

A. They were put in there according to his directions.

Q. Were they concealed in that condition ?

A. Yes, sir : I put them in there. I stated to Colonel Wells, through mistake, that Surratt put them there; but I put them in there myself. I carried the arms up myself.

Q. How much ammunition was there ?

A. One cartridge-box.

Q. For what purpose, and for how long, did he ask you to keep those articles ?

A. I am very positive that he said he would call for them in a few days. He said he just wanted them to stay for a few days, and he would call for them.

Q. What kind of carbines were they ?

A. I did not examine them : they had covers over them.

Q. Will you state whether or not, on the Monday or Tuesday

preceding the assassination of the President, Mrs. Surratt came to your house?

A. I was coming to Washington, and I met Mrs. Surratt at Uniontown on the Monday previous.

Q. Did she say any thing to you in regard to those carbines?

A. When she first broached the subject to me, I did not know what she had reference to: then she came out plainer; and I am quite positive she asked me about the "shooting-irons." I am quite positive about that, but not altogether positive. I think she named "shooting-irons," or something to call my attention to those things; for I had almost forgotten about their being there. I told her that they were hid away far back; that I was afraid the house would be searched, and they were shoved far back. She told me to get them out ready: they would be wanted soon.

Q. Was her question to you, first, whether they were still there? or what was it?

A. Really, I cannot recollect the first question she put to me. I could not do it to save my life.

Q. Was it so indistinct, that you did not understand what was meant?

A. It was put in a manner as if she wanted to draw my attention to something so that anybody else could not understand. Finally she came out bolder with it.

Q. And said they would be wanted soon?

A. Yes, sir.

Q. And then she said they would be wanted soon?

A. Yes, sir. I told her at the same time that I had an idea of having them buried; that I was very uneasy about having them there.

Q. Will you state now whether or not, on the evening of the night on which the President was assassinated, Mrs. Surratt came to your house with Mr. Weichmann?

A. I went to Marlboro' on that day to attend a trial there in court; and in the evening it was probably late when I got home. I found Mrs. Surratt there when I got home. I should judge it was about five o'clock.

Q. What did she say to you?

A. She met me out by the wood-pile as I drove in, having fish and oysters in the buggy; and she told me to have those shooting-irons ready that night, — there would be some parties call for them.

Q. Did she ask you to get any thing else ready for those parties besides the shooting-irons?

A. She gave me something wrapped up in a piece of paper. I did not know what it was till I took it up stairs; and then I found it to be a field-glass.

Q. Did she ask you to have any whiskey prepared for them?

A. She did.

Q. What did she say about that?

A. She said to get two bottles of whiskey also.

Q. And said they were to be called for that night?

A. Yes: they were to be called for that night.

Q. State now whether they were called for that night by Booth and Herold.

A. The carbines and ammunition were called for that night; but the whiskey was not. They drank what whiskey they wanted out of the bottle, and did not carry any bottles of whiskey with them.

Q. When they came there, did they ask for the carbines?

A. They did not ask for the carbines. Booth did not come in: Herold came in.

Q. At what time was that?

A. Just about midnight, I think, on Friday night: not over a quarter-past twelve o'clock. I did not know Booth; the person was a stranger to me; he remained on his horse. Herold came into the house and got a bottle of whiskey, and took it out to him; and Herold drank some out of a glass, I think, before he went out.

Q. Do you remember in what terms Booth asked you for that whiskey?

A. I think he did not ask for the whiskey. He might possibly have asked for something to drink; but he called for the carbines in such terms that I understood what he wanted. He told me, "Lloyd, for God's sake, make haste and get those things!" He might have included whiskey and all for what I know.

Q. He had not before that said to you what "those things" were?

A. He had not.

Q. Did he not seem, from the manner of his language, to suppose that you already understood what he called for?

A. From the way he spoke, he must have been apprised that I already knew what I was to give him.

Q. What did you say?

A. I did not make any reply, but went up stairs and got them.

Q. Did you not give him all the articles, — the field-glass and the monkey-wrench and the rope?

A. No: the rope and monkey-wrench were not what I was told to give him. I gave him such things as I was told to give by Mrs. Surratt.

Q. She told you to give him the carbines and whiskey and field-glass?

A. Yes, sir; and the whiskey they did not take with them.

Q. How long did they remain at your house?

A. I do not think they were over five minutes.

Q. Did they take one or both of the carbines?

A. Only one.

Q. Did they explain why the other was not taken?

A. Booth said that he could not take his, because his leg was broken.

Q. Did he take a drink also?

A. He drank while he was sitting out on his horse.

Q. Did Herold carry the bottle out to him?

A. Yes, sir.

Q. Did they say any thing in regard to the assassination as they rode away?

A. Just as they were about leaving, the man who was with Herold [Booth] said, "I will tell you some news if you want to hear it," or something to that effect. I said, "I am not particular: use your own choice about telling news." — "Well," said he, "I am pretty certain that we have assassinated the President and Secretary Seward." I think that was his language as well as I can recollect: "We have assassinated" or "killed the President and Secretary Seward."

Q. Did he say that in Herold's presence?

A. I am not positive now whether Herold was present at the time he said that, or whether he was across the street. Herold rode across the street towards the stable. I was so much excited and unnerved at it, that I did not know whether it was said in Herold's presence or not. Herold, as soon as he rode back to where we were, got right between me and this other man, and rode off.

Q. What hour the next morning was the news of the assassination of the President received there ?

A. I suppose between eight and nine o'clock the next morning. I think it was about nine o'clock; but I am not sure.

Q. As the news spread, was it spoken of always that Booth was the assassin ? Was his name used ?

A. I think it was. I think on several occasions I heard it used there as being the one.

Q. Did you see Dr. Mudd during the day.

A. I never saw Dr. Samuel Mudd : I am not acquainted with him. I have a slight acquaintance with Dr. George Mudd.

Q. I understood you to say that Herold's language was, "For God's sake, make haste and get those things ! "

A. Yes, sir : that was what Herold said to me first.

Q. And you went straight and got the carbines ?

A. Yes, sir ; supposing they were the parties Mrs. Surratt had referred to. She did not mention any names. She did not say who was to come.

Cross-examined by MR. AIKEN :

Q. At what time did you rent this house of Mrs Surratt ?

A. As well as I can remember now, without any thing to go by, I think it was about the 1st of December last.

Q. Has she been there quite frequently since that time ?

A. Mrs. Surratt has been there right often. Sometimes I would be at home, sometimes not. I do not know how often she has been there, but frequently.

Q. At the time you commenced the occupancy of the premises, did you find any arms in the house ?

A. I did not.

Q. Did you know any thing of a pistol or gun being there?

A. I knew of a broken gun being there — a double-barrelled gun — in the back room. It was there some time; and John Surratt took it away.

Q. Did you keep a bar?

A. I did.

Q. Will you detail the first conversation you had with Mrs. Surratt on the first of the last two occasions that you saw her? I refer to the time you met her at Uniontown.

A. The conversation that ensued there was this: We had passed each other somewhat; and I did not recognize Mrs. Surratt, and I do not know that she recognized me. I was coming to Washington; and she was going down to my place, I supposed. I stopped, and so did she. I then got out, and went to her buggy. It had been raining, and was very muddy. She spoke to me in a manner trying to draw my attention to those things, the carbines, but so that I did not understand.

Q. The word "carbine" was not mentioned?

A. No. She finally came out, and, I am quite positive, but cannot be determined about it that she said "shooting-irons," asked me in relation to them.

Q. Had she asked you any question in reference to the soldiers about those premises previous to this?

A. I had told her that I expected the place would be searched, I think, at that time; but I am not positive whether it was not previous to that. I think it was at that time a conversation ensued as to the place being searched by soldiers.

Q. Immediately after this remark in regard to the soldiers, did Mrs. Surratt speak of the "shooting-irons"?

A. I cannot say now whether it was before or after that remark. It was during the conversation that ensued. It was a very quick and hasty conversation; and, consequently, I cannot remember distinctly whether it was before or after.

Q. Can you swear on your oath that Mrs. Surratt mentioned the word "shooting-irons" to you at all?

A. I am very positive she did.

Q. Are you certain?

A. I am very positive that she named "shooting-irons" on both occasions, — not so positive as to the first as I am about the last : I know she did on the last occasion.

Q. At what time in the day did you meet Mrs. Surratt on Friday ?

A. I did not meet Mrs. Surratt on Friday at all.

Q. You did not see her ?

A. I saw her, but did not meet her. I was at Marlboro' that day ; and, when I arrived home, I found Mrs. Surratt there.

Q. What time in the evening was that ?

A. In the neighborhood of five o'clock, or thereabouts : I do not know exactly.

Q. How long did Mrs. Surratt remain at your house after your return ?

A. I do not think she was there over ten minutes then.

Q. Now state again the conversation that occurred between you and Mrs. Surratt during those ten minutes.

A. I was not in Mrs. Surratt's company during all those ten minutes. When I first drove up to the kitchen or wood-yard with fish and oysters in the buggy, Mrs. Surratt came out to where I was. The first thing she said to me was, "Talk about the Devil, and his imps will appear," or something to that effect. I said, " I was not aware that I was a devil before." — "Well," said she, " Mr. Lloyd, I want you to have those shooting-irons ready : there will be parties here to-night who will call for them." At the same time, she gave me something wrapped up in a newspaper. I did not undo it until I got up stairs.

Q. Did you undo it immediately after you got up stairs ?

A. As soon as I got up stairs and saw what it was.

Q. Did you lay it down, and leave the package anywhere before it was undone ?

A. No, sir : I undid it when I laid it out of my hands.

Q. Are you positive again that Mrs. Surratt told you, at that time, that shooting-irons would be called for that night ?

A. I am very positive.

Q. At what time in the evening did you state that you had this conversation with Mrs. Surratt ?

A. I judge it was in the neighborhood of five o'clock. I have nothing to go by particularly, without going to the house. I took no particular pains to see. It might have been a little later than five o'clock.

Q. Did she say to you that some things would be called for that night?

A. She told me to have those shooting-irons ready; there would be parties call for them that night. That was the language she made use of; and she gave me this other thing to give to whoever called.

Q. Were any other remarks made with reference to it?

A. Nothing more. I carried the fish and oysters into the house; and the conversation ensued while I was at work carrying them in. That is about all the conversation I had with Mrs. Surratt. I went into the bar. Mrs. Surratt then requested me to fix her buggy for her. The front spring-bolts were broken. The spring had become detached from the axle. I tied them with some cord, and that was the only fixing I could give them.

Q. Were any other persons present at this interview?

A. Mrs. Offutt was there. I do not know whether she heard the conversation or not. She was in the yard, I believe.

Q. This conversation occurred in the yard?

A. It occurred in the yard.

Q. Was Mrs. Offutt within hearing distance?

A. I suppose so: I do not know.

Q. Is Mrs. Offutt a neighbor of yours?

A. She is a sister-in-law of mine.

Q. What is her given name?

A. Emma Offutt. She is now very low, — very sick in bed: so Captain Cunningham told me to-day.

Q. Were these shooting-irons called for that night?

A. They were.

Q. Who called for them?

A. David E. Herold, and another man that I did not know.

Q. Did Mrs. Surratt tell you to give the field-glass and the whiskey to them?

A. She did.

Q. Why did you not do it?

A. I gave the field-glass; but they did not take the whiskey with them.

Q. When were you first interrogated, after this occurrence, in regard to what was said at that time?

A. I gave the full information, all the particulars of the information, to Colonel Wells, on the Saturday week following. I gave part of the information to Lieutenant Lovett and Captain Cunningham some time during the middle of the week, but did not detail all this minute conversation.

Q. Was that the first time you detailed the conversation?

A. It was the first time that I gave the full conversation between us.

Q. Had you given any part of the conversation to any one before?

A. No, sir; no part of the conversation.

Q. Had you related any of these circumstances to any person?

A. I only told Lieutenant Lovett and Captain Cunningham that it was through the Surratts I got myself into the difficulty: if they had never brought me on there, I never would have got myself into difficulty, or words to that effect.

Q. Were Captain Cunningham and Lieutenant Lovett present together? Did you tell them both together?

A. They were both present: they were then going from Mr. Roby's to my house, which was close by.

Q. Do you know where they are stationed?

A. They were here to-day.

Q. Are you sure that was all you told them?

A. I am quite sure that was all I told them at that time. I told Captain Cunningham further about it afterwards.

Q. Do you recall the name of any other person to whom you detailed any of these occurrences?

A. I do not remember.

Q. Did you talk with Mrs. Offutt in regard to them?

A. I do not know that I did; but I will not be quite positive about it. I do not think I did, because the time was so short. The soldiers were coming there, and I had to be in the bar-room all Friday; and I do not think I saw Mrs. Offutt from the time I got up, only at meal-times, except once.

Q. How soon after Herold and Booth left you did you learn positively of the assassination of the President?

A. I learned it from them.

Q. But how soon did you learn it positively from other parties?

A. I suppose it was between eight and nine o'clock when the soldiers came down through our place next morning.

Q. Did you have a conversation with the soldiers in regard to it?

A. I did not have much conversation with them in regard to it.

Q. Did you have any conversation?

A. I only deplored the circumstances; that was all.

Q. Did you tell them any thing of the circumstance of Booth and Herold having been at your place?

A. I did not; and I am only sorry that I did not. There is where I blame myself: it is the only difficulty I labor under.

Q. What day did you tell Captain Cunningham and Lieutenant Lovett?

A. I am not altogether prepared to state positively whether it was on the Wednesday following or not. I went down after my wife, who was in Charles County, on Monday or Tuesday. On my return home, I was arrested on the road. I think it was Wednesday I told them.

Q. Did you have any information from Mrs. Surratt as to what those things were that were left in your charge?

A. She spoke of those "shooting-irons;" that is all.

Q. Did Mrs. Surratt ever bring any "shooting-irons" to your house?

A. Not to my knowledge.

Q. Did she ever have any conversation with you with reference to any conspiracy?

A. Never.

Q. What did she say to you when she was about leaving your house?

A. On that Friday, she said, when leaving, nothing; only bade me good-evening. That was the last interview I had with her when fixing the buggy.

11*

Q. Did she not give you any charges ?

A. The only charges she gave me in regard to those things, the shooting-irons, was when she first saw me.

Q. Was that at Uniontown ?

A. When I first drove up. I was at home then : it was after I arrived from Marlboro' when I first saw her that day.

Q. Did Mrs. Surratt hand any package to you ?

A. She handed me a package at the same time that she was telling me to deliver those shooting-irons to the parties who would call for them, and to give them a couple of bottles of whiskey.

Q. Have you a family ?

A. I have a wife.

Q. Have you a son ?

A. No, sir.

Q. Have you any person to work for you ?

A. Yes, sir ; a colored man and a colored boy : and there was a woman there sometimes who used to live with Mrs. Surratt ; but she was not there on this occasion.

Q. Were the colored man, woman, and boy, all or either of them, present ?

A. No, sir : I do not think they were.

Q. Was the package handed into your hands by Mrs. Surratt, or by another person ?

A. It was handed to me by Mrs. Surratt herself.

Q. Whereabouts were you standing when the package was handed to you ?

A. I was standing near the wood-pile. I had just got out of my buggy.

Cross-examined by MR. EWING :

Q. Can you recollect who it was, after Booth and Herold left your house that night, first told you that it was Booth who killed the President ?

A. I cannot. It was spoken of there in the bar-room ; and I cannot for the life of me tell you who it was.

Q. When was it spoken of in the bar-room ?

A The next morning.

Q. At what time in the morning?

A. I should judge, between eight and nine o'clock: it was spoken of all through the day.

Q. Were the circumstances told, — the manner in which he had done it?

A. No, sir; not to my knowledge. I do not remember that any circumstances were told in connection with it.

Q. Do you know whether the soldiers who first came out to the house in the morning knew that it was Booth who had killed the President?

A. I do not suppose that they knew it more than I did; only that they heard so.

Q. Did they bring the report from the city?

A. I believe they brought the report, so far as I could get hold of it.

Cross-examined by Mr. STONE:

Q. How long was it before the assassination that the three gentlemen to whom you referred came to your house?

A. I judge, as well as my memory will serve me, that it was five or six weeks before the occurrence.

Q. Had they one or two buggies?

A. Two buggies: there was a man in each buggy, and a man on horseback.

Q. Who were in the buggies?

A. John Surratt and Dave Herold, I think, were in the buggies. Atzerodt was on horseback.

Q. Did they all arrive together?

A. They all came up together, and at a very fast gait up the road. I saw them when they came up.

Q. Two of them passed on?

A. No: all came up to the house, and stopped the horses and buggies. One of them stopped right at the front-yard gate; and the other stopped about the corner, as well as I remember. I thought nothing much of it at the time, and cannot locate them distinctly: only I noticed the one at the front gate with the sorrel horse; and the other, I think, was about the corner. I paid no material attention to them.

Q. Who went on down the road towards the place called T. B. ?

A. That morning, when they first came down, John Surratt and Atzerodt. When they first came down from, as I supposed, Washington, or up this way, they stopped at my house, and started towards T. B.

Q. Was Herold with them then?

A. Herold came back with them. After they were gone half an hour, all three returned.

Q. Herold did not come to your house that morning?

A. No: he was there the night before.

Q. Had he gone down the country?

A. He told me that night that he had to go down to T. B.

Q. When Atzerodt and Surratt came and remained a while, they went on down towards T. B. ?

A. Yes, sir; down that direction.

Q. How long were they gone?

A. Not over half an hour before they returned again.

Q. Who handed the carbines to you?

A. When they came into the bar, after being there a few minutes, John Surratt told me he wanted to see me; and he took me to the front parlor; and on the sofa in the front parlor these carbines and things were lying.

Q. Then Mr. Surratt was the one who gave the arms into your charge?

A. Mr. Surratt was the one who requested me to receive them for him.

Q. Do you know which buggy brought them up?

A. I did not see the arms taken out of the buggies at all; I did not see any thing of any arms until they were shown to me on the sofa: but, from the position of Herold's buggy, I supposed he was the one who brought them.

Q. Your only reason for supposing they came from Herold's buggy was the position of the buggy being at the front gate, whereas the other buggy was at the corner?

A. That is all.

Q. What became of that rope?

A. The rope was not taken away. It was put into the store-room with the monkey-wrench, and, I suppose, remained there, unless they have got it away since. I told the colonel at the Old Capitol of it; and I suppose he sent down for it, but I do not know. It was left there.

Q. At that time you had no conversation either with Atzerodt or Herold about the arms: it was entirely with Mr. Surratt?

A. With Mr. Surratt altogether.

Q. I think the roads cross at your house?

A. I do not suppose it is more than seventy or seventy-five yards below the house where the roads cross.

Q. Did you see Booth and Herold when they left the house, after they got the carbines, on the night of the assassination?!

A. I did.

Q. Which road did they take!

A. They took the road towards T. B.

Q. Did they both start off together?

A. Yes, sir. Herold came from towards the stable, and came between me and the man who was on the light-colored horse; and they rode right off at a pretty rapid gait.

Q. You cannot say whether it was in Herold's presence that Booth announced to you that he had assassinated the President?

A. I am not positive whether it was in his presence or not, because he rode across the street.

Q. Did any one say any thing to you about the rope and the wrench afterwards?

A. I think not until I told it myself.

Q. Had you seen Herold pass there that day, before the assassination, on the same day?

A. I had not. I had not seen Mr. Herold for some time before that.

Q. You say you think you were arrested on Tuesday?

A. I was arrested on the Tuesday following.

Q. Where were you arrested?

A. I was arrested, I suppose, within about two or three hundred yards of T. B., just the other side, on my way home with my wife.

Q. Did Herold that night take a drink at the bar?

A. He did.

Q. And carried a bottle out to Booth?

A. Yes, sir.

Q. Did he bring the bottle back to you?

A. He brought the bottle back into the house.

Q. Did he pay for the drink he took?

A. He remarked to me, "I owe you a couple of dollars;" and said he, "Here." I looked at it when it got light next morning, and found it to be one dollar, which just about paid for the bottle of liquor they pretty nearly drank.

Q. He gave you the dollar?

A. Yes, sir.

By the JUDGE ADVOCATE:

Q. Was it light enough for you to observe the kind of horses they rode?

A. The moon was shining.

Q. What kind of horses were they?

A. One I took to be a gray horse. It was a light-colored horse, almost a white horse. I supposed it to be a gray horse, in the moonlight. The other was a bay horse. The light horse was a large horse, — I suppose, some sixteen hands high : the other was not so large.

Q. Which rode the light horse?

A. The one who broke his leg was on the light horse : Herold was riding the bay.

Q. You say, that, although Mrs. Offutt was in the yard where the conversation took place between you and Mrs. Surratt, you are not certain that she was near enough to hear it?

A. I am not positive whether she was or not.

Q. Was it in a low tone of voice that Mrs. Surratt spoke to you?

A. No, sir, not very : not very loud, either, — loud enough to hear.

Cross-examined by MR. DOSTER:

Q. You say you have met Mr. Atzerodt in company with Surratt and Herold?

A. He came to my place, I judge, about five or six weeks before, in company with Surratt.

Q. Did you know him before?

A. He had been in my place several times before.

Q. Did you have any conversation with him on this occasion?

A. No, sir : I had no conversation particularly with him. They did not stay any great while.

Q. Did he deliver to you any thing?

A. No.

Q. You had no conversation with him of any importance?

A. No.

Q. Have you seen him since the assassination?

A. Not until now.

By the JUDGE ADVOCATE :

Q. Have you known Atzerodt by any nick-name, — "Port Tobacco"?

A. I heard him called that. I used to call him "Miserable;" and then I called him, for a long time, "Stranger." I did not know his name very well. I do not think I had been acquainted with him over two months before the assassination.

By MR. DOSTER :

Q. Did you know his name to be Atzerodt when he was down there?

A. I did not know his name to be Atzerodt, until, I suppose, about two or three weeks at farthest before the assassination. I never knew his full name.

By MR. EWING :

Q. Did you ever see the prisoner Arnold, the one in the corner?

A. I do not know him.

By MR. STONE :

Q. Did Booth take a carbine with him?

A. He did not. Mr. Herold took one.

Q. Did you hand Booth one?

A. I told him I would go up after the other one ; but he said he could not carry it.

Q. You never brought but one down?

A. That is all.

Q. Had you those carbines convenient when they came?

A. They were in my bed-chamber.

Q. When did you bring them down?

A. Not till they came.

Q. When did you bring them from the store-room in which they were originally placed?

A. No great while after Mrs. Surratt left, according to her orders to get them out, and have them ready.

By the COURT:

Q. The same evening?

A. The same night.

By MR. STONE:

Q. You say that you had them in your bed-chamber when they called?

A. Yes.

Q. Did you give them the carbines before or after they told you they had killed the President?

A. They were given to them before. They never told me about killing the President until they were about riding off.

Q. Have you any colored servants about your establishment?

A. Two there generally; and a man who used to live with Mr. Surratt used to stay there also.

Q. Were any of those about the yard when they called?

A. I suppose the old colored man was there in his room.

Q. You do not know that he saw them?

A. I do not.

Q. Had you retired?

A. I had been to bed and asleep.

Q. They waked you up?

A. I woke up just as the clock struck "twelve." I went to bed between eight and nine o'clock, I judge. I was right smart in for liquor on that evening, and after night I got more so; and I went to bed very early, and slept very sound until twelve o'clock. At twelve o'clock, I roused up.

Q. Between the Saturday and the next Tuesday, had you not a great many inquiries made you about suspicious characters passing that way?

A. All the inquiries I had, pretty much, were on Saturday. They were not many, although a good many soldiers came there. There were so many persons about the establishment, that they would ask others almost as quick as they would me. On Sunday morning, I took a walk around an old neighbor's place with him. In the evening, when I came back, there was a crowd of persons who occupied my attention pretty much home all the time, until I drove them out of the house, and locked the doors. They got pretty high. I was not troubled that night any more until the soldiers came, and searched the place that night.

Q. What account did you give when asked?

A. When they asked me if I had seen two men pass that way in the morning, I told them I had not. That is the only thing I blame myself about. If I had given the information that was asked of me, I should have been perfectly free as regards it. That is the only thing I am sorry that I did not do.

By MR. AIKEN:

Q. Did you have any conversation with Mrs. Offutt in regard to the package after Mrs. Surratt went away?

A. I think, but I will not be positive about that, I told Mrs. Offutt that it was a field-glass.

Q. Did Mrs. Offutt have any thing to say to you about a package after Mrs. Surratt went away?

A. I do not know, indeed. I cannot remember.

Q. Did she tell you that Mrs. Surratt gave her a package?

A. She did not.

Q. How large is the yard in front of your house?

A. I suppose that from the front of the house to the gate is about as far as from here, where I am standing, to the door coming into this room.

Q. How near to the door of the house were you standing when Mrs. Surratt drove away?

A. I did not see her drive away; but, when I tied up the springs of her buggy, I bade her good-by.

Q. Where were you standing when you had the conversation with her last ?

A. Which conversation have you reference to ?

Q. The one in which she made the remark about the " shooting-irons."

A. I was standing then near the wood-pile, in the back yard; the kitchen-yard, we call it.

On motion, the Commission adjourned until Monday morning, May 15, at ten o'clock.

MONDAY, May 15, 1865.

The Court again met on Monday, and proceeded with the examination.

Edward Spangler, who has hitherto had no counsel, was this day added to the list of those for whom Mr. Ewing appears : and, as the other prisoners had severally done before, he asked leave to withdraw for the time his plea of " Not guilty," heretofore filed, so that he might plead to the jurisdiction of the Court. He said, through his counsel, that he had not heretofore had counsel to advise him as to the pleas which it would be expedient for him to make.

The application was granted ; and thereupon, through his counsel, he presented the plea that the Court had no jurisdiction in this proceeding against him, because, he says, he has not been in the military service of the United States. And, for further plea, he said that loyal civil courts, in which all the offences charged are triable, exist, and are in full and free operation, in all the places where the several offences charged are alleged to have been committed.

And further, that this Court has no jurisdiction in the matter of the alleged conspiracy, so far as it is charged to have been a conspiracy to murder Abraham Lincoln, late President of the United States, and William H. Seward, Secretary of State. The same plea is made in reference to the charge of murdering the late President, &c, because the offences were alleged to have been committed in the city of Washington, in which are loyal civil courts in full operation, in which all such offences are triable.

The Judge Advocate presented a replication in answer to the special plea, affirming the jurisdiction of the Court; and the Court, as in other cases, overruled the plea.

The same prisoner then, as others had done, applied for a separate trial, for the reason that he believes his defence will be greatly prejudiced by a joint trial.

The Commission overruled the application for a severance; and Spangler renewed his plea of "Not guilty" to the specification of the charge and to the charge.

Michael O'Laughlin, through his counsel, pursued the same course with the same result.

Louis J. Weichmann

was recalled by leave of the Court, and cross-examined.

By Mr. Ewing:

Q. In your testimony, you mentioned, that, as Dr. Mudd and Booth were walking up Seventh Street, you and Surratt were walking down; and Dr. Mudd called out to Surratt, and Surratt turned round. Were you and Booth on the same side of the street?

A. Yes, sir.

Q. Then you had passed each other?

A. Yes, sir: we had passed each other before Mudd recognized Surratt; and I said, "John, some one is calling you;" and he turned round, and recognized Dr. Mudd.

Q. By whom have you heard Dr. Samuel Mudd spoken of in the Surratt Family before this meeting?

A. Miss Surratt has spoken of him. She was educated at Bryantown; and I think she was acquainted with the Mudd Family.

Q. Are you sure that she spoke of Dr. Samuel Mudd?

A. I have heard the name mentioned in the house; but, whether it was she who mentioned it, I cannot positively say. I have heard the name of Dr. Samuel Mudd and of Dr. George Mudd mentioned in the house.

Q. You think it was she who mentioned the name?

A. Yes, sir; and I also heard a Miss Angela Mudd mentioned. These are the only Mudds I ever heard spoken of.

Q. Do you know whether Dr. Samuel Mudd lives near Bryantown?

A. I have heard it said, in Charles County; but in what particular portion of the county he resides, I do not know.

Q. Is Bryantown in Charles County?

A. I could hardly tell that: I think it is. I have never been there.

By Mr. Johnson:

Q. I understood you to say on Saturday that you went with Mrs. Surratt the first time to Surrattsville, on the Tuesday before the assassination, in a buggy with her. Do you recollect whether you stopped on your way to Surrattsville?

A. Yes, sir.

Q. Where?

A. We stopped on two or three different occasions.

Q. Did you stop at Uniontown?

A. I do not know the name of the particular town. I do not know where Uniontown is.

Q. Did you stop at a village?

A. We stopped on the road: I do not remember any particular village that could be seen.

Q. Do you know Mr. Lloyd?

A. I have met him three times.

Q. Did you know him as the keeper of the hotel at Surrattsville?

A. I knew him as the man who had rented Mrs. Surratt's house from her, because I copied off the instrument.

Q. Do you recollect seeing him by the buggy at any time on your way between Washington and Surrattsville on that Tuesday?

A. Yes, sir: we met his carriage. His carriage drove past ours; and Mrs. Surratt called after Mr. Lloyd; and Mr. Lloyd got out and approached the buggy; and Mrs. Surratt put her head out, and had a conversation with him.

Q. From the buggy?

A. Yes, sir.

Q. Did you hear it?

A. No, sir.

Q. Did you hear any thing that was said?

A. No, sir.

Q. Any thing about shooting-irons?

A. There was nothing mentioned at all about shooting-irons. Mrs. Surratt spoke to Mrs. Offutt about this man Howell. Mrs. Surratt was in the carriage: she said she was going to see him, and see if he would not take the oath of allegiance and get released, and that she was going to apply to General Augur and Judge Turner for the purpose.

Q. How long was the interview between Mr. Lloyd and Mrs. Surratt on that occasion?

A. That I could not say exactly: I do not think it was over five or eight minutes. I do not carry a watch myself, and I had no precise means of judging.

By the JUDGE ADVOCATE:

Q. I understood you to say at first that you did not hear the whole of this conversation?

A. I did not hear the conversation between Mr. Lloyd and Mrs. Surratt, but between Mrs. Surratt and Mrs. Offutt, who was at some distance in the carriage.

Q. It is the conversation between Mrs. Surratt and Mr. Lloyd that we are talking of. You could not hear that?

A. I could not hear it.

By MR. JOHNSON:

Q. Do you reccollect whether it was raining?

A. I do not think it was raining at the particular time. It was a murky day, a very cloudy day; but I could not say whether it was raining or not: I did not remember that.

JOHN W. LLOYD recalled by leave of the Court.

By the JUDGE ADVOCATE:

Q. [Exhibiting to the witness two carbines.] Are these the carbines that John H. Surratt left at your house?

A. They were brought in with covers. One of these has a cover on: it looks like the cover that was on them. These look like tho carbines that were brought there.

Q. You did not see them with the cover off?

A. I took the cover off one; and the peculiar kind of breech attracted my attention. I never saw one like it before. Both the carbines left at my house had covers. I did not examine both of them: I only slipped the cover off one, and looked at it.

The witness added, —

I desire to make a statement, if the Court will permit me. I said, on Saturday, that it was on Monday that I met Mrs. Surratt at Uniontown. I got the days confounded by being summoned to Court on two Mondays in succession. The first Monday I was summoned to Court, I did not go, but came to Washington; and I was under the impression that it was on that Monday I met Mrs. Surratt: but in fact, on the Monday that I said here I met Mrs. Surratt, I went to Court; and, consequently, it was on Tuesday that I met her at Uniontown. I say so now on reflection. In the last of my examination, in stating with regard to the bundle Mrs. Surratt gave me, I did not exactly recollect, but was pretty positive that I carried it directly up stairs; but I cannot say now that I am positive. I carried it up stairs. The whole thing was very hurried; and I had liquor at the time, so that I cannot distinctly recollect: but I think it likely that I laid it upon a safe in the dining-room, and that is my impression.

By the JUDGE ADVOCATE:

Q. You are sure it was the same package you examined afterwards?

A. Yes, sir: it was tho same.

Q. And it was a field-glass?

A. Yes, sir.

Q. The same one you handed to Herold?

A. Yes, sir.

By MR. AIKEN:

Q. I do not know that I fully understand the witness; and I should like to ask one question. Do I understand you as stating that you were in liquor at the time you had the conversation with Mrs. Surratt?

A. I was somewhat in liquor at the time that I was in conversation with Mrs. Surratt, as I said on Saturday.

Q. On that account, you do not feel able to give clear testimony? Is that the explanation you want to make?

A. I wanted to explain that I was not positive whether the package was carried up-stairs or not. It was a hurried piece of business with me, and, consequently, I did not reflect over it.

MARY VAN TINE,

a witness called for the prosecution, being duly sworn, testified as follows : —

By the JUDGE ADVOCATE:

Q. Do you reside in the city of Washington?

A. Yes, sir : at 420, D Street.

Q. Do you keep rooms to rent?

A. I do.

Q. Will you look at the prisoners at the bar here, and state whether, in the month of February last, you saw any one of them, and which one?

A. Yes, sir : I see two gentlemen who had rooms at my house.

Q. Which two?

A. Mr. Arnold and Mr. O'Laughlin.

Q. What time in February last was it?

A. As near as I can recollect, it was on the 10th of February they came. I could not be positive as to the day; but I think it was the 10th.

Q. Did you know J. Wilkes Booth?

A. I knew him by coming to the house to see the gentlemen who had rooms there.

Q. Did he or not come very often to see the prisoners, O'Laughlin and Arnold?

A. Yes, sir : frequently.

Q. Would he remain a good while in conversation with them?

A. Not as a general thing, I believe; but he was admitted in the room, and I saw nothing further of them.

Q. Did these prisoners leave the city, and return several times?

A. Yes, sir: they frequently left on Saturday for Baltimore, as I understood, their homes.

Q. Do you know whether Booth accompanied them or not?

A. I think not.

Q. Were these interviews between Booth and them alone, or was Booth accompanied by other persons?

A. I never saw any one in company with them.

Q. They told you themselves that his name was J. Wilkes Booth, did they?

A. Yes, sir: Mr. Arnold did. I inquired who he was. He told me his name was J. Wilkes Booth.

Q. Did he call for them frequently, and find them out?

A. Sometimes.

Q. Did he, or not, manifest much anxiety to see them on these occasions?

A. Frequently, when they were away: sometimes he came two or three times before they returned. He generally appeared very anxious for their return.

Q. Did he leave messages for them?

A. Sometimes he requested, that, if they returned before he called again, they should come to the stable; or he sometimes left a note, going into the room, and writing a note.

Q. Will you look at that photograph [Exhibit No. 1], and see if you recognize it as that of the man you call Booth?

A. Yes, sir; I think so: but I cannot see very well without my glasses. [Puts on her spectacles.] I should not call it a good likeness. I think him a better-looking man than that is; but I should think it was the man I saw; but it is a poor likeness of him.

Q. Do you remember the last time Booth played in the city, about the 18th or 20th of March?

A. Yes, sir: somewhere about that time.

Q. Did these prisoners bring you complimentary tickets from Booth on that occasion?

A. Yes, sir: I expressed a wish to see him; and Mr. O'Laughlin gave me the tickets.

Q. Did he seem to be more confidential and intimate with one of these prisoners than with the other?

A. Sometimes he would inquire for one, sometimes the other; though I think he more frequently inquired for O'Laughlin.

Q. Did you see any arms in their rooms?

A. I saw a pistol once; only once.

Q. Do you remember at any time seeing a man call, a very rough-looking person, a laboring man or mechanic?

A. Not a laboring man. A man used to come sometimes there, and I think he passed one night with them; but I am not certain. By his leaving the room very early one morning, I thought so; but he might have come in with them, and gone out early in the morning. I never heard his name. I should know him if I saw him.

Q. Can you give a description of him?

A. Not what you call a gentleman in appearance, but a very respectable-looking mechanic.

Q. Could you describe him at all?

A. Not very minutely. His skin was hardened, as of a man who had been exposed to weather; and he had sandy whiskers.

Q. Do you recognize him among these prisoners?

A. No, sir.

Q. Did they represent themselves to have any business transactions with Booth; and if so, of what character?

A. They said they were in the oil trade; but they did not say they were connected with him in it. They merely said they were in the oil business.

Q. Did they seem to have an extensive correspondence? Did many letters come to them?

A. Not a great many: some letters came.

Q. Where did they generally come from, if you noticed?

A. I never noticed: I merely took the letters in, and laid them down.

Q. They were addressed to the names you gave now, O'Laughlin and Arnold?

A. Sometimes to one, sometimes to the other.

Q. You say Booth came there frequently, by day and night?

A. Not in the night frequently. I do not know that I ever saw him at night. He might have come without my seeing him. It was the winter season, when I sit back ; and persons might come into the other part of the house without my seeing them.

Q. You do not know whether, when they went out at nights and staid late, they were with Booth or not ?

A. No, sir.

Q. You have not seen them since the time they left your house ?

A. Never till the present time.

Q. Was that about the 20th of March ?

A. I think that it was the Monday after Booth played : on Saturday they left.

Q. Did you ever see Booth riding out with either of these men ?

A. No, sir : I do not think I ever did. I cannot say positively whether I did or not. I would not like to say on my oath that I saw that, though he frequently came to the house in a carriage and inquired for them ; but I never saw them riding, that I recollect.

Cross-examined by Mr. Cox :

Q. Can you state with certainty whether these gentlemen said they were then in the oil business, or had been ?

A. That they were then in the oil business.

Q. Was that during the first part of their stay, or at what time during their occupation of your room ?

A. I think they had been there two or three weeks.

Q. They had been there two or three weeks when they told you that ?

A. Yes, sir. Mr. Arnold told me.

Q. That would bring it to the beginning of March ?

A. Somewhere about that.

Q. Did they say any thing to you when they went away about where they were going to ?

A. Pennsylvania, I understood.

Q. They said they were going to Pennsylvania when they left your house ?

A. Yes, sir.

Q. Did they say any thing to you about having abandoned the oil business ?

A. No, sir. I had very little conversation with them at any time.

Q. Were they much in their room, or moving about ?

A. They did not stay a great deal in the room.

Q. Did they occupy it regularly at night ?

A. They were out some nights all night.

Q. Can you fix the 20th of March with certainty as the day they left ?

A. If you could ascertain what night Booth played. I know it was the Monday following.

Q: What was he playing ?

A. Pescara.

Q. You do not speak with certainty of any one else visiting them besides Mr. Booth ?

A. No, sir : not any one else that I know. Persons might have often gone into the room, and we not see or know them.

Q. The only person you remember is a respectable-looking mechanic, whom you do not identify as one of the prisoners ?

A. That was all ; and he is not present. I should know him if I was to see him anywhere.

Q. When were Booth's visits most frequent, — during the month of February, or the latter part of their stay in March ?

A. I think pretty much the same all through the time they were there. He was a constant visitor.

Q. You do not think his visits fell off in point of frequency towards the close of the stay ?

A. I do not.

Q. Were you present at any conversation between them at any time ?

A. No, sir.

Q. You never heard any of their conversation ?

A. No, sir.

Q. Was their room up stairs ?

A. No, sir : they had the back parlor. The doors were always closed ; and it was none of my business to pry into the conversation of my lodgers.

Q. Of course not : I mean whether you casually overheard any conversation ?

A. No, sir : never.

BILLY WILLIAMS,

(colored,) a witness called for the prosecution, being duly sworn, testified as follows : —

By the JUDGE ADVOCATE :

Q. Will you state to the Court whether you are acquainted with the prisoners O'Laughlin and Arnold ? Look at them, and see if you have ever met with them before.

A. I know Mr. O'Laughlin, and I know Mr. Arnold by sight.

Q. Have you ever met with them before ?

A. I have met Mr. O'Laughlin.

Q. Where did you meet with him ?

A. I met Mr. O'Laughlin when I carried the letters to him and gave them to him at the theatre.

Q. Where was that theatre ?

A. In Baltimore.

Q. When was that ?

A. It was in March; but I do not know what time.

Q. This last March ?

A. Yes, sir.

Q. From whom did you carry letters to him ?

A. Mr. Booth.

Q. J. Wilkes Booth, the actor ?

A. Yes, sir.

Q. Did you carry them to O'Laughlin alone, or to him and to Arnold ?

A. I carried one to Mr. Arnold; and I gave it to a lady there at the door, and she said she would send them up. I then went off. I was in a hurry.

MR. COX. Unless that is followed up by something on the part of O'Laughlin, I hardly think it competent evidence, — the carrying of a letter to him.

Q. You say you delivered the letter at the boarding-house of O'Laughlin ?

A. Yes, sir. When I carried the letters, — there were two, — I was going by Barnum's at the time; and Mr. Booth came down the steps, and asked me if I would take it. I told him I had to go to the country; but he said it would not take any time.

Q. Did he tell you where O'Laughlin lived?

A. In Exeter Street, he told me.

Q: He told you it was for O'Laughlin?

A. Yes, sir.

Q. Did you ever carry a letter to the prisoner Arnold?

A. I carried a letter up there: I do not know who it was for.

Q. Who gave it to you?

A. I gave it to a lady.

Q. Who was it from?

A. Mr. Booth.

Q. Did he state to you whom it was for?

A. No, sir. He just told me, — he called me Bill, — said he, "Here is a letter; and I want you to carry it up to this number." I went up with it. I did not know where the number was, I did not know that I was on the right street; and I asked a lady who was coming out of a door where was the number, and she told me on that side; and I went down there.

Q. And delivered the letter?

A. Yes, sir.

Q. You did not know for whom it was?

A. No, sir.

Q. You said that Booth did not tell you for whom it was?

A. No, sir: he told me just to carry it to the number that was on it. There was a colored fellow with me; and I asked him to look at it, and see what it was, as I could not read writing.

Q. Were there more than one?

A. Two.

Q. To Arnold?

A. Two letters I had to carry, — one up town, and one down town.

Q. To whom did you deliver the second?

A. I delivered it to Mr. O'Laughlin.

Q. When did you deliver it to him?

A. I gave it to him at the theatre. It was in the evening.

Q. Did you know for whom it was?

A.   He told me.   I knew the name.   I had almost forgotten it; but I had to go to the theatre, and I went there, and saw O'Laughlin there ; and I told him he had saved me a smart deal of trouble, and handed it to him.

Q.   He told you it was for Arnold, did he?

Mr. Ewing.   I certainly object to that.

The Judge Advocate.   The theory is, that these men were co-conspirators ; and, if that is established, their declarations are certainly evidence against each other.

Mr. Ewing.   I object to that question as it is put down ; and I should like to have my objection entered.

By the Judge Advocate :

Q.   I asked you for whom O'Laughlin said the letter was ?

A.   I said, when I carried the letter to him, " Mr. O'Laughlin, here is a letter Mr. Booth gave to me ; " and I handed it to him. That is all I know.   When Mr. Booth told me I had to carry the letter, I said, " Certainly, I will carry it ; but I will take my own time ; " and he gave me it to carry, and I thought no more of it.

Q.   Booth told you this letter was for O'Laughlin, did he ?

A.   Yes, sir.

Mr. Cox.   I must object to the whole of this evidence.   I made the objection a short time ago, in the expectation that it would be followed up by some evidence of the act of O'Laughlin on the receipt of the letter.   Nothing of that sort is produced.

The Judge Advocate.   He states that O'Laughlin received the letter.

Mr. Cox.   Yes, sir ; but that is not sufficient.   I object to the whole of the evidence of the delivery of this note to O'Laughlin ; and I desire, if the objection is sustained, that it be struck out of the record.

The Judge Advocate.   If the Court please, it is simply going to establish the intimacy of these men, their close personal relations with each other, as evidenced by their correspondence ; and I think, in that point of view, it is clearly competent.   We have presented them as visiting each other constantly.   Now we present them as coresponding with each other constantly.   Both facts go to establish an intimacy which is in accordance with the theory of the prosecution ; which is, that they are co-conspirators.

The PRESIDENT. What was the objection of counsel ?

MR. COX. I object to any evidence of the acts of Booth himself. The act of sending a note to an individual, no matter what may be the contents of that note, would be no evidence against that individual, unless the contents were accepted and acted upon by him. The mere fact of intimacy alone is an innocent fact on the part of the accused, and therefore is not evidence, I think, of a conspiracy. I therefore object to it in the first place as an act of Booth to which the defendant is not a party at all. He could not help receiving a letter from Booth. The act of receiving a letter was an entirely innocent one. I object furthermore, that, even if it tends to show intimacy, it does not tend to prove the guilt of the party of the charge now made against him.

The JUDGE ADVOCATE. We have established that intimacy clearly in their association in Washington. We are simply following them to Baltimore, and showing that there they were in correspondence with each other. It is a fact of the same order ; and, although it may not have the same force with the other fact, its tendency certainly is in the same direction. We do not offer the contents of the letter. We offer the fact of their correspondence with each other.

The Court overruled the objection.

Cross-examined by MR. COX:

Q. I did not understand you to state when that note was carried.

A. No, sir : I do not know when it was carried. I did not think any thing about it.

Q. You do not recollect the date ?

A. No, sir : it was in March, I am pretty sure.

Q. You are sure it was in March last ?

A. Yes, sir.

Q. What makes you certain of that ?

A. I think it was that time, because I heard Tom Johnson — I had never taken much notice of the months — he said it was in March ; but I do not know what.

Q. What another person told you will not do. Is there nothing that you recollect that fixes it in your mind certainly?

A. I am almost sure it was in March.

Q. Was it in the beginning, or late in the month?

A. It was in the middle, I think, or nearly the last, because I had something to get for customers; and it put me back in my business, and I could get nothing. It was cold then.

Q. You said Booth gave you this note at the door of Barnum's Hotel in Baltimore?

A. Yes, sir: I was coming along; and, just as I was coming up about to the saloon underneath Barnum's, he asked me to carry the letter. I told him that I could not do it; that I had to go to the country. He said it would take me no time, and I carried them.

Q. You took them where?

A. One in Fayette Street; but I did not know the number, for I had to look for it.

Q. Was that the house of O'Laughlin?

A. That was up town. The other was in Old Town that I had to go.

Q. You said something about taking a note to the theatre. When was that?

A. I went with one to the theatre.

Q. What theatre?

A. Holliday-street Theatre. I went around there first, and had the letter in my hand, and was going to put a pitcher and some things away, and then I gave it to that gentleman [O'Laughlin].

Q. You found him there at that theatre?

A. Yes, sir.

Q. What part of the theatre?

A. In the dress circle.

Q. At what time?

A. In the afternoon.

Q. How did you find him?

A. I know Mr. O'Laughlin right smart.

Q. How did you know where to look for him in the theatre?

A. I was not looking for him. I went up stairs with the pitcher, and saw him there. After I put the pitcher away, I was going to run over there and look for the number.

Q. That is all you know about it : you gave him the note, and came off?

A. Yes, sir.

Cross-examined by MR. EWING :

Q. What did Mr. Booth say to you when he gave you this other letter, the one not for Mr. O'Laughlin ?

A. Mr. Booth told me that one was to go up Fayette Street. He said it was in Fayette Street, above Hart. I went up there. I did not think it was that low down. I was on the right-hand side, going up on Fayette ; and I asked a lady at a door where it was, and she read it to me.

Q. Did he say any thing more ?

A. No, sir. I asked him how his mother was; and he said, "Very well;" and he said he was going away to New York at half-past three o'clock.

Q. You asked Booth ?

A. Yes, sir. When I came back, I did not look for him.

Q. Mr. Booth just gave you the number of the house to which the letter was directed ?

A. Yes, sir : it was on it, — some writing.

Q. He did not tell you to whom it was addressed ?

A. No, sir. I could not read it.

BERNARD J. EARLY,

a witness called for the prosecution, being duly sworn, testified as follows : —

By the JUDGE ADVOCATE :

Q. Are you acquainted with the prisoners O'Laughlin and Arnold, or either of them ?

A. I am acquainted with O'Laughlin, and with Mr. Arnold slightly.

Q. Do you remember to have been on the cars with them coming from Baltimore to this city at any time ?

13*

A. Yes, sir: with O'Laughlin. I came down with Mr. O'Laughlin on the Thursday previous to the assassination.

Q. Was Mr. Arnold on the cars?

A. No, sir: he was not, — not to my knowledge.

Q. That was on the day preceding the assassination?

A. Yes, sir: Thursday, the night of the illumination.

Q. Do you know where he went in the city after he came?

A. After we came out of the cars in company, — there were four of us together, — one stopped to get shaved on the avenue, between Third and Four and a Half Streets; and O'Laughlin asked me to walk as far as the National Hotel with him.

Q. Do you know whether he took a room there that night?

A. No, sir: he did not.

Q. Did you see him at any time associating with J. Wilkes Booth?

A. No, sir: I never saw Mr. Booth in my life, except once on the stage.

Q. Did you hear him make inquiry for Booth?

A. That evening I cannot say as he did. I cannot recollect what inquiry he made at the desk.

Q. Did you see him during the day on Friday?

A. Yes, sir: I was with him the greater part of that day.

Q. Where?

A. We stopped that Thursday night at the Metropolitan Hotel. The next morning we got up and went down to Welch's (Welcker's), on the avenue, and had breakfast. After that we came up the avenue, — there were four of us in company at the time; and, when passing by the National Hotel, I stopped to go in back to the water-closet; and, when I came out of there, I met Mr. Henderson, one of the company, sitting down. I was going out; but he called me back, and told me to wait for O'Laughlin, who was gone up stairs to see Mr. Booth.

Q. That was at the National Hotel?

A. Yes, sir.

Q. How long was he gone up there?

A. I cannot say. We staid there, I should judge, for about

three-quarters of an hour, waiting for O'Laughlin to come down stairs; and, he not coming down, we went out.

Q. Did you see him in the course of the day?

A. Yes, sir: I saw him in about an hour, I should judge, after that. I met him in a restaurant on the avenue, between Third and Four and a Half Streets. He came in there while we were there.

Q. What hour did you say it was that he went up to see Booth on Friday?

A. It was after getting breakfast at Welch's. We got up at seven in the morning. I should say it was about nine o'clock, perhaps.

Q. What was the latest hour at which you saw him on that day?

A. We had been drinking considerable; and I distinctly recollect seeing Mr. O'Laughlin, that Friday night, going out of this restaurant with Mr. Fuller. I cannot say whether it was before or after the assassination; but I believe it must have been after it: it was pretty late.

Q. How long had he been in there, do you know?

A. He had been in there from the time we had supper. We went up and had supper at Welch's, — me and O'Laughlin and Henderson.

Q. Will you give me the name of that restaurant?

A. I believe the proprietor's name at present is Lichau.

Q. Did you see O'Laughlin at the time or immediately after you heard of the assassination of the President?

A. I cannot say as I did; for I went to bed myself shortly after that.

Q. You are not certain, but you think he remained there until after the assassination?

A. I think he did: I would not be certain of it; but I distinctly recollect him that night being there, and going out in company with this Mr. Fuller.

Q. Who is Mr. Fuller?

A. I do not know what he is doing at present: he used to be employed by O'Laughlin's brother here once. I have seen him several times in Baltimore.

Q. They went out, and you did not see them afterwards?

A. Not that night.

Q. Did O'Laughlin go with you to Baltimore the next day?

A. Yes, sir.

Q. At what hour?

A. We went up on the train in the afternoon, either at three or half-past three o'clock.

Q. Where did he go in Baltimore? Do you know, after you arrived there?

A. After arriving in Baltimore, we went down Baltimore Street, and up as far as High Street, and down High Street to the corner of Fayette; where I asked him to walk down as far as the store with me, to let them know that I had arrived in town again. From there he asked me if I would not go over as far as a Mr. Hoffmann's house to see his wife. Mr. Hoffmann was lying sick in Washington here at the time with rheumatism. We went over as far as Hoffmann's wife's house, and saw her. Mr. O'Laughlin had some communication to make to her from her husband, who was lying here sick. Then we came down, and went to Mr. O'Laughlin's house. He asked me if I would walk that far. In going down to his house, we met his brother-in-law on the way; and he walked along with us. He told Mr. O'Laughlin that there had been parties there that morning looking for him. Mr. O'Laughlin went into the house, and asked me if I would remain there, and then came out and invited me to come in. I went in, and sat in the parlor while he went up stairs to see his mother: he remained a few minutes, and then came down, and said he was not going to stay-home that night.

Q. Did he manifest much excitement about the assassination of the President?

A. I cannot say as he did. He did not appear to be anyways excited much to me, only when he heard there were parties after him; and his brother-in-law, I suppose it was, made the remark that they were after him because of his known intimacy with Booth, having been acquainted with him, and been in the habit of going with him, and supposed to be connected in the oil business with him.

Cross-examined by Mr. Cox:

Q. Who were the parties that came down with you?

A. Mr. Henderson, Edward Murphy, O'Laughlin, and myself.

Q. Who is Mr. Henderson?

A. Mr. Henderson, I believe, is a lieutenant in the United-States Navy.

Q. For what purpose did you come down, all of you?

A. I was invited down by Mr. Henderson. He came to the store after me that afternoon, and asked me to come down with the intention of having a little good time, he said, and see the illumination.

Q. Were the others invited by him also?

A. I do not know. I have heard Mr. Murphy say they were.

Q. Where did Mr. O'Laughlin join you in Baltimore?

A. He came to the store along with Mr. Henderson.

Q. And Mr. Henderson invited you to go along?

A. Yes, sir: Mr. Henderson invited me to go along. I was making a pair of pantaloons for Mr. Henderson; and they were not done at the time. They were to be done that evening; but they were not done when he called for them, and he persuaded me to go down with him.

Q. Mr. Henderson came to the store with O'Laughlin and Mr. Murphy, and invited you to go down with them to see the illumination and have a good time?

A. That is the remark he made.

Q. On Thursday night, where did you stay?

A. On Thursday night, we stopped at the Metropolitan Hotel.

Q. All of you?

A. All of us. Me and Henderson and Murphy slept in one room, it being a three-bedded room; and, O'Laughlin's name coming last as we signed our names, they gave him a room to himself.

Q. Was it adjoining the room in which you were?

A. I cannot say whether it was an adjoining room or not; but it was on the same floor, the second or third door from it, anyhow.

Q. Who arranged that he should sleep separately? Was it arranged among the party?

A. No. Our names came in rotation, and he was the last one that signed his name on the book; and the clerk assigned those rooms to us.

Q. Did he stay there all night?

A. He did.

Q. You saw him early in the morning?

A. Yes, sir. I went and woke him up. I rapped at the door, peeped in the keyhole, and saw that he was in the room.

Q. How late was it that night when you went to bed?

A. I should judge it was about two o'clock on Friday morning before we went to bed.

Q. And he was with you during all that time?

A. All that time, — from the time we left Baltimore until we went to bed in the Metropolitan Hotel.

Q. You woke him up in the morning?

A. I went and rapped at his door (he was asleep), and woke him up.

Q. And then you went down the street to get breakfast at the Lichau House?

A. No, sir : at Welch's, I believe it is.

Q. Where is that?

A. On the avenue ; I guess about Tenth Street : I do not know exactly.

Q. And after breakfast, about nine o'clock, you think, you called at the National Hotel?

A. Yes, sir.

Q. Do you know for what purpose he went to see Mr. Booth?

A. I should judge —

ASSISTANT JUDGE ADVOCATE BINGHAM. You need not state what you judge.

Q. Did you hear Mr. O'Laughlin state what he was going to see Mr. Booth for?

A. No, sir : I did not.

Q. To refresh your recollection, I will ask you to state whether he said any thing about getting money that Booth owed him?

A. Not at that time : I did not hear him make that remark.

Q. Booth had not come down from his room when you called there?

A. I do not know.

Q. Mr. O'Laughlin went up stairs to see him?

A. He went up stairs, and I went to the rear of the building: at least, I was told that he went up stairs; I did not see him go up.

Q. You do not know whether he actually saw Booth or not?

A. I do not.

Q. But in about an hour's time, I think you stated, he rejoined you at the Lichau House?

A. We remained in the hotel — Mr. Henderson and myself — for, I should say, three-quarters of an hour, waiting for him, and thought he was up stairs; and, not coming down, Henderson concluded to go out. As he went out, he had some cards written by the card-writer there, and said he would call for them in about ten minutes. We then went out, and walked down the avenue as far, I think, as this Lichau House, to see if Mike — Mr. O'Laughlin — had been down there; and, he not being there, we returned back, and got the cards; and the card-writer asked me what was his name, and wrote me a sample card at the same time, and wrote it wrong, and afterwards corrected it. Mr. Murphy, in the mean time, had joined us on the avenue; and I forget who it was that proposed to send cards up to Mr. Booth's room for Mr. O'Laughlin, so that, if he was in there, he might take it as a hint to come down, that we were tired of waiting. The cards were returned down, that there was nobody in the room.

Q. Where were the cards put then? Were they left at the bar?

A. They were left at the bar.

Q. Or at the clerk's office?

A. At the desk of the clerk.

Q. And, in about an hour's time, he rejoined you at the Lichau House?

A. Yes, sir.

Q. How long during that day was he in your company?

A. We took a stroll around the city in different parts; and me and him and Mr. Murphy and Henderson had dinner again at Welch's.

Q. You strolled around the city all together?

A. Yes, sir.

Q. And dined at Welch's?

A. Yes, sir.

Q. At what hour?

A. I cannot state correctly the hour. I guess it was some time between twelve and two o'clock.

Q. Do you know where Wall and Stephens's dry-goods and clothing store is?

A. Yes, sir.

Q. Was it over that store that you dined?

A. I cannot say that it was. I think it was farther up on the avenue. I have seen it several times; but I never took notice of what store it was over.

Q. You dined at two o'clock. At what time did you get through dinner?

A. I do not think it took over an hour, getting it ready and so on.

Q. That would be about three o'clock?

A. I should think, maybe, we got through dinner and all between those two hours. I could not say correctly.

Q. After dinner, where did you go?

A. We went around the town again to different places.

Q. You visited the different places in town?

A. Yes, sir. I cannot say that we went to any particular place.

Q. Was O'Laughlin with you during all the time?

A. I cannot say whether O'Laughlin was with me later; that is, after dinner. We had been drinking pretty freely all of us; but I recollect, between four and five o'clock I should think it was, O'Laughlin went with me to a friend's house of mine.

Q. To pay a visit?

A. Yes, sir: I was not acquainted in town very well, and did not know the way the streets ran; and I asked him to go along with me to help to find a place.

Q. To pay a visit to a lady?

A. Yes, sir; and there we had dinner the second time: she invited us to have dinner. She took our hats, and we had to stay.

Q. That was on Friday, you say, between four and five o'clock?

A. Yes, sir.

Q. At what time did you leave there?

A. We staid there to dinner, then sat down and had a little talk, and left there, I suppose, about six o'clock.

Q. You stated that you are not certain of O'Laughlin's being with you all the afternoon; but do you not suppose, or do you strongly think, that he was with you between the first and the second dinner?

A. I cannot say positively as to that. He might have been in company with us; but I think we separated; that is, O'Laughlin and Henderson went one way, or me and Michael went together: I cannot say which.

Q. You are not certain whether O'Laughlin went with you or Henderson?

A. I cannot say; but I know me and him started together again about four o'clock, and went to this lady's house.

Q. At six o'clock, where did you go?

A. We took the cars: the place was down near the depot; but we went out the other side of the town to hunt it, and found that the numbers ran down that way.

Q. It was on D Street, near the Baltimore Depot, where you paid the visit?

A. Yes, sir.

Q. You left there about six o'clock, you say: where did you go then?

A. After that, we turned back to the Lichau House, and were found there by Murphy and Henderson.

Q. How late were you there?

A. We staid there around that place until about seven or eight o'clock, I guess; when we went back to Welch's, and had supper. I know that we were in Welch's at the time the procession passed up the avenue of Navy-Yard men. I do not believe Mr. Murphy went up to supper: I think O'Laughlin, Henderson, and I went and had supper.

Q. And you were in there when the procession passed up from the Navy Yard?

A. Yes, sir.

Q. Do you know what time that was?

A. I could not say: I should judge between eight and nine o'clock.

Q. How late did you stay there?

A. I could not say exactly what length of time: we staid there till we ate our meal, and while it was getting ready for us; and then returned back to the Lichau House, and staid there the balance of the night up to the time I went to bed.

Q. You staid there until you had finished supper. Cannot you fix the hour exactly?

A. No, sir: I could not.

Q. And then you went back to the Lichau House, and staid there until you went to bed, you say?

A. Yes, sir: I did.

Q. Was O'Laughlin there too?

A. O'Laughlin was there the best part of that night.

Q. Did I understand you to say that you were there when you heard of the assassination?

A. Yes, sir: I was there when I heard of the assassination.

Q. Where is the Lichau House?

A. I do not know whether they call it the Lichau House or not; but that is the man's name.

Q. Where is the house?

A. It is situated between Third and Four and a Half Streets: I believe it is the second door from the "Globe" office.

Q. You spoke of O'Laughlin going out with Fuller?

A. Yes, sir.

Q. Are you not certain that that was after you had received the news of the assassination?

A. No, sir: I am not certain whether it was after that or not. I recollect it, and that is all. I had been drinking considerable myself.

Q. Where did you stay that night?

A. I slept in that house, — the Lichau House.

Q. Did O'Laughlin stay there too?

A. No, sir: not that I know of.

Q. You do not remember?

A. No, sir.

Q. Had you been drinking sufficiently not to notice the fact at that time?

A. Yes, sir: I had.

Q. Then, if he did stay there, you might not have known it?

A. I might not have known it; but I understood from parties that he slept at some other place that night.

Q. He went out with Mr. Fuller?

A. Yes, sir.

Q. I should like you to charge your memory particularly, and state whether that was not after the report of the assassination reached you there. How late by the clock do you make it?

A. I should judge it to be about ten o'clock, as I said before. I could not say whether I saw him there at the time the news came, or not.

Q. Where was Murphy then?

A. He had left us on the avenue previous to that, and stopped at the Metropolitan Hotel.

Q. He was not with you at the time when you heard of the assassination?

A. No, sir.

Q. Where was Mr. Henderson?

A. He was there in the bar-room, I believe.

Q. I will ask you, when you came down on Thursday, whether the whole party had not arranged to go back on Friday?

A. Yes, sir; that was our intention.

Q. It was the intention of the whole party to return on Friday?

A. Yes, sir: at least, I understood so.

Q. During this visit, did you see any thing in Mr. O'Laughlin that betrayed a knowledge of any thing desperate which was to take place?

ASSISTANT JUDGE ADVOCATE BINGHAM objecting to the question, it was varied as follows:—

During this visit, state what his conduct was.

A. His conduct was the same as I usually saw him,—jovial and jolly as any of the rest of the crowd.

Q. In good spirits?

A. Yes, sir: he was particularly so coming down in the cars with us that Thursday evening.

Q. No nervousness?

A. No, sir.

Q. I will ask you whether you were anywhere near Willard's Hotel during Friday or Friday evening? Did you go as far up town as that?

A. I do not recollect passing there.

Q. What induced you to stay later than Friday afternoon?

A. I guess it was the liquor we had aboard.

Q. Did Lieutenant Henderson press you all to stay?

ASSISTANT JUDGE ADVOCATE BINGHAM objected to the question, as an attempt to bring in the declaration of a third party.

Mr. Cox stated that he proposed to show not merely the declaration of a third party, but the action of the accused, and those who were with him, based on those declarations.

The Commission sustained the objection.

Q. You have stated that probably the liquor that you drank kept you down here in Washington. I will ask you if any thing else kept you here?

A. I cannot say that there was any thing else.

Q. State what time in the morning you went up to Baltimore.

A. We did start to go in the morning train, at eleven o'clock, I believe, on Saturday morning. We went as far as the depot, and Mr. Henderson went and got the tickets: but Mr. Henderson finally concluded that he thought he would stay over until the afternoon; but, if we all pressed on him going up, he would go. Mr. O'Laughlin was wanting to go up; and I told Mr. Henderson, "If you press on Mike's staying, he will stay until the afternoon." So we all concluded to stay until the next train, at three o'clock in the afternoon.

Q. And then you went up at three o'clock in the afternoon?

A. Yes, sir.

Q. You have stated that you went with O'Laughlin to his house, and met his brother-in-law on the street?

A. Yes, sir: previous to going there.

Q. And then you went to his house, and he went up stairs, you supposed, to see his mother; and, on returning, he said he would not stay at home that night? Did he tell you why?

A. The remark he made was, that he would not like to be arrested in the house; that it would be the death of his mother.

Q. Where did you part with him?

A. His brother-in-law went along with us up as far as the corner of Fayette and Exeter Streets; and we stopped there, and had a conversation. I told Mr. O'Laughlin that I thought it best for him to stay home until the parties who were looking after him would come again; but he said, "No: it would be the death of his mother if he was taken in the house." So then he asked me to go up town with him; and we went up as far as the corner of Calvert and Fayette Streets, at Barnum's Hotel there, where he got a hack, and we drove up town in it. I accompanied him as far as some street up town, — I do not recollect the street, — where he got out, and I returned home.

By the JUDGE ADVOCATE:

Q. Will you tell me at what hour O'Laughlin joined you at the Metropolitan Hotel on Thursday night, the 13th of April?

A. We, all four of us, went in there together.

Q. At what hour?

A. About between one and two o'clock, I suppose.

Q. Do you mean one or two o'clock on Friday morning?

A. Yes, sir: that is the time we went to bed.

Q. Where had he been during the previous part of the night?

A. After having supped, we went up to see the illuminations: we went a considerable piece up the avenue; returned back; and, on the invitation of Mr. Henderson, we went into the Canterbury Music Hall.

Q. All of you?

A. Yes, sir.

Q. Did you all continue together until one or two o'clock?

A. Yes, sir.

Q. You say you went up to the Canterbury: were you anywhere else? Were you out on K Street or L Street?

14*

A. I cannot say : I do not know where that street is myself.

Q. O'Laughlin, you say, was not separated from you during the night ?

A. No, sir : he was not.

Q. Will you state where you were that evening besides being at the Canterbury ?

A. After coming out of the Canterbury —

Q. Before you went there.

A. We had supped previous to that, and took a walk up the avenue.

JAMES B. HENDERSON,

a witness called for the prosecution, being duly sworn, testified as follows :—

By the JUDGE ADVOCATE :

Q. State whether you are acquainted with the prisoner O'Laughlin.

A. Yes, sir.

Q. Did you not see him in this city on Friday, the 14th of April?

A. On Thursday and Friday, the 13th and 14th.

Q. Do you know whether, on either of those days, he visited J. Wilkes Booth?

A. He told me on Friday he was to see him in the morning.

Cross-examined by MR. COX :

Q. Did he tell you he was to see him, or wanted to see him ?

A. That he was to see him on Friday morning.

Q. Did he say it in such a way as to imply that he had an engagement ?

A. He only told me he was to see him. I cannot tell whether he said he had an engagement or not.

Q. Did he tell you what for ?

A. No, sir.

Q. That is all you know about it ?

A. It is all I know about it.

SAMUEL STREETT,

a witness called for the prosecution, being duly sworn, testified as follows :—

By the JUDGE ADVOCATE :

Q. State to the Court whether you are acquainted with the prisoner O'Laughlin.

A. Yes, sir : I have known him from youth.

Q. Did you see him in this city, or not, during the month of April last, before the assassination of the President ?

A. I will not be positive about it being April ; but it was well on to the first of April.

Q. Did you, or not, see him with J. Wilkes Booth ?

A. I did.

Q. Did their association seem to be of an intimate character, or not ?

A. It did.

Q. Did you observe them conferring together in a confidential manner ?

A. I did.

Q. On more than one occasion ?

· A. Only one.

Q. Where was that ?

A. I do not know the house ; but I know it was on the right-hand side of the avenue, going towards the Treasury Department.

Q. Were they in the house, or out of it ?

A. On the stoop of the house.

Q. You do not know whether either of them was living there, or not ?

A. I know nothing about that, not having met them for years.

Q. Were they alone, or was there a third party with them ?

A. There were three in company.

Q. Did the third party also appear to be engaged in the same kind of conference ? What part did he take in it apparently ?

A. I did not pay particular attention ; but I think Booth was the speaker of the party, and the third party was the attentive listener.

I addressed O'Laughlin first, having known him more familiarly than Booth.

Q. Did they suspend the conference while you were present?

A. O'Laughlin called me to one side, and told me Booth was busily engaged with his friend, or was talking privately.

Q. Was the tone very low?

A. It was.

Q. Have you seen that person since?

A. I have not.

Q. Could you give a description of him?

A. I should judge he was a man about my own height; and his hair, if I remember correctly, was a kind of curly: he had on at the time a slouch hat, and was in a stooping position, as though talking to Booth in a low tone, or very attentively listening to Booth's conversation. I thought it ill manners to put my ear towards them, and pay any further attention to them.

Q. Is he one of these persons?

A. In the present dress of the prisoners, I would not swear against a man's life. I do not recognize the man here.

Q. Have you an opinion that either of them is the man?

A. I feel it my duty to detect the man; but it is a delicate question, — a man's life, — let him be who he may. [After looking at the prisoners.] No, sir: I will not swear that the man is there.

Q. I am not sure whether you are the person. It is a person of your name, I believe, who is reported to have seen Booth and Herold on the night after the assassination. Are you the person?

A. No, sir: I do not know the man Herold. I saw Booth but once afterwards.

Cross-examined by Mr. Cox:

Q. You say you saw this conference between Booth and O'-Laughlin at a house on Pennsylvania Avenue: you did not state where it was on the avenue.

A. I paid no attention to the locality; but it was between Ninth and Eleventh Streets, to the best of my recollection. I was on my way to Eleventh Street and the avenue.

Q. You cannot speak with any certainty about the date, except that you think it was nigh on to April?

A. If I had the assistance of the passes I obtained since I was at Camp Stoneman, I could tell you exactly: I cannot state positively the date.

Q. Did I understand you to say that O'Laughlin made a remark about Booth being engaged with his friend?

A. He did: he called me aside, and said they were engaged in conversation.

Q. In making that remark, did you not ask him to propose to Mr. Booth to take a drink? and did he not reply, that Booth was busy with his friend?

A. I may have done so.

Q. Do you think, on reflection, that you did?

A. I am not anyways stingy. I presume I may have done so.

Q. Was it not that which induced the remark, that Booth was engaged with a friend?

A. I did not see the interior of Mr. O'Laughlin's mind. I cannot tell.

Q. Was not that remark of his an answer to your invitation to him to ask Mr. Booth to take a drink?

A. According to the art of language, it may have been. I cannot tell what the remark was made for.

Lyman S. Sprague,

a witness called for the prosecution, being duly sworn, testified as follows: —

By the Judge Advocate:

Q. You have been clerk at the Kirkwood House, in this city?

A. Yes, sir.

Q. Were you present when the room of the prisoner Atzerodt was broken open?

A. Yes, sir: I went to the room with Mr. Lee.

Q. Will you state what was found there?

A. All I saw was the revolver found under the pillow as I went into the room with Mr. Lee.

Q. Do you remember whether, in the course of the day, a man called at the Kirkwood House, inquiring for Atzerodt?

A. No, sir: I do not, — not at the time I was in the office.

Cross-examined by Mr. Doster:

Q. Were you at the desk in the Kirkwood House at noon?

A. Yes, sir: at twelve o'clock I went off duty. I was in from eight in the morning until twelve at noon.

Q. Did you observe anybody calling, and asking for Mr. Atzerodt?

A. No, sir: I did not.

David Stanton,

a witness called for the prosecution, being duly sworn, testified as follows: —

By the Judge Advocate:

Q. Look upon the prisoner O'Laughlin, and state to the Court whether you have seen him at any time before; and, if so, when and where?

A. I saw him [pointing out Michael O'Laughlin]. He is the man with the black mustache.

Q. When and where did you see him last?

A. I saw him on the 13th of April, the night before the assassination, at the Secretary of War's.

Q. In the house of the Secretary of War?

A. Yes, sir.

Q. State what occurred there, and under what circumstances he was there.

A. I simply saw him pass in the door, and take a position on one side of the hall; and he remained there some minutes, until I requested him to go out. He followed me out as far as the gate of the house, on the left-hand side of the house. That was the last I saw of him.

Q. Did you have any conversation with him in the house?

A. I asked him what his business was. He asked me where the Secretary was. I told him he was standing on the steps. He did not say any thing further; and finally I requested him to walk out.

Q. Did he ask for anybody else besides the Secretary?

A. No, sir.

Q. Did he explain at all why he was there?

A. No, sir.

Q. He came in uninvited, did he?

A. Yes, sir. I presumed he was intoxicated, at first; but I found out, after having some conversation with him, that he was not.

Q. Was General Grant there that night?

A. Yes, sir: he was in the parlor.

Q. Did he ask any thing in regard to him?

A. I do not remember that he did.

Q. Did he see him from his position?

A. Yes, sir.

Q. Did he go away from the house when you put him out?

A. I went into the house. I did not see whether he left or not, there was such a crowd there.

Q. What hour was that?

A. I presume, about half-past ten. They were serenading the Secretary and General Grant.

Q. Were you at the Secretary's the night of the assasination?

A. I was there after it, and staid there all night.

Q. Do you know any thing of a man being seen lurking or hanging about the premises that night?

A. No, sir. It was eleven o'clock before I got there.

Q. Was the inquiry of O'Laughlin simply after the Secretary of War?

A. Yes, sir: I pointed him out. He did not seem to go to see him, and did not tell what his business was.

Cross-examined by Mr. Cox:

Q. Was that the first time you ever saw this man?

A. Yes, sir.

Q. When did you see him since?

A. I never saw him since, until I saw him on the monitor as a prisoner.

Q. How long afterwards was that?

A. I do not remember the date: it was the day that they took Booth's body away from the vessel.

Q. You say it was half-past ten o'clock at night when you first saw him on the steps?

A. About that: I had not a time-piece. The fireworks commenced at nine o'clock, and lasted about an hour and a half. It was after they were over.

Q. Was there a crowd there at the time?

A. Yes, sir.

Q. Was it very light or dark?

A. It was not very light.

Q. Was it moonlight or gas?

A. No, sir: it was dark.

Q. How was he dressed?

A. In a black suit.

Q. What kind of hat?

A. I think a black slouch hat. He had it off in his hand. I did not pay particular attention to that.

Q. When you say a black suit, do you mean his whole suit was black?

A. Yes, sir.

Q. What kind of coat?

A. It was a dress coat.

Q. Black vest and pants?

A. Yes, sir.

Q. I do not know exactly where the Secretary's house is. Where is it?

A. Fourteenth and K Streets; the second house from the corner of Fourteenth and K. There is a vacant lot between that and the Rugby House: it is No. 320.

Q. Opposite Franklin Square?

A. Yes, sir: about opposite the centre of the square.

Q. What particularity about his appearance was there that enabled you to identify him when you saw him in the entry?

A. The hall was very well lit up: I was almost in contact with him when I addressed him, — directly in front of him.

Q. How far inside of the door was he?

A. About ten feet. He was next to the library-door.

Q. After having seen him on that occasion, and before you saw him again, did you recollect his size? He was standing in the hall, of course?

A. He was standing in the hall. About my height, — five feet four inches about.

Q. When you saw him on the monitor, was he standing or sitting or lying down?

A. He stood up. I had a very indistinct view of him, though, because it was so dark.

Q. You thought at first he was intoxicated, but discovered that he was not?

A. I presumed he was, from the way he came into the house. I inquired before I went to him, of different members of the family, if they knew him. Finding they did not know him, I addressed him.

Q. When he walked out, did he seem unsteady in his gait?

A. He followed me out. I requested him to go out, and he did, going after me.

Q. Were plenty of people about?

A. Yes, in front of the house.

Q. Was anybody else in the hall or on the doorsteps?

A. The Secretary of War was on the doorsteps, and Major Knox.

Q. This man had got behind them?

A. Yes, sir.

Q. Was General Grant sitting in the parlor?

A. Yes, sir.

Q. Was that lit up?

A. Yes, sir.

Q. Had he the same mustache and beard that he has now?

A. I think so: I do not see any change, with the exception of that caused by want of shaving.

DAVID C. REED,

a witness called for the prosecution, being duly sworn, testified as
follows : —

By the JUDGE ADVOCATE

Q. Are you acquainted with John H. Surratt, of this city?

A. I have not any personal acquaintance with him.

Q. But do you know him when you see him?

A. I do.

Q. When did you last see him?

A. I saw him on the 14th of April, the same day of the assassination.

Q. In this city?

A. Yes, sir.

Q. Where did you see him?

A. I was standing on the stoop of a store just below the National
Hotel as he passed.

Q. At what hour of the day was it?

A. Probably half-past two o'clock.

Q. Was he alone?

A. He was alone.

Q. Do you remember how he was dressed?

A. Yes, sir.

Q. State how he was dressed.

A. He was dressed in a country-cloth suit, very fine in its texture
and appearance, very genteelly got up. He had a little round-
crowned drab hat. But, as he passed me, I particularly noticed
his spurs: he had on a pair of new brass-plated spurs, with very
large rowels.

Q. Was he on foot?

A. He was on foot.

Q. What did you say was the color of his clothes?

A. They were drab.

Q. Did you speak to him?

A. I bowed as he passed.

Q. How long did you know him?

A. I knew him a great while. I knew him when quite a boy

at his father's house : I had seen him out gunning. He grew pretty much out of my recollection. Still I knew him, though I had no intimacy.

By the JUDGE ADVOCATE :

Q. You have no doubt that you saw him that day ?

A. I am positive that I saw him.

Cross-examined by MR. AIKEN :

Q. How long have you known Mr. Surratt ?

A. I do not know that I can just state exactly what length of time.

Q. Have you been in the habit of seeing him frequently within the last year ?

A. No; I cannot say that I have : I do not recollect seeing him very often.

Q. When did you see him last before the time you now refer to on the 14th of April ?

A. I cannot say positively ; but I think I saw him some time last fall, — probably about October. He was in the city : there had been a trotting-race or something of that kind across the river.

Q. Will you describe his appearance ?

A. I will as near as I can. He was a light-complected man, with rather singular colored hair : it is not red ; it is not white ; it is a kind of sandy ; and it was cut rounded, so as to lie down low on his collar, and a little heavy.

Q. How tall a man ?

A. I suppose about five feet ten inches : I should take him to be that.

Q. Did he wear whiskers at the time you last saw him ?

A. I do not recollect seeing any hair on his face at all. If there was any, it was very light.

Q. Did you see any thing of a goatee or mustache ?

A. I did not : I was more attracted by the clothing he had on.

Q. What do you mean by "drab" ? — a regular drab or gray ?

A. Light country cloth. It is a drab ; you cannot term it any thing else : it is the term used for that color.

Q. Did I understand you to say that you were standing on the steps of the National Hotel?

A. No, sir: it was Hunt and Goodwin's, the store below.

Q. Was he walking?

A. Yes, sir.

Q. He made no stop?

A. No stop.

Q. You had no conversation with him?

A. None : I never exchanged a word with him in my life, to my knowledge.

Q. Accidentally you saw a gentleman whom you supposed to be Surratt pass by you?

A. Yes, sir.

Q. Are you able to swear positively that it was John H. Surratt?

A. Well, the best of us is liable to be mistaken; but I am as certain it was Surratt as that I stand here.

Q. What is the color of Surratt's eyes?

A. That I cannot say.

Q. What is the shape of his forehead?

A. That could not be seen ; and I do not know, because he had a hat on, and I was not picking him out particularly·: I was only looking at him as he passed, admiring the style of his clothes, and my attention was taken to his spur. His pantaloons were a little short, and the tremendous size of the rowel that was in the spur attracted my attention.

Q. You observed the rowel and the clothes that were passing more than you did the man's face?

A. I cannot say that I dwelt on his face at all.

Q. How large a man is Surratt? I do not mean his height now.

A. He is not a stout man. He is rather a delicate man. I do not suppose he would weigh over a hundred and forty pounds, judging from his build. He is not a heavy built man. He is a little stooped : he walks so.

Q. Did you have any conversation with any one at the time he was passing? Did you call any one's attention to him?

A. No.

Q. About how long did you have your eyes on him?

A. When I noticed him, he was about opposite Lutz's, coming up the avenue; and, as he passed, I turned and looked at him.

Q. Was he on the same side of the avenue?

A. Yes, sir: he passed within three feet of me.

Q. Did you see him again during the day?

A. No, sir.

Q. Did you ever see him in that dress before?

A. No, sir.

By the JUDGE ADVOCATE:

Q. Did Mr. Surratt recognize you when you recognized him?

A. He bowed.

Q. Did he return your bow, or did you bow first?

A. I cannot be positive which.

Q. You have given us a very particular description of his clothing. Are you in the habit of noticing those things?

A. Yes, sir: I make clothes.

JAMES W. PUMPHREYS,

a witness called for the prosecution, being duly sworn, testified as follows: —

By the JUDGE ADVOCATE:

Q. Do you reside in Washington City?

A. I do.

Q. What is your business?

A. I keep a livery-stable.

Q. Were you acquainted with J. Wilkes Booth?

A. I was.

Q. Do you remember to have seen him on Friday, the 14th of April?

A. Yes, sir: he came to my stable about twelve o'clock on that day, and engaged a saddle-horse.

Q. For immediate use?

A. No: he said he wanted him about four or half-past four

o'clock that day. He had been in the habit of riding a sorrel horse, and he came to get it; but that horse was engaged, and I could not let him have it.

Q. What kind of a horse did you let him have?

A. A small bay mare, about fourteen or fourteen and a half hands high.

Q. At what time did he obtain that mare?

A. About four or half-past four o'clock.

Q. Was the mare returned to you?

A. I have never seen her since.

Q. What description would you give of her besides that you have mentioned? Was there any thing peculiar about her mane and tail?

A. She was a little rubbed behind. She was a mare that I should call about fourteen or fourteen and a half hands high, as well as I can remember; blood, bay, black legs, black mane and tail. I think the off front foot had white spots: you could not call it a white leg. She had a star in the forehead.

Q. Was he in the habit of hiring horses there?

A. About a month or six weeks before the assassination of the President, he called at my stable, and said he wanted a saddle-horse. He was then in company with young Surratt.

Q. John H. Surratt?

A. I think that is his name: they called him "John." Booth asked for the proprietor: I told him I was the man. He said he wanted a good saddle-horse. Said I, "I am your man: I can let you have him." — "Have you a good one?" he asked; and I said, "Yes." He said, "I should like to have him: I want to take a ride." Said I, "Before you get him, you will have to give me reference, or security: you are a stranger to me." He said to me, "If you don't know me, you have heard of me: I am J. Wilkes Booth." Said I, "If you are J. Wilkes Booth, I will let you have a horse; but I don't know whether you are J. Wilkes Booth or not yet." Mr. Surratt spoke up, and said, "This is Mr. J. Wilkes Booth, Mr. Pumphreys: he and I are going to take a little ride; and I will see to it that you are paid for the horse." I let him have the horse: the price was paid.

Q. When was that?

A. It was a month or six weeks before the assassination.

Q. [Exhibiting to the witness the photograph of J. Wilkes Booth, Exhibit No. 1.] Look at that photograph, and see if you recognize it as J. Wilkes Booth.

A. That is the man.

Q. On that Friday, did he ask for any thing besides the horse and saddle? Did he ask for any thing to hitch or tie the horse?

A. On the Friday that he came in the afternoon for the saddle-horse, he asked me to give him a tie-rein to hitch the horse; and I told him not to hitch the horse, as she was in the habit of breaking the bridle. A gentleman had had her a day or two before; and he had hitched her, and she broke the bridle. I told him that; and he said that he wanted to tie her while he stopped at a restaurant and got a drink. "Well," said I, "get a boy at the restaurant to hold her." He said he could not get a boy. "Oh," said I, "you can find plenty of boot-black boys about the street to hold your horse." Then said he, "I am going to Grover's Theatre to write a letter; and there is no necessity of tying her there; for there is a stable in the back part of the alley, and I will put her there." Then he asked me where was the best place to take a ride to. I told him, "You have been some time around here, and you ought to know." He asked, "How is Crystal Spring?" I said, "A very good place; but it is rather early for that." — "Well," said he, "I will go there after I get through writing a letter at Grover's Theatre." He left then, riding off on the mare; and I have never seen Booth since.

Q. You say that was between four and five o'clock?

A. I think it was between four and five o'clock.

Q. Do you know any of the other prisoners here?

A. No, sir: I do not know any of them at all.

Cross-examined by MR. AIKEN:

Q. Was Mr. Surratt with Mr. Booth when he first came to your place?

A. He was, the first time Booth came to my place: that was the only time he ever came with him.

Q. When was that first time?

A. A month or six weeks before the assassination.

Q. He was not with Mr. Booth on the Friday?

A. No, sir: Booth always came there alone after that.

Q. What sort of looking man was John H. Surratt?

A. A young man: I suppose about five feet ten or eleven inches high; sandy hair, and a very light goatee I think he wore; his eyes sunk a little in his head; thin features. That is about as good a description as I could give of him.

Q. How was he dressed when you saw him?

A. I think he had on a gray suit: I am not certain as to the coat, but I think a plaid coat. I do not remember exactly the suit of clothes he had on.

Q. Have you stated all the remarks he made in reference to Booth?

A. All; and it was the only time I ever saw him with Booth.

Q. Did Booth afterwards ever refer you to his introduction by Mr. Surratt to you?

A. Not at all.

BROOKE STABLER,

a witness called for the prosecution, being duly sworn, testified as follows:—

By the JUDGE ADVOCATE:

Q. Do you live in Washington City?

A. Yes, sir.

Q. In what business are you engaged?

A. In a livery-stable on G Street.

Q. Will you state whether or not you were acquainted with J. Wilkes Booth?

A. Yes, sir: I was acquainted with him.

Q. Were you also acquainted with John H. Surratt?

A. Yes, sir.

Q. And with the prisoner Atzerodt?

A. Yes, sir.

Q. Did you see them often together at your stable?

A. Frequently together, — almost always together when there.

Q. To what time did this intimacy continue?

A. Three or four of them were there together down to about the 29th of March : then the other three were there frequently.

Q. Were they unusually intimate? How often were they there together, say, in the course of a day?

A. Sometimes they would be there three or four times a day; sometimes several days would intervene.

Q. Did either of them keep horses there?

A. Mr. Surratt kept two there.

Q. Did he allow Atzerodt to use his horses when he pleased?

A. No, sir: he rode out occasionally with Surratt.

Q. I have in my hand a note, which reads, —" Mr. Howard will please let the bearer, Mr. Atzerodt, have my horses whenever he wishes to ride; also my leggins and gloves; and oblige yours, &c., (signed) J. H. Surratt, Feb. 22, 1865." Who is Mr. Howard?

A. The proprietor of the stable.

Q. Will you state whether or not under that order he rode the horse of Mr. Surratt?

A. Several times, perhaps, he rode it; but, after the date of that, I think the order was rescinded to me : I was manager of the concern.

Q. [Exhibiting to the witness the note just read, signed " J. H. Surratt."] Look at that note, and see if you identify it in any way.

A. Yes; I know the note : it passed through my hands.

Q. How did that note reach the hands of Mr. Howard? Do you know any thing about that?

A. It was sent there by Mrs. Surratt : I put it on file.

[The note was offered in evidence without objection, and is annexed to this record, marked Exhibit No. 27.]

Q. You acted under that note, and let the horses go accordingly?

A. Yes, sir.

Q. Do you remember what the prisoner Atzerodt said in regard to John H. Surratt's visit to Richmond? Did he speak to you of his having been there, and of his return, and of the trouble in which he seemed to be involved in consequence?

A. He told me that he had been to Richmond, and that, in coming back, he got into difficulty; that the detectives were after him: but he thought it would soon be over; he would soon be relieved of the difficulty.

Q. Do you remember what time in April that was?

A. It was in the early part of April.

Q. Did Atzerodt himself hire of you?

A. No, sir: I think not at that period.

Q. Did he or not take away a horse blind of one eye?

A. Yes, sir: under an order from the then owner.

Q. Who was the owner?

A. Surratt was the owner then: a bay horse, blind of one eye.

Q. When did he take that horse away?

A. They were taken away on the 31st of March; paid for on the 29th, according to my book.

Q. Will you describe the animals that were taken?

A. Both of them were bay horses: one larger than the other, blind of one eye, a fine racking horse; the other was a smaller horse.

Q. Did he pay for keeping them?

A. Mr. Booth paid for keeping them.

Q. Did you see that horse afterwards?

A. Yes, sir.

Q. Where?

A. At the stable. He took them there to sell to Mr. Howard.

Q. When was that?

A. Very soon after they were taken away?

Q. Atzerodt took him there?

A. Yes, sir.

Q. He failed to sell him, and took him away.

A. Yes, sir.

Q. Did you see the horse afterwards?

A. No, sir; not that one. He brought two to sell.

Q. Who claimed to own those horses at first?

A. Surratt.

Q. Then Surratt claimed them, Booth paid for their keeping, and Atzerodt took them away. I so understand you?

A. Yes, sir. Another gentleman came the evening the horses went away, and rode on one of them away.

Q. Who was that?

A. I do not know.

Q. Do you think you would recognize that horse blind of one eye, if you were to see him?

A. I think so.

The witness was here requested to go to a stable at Seventeenth and I Streets, and look at a horse there; and his further examination was deferred till the witness should return.

Peter Taltavull,

a witness called for the prosecution, being duly sworn, testified as follows: —

By the Judge Advocate:

Q. State to the Court whether you were acquainted with J. Wilkes Booth during his lifetime.

A. Yes, sir.

Q. What is your business?

A. I keep the restaurant next to Ford's Theatre, the Star Saloon, on this side of Ford's Theatre.

Q. Did you or did you not see Booth in your restaurant on the evening of the 14th of April?

A. Yes, sir: he was there just about, I judge, a little after ten o'clock.

Q. State what occurred; under what circumstances you saw him.

A. He just walked into the bar, and called for some whiskey. I gave him the whiskey; put the bottle on the counter; and he called for some water. I did not give him water right off: it is customary to give water, but I did not give him water right off; and he called for some water, and I gave him some water. He put the money on the counter, and went right out.

Q. How near the theatre?

A. Adjoining the theatre.

Q. Did you observe where he went from there?

A. I only saw him go out of the bar.

Q. Was he alone?

A. Alone.

Q. Was he there in the afternoon of that day?

A. I did not see him.

Q. How many minutes do you think he went out before you heard the report of the pistol?

A. I did not hear the report of the pistol.

Q. Before you heard the cry that the President was assassinated?

A. I judge it was about from eight to ten minutes; that is, as near as I could recollect. I could not form an accurate idea of it; but that is as near as I could come to it.

Q. Are you acquainted with the prisoner Herold?

A. Yes, sir.

Q. When did you see him?

A. I saw him there the night of the murder, or the night previous to that: he came into my place. I was behind the bar; and he walked to me, and asked me if Mr. John Booth had been there in the afternoon. I told him I had not been there myself in the afternoon. And then said he, "Was he not here this evening?" I said, "No, sir;" and he went right out.

Cross-examined by MR. STONE:

Q. You cannot positively fix whether that was Thursday or Friday evening?

A. I cannot positively swear as to that.

Q. Were there not two other gentlemen with Herold the evening he came into your restaurant?

A. I did not see them.

Q. Did he come in alone?

A. I think he came alone to the bar. There might have been some other gentlemen outside the restaurant; but I did not see anybody come in there with him.

Q. How long have you known Herold?

A. I have known Herold ever since he was a boy.

Q. He only asked you about Booth the evening he came in: what time of the evening was it?

A. As near as I can recollect, it must have been between six and seven o'clock.

SERGEANT JOSEPH M. DYE,

a witness called for the prosecution, being duly sworn, testified as follows :—

By the JUDGE ADVOCATE :

Q. State whether or not, on the evening of the 14th of April last, you were in front of Ford's Theatre, and at what hour you were there.

A. I was sitting in front of Ford's Theatre about half-past nine o'clock.

Q. Did you observe several persons, whose appearance excited your suspicions, conferring together upon the pavement in front of the theatre ?

A. Yes, sir.

Q. Describe their appearance, and what they did.

A. The first appearance was an elegantly dressed gentleman, who came out of the passage, and commenced conversing with a ruffianly-looking fellow. Then there was another one appeared, and the three conversed together. After they had conversed together, it was drawing near the second act. The one that appeared to be the leader of them, the well-dressed one, said, " I think he will come out now ; " referring to the President, I supposed.

Q. Was the President's carriage standing there ?

A. Yes, sir. One of them had been standing out, looking at the carriage on the curbstone, while I was sitting there, and then went back. They watched a while, and the rush came down : many gentlemen came out, and went in and had a drink in the saloon below. Then, after they went up, the best-dressed gentleman stepped into the saloon himself, remained there long enough to get a drink, and came out in a style as if he was becoming intoxicated. He stepped up and whispered to this ruffian (that is, the miserablest-looking one of the three), and stepped into the passage, — the passage that leads to the stage there from the street. Then the smallest one stepped up and called the time, just as the best-dressed gentleman appeared again, from the clock in the vestibule. Then he started up the street and remained there a while, and came down again, and called the time again. Then I began to think there was something going on, and looked towards this man as he called the time. Presently he went up again, and came down then, and called the time again. Then I began to think there was something going on, and looked towards the man as he called the time. Presently he went up again, and then came down and called the time louder. I think it was ten minutes after ten that he called out then.

Q. Was he announcing it to the other two?

A. Yes, sir: then he started on a fast walk up the street; and the best-dressed one among them started into the theatre, and went inside. I was invited by Sergeant Cooper to have some oysters; and we had barely time to get in the saloon and get seated, and order the oysters, when a man came running in, and said the President was shot.

Q. Would you recognize that well-dressed person from his photograph if you were to see it now?

A. Yes, sir.

Q. [Exhibiting Booth's photograph, Exhibit No. 1.] Look at that photograph.

A. That was the man; but his mustache was heavier and his hair longer than in this picture.

Q. But do you recognize the features?

A. Yes, sir: this is the man; these are his features exactly.

Q. What restaurant did that man go into to drink?

A. The restaurant just below the theatre, towards the avenue.

Q. Did he go in alone?

A. Yes, sir: he went in alone.

Q. Can you give a more particular description of the ruffianly-looking man whom you saw? What was his size? and what was it that gave him such a ruffianly appearance? Was it his dress?

A. He was not as well dressed as the rest of them.

Q. Was he shabbily dressed or dirtily dressed?

A. His clothes had been worn a considerable time; and he had a bloated appearance.

Q. Was he a stout man?

A. Yes, sir; and a rough face.

Q. Which way did he go?

A. He remained there at the passage, and the other one started up the street.

Q. The time was announced to the other two men three times by him, was it?

A. Yes, sir: three times.

Q. The last, you think, was ten minutes after ten?

A. The last time he called out was ten minutes after ten.

Q. Immediately on announcing that, did Booth leave, and go into the theatre?

A. He whispered to the ruffian, and started in.

Q. Look at these prisoners, and see whether you recognize any of them as either of the persons present on that occasion.

A. If that man [pointing to Edward Spangler] had a mustache, it would be just the appearance of the face exactly.

Q. Do you mean that the rough-looking man was like him, except that he had a mustache?

A. Yes, sir. He was standing at the entrance of the passage; but I think he had a mustache, — a heavy one. It was rather dark back there: the gas-light did not shine very much on it; but I saw the mustache.

Q. I understand you to state that the call was made from the clock in the hall of the theatre?

A. Yes, sir. He stepped up there, and called the time right in front of the theatre.

Q. Can you tell at what time the other calls were made? You have stated that the last was at ten minutes past ten.

A. They were all between half-past nine and ten minutes after ten.

Q. Do you think you could recognize either of the other persons?

A. The one that called the time was a very neat gentleman, well dressed; and he had a mustache.

Q. Do you see him here?

A. He was better dressed than any I see here. He had on one of the fashionable hats they wear here in Washington, with round tops and stiff brim.

Q. Can you describe his dress as to color and appearance?

A. No, sir : I cannot exactly describe it.

Q. How was this well-dressed man as to size ?

A. He was not a very large man, — about five feet six inches high.

Q. You have never seen that man before or since ?

A. No, sir.

Q. Do you remember the color of that man's clothes ?

A. His coat was a kind of drab color.

Q. What color was his hat ?

A. His hat was black, — similar to the one I had on the same night.

Q. Did you observe whether they had spurs on any of them ?

A. I did not observe that.

Cross-examined by MR. AIKEN :

Q. You say that the well-dressed man wore a black hat, and was about five feet six inches high ?

A. Yes, sir.

Cross-examined by MR. EWING :

Q. How long did you observe the slouchy man ?

A. I observed him while I was sitting there.

Q. About how long ?

A. While I was sitting there, and until I left.

Q. Could you not fix some time ?

A. I was there till the last time was called ; and I was there from about twenty-five minutes after nine or half-past nine.

Q. You went there at twenty-five minutes after nine or half-past nine, and left when this man called ten minutes past ten ?

A. Yes, sir.

Q. Was the slouchy man there during the whole of that time, — the man dressed in slouched clothes ?

A. Yes, sir : he remained at the passage.

Q. Was he there during the whole of that time ?

A. Yes, sir.

Q. Will you describe the several articles of his dress as near as you can ?

A. I could not observe him well : he was back, and it was rather dark there.

Q. Could you see his countenance ?

A. Yes, sir.

Q. Did you notice the color of his eyes ?

A. No, sir : I did not observe that.

Q. Did you notice the color of his mustache ?

A. The mustache was black.

Q. Did you notice the color of his hair ?

A. No, sir : because he remained in one position.

Q. What shaped hat had he on ?

A. A slouched hat, — one that had been worn some time.

Q. Had he an overcoat on ?

A. I did not observe that.

Q. Do you recollect any thing as to the color of the coat ?

A. No, sir : he did not move around, and I did not pay any particular attention ; only that I observed the well-dressed gentleman would whisper to him ; that was all.

Q. Exactly where did he stand ?

A. Right at the passage.

Q. Inside ?

A. No, sir : right at the end of the passage.

Q. On the pavement ?

A. Yes, sir.

Q. Near the President's carriage ?

A. No, sir : the President's carriage was at the curb-stone.

Q. Did he occupy the same position during the whole of this time ?

A. That man did.

Q. You refer to the man of slouched dress ?

A. Yes, sir.

Q. Which way did Booth enter the last time ?

A. He just stepped right up into the front door.

Q. Did you see the man in slouched dress standing there at that time ?

A. When Booth whispered to him, and left him, I did not see him change his position, because I was observing Booth. As soon

16*

as Booth stepped into the theatre, we started. The other man started on a fast walk up the street.

Q. You do not know whether the man in the slouched dress did not come out on the pavement before Booth went out?

A. I do not recollect his coming out on the pavement.

Q. What attracted your attention to that man?

A. This elegantly-dressed, gentlemanly-looking man addressing him.

Q. When did you notice him speak to him first?

A. When I first came there.

Q. At about twenty-five minutes past nine or half-past nine?

A. Yes, sir.

Q. How long after Booth entered the theatre was it that you heard the news of the assassination?

A. I cannot state the precise time.

Q. About what time?

A. Well, fifteen minutes, I presume.

Q. Do you think it was as long as that?

A. It might not have been as long; but I cannot be certain.

Q. What did you do in the mean time?

A. We started, turned the corner, and went into a saloon; debated a while which saloon to go to. I do not know how long it took us. We had just got in and ordered oysters as a man came in telling us the news.

Q. Do you think it was not exceeding fifteen minutes?

A. I think so.

Q. Do you think it may have been less?

A. I do not know about that: I am not certain.

Q. About how high do you think the man dressed in the slouched clothes was?

A. He was about five feet eight or nine inches.

By Mr. AIKEN:

Q. Will you state, as near as you can recollect, the time you first observed those gentlemen in front of the theatre?

A. Twenty-five minutes or half-after nine o'clock.

By the COURT:

Q. Do you say without hesitation that Spangler was the man?

A. I say that was the countenance, except the mustache.

Q. Do you say that was the man?

A. I say the countenance was the same: he resembled that face as much as possible.

By MR. EWING:

Q. Have you seen this man since the assassination of the President?

A. Yes, sir.

Q. Where?

A. In the Capitol Prison.

Q. In the presence of what persons?

A. In the presence of the proprietor, I presume, Sergeant Cooper, and another prisoner.

Q. Did it seem to you then that he was the man?

A. All but the mustache.

Q. But you say that he was under the shadow, so that you could not observe his features distinctly?

A. I remember the face, the expression of his countenance.

Q. But you did not see his eyes?

A. No, sir.

JOHN E. BUCKINGHAM,

a witness called for the prosecution, being duly sworn, testified as follows: —

By the JUDGE ADVOCATE:

Q. Do you reside in Washington?

A. Yes, sir.

Q. What business were you engaged in during the month of October?

A. I am at night doorkeeper at Mr. Ford's Theatre; and in the daytime I am employed in the Washington Navy Yard.

Q. Were you acquainted with J. Wilkes Booth during his lifetime?

A. Yes, sir. I knew him by coming to the theatre.

Q. You knew him by sight?

A. Yes, sir.

Q. Will you state whether or not you saw him on the evening of the 14th of April, at what hour, and what occurred in connection with it?

A. I should judge it was about ten o'clock that he came there to the theatre, walked in, and walked out again; and he returned, I judge, in about two or three minutes. He came to me, and asked me what time it was. I told him to step into the lobby that leads out into the street, and he could see. He stepped out, and walked in again, and stepped into the door that leads to the parquette and dress-circle, and returned immediately; came out, and went up the stair-way to the dress-circle. The last I saw of him was, he alighted on the stage from the box, running across the stage with a knife in his hand. He was uttering some sentence; but I could not understand it well at the time: I was too far back from him, at the front door.

Q. He went into the President's box, did he?

A. I could not say.

Q. He was on that side of the dress-circle?

A. I was down below, underneath. The dress-circle extends over my doorway, so that I could not see.

Cross-examined by MR. EWING:

Q. Are you acquainted with the prisoner, Edward Spangler?

A. Yes, sir; knowing him at the theatre.

Q. You have known him?

A. I have known him to be there at the theatre.

Q. Did you see him enter or come out of the front of the theatre during the play?

A. I did not.

Q. State the position of your box. Is it that you would be likely to see any persons who entered from the front of the theatre?

A. Yes, sir: every person has to pass me on entering the theatre; that is, in the lower part, for the parquette, dress-circle, and orchestra.

Q. Do you observe the persons that go in?

A. No: I do not take notice of the persons.

Q. Do you see that persons do not go in who are not authorized to do so?

A. Yes, sir.

Q. If this man Spangler had gone in from the street, entering at the front of the theatre, would you have seen him?

A. Yes, sir.

Q. Would you have been pretty sure to see him?

A. Yes, sir: he could not have passed me without my seeing him.

Q. Are you certain he did not pass, then?

A. I am perfectly satisfied that he was not in the front part of the house that night.

Q. Did you see him that night at all?

A. Not to my recollection.

Q. Did you ever see him wear a mustache?

A. No, sir: not as I can recollect of.

JAMES P. FERGUSON,

a witness called for the prosecution, being duly sworn, testified as follows: —

By the JUDGE ADVOCATE:

Q. Do you reside in Washington City?

A. Yes, sir.

Q. What business are you engaged in?

A. The restaurant business.

Q. Where?

A. No. 452, Tenth Street.

Q. Near Ford's Theatre?

A. Adjoining the theatre on the upper side.

Q. Did you know J. Wilkes Booth in his lifetime?

A. I did.

Q. Did you see him on that evening?

A. I saw him that afternoon: I do not recollect exactly what time; but it was some time between two and four o'clock, I think. He came up in front just below my door on the street. I walked out to the door, and saw Mr. Maddox standing out by the side of his horse, — a small bay mare. Mr. Maddox was standing aside of him, with his hand on the horse's mane, talking. I stood on the porch a minute; and Booth looked round, and said, "See what a nice horse I have got!" As I stepped out near him, he said, "Now, watch : he can run just like a cat!" and struck his spurs into the horse, and off he went down the street. I did not see him any more until that night, — somewhere near ten o'clock, I should think. Along in the afternoon, about one o'clock, Harry Ford came into my place, and said to me, "Your favorite, General Grant, is going to be in the theatre to-night ; and, if you want to see him, you had better go and get a seat." I went and secured a seat directly opposite the President's box, in the front of the dress-circle. He showed me the box that he said the President was to be in ; and I got those seats directly opposite. I saw the President and his family when they came in, and some gentlemen in plain clothes with them. I did not recognize him ; but I knew from the appearance of the man that it was not Grant. I supposed that probably Grant had remained outside, so as not to create any excitement in the theatre, and would come in alone, and come in the box ; and I made up my mind that I would see him before he went in ; and I watched every one that passed around on that side of the dress-circle towards this box. Somewhere near ten o'clock, I should think it was (it was the second scene in the third act of the play they were playing, "Our American Cousin"), I saw Booth pass along near the box, and then stop, and lean against the wall. He stood there a moment. Something directed my attention on the stage ; and I looked back and saw him step down one step, put his hands to the door, and his knee against it, and push the door open, — the first door that goes into the box. I did not see any more of him until I saw him make a rush for the railings that ran around the box, to jump over. I saw him put his left hand on the railing, and he seemed to strike back with the right with a knife. I could see the knife gleam, and that moment he was over the box. The President sat in the left-hand corner of the box, and Miss Harris in the right-hand corner. Mrs. Lincoln sat to the right of the President, as I am sitting here. Then the gentleman in citizen's clothes, whom I learned afterwards was Major Rathbone, sat back almost in the corner of the box. The President, at the time he was shot, was sitting in this position : he was leaning his hand on the rail, and was looking down at a person in the orchestra, — not looking on the stage. He had the flag that decorated the box pulled around, and was looking between the post and the flag. As the person lit on the stage, just as he jumped over, I saw it was Booth. I saw the flash of the pistol back right in the box. As he struck on the stage, he rose and exclaimed, *"Sic semper tyrannis!"* and ran right directly across the stage to the opposite door, where the actors come in. I did not see any thing more of him that evening. I got out as quick as I could. I had a little girl with me, who lived on E Street. As I understood General Grant was to be at the theatre that night, I took her with me to see him. I got her home as quick as I could, and then ran down Ninth Street to D, and through D to the police station; went up stairs, and told the Superintendent of Police, Mr. Webb. I then ran up Tenth Street to the house where the President was. Some one told me that General Augur was up there, or Colonel Wells. Colonel Wells was standing out on the step of Mr. Peterson's house. I told him I had seen it all, and knew the man that jumped out of the box. He told the guard to pass me through; and I went in and stated it to him. I then went over the street, and went to bed. In the morning, when I got up, I saw Mr. Gifford; and he said to me, "You made a hell of a statement about what you saw last night. How could you see the flash of the pistol, when the ball was shot through the door?" I said to him, "Mr. Gifford, that pistol never exploded in any place but in the box: I saw the flash." Said he, "Oh, hell! the ball was shot through the door; and how could you see it?" I studied about it all day. On Sunday morning, Miss Harris came down, and her father, Senator Harris, and Judge Olin and Judge Cartter; and I went into the theatre with them. We had a great deal of difficulty in getting the theatre open. Maddox and Gifford were in the theatre, but would not open the door. I sent a young man through my back way, and he broke a window in; and then Maddox came to the front door, opened the theatre, and let us in. We got a candle and examined this hole, where Mr. Gifford said the ball was shot through. It looked to me like as if it had been bored by a small gimlet, and then cut around the edge with a knife; and in several places it was scratched down as if with a knife. This thing had bothered me all night on Saturday night; and, after this examination, I was satisfied that I saw the flash of the pistol. Mr. Gifford's accusing me of making this statement bothered me all night. I saw him on Monday, and said to him, "Mr. Gifford, you are a very smart man! You knew that ball was not shot through the board." Said he, "I have understood since that it was cut through." Said I, "Did you not know it was cut through?" Said he, "No: how did I know any thing about it?" and walked away, and left me.

Q. Is Gifford the chief carpenter of the theatre?

A. Yes, sir: he had charge of the theatre altogether. He was chief carpenter, and then he had the management of the theatre: he had full charge of it; at least, I always understood so. I recollect, that, when Richmond was surrendered, I mentioned to him, "Have you not got any flags in the theatre?" He said to me, "Yes, I have: I guess there is a flag about." I said to him, "Why do you not run it out on that roof?" and he said, "There is a rope: is not that enough?" Said I, "You are a hell of a man: you ought to be in the old Capitol," and walked away, and left him. He did not like me anyhow.

Q. The President's box was on the south side of the theatre?

A. Yes, sir: he always had that box every time I ever saw him at the theatre.

Q. Did you hear any other exclamation besides " *Sic semper tyrannis* "?

A. I heard some one halloo out of the box, — I do not know that it was him; I suppose it was, though; it must have been, — " Revenge for the South! " just as he was putting his foot over this railing. There was a post there, and the President was right in the corner; and he jumped in between the President and the post. Just as he went over the box, I saw the President raise his head; and then it hung back, and I saw Mrs. Lincoln catch him on the arm. I was satisfied then that he was hurt. By that time, Booth was across the stage.

Q. Did Booth's spur catch in the flag?

A. His spur caught in the flag that was stretched around the box. There was also a flag decorating this post. His spur caught in the blue part of it. I thought it was a State flag at first, by the looks of it; but I saw afterwards, when I examined it, that it was the blue part of the American flag. As he went over, his spur caught in the moulding that ran round the edge of the box, and also in this flag, and tore a piece of the flag as he struck on the stage; and it was dragged half-way across the stage on his spur. I saw that the spur was on his right heel.

Q. Did you observe that hole closely, to see whether it had been freshly cut?

A. No, sir: I could not tell. It looked as though it was just done. Miss Harris remarked that morning, "There is one thing I want to examine: I am satisfied there was a bar across the door when I jumped off my seat and called for assistance." We went and looked; and there was a square hole cut in the wall, just big enough to let in a bar, and this ran across to the door. The door stands in a kind of an angle; and, this bar being placed in the wall, the other end came against the door, and you could not open it. That had been cut with a penknife, as it looked to me. There was a scratch down the wall.

Q. Could you observe the character of the spur at all? or did he move too rapidly for that?

A. I could not observe that. The way I noticed the spur was, when I saw the flag pulled down, I watched to see what it was caught to as he went over the edge of the box.

Q. You did not see him after he disappeared behind the scenes?

A. No, sir: I did not see him afterwards. He ran right across the stage. I was up in the dress-circle, and he ran out the side door. A young man named Hawk was the only one on the stage at the time. As he went over, he had the knife raised, the handle up, and the blade down.

Q. He went out on the opposite corner of the stage from the President's box?

A. Yes, sir: he ran right straight across the stage.

Cross-examined by Mr. Ewing:

Q. Did you see the bar?

A. I did not. We could not find it. There was no bar there on Sunday morning.

Q. Do you know Edward Spangler, the prisoner at the bar?

A. I know Mr. Spangler.

Q. Did you see him that night?

A. I do not recollect seeing him that night at all. I was in the theatre all the night. I went in, I think, at about twenty minutes to eight o'clock. I wanted to be there before the party came there; and I went in early. I did not see Mr. Spangler that night at all, that I recollect.

Q. Do you know him well?

A. Yes, sir: he worked at the theatre.

Q. Did you ever see him wear a mustache?

A. I do not think I ever did. I do not recollect ever seeing him wear a mustache. He never wore any mustache, I think, since I have been there.

CAPTAIN THEODORE McGOWAN,

a witness called for the prosecution, being duly sworn, testified as follows: —

By the JUDGE ADVOCATE:

Q. Did you know J. Wilkes Booth?

A. I knew him by sight, having seen him.

Q. Did you see him on the night of the assassination of the President?

A. Yes, sir.

Q. Will you describe what you saw on that occasion?

A. I was sitting in a chair in the aisle leading by the wall toward the door of the President's box on the night of the murder, when a man came and disturbed me in my seat, causing me to push the chair forward to permit him to pass, and who then stopped about three feet from where I was sitting, and leisurely took a survey of the house. I looked at him, because he happened to be in my line of sight. He took a small pack of visiting cards from his pocket; and, selecting one and replacing the others, stood a second, perhaps, with it in his hand, and then showed it to the President's messenger, who was sitting just below him. Whether the messenger took the card in the box, or, after looking at it, allowed him to go in, I do not know; but, in a moment or two more, I saw him go in the box and close the door, — the door of the lobby leading to the box.

Q. Did you see him after the pistol was fired?

A. Yes, sir. I saw the body of a man descend from the front of the box towards the stage. He was hid from my sight for a moment by the heads of those who sat in the front row of the dress-circle: but in another moment he re-appeared, and strode across the stage towards the entrance on the other side; and, as he passed, I saw the gleaming blade of a dagger in his right hand. He disappeared behind the scenes in a moment, and I saw him no more.

Q. Was it a large weapon that he held in his hand?

A. Yes, sir. The blade I should suppose to be five or six inches in length, from the length of the gleam I saw.

Q. You stated that that was Booth, as I understood you?

A. I did not say so.

Q. I thought you said you knew him?

A. I do know him; but I did not recognize that man as Booth, not having seen his face fully.

Q. You did not see his face?

A. No, sir; not fully.

Major Henry R. Ratubone,

a witness called for the prosecution, being duly sworn, testified as follows : —

By the Judge Advocate:

Q. Will you state to the Court whether or not you were in the box. of the President on the night of his assassination at Ford's Theatre?

A. I was.

Q. State all the circumstances that came under your observation in connection with that crime.

A. On the evening of the 14th of April last, at about twenty minutes past eight o'clock, I, in company with Miss Harris, left my residence at the corner of Fifteenth and H Streets, and joined the President and Mrs. Lincoln, and went with them, in their carriage, to Ford's Theatre in Tenth Street. On reaching the theatre, when the presence of the President became known, the actors stopped playing; the band struck up "Hail to the Chief!" the audience rose, and received him with vociferous cheering. The party proceeded along in the rear of the dress-circle, and entered the box that had been set apart for their reception. On entering the box, there was a large arm-chair that was placed nearest the audience, farthest from the stage, which the President took, and occupied during the whole of the evening, with one exception, when he got up and put on his coat, and returned and sat down again. When the second scene of the third act was being performed, and while I was intently observing the proceedings upon the stage, with my back towards the door, I heard the discharge of a pistol behind me, and, looking round, saw, through the smoke, a man between the door and the President. At the same time, I heard him shout some word, which I thought was "Freedom!" I instantly sprang towards him, and seized him. He wrested himself from my grasp, and made a violent thrust at my breast with a large knife. I parried the blow by striking it up, and received a wound several inches deep in my left arm, between the elbow and the shoulder. The orifice of the wound was about an inch and a half in length, and extended upwards towards the shoulder several inches. The man rushed to the front of the box; and I endeavored to seize him again, but only caught his clothes as he was leaping over the railing of the box. The clothes, as I believe, were torn in the attempt to seize him. As he went over upon the stage, I cried out with a loud voice, "Stop that man!" I then turned to the President. His position was not changed: his head was slightly bent forward, and his eyes were closed. I saw that he was unconscious, and, supposing him mortally wounded, rushed to the door for the purpose of calling medical aid. On reaching the outer door of the passage-way, I found it barred by a heavy piece of plank, one end of which was secured in the wall, and the other resting against the door. It had been so securely fastened, that it required considerable force to remove it. This wedge or bar was about four feet from the floor. Persons upon the outside were beating against the door for the purpose of entering. I removed the bar, and the door was opened. Several persons who represented themselves as surgeons were allowed to enter. I saw there Colonel Crawford, and

requested him to prevent other persons from entering the box. I
then returned to the box, and found the surgeons examining the
President's person. They had not yet discovered the wound. As
soon as it was discovered, it was determined to remove him from the
theatre. He was carried out; and I then proceeded to assist Mrs.
Lincoln, who was intensely excited, to leave the theatre. On
reaching the head of the stairs, I requested Major Potter to aid me
in assisting Mrs. Lincoln across the street to the house where the
President was being conveyed. The wound which I had received
had been bleeding very profusely; and on reaching the house, feeling very faint from the loss of blood, I seated myself in the hall,
and soon after fainted away, and was laid upon the floor. Upon
the return of consciousness, I was taken to my residence. In a
review of the transactions, it is my confident belief that the time
which elapsed between the discharge of the pistol and the time when
the assassin leaped from the box did not exceed thirty seconds.
Neither Mrs. Lincoln nor Miss Harris had left their seats.

Q. You did not know Booth yourself, did you?

A. No, sir.

Q. Do you think you would recognize him from a photograph?

A. I should be unable to do so as being the man in that box. I
myself have seen him on the stage some time since.

By the COURT:

Q. What distance was the assassin from the President when you
first saw him after hearing the report?

A. The distance from the door to where the President was sitting,
to the best of my recollection, was about four or five feet; and this
man was standing between the door and the President.

By the JUDGE ADVOCATE:

Q. Will you look at that knife [exhibiting a knife to the witness],
and say if it appears to you to be such a one as he used? I believe
the blood is still on the blade.

A. I think this knife might have made a wound similar to the
one I received. I could not recognize the knife. I merely saw the
gleam.

17*

[The knife was offered in evidence without objection, and is marked Exhibit No. 28.]

Q. Did you notice how the blade was held in the hand of the assassin when he held it?

A. The blade was held in a horizontal position, I should think; and the nature of the wound would indicate it. It came with a sweeping blow down from above.

WILLIAM WITHERS, JUN.,

a witness called for the prosecution, being duly sworn, testified as follows : —

By the JUDGE ADVOCATE :

Q. Did you belong to the orchestra of Ford's Theatre?

A. Yes, sir.

Q. Were you there on the night of the assassination of the President?

A. Yes, sir.

Q. Did you see J. Wilkes Booth?

A. Yes, sir.

Q. State what you saw of him.

A. I had some business on the stage with our stage-manager that night in regard to a national song that I had composed; and I went to see in what costume they were going to sing it in, as it was the afterpiece. I went up on the stage and talked with the stage-manager a little while; and he told me that they would sing it in the costume they wore in the piece. After that was over, I went to return under the stage, where my orchestra was, and went very leisurely along; and I heard the report of a pistol just as I was in the act of going under the stage. I stood with astonishment to think why they should fire a pistol off in "Our American Cousin," as I had never heard of such a thing before. As I turned around, I heard a confusion, and met this man [Booth] running towards me, with his head down. I stood completely paralyzed at the time. I did not know what was the matter. As he ran, I could not get out of his way; so he hit me on the leg and turned me around, and made two cuts at me, — one in the neck and one on the side, and knocked me from the third entrance down to the second. The scene saved me. As I turned, I got a side-view of him; and I saw it was John Wilkes Booth. He then made a rush for the door, and out he went. After that was over, I returned on the stage; and I heard then that the President was killed; and I saw him in the box, apparently dead.

Q. Which way did he go out of the theatre?

A. Out of the back door.

Cross-examined by Mr. EWING:

Q. Are you acquainted with the prisoner Edward Spangler?

A. I have known him ever since I have been in the theatre.

Q. Did you see him that night?

A. No, sir: I do not recollect of seeing him that night. I only happened to go on the stage in that act that night to see the stage-manager, Mr. Wright.

Q. Which side of the stage did you go on?

A. The right-hand side, facing the audience.

Q. That was the side farthest from the President's box?

A. Yes, sir.

Q. What was the position of this man Spangler? What place had he on the stage, if any?

A. His position ought to have been at the scene, if it should be changed, right in the centre of the stage. His business there is to change the scenes; and he ought to have been there, either at the wing, or right behind the scenes.

Q. On which side?

A. I really do not know. There are two that shift the scenes; but I do not know which position he had there.

Q. You do not know which side was his position?

A. No, sir.

Q. Do you know whether the passage through which Booth passed out of the door is obstructed generally.

A. Sometimes there are a great many scenes there, so that you cannot pass. During some of the pieces while Mr. Forrest was there, there were a great many scenes put up against the wall, and generally there are a lot of tools lying close by this door; but on that night every thing seemed to be clear. I met nobody there that night that I met John Wilkes Booth.

Q. Was there a necessity for many shiftings of the scenes in the play that night?

A. There was a very long wait in that scene. I think it was the time Asa Trenchard was to meet Mary Meredith, and propose to her. After he does that, they both go off; and the scene changes there. I do not think it wanted many minutes until the scene changed.

Q. Was it a time in the scene, and such a scene, where the stage and that passage-way would probably, in the ordinary course of things, have been obstructed?

A. A little, by some of the scene-shifters. They might have been there, and the actors: some of them had to go on the next scene, which required their presence.

Q. Where is the actors' room?

A. The actors' room is to the right, facing the audience as you go up the stairs; the green-room is about two yards from the stage; there is a wall partition that separated the stage and the green-room; and then there is the stars' room, on the first floor; and up stairs are the dressing-rooms for the actors.

Q. The green-room is the place where the actors wait before going on the stage?

A. Yes, sir: they are called from this room to prepare to go on the stage about five minutes or sometimes two minutes before they go on the stage; and they sit down there and wait for the call-boy to call them and go on in the respective scenes.

Q. Did Booth pass between the scenes and the green-room?

A. Yes, sir.

Q. How wide is that passage between the scenes and the green-room?

A. I should judge it to be about as wide as this railing (about four feet). The door faces right on the stage. There is another scene that comes to separate it; but this leaves the door from the scene. You look from the scenes to the dressing-room. Here is a scene, and there also; and from here there is a prompter's desk, and this scene is open from the door that leads into the dressing-room. Then there is an open space that leads right on to the stage, and nothing to obstruct the passage.

Q. I mean from the door out of which he passed?

A. It is not so large as the dressing-room door there; and there are some scenes there that obstruct the passage for anybody. Where we go down under the stage, there is a little box made, where the carpenters put their tools on sometimes. You have to stoop as you go under to get to the orchestra, and there is only a little narrow passage as you get out of this door. It is narrower, about two yards, before you get to the door than before.

Q. And, in passing from where Booth leaped on the stage to where he made his exit, he would leave the green-room to the left?

A. Yes, sir.

Q. As he would pass between the scenes and the green-room?

A. No: he would pass the green-room door. There is a partition that separates the green-room. You have to go in about two yards after leaving this door to get into the green-room; and, when that is shut, the stage is all open.

Q. Did you ever see Spangler wear a mustache?

A. No. I have seen him as he appears now. I do not recollect ever seeing him wear a mustache.

Q. How long have you known him?

A. Ever since Ford's Theatre was opened. I played there when it first opened.

Q. How long?

A. That is going on two years now.

By the JUDGE ADVOCATE:

Q. Will you state if there is not a side way by which the theatre can be entered without passing through the door; passing between the saloon and the theatre?

A. Not that I know of.

Q. Can not it be entered from the street in that way, going in the back way?

A. Not that I know of. There is only one little passage, where the actors and the orchestra get in, that leads out of the saloon.

There is a door that leads into the saloon, and from this passage leads into the theatre.

Q. That is used by the actors and persons connected with the theatre?

A. Yes, sir. It was used when the theatre first opened, so that the actors could go out, without being observed, to get a drink sometimes. This little door leads into the bar-room.

Q. Is there a passage-way from the rear of the theatre to the front without passing through that front door?

A. Not that I know of.

By the COURT:

Q. When you met Booth on the stage, as he was passing out, could you see the door where he went out?

A. Yes, sir.

Q. Was there any door-keeper standing around there that you saw?

A. I did not see one.

Q. Was the door open?

A. I do not think it was, because, as I turned round when I heard the report of the pistol (I was astonished that a pistol should be fired off in that place), I looked at the door, because the door was only a yard from me.

Q. There was nothing to obstruct his passage out?

A. No, sir: nothing.

Q. Was not that an unusual state of things?

A. It seemed strange to me.

Q. Was it not unusual?

A. Yes, sir.

Q. Was there any check at the door? or was it open before?

A. No, sir. When he gave me the blow that knocked me down in the scene, and when I came to and got a side-view of him, it seemed to me that he made one plunge at the door; and, as soon as he made the plunge, he was out.

Q. The door opens out?

A. I think it opens inward on the stage.

Q. Was it your impression that the door was opened for him? or did he open it himself?

A. I do not know.

Q. What was your impression?

A. It seems to me I tried it myself, the day I went to rehearsal, to get a hold of the door, because it surprised me that he made a jump, and went out of the door.

Q. There was no delay; but he passed right out?

A. There was no delay. From the jump he made, he went right out.

Q. Was it your impression that some one assisted him to get out by opening the door?

A. I could not say. I tried the door to see if the knob would come that way. I did not see anybody, only him, go out.

By the JUDGE ADVOCATE:

Q. Do the scenes stand at this moment just as they were left at that time? or have they been changed?

A. I really do not know.

By the COURT:

Q. Did you say there was no way for any person getting out from the rear of the theatre, except out of the front entrance?

A. You have to come to the front, without you go to the alley, and come in the front.

BROOKE STABLER recalled.

By the JUDGE ADVOCATE:

Q. Will you state to the Court, whether, since you left here, you have been to the stable and examined that horse?

A. Yes, sir.

Q. Do you recognize that animal as the same horse?

A. It is the same — a one-eyed bay horse — that Atzerodt took away on the 31st of March, and brought back again for sale some days afterwards. It is the same horse.

By the COURT:

Q. That was Surratt's horse at one time?

A. He was held in the stable as Surratt's horse until Booth paid the livery and took him away.

Q. In whose stable did you find him to-day? Where is he kept now?

A. Near the corner of Seventeenth and I Streets.

Q. Whose stable is it?

A. It is a Government stable.

Cross-examined by MR. DOSTER:

Q. Are you the owner of the stables where those horses were kept?

A. No, sir.

Q. What is your business there?

A. I keep the books, and attend to the reception and delivery of horses, hiring them, and general oversight.

Q. You are certain, then, that Surratt owned those horses?

A. I suppose he did. He brought them there in his own name, and paid the livery from time to time.

Q. I understood you to say that some one else paid for them?

A. That was when they were taken away: finally, Mr. Booth paid for them.

Q. Just now, you said that Surratt paid for them.

A. Surratt paid for them at the end of the month previous.

Q. When Booth settled the bill, did Booth claim the horses as his?

A. Not at that time.

Q. Did he state to whom they belonged at that time?

A. He brought an order from Surratt to pay for the horses and take them away.

Q. You say that the horse you have just been to identify was sold from your stables?

A. Not sold.

Q. It was brought there for sale?

A. It was brought there in October for livery; and, on the 29th of March, Booth paid the livery for the month ending the 31st of March; and, some days after that, Atzerodt brought them back there, one at a time, to sell to Mr. Howard.

Q. When did you see this horse last, before to-day?

A. I saw him about, I should think, the 4th or 5th of April; the time he brought it there to sell it, — about that time. I do not recollect the date exactly.

Q. Have you seen that horse in the possession of Atzerodt since, between to-day and that time when you saw him, that you just mentioned?

A. Not since the day he brought them there to sell.

JOE SIMMS (colored),

a witness called for the prosecution, being duly sworn, testified as follows : —

By the JUDGE ADVOCATE :

Q. Do you live in this city?

A. Yes, sir.

Q. What connection have you had with Ford's Theatre?

A. I worked there two years. I came there when I first came to Washington.

Q. Were you there on the night the President was assassinated?

A. I was up on the flies to wind up the curtain.

Q. Did you see Booth there that evening?

A. I saw Mr. Booth that evening between five and six o'clock.

Q. State where you saw him, and what he did and said.

A. When I saw him, he came in on the back part of the stage, and went through to the front of the house. I was in front of the house; and Mr. Booth came out there, and went out and into one of the restaurants by the side of the theatre. I saw him no more that night until the performance was. During the performance I heard the fire of a pistol, and looked immediately to see where it was. When I looked, I saw him jumping out of the private box down on to the stage, with a bowie-knife in his hand, and then making his escape across the stage. I saw no more of him.

Q. Did you hear any thing that he said?

A. No, sir : not a word.

Q. Who was with him when he went out to drink?

A. There was nobody with him then; but one of the men, a

man named Spangler, was sitting out in front, and he invited him to take a drink.

Q. Is that the man who is here?

A. That is the man [pointing to Edward Spangler].

Q. Did you hear a word said between them?

A. Not a word. They went into the restaurant and took a drink : that was all I saw or heard.

Q. Did you see or hear Booth when he came up to the back of the theatre with his horse?

A. I did not hear him myself, neither did I see him ; but the other colored man that works with me saw him.

Q. Is he here?

A. He is here.

Q. You know Mr. Spangler very well?

A. Yes, sir.

Q. Were he and Booth very intimate?

A. They were quite intimate together ; but I know not of any thing between them.

Q. You only saw them often together?

A. Yes, sir.

Q. Drinking together?

A. Yes, sir.

Cross-examined by Mr. Ewing :

Q. Did Mr. Spangler have any thing to do with Booth's horses?

A. No more than he used to have them attended to while Mr. Booth was away.

Q. He had charge of the horses?

A. Yes, sir.

Q. Saw to their being fed and watered?

A. Yes, sir.

Q. Was he hired by Mr. Booth?

A. Mr. Spangler was not ; but there was a young man hired by Mr. Booth. I suppose Mr. Booth thought this young man might not do right by his horses; and he got Mr. Spangler to see that it should be done right when he was not there.

Q. What position had Mr. Spangler in the theatre?

A. Mr. Spangler was one of the stage-managers; one that shoved the scenes at night, and worked on the stage all day.

Q. On what side of the stage was his usual position in the theatre?

A. On the back part of the stage; there was his particular place.

Q. On which side?

A. On the right-hand side of the stage.

Q. As you face it from the audience?

A. Yes, sir.

Q. That was the side of the President's box, was it? or was it not?

A. No, sir: the President's box was on the left-hand side.

Q. The left-hand side looking out from the stage?

A. Yes, sir.

Q. Mr. Spangler's place, you say, was on the other side?

A. Yes: next to the back-door leading out to the alley.

Q. Where was your position?

A. Right on the flies, where we wind the curtain up, on the third story.

Q. Did you see Mr. Spangler that night after five o'clock?

A. Oh, yes! Mr. Spangler was there on the stage, attending to his business as usual.

Q. At what time did you see him?

A. In the early part of the night; I cannot tell exactly when: I never inquired to know the particular time. We had no time up there where we were. Only two men worked up there.

Q. How long did you see him before the President was shot?

A. I did not see Mr. Spangler at all before the President was shot. I myself was not thinking about any thing like that going on. I was busy looking at the performance until I heard the report of a pistol.

Q. Did you not see Mr. Spangler during the play that night?

A. Yes, sir: he was there. He was on the stage during the play: he was obliged to be there.

Q. Did you see him in the first act?

A. Yes: he was there in the first act. I saw him then.

Q. Did you see him in the second act?

A. I do not remember seeing him in the second act.

Q. Were you down off the flies?

A. I was not off the flies. I could see him very well from the flies, on the opposite side of the stage, next to the side where the President was sitting in his box. I could see from my side over to that side of the stage.

Q. Were you on the side that the President's box was on?

A. No: I was on the other side.

Q. And Mr. Spangler's place was on the opposite side below?

A. Yes, sir.

Q. You say you did not see him during the second act?

A. I did not see him during the second act.

Q. Were you looking for him?

A. No, sir: I was not looking for him during the second act.

Q. Was he a sort of assistant stage-manager?

A. Yes, sir: he was one of the regular stage-managers to shift the scenes at nights.

Q. From where you were, could you see into the President's box?

A. I could. From where I was, I could see him plain.

Q. And could you see also where Mr. Spangler was in the habit of being?

A. Yes, sir.

Q. Both of them were on the opposite side of the theatre from you?

A. Yes, sir: on the opposite side.

Q. Both of them, then, were on the same side with each other?

A. Yes, sir.

Q. What time in the first act did you see Spangler?

A. In the first act, I saw him walking around the stage, looking at the performance.

Q. Did he have his hat on?

A. Yes: he always had his hat on in the back entries.

Q. How was he dressed?

A. I cannot tell exactly what kind of clothes he had on, but just a common suit.

Q. Did he look as he does now?

A. Oh, no, sir! he did not look as he looks now.

Q. How was his face?

A. It is just as natural now as it was then.

Q. Did you ever see Mr. Spangler wear a mustache?

A. No, sir: I never did.

Q. From where you were up on the flies, you could sometimes see him where he was; and sometimes, when he would change his position, you would not see him?

A. I could not see him then.

Q. You just saw him occasionally; and his position generally was around on the side opposite to that where you were?

A. Yes, sir.

JOHN MILES (colored),

a witness called for the prosecution, being duly sworn, testified as follows: —

By the JUDGE ADVOCATE:

Q. Do you belong to Ford's Theatre? and have you been working there?

A. Yes, sir.

Q. Were you there on the night of the assassination of the President?

A. Yes, sir.

Q. Did you see J. Wilkes Booth there?

A. I saw him when he came there.

Q. What hour did he come? Tell us all you saw.

A. He came there, I think, between nine and ten o'clock; and he brought a horse from the stable, and came to the back door and called " Ned Spangler " three times out of the theatre. Ned Spangler went across the stage to him. After that I did not see what became of Booth, and never noticed him any more until I heard the pistol go off. I then went up in sight of the President's box. The man up with me said some one had shot the President. The President had then gone out of sight. I could not see him. I went in a minute or two to the window; and I heard the sound of horses' feet going out the alley.

Q. Did you see anybody holding the horse out there?

18*

A. I saw the boy holding the horse there: from the time I saw him, he held him fifteen minutes.

Q. Was that after he called for Spangler?

A. Yes, sir.

Q. You mean Spangler the prisoner here?

A. Yes, sir.

Q. You do not know what was said between them?

A. No, sir: I do not know any thing about what was said between them. I did not understand a word. I only heard him call " Ned."

Q. You say he came up to the door with his horse between nine and ten o'clock. Do you know at what hour he put his horse in the little stable back of the theatre?

A. He had put his horse in the stable when I came over there. He and Ned Spangler and Jim Maddox came up from the stable in the evening, I think, about three o'clock. I judge it was about that time. I did not notice the time particularly. It was the time he came right through the theatre.

Q. How far is the little stable in which he kept the horse from the theatre?

A. Not more than fifty yards, if that.

Cross-examined by MR. EWING:

Q. Was the play going on when Booth rode up and called for Spangler?

A. They had just closed a scene, and were getting ready to take off that scene at the time he called for Spangler. Spangler was at the second groove then, and pushed a scene across. Booth called him three times.

Q. Where were you then?

A. Up on the flies, about three and one-half stories from the stage.

Q. Was that in the third act?

A. I think it was in the third act.

Q. How long was it before the President was shot?

A. The President came in during the first act; and I think it was in the third act he was shot.

Q. About how long do you think it was from the time Booth came up there until the President was shot?

A. From the time he brought the horse there until the President was shot, I think was about three-quarters of an hour. I saw Booth when he brought the horse from the stable to the door; and from that time until the President was shot, I think, was three-quarters of an hour.

Q. Do you know who held the horse?

A. John Peanuts held him: he was lying on a bench holding the horse when I noticed him. I was at the window pretty nearly all the time from the time Booth brought the horse until he went away. Every time I looked out the window, John Peanuts was lying on the bench, holding the horse. I did not see any one else hold him.

Q. Was John Peanuts there when Booth came up?

A. I do not know: he was at the theatre; but I do not know whether he was at the door.

Q. Did you look out to see who was there?

A. There was nobody there when Booth came up, that I saw, because I was looking out of the window.

Q. Did Spangler go out?

A. He went to Booth. I supposed Booth was at the door.

Q. Spangler went to him?

A. He ran across the stage when Booth called him. Some person told him that Booth called him; and he ran across the stage to him.

Q. Do you know whether he went out of the door?

A. I do not know whether he did or not. I did not see him go out.

Q. Do you know how long Spangler staid there?

A. No: because, when I looked out again, his boy was holding the horse.

Q. How long was that after he called Spangler?

A. Not more than ten or fifteen minutes.

Q. Do you know what Spangler had to do with Booth?

A. No, sir: only I saw him appear to be familiar with him, and keeping his company and so on when he was round about there.

Q. Did Booth treat him?

A. I do not know: I never saw him treat him.

Q. Did Spangler have any thing to do with Booth's horses, — hitch them up, or saddle them, or hold them?

A. Yes, sir: I have seen him hold them down at the stable.

Q. Did you know any thing about his hitching Booth's horse, or saddling him up?

A. I never saw him hitch any up there; but I have seen him hold the horse there at the stable-door. John Peanuts always attended to the horses. I never saw Spangler put any gear on any of them.

Q. Do you know what place on the stage Spangler generally occupied?

A. He worked on the right-hand side, — the side next to E Street.

Q. The side the President's box was on?

A. Yes, sir: on that side.

Q. Could you see from where you were up in the flies?

A. I could see right straight down through the scenes on that side of the stage; and I always saw him work on that side.

Q. Was he on that side when Booth called him?

A. Yes, sir: he was.

Q. What was Spangler's business on that side? What kept him on that side?

A. He shoved the scenes at night on that side.

Q. Was there another man shoving from the other side?

A. Yes, sir: there was another man opposite to him.

Q. Did you see Spangler after you saw that Peanut John was holding Booth's horse?

A. I never saw him any more until I came down. I came down the stairs after the President was shot, and Spangler was out there at the door.

Q. At what door?

A. At the same door Booth went out when I came down stairs.

Q. Were there others out there?

A. Yes; there were some more men out there: I did not notice who they were, but some more besides him.

Q. More men of the theatre?

A. That were at the theatre that night: there were some strangers out there then, I believe; because every person had got over the stage then that wanted to go over.

Q. How many men were out at the back door at that time?

A. Not more than two or three out of the door when I came down, because I came down in a very short time after I understood what it was; and Spangler came out, and I asked him who it was that held the horse; and he told me, "Hush! not to say nothing;" and I did not say any more, though I knew who it was, because I saw the boy who was holding the horse. I knew that the person who brought the horse there rode him away again.

Q. You could not see Spangler all the time when he was on the stage, could you, from where you were?

A. When he was working on that side, I could see him all the while if I looked for him.

Q. Did you look for him that night?

A. No: I did not notice him particularly that night more than usual. I would not have noticed him when I did, only I heard Booth call him; and I noticed where he was when he went to Booth.

Q. He might have been on that side all night without your noticing it?

A. He might.

Q. You do not know, then, whether he was on that side or not?

A. He was on that side when I saw him before then, and he was on that side then.

Q. But you did not look for him after that?

A. I did not look for him at all.

Q. What was it you asked Spangler when you came down?

A. I asked him who it was holding the horse at the door of the theatre.

Q. What did he say?

A. He told me to hush; not to say any thing at all to him; and I never said no more to him.

Q. Was he excited?

A. He appeared to be.

Q. Was everybody excited?

A. Every person appeared to be very much excited.

Q. When you asked him who it was who was holding the horse, he said, " Hush! don't say any thing to me "?

A. Yes, sir.

Q. And you say, " Hush! don't say any thing to me "?

A. I mean the same thing, to hush, not say any thing about it. That was the word. Not thinking at the time, I said, " Do not say any thing to me ; " but he said, " Don't say any thing about it." That was the word ; that was what he said, " Don't say any thing about it."

Q. Do you know Spangler well?

A. Oh, yes! at least, I know him when I see him.

Q. Did you ever see him wear a mustache?

A. No, sir : I do not think I ever saw him wear a mustache.

By the JUDGE ADVOCATE :

Q. This remark he made to you, " Hush! don't say any thing about it," was immediately after the killing of the President, was it?

A. Yes, sir : right at the door when I went out doors.

Q. Did he make any other remark as a reason why you should not say any thing about it?

A. No, sir : not a word to me.

Q. He made no other remark?

A. No, sir : not a word to me.

Q. Did you see Booth go out of the door?

A. No, sir : I did not see him go out of the door; but I heard his horse when it went out of the alley. Whether it went right or left, I cannot tell; but I heard the rapping of his feet on the ground.

Q. Was the door left open at that time when Booth was gone? or was it shut?

A. It was open when I came down stairs. I do not know whether it was left open from the time he came in and went out, or not ; but it was open when I got down stairs. I had to go down three and a half stories before I got down on the stage ; and when I got down it was open.

Q. Do you know anybody who probably heard your remark to Mr. Spangler, and his reply to you?

A. No, sir: I do not know any person that was noticing the words at all. There were a good many persons around; but I do not know that any of them was noticing the words used.

By the Court:

Q. When Booth called for Ned Spangler the first time, did you see where Spangler was?

A. Yes: when I noticed where Spangler was, he was right across the stage.

Q. You say Booth called him three times: when he called the first time, did you see where Spangler was?

A. I did not see where he was then, because I did not notice where he was until Booth called him the third time: then I saw where he was standing.

Q. Where did Spangler meet Booth then?

A. He went towards the door. After he got underneath the flies, I could not see him any more.

Q. Then you lost sight of him as he was going to the door?

A. Yes, sir: as he went across the stage.

Q. How long was he with him? Can you tell?

A. I cannot tell, because I did not see Spangler again until I came down from off the flies.

Q. When Spangler told you to hush, not to say any thing about it, was he near the door?

A. He was, I suppose, about a yard and a half from the door.

Q. Was anybody else near the door but him?

A. There was nobody else near the door that I could see; that is, there was nobody else between him and me and the door.

Q. Did he have hold of the door at that time?

A. No: he was walking across the door when I spoke to him; he was walking across the door, in front of the door, outside the door. There was nobody else between him and me and the door, because I brushed right up to him, and asked who was holding the horse.

Q. Right at that door, was it light or dark?

A. Dark right at the door; and it was a dark night anyhow.

Q. But there was no light right there?

A. No light there.

By Mr. Ewing:

Q. Were you and Spangler inside of the door, or outside of the door?

A. Outside.

Q. Where were the other people that you say were about there?

A. They were standing just round about there, some of them a little farther from the door.

Q. Still farther outside the door?

A. Yes: farther outside the door.

Q. You were between those people and the door?

A. Yes, sir.

Q. And all were in the alley?

A. Yes, sir.

By the Court:

Q. Did he appear to be covering that door?

A. No, sir: he did not appear to be covering it at all.

Q. Did he act as if he was trying to prevent persons getting in or out that door?

A. No. He did appear to be excited. That was the only thing I discovered about him, — very much excited.

Q. At that time, Booth had gone out of the alley?

A. Yes, sir: he had gone out of the alley.

John F. Sleickmann,

a witness called for the prosecution, being duly sworn, testified as follows: —

By the Judge Advocate:

Q. Have you been connected with Ford's Theatre in this city?

A. Yes, sir.

Q. Were you there on the night of the assassination of the President?

A. I was.

Q. Do you know J. Wilkes Booth?

A. Yes, sir.

Q. Did you, or not, see him on that night? and if so, at what hour, and under what circumstances?

A. I saw him about nine o'clock, I guess it was. He came up on a horse, and came in a little back door to the theatre. Ned Spangler was standing there by one of the wings; and Booth said to him, "Ned, you will help me all you can, won't you?" and Ned said, "Oh, yes!"

Q. I understand you to say, that, as Booth came up to the door with his horse, he said that?

A. When he came in the door, after he got off the horse.

Q. Was that his salutation, the way he first addressed Spangler? Were those the first words he spoke?

A. Yes, sir: the first words that I heard.

Q. "Ned, you will help me all you can, won't you"?

A. Yes, sir; and Ned said, "Oh, yes!"

Q. How long was that before the President was shot?

A. I should judge it to be about an hour and a half.

Q. Did you observe the horse afterwards, by whom it was held?

A. I did not.

Q. You did not see Booth any more?

A. I just got a glimpse of him as he was going out the first entrance on the right-hand side.

Q. What hour was that when you saw him going out of the first entrance?

A. About half-past ten o'clock, I think. That was after he shot the President.

Q. You mean he went out the back door?

A. I do not know where he went after that. I did not see him.

Q. You say you saw him going out?

A. I saw him going out the entrance near the prompter's place.

Q. That is near the back door?

A. Yes: you go there, and turn to your right to go out the door.

Cross-examined by MR. EWING:

Q. Did you hear Booth calling for Spangler?

A. No, sir. He just came up, and said, " Ned, you will help me all you can, won't you?" and Ned said, " Oh, yes!"

Q. Where were they then?

A. Right by the back door.

Q. Did Booth ride up?

A. I guess so. I did not see him on the horse; but the horse was standing there when he came in the back door.

Q. Was anybody holding the horse then?

A. I did not see anybody holding the horse at all.

Q. Was not Spangler holding him?

A. No: Booth was talking to Ned.

Q. Was Booth holding the horse?

A. No: Booth had come inside the door.

Q. Did you see the horse?

A. I saw the horse: he left the door open.

Q. But you cannot say whether anybody was holding the horse or not.

A. I cannot: it was dark out there; and I could not tell much about it.

Q. What was your place in the theatre?

A. I was assistant property-man.

Q. What was your position on the stage? any particular place?

A. We have to set the furniture and every thing of that kind on the stage.

Q. What was Spangler's position on the stage?

A. Stage-carpenter, shoving the scenes, and so on.

Q. Is he the principal stage-carpenter?

A. No, sir: Mr. Gifford is the principal stage-carpenter.

Q. Spangler is just a rough carpenter?

A. He was helping Mr. Gifford there: hired by Mr. Gifford.

Q. What was Spangler's place on the stage during a play?

A. He had to shove the scenes together.

Q. On which side?

A. I do not know which side particularly.

Q. Were you about that night?

A. Yes, sir.

Q. Were you on the stage?

A. I was.

Q. During the whole play?

A. I had to go down to the apothecary store to get a few little articles to use in the piece : I do not believe I was out more than that, except when I went into the restaurant next door.

Q. Did you notice these *employés* that night at all? Could you see whether Spangler was there through the play or not?

A. I could not. I saw him after the assassination. He was standing up on the stage, by one of the wings, with a white hand-kerchief in his hand : he was very pale, wiping his eyes. I do not know whether he was crying or not.

Q. How long was that after the President was shot?

A. About ten minutes, I suppose.

Q. Did not Spangler frequently hold Booth's horse?

A. I did not see that at all.

Q. Did he not frequently hold Booth's horse, hitch him, and saddle him? or do you know?

A. He might have done it; but I never saw it that I recollect.

Q. Was Booth an *habitué* of the theatre? Did he go back and forth frequently?

A. Yes, sir.

Q. Was he familiar with the actors and employes?

A. Yes : I think he was.

Q. Knew them all pretty intimately?

A. Yes, sir.

Q. Did he not have access to the theatre at all times?

A. Yes, sir.

Q. Came about behind the scenes, in the green-room, &c.?

A. Yes, sir : anywhere about the theatre.

Q. Just as though he were in the employment of Mr. Ford?

A. Yes, sir.

Q. Is Spangler a drinking man?

A. Yes : I think he is.

Q. Did Booth treat him much?

A. I cannot tell that : I do not know.

Q. Were you around in front of the theatre at any time during the performance?

A. I do not recollect being in front.

Q. Or on the pavement in front?

A. I was on the pavement in front.

Q. Did you see any thing of Spangler in front there?

A. No, sir.

Q. What time were you there?

A. I was there about seven o'clock or half-past seven, until the assassination.

Q. And you were there, then, until the assassination?

A. Yes, sir.

Q. Did you notice the people who were about there?

A. I did not.

Q. If Spangler had been there, you would have probably seen him and noticed him?

A. I guess I would.

Q. You did not see any thing of him there?

A. No, sir.

Q. Did you notice the President's carriage there?

A. Yes, sir.

Q. Did you ever see Spangler wear a mustache?

A. No, sir: I do not think I did. I saw him wear side-whiskers; but I do not recollect his ever wearing a mustache.

Q. How was his face about that time, — smooth shaved as it is now?

A. I think it was.

Q. You say you were in front of the theatre constantly from seven or half-past seven o'clock?

A. Not constantly.

Q. But frequently in front of the theatre from seven or half-past seven to the time of the assassination?

A. No, sir: I got to the theatre about half-past seven or eight; and I was about the theatre from that time till the assassination.

Q. How much of the time were you in front of the theatre?

A. I was in front of the theatre two or three times.

Q. Were you there during the third act?

A. No, sir: I was on the stage during the third act.

Q. Were you in front during the second act?

A. I think I was. I was in the restaurant, next door.

Q. How long before the close of the second act?

A. About ten or fifteen minutes.

Q. You think, that, if Spangler had been there, you would have seen him?

A. Yes, sir.

By the COURT:

Q. How did you get from the rear to the front of the theatre?

A. There was a side-entrance to go out to the front on the left-hand side of the theatre, — a little alley-way.

Q. You did not go through the front door?

A. I did not.

Q. Did you see Booth in front of the theatre?

A. I saw him that afternoon, between four and five o'clock, I think, in the restaurant, next door. I went in to look for James Maddox; and I found several there drinking, — Booth, Ned Spangler, Jim Maddox, Peanuts, and a young gentleman by the name of John Mouldey, I think. Maddox asked me if I would not take a drink. I said yes, and went up and took a glass of ale.

Q. Did you see Booth in front of the theatre when you were out on the pavement that night?

A. No: I did not see him after he rode up there until after the assassination.

By MR. EWING:

Q. How close were you to Booth and Spangler when Booth said those words to him on entering the theatre from the door?

A. About as far as I am from you [a distance of about eight feet].

Q. How far was Spangler from him?

A. Spangler was standing as close to him as the gentleman next to you is to you [about three feet].

Q. How many feet were you distant from Booth then?

A. I should judge it to be about eight feet.

Q. How many feet was Spangler from Booth?

19*

A. Two or three feet.

Q. Ho spoke, then, in a loud voice?

A. Yes, sir.

Q. Did Booth see you?

A. I do not know. He went right behind the scenes after that.

Q. Could he have seen you from where he was standing?

A. Oh, yes!

Q. Was there anybody else by but you?

A. I did not take notice at that time.

Q. Was not Spangler in liquor that night?

A. That I cannot say: I do not know.

Q. Did you often see him in liquor?

A. I have seen him in liquor; but I could not tell when he was drunk, and when not.

Q. Was he not habitually pretty well soaked?

A. I do not know, indeed.

By the COURT.

Q. Was there any thing unusual in the furniture on the stage that night?

A. No, sir.

Q. Was it all in its proper place, according to the performance that was going on?

A. Yes, sir: every thing.

Q. The scenes, and every thing?

A. Yes, sir.

By the JUDGE ADVOCATE:

Q. Do you know whether the scenes remain now as they were left that night?

A. I do not know. I have not been in the theatre but once or twice since that.

Q. Do you know what Spangler had to do with the decoration or arrangement of the President's box?

A. I do not.

The JUDGE ADVOCATE suggested to the Court the propriety of a visit to Ford's Theatre. Testimony having been given in relation to the murder, and the condition of affairs at and in the rear of the theatre, it would, perhaps, be more satisfactory to the Court to make a personal inspection of the premises.

The suggestion was acquiesced in ; and the Commission adjourned to meet informally at the theatre at half-past nine o'clock on Tuesday morning.

TUESDAY, May 16, 1865.

The Commission met informally at the theatre at half-past nine o'clock ; and, after an inspection of the premises by the members of the tribunal and the counsel concerned in the case, proceeded to the Penitentiary building, in which its sessions are held.

The roll was called ; and, all the members being present, the following proceedings took place : —

The PRESIDENT. One of the members of the Court has moved that the reading of the record be dispensed with, inasmuch as the counsel on the part of the prisoners are furnished with an official copy of the record, and have an opportunity of examining it during the intervals between the meetings of the Court, and can object to any thing that is incorrect when they come into Court, if they find any thing incorrect.

COL. TOMPKINS. Besides, it is very accurately published in the morning papers.

MR. EWING. If the Court will allow me, I will state that the reporters are not able to furnish us immediately with an official copy of the record ; it is behind-hand always a day or more : but inasmuch as the record is published quite accurately in the " Intelligencer," and in fact published, I think, from the notes of the reporters, if the Court would allow us the privilege at any time, even though it be not the day after the examination of a witness, in case we discover an error, to ask that the witness be recalled, it would be satisfactory, so far as I am concerned.

GEN. KAUTZ. That can be done at any time. Under any circumstances, a witness may be recalled.

MR. EWING. If the arrangement proposed is made, it will be

necessary for the Judge Advocate to detain witnesses for, say, two days after their examination, so that we may have time to read the testimony as published in the paper, or as furnished us by the reporters. We have not been furnished yet with the last of yesterday's proceedings, nor has that portion been published in the paper.

The PRESIDENT. I should think a detention of one day would be ample.

MR. EWING. If the witnesses who were examined yesterday were detained until after the Court meets to-morrow, I think that would be sufficient. The evidence of the last witnesses examined yesterday will probably be published in the "Intelligencer" to-morrow.

The PRESIDENT. Has the Judge Advocate any objection to that arrangement?

The JUDGE ADVOCATE (GEN. HOLT). I do not wish to embarrass the Court, certainly, by any suggestions of mine. I am as anxious for the despatch of business as anybody can be; but, if this precedent is now established, it will be, I think, not only the first one which has been set in the military service, but the first in the civil service. I never, in my whole life, have been in connection with any court, the proceedings of which were not read over in the hearing of the court itself, before they were declared by the court to be accurate and complete. Although I have as much confidence in the accuracy of our reporters as anybody can have, I think it would be a dangerous example to set; and I would rather see it in any case that has arisen in the military service of the country than in this, where there are so many lives at stake, and where it is so vastly important, not only that there should be strict accuracy, but that the country should feel assured that it is so, and that all the precautions necessary to secure that result have been resorted to. If it shall be known hereafter, in connection with this trial, that the Court departed from the usages of the service, and did not even have its own record read over, but trusted simply to the reporters for accuracy, it might go very far to shake the confidence of the country in the accuracy of these reports, and would certainly leave an opening for criticism.

GEN. FOSTER. I think the reading should be proceeded with every morning for the purpose of corection, if any correction should be necessary.

The PRESIDENT. I am very much inclined, after hearing the opinion of the Judge Advocate General, to change my first impression on the subject; and I will vote against the proposition, though I thought favorably of it at first.

The motion was then withdrawn; and the record was read and approved.

JOSEPH BORROUGH,

a witness called for the prosecution, being duly sworn, testified as follows : —

By the JUDGE ADVOCATE :

Q. State whether or not you have been connected with Ford's Theatre in this city.

A. Yes, sir : I have been.

Q. In what capacity?

A. I used to stand at the stage-door, and then carry bills in the daytime ; and I used to attend Booth's horse, — see that he was fed and cleaned.

Q. Did you know John Wilkes Booth in his lifetime?

A. I knew him while he kept his horse there in that stable.

Q. Do you speak of the stable immediately back of the theatre?

A. Yes, sir.

Q. Did you see him on the afternoon of the 14th of April?

A. I saw him when he brought his horse to the stable, between five and six o'clock.

Q. State what he did.

A. He brought the horse, and hallooed out for Spangler.

Q. Did Spangler go down to the stable?

A. Yes, sir : he went out there. Mr. Booth asked him for a halter : he had none there, and he sent Jake after one up-stairs.

Q. How long did they remain together then?

A. I do not know. Jim Maddox was down there then too.

Q. Did you see him again at a later hour that evening?

A. I saw him on the stage that night.

Q. Did you or not see him when he came with his horse between nine and ten o'clock that night?

A. No, sir: I did not see him when he came up the alley with his horse.

Q. Did you see the horse at the door?

A. I saw him when Spangler called me out there to hold the horse.

Q. State all that happened at that time, — what was said and done.

A. I cannot.

Q. Why? Do you not recollect it?

A. No, sir.

Q. Did you see Booth when he came there with his horse?

A. No, sir: I did not see him.

Q. Did you hear him call for Ned Spangler?

A. No, sir: I heard Deboney calling Ned, that Booth wanted him.

Q. Who held Booth's horse that evening?

A. Nobody but me: I held him that night.

Q. Who gave you the horse to hold?

A. Spangler.

Q. At what hour?

A. I cannot tell exactly what hour; between nine and ten, I think.

Q. How long was it before the President was shot?

A. I held the horse about fifteen minutes.

Q. What did Spangler say when he asked you to hold the horse?

A. He just told me to hold it. I said I could not; I had to go in and attend to my door. He told me to hold the horse, and, if there was any thing, to lay the blame on him. So I held the horse.

Q. Did you hold him near the door?

A. No: I was sitting over against the house there, on a carpenter's bench.

Q. Did you hear the report of the pistol?

A. Yes, sir.

Q. Were you still on the bench when Booth came out?

A. I had got off the bench then.

Q. What did he say when he came out?

A. He told me to give him his horse.

Q. Had you got up to the door?

A. No: I was still out by the bench.

Q. Did he do any thing besides that?

A. He knocked me down.

Q. With his hand or not?

A. He struck me with the butt of a knife.

Q. Did he do that as he mounted his horse?

A. Yes, sir: he had one foot in the stirrup.

Q. Did he also strike or kick you?

A. He kicked me.

Q. As he got on the horse?

A. Yes, sir.

Q. Did he say nothing while getting on the horse?

A. He said nothing else: he only hallooed to me to give him his horse.

Q. Did he ride off immediately?

A. Yes, sir.

Q. State whether or not you were in the President's box that afternoon.

A. Yes, sir: I was up there.

Q. Who decorated or fixed the box for the President?

A. Harry Ford put the flags around it.

Q. Was or was not the prisoner Spangler with you in the box?

A. He was up there with me. I went after him to take out the partition.

Q. What was he doing?

A. Harry Ford told me to go in with Spangler, and take out the partition of the box, as the President and General Grant were coming there. I then went after Spangler.

Q. Do you remember whether, while Spangler was doing that, he said any thing in regard to the President?

A. He made remarks, and laughed.

Q. What were they?

A. He said, " Damn the President and General Grant!"

Q. While damning the President, or after damning him, did he say any thing else?

A. I said to him, "What are you damning the man for, — a man that has never done any harm to you?" He said he ought to be cursed when he got so many men killed.

Q. Did he or not say any thing in regard to what he wished in that connection?

A. I do not remember that.

Q. Did he or did he not say what he wished might happen to General Grant?

Mr. Ewing objected to the question.

A. I do not remember that.

Q. Was or was there not any thing said, in the course of that conversation, as to what or might not be done to the President or General Grant.

Mr. Ewing objected to the question.

A. No, sir : I did not hear any thing.

Cross-examined by Mr. Ewing :

Q. You say you did not hear anybody calling out for Spangler?

A. I heard Deboney call for him ; and he told him Mr. Booth wanted him out in the alley.

Q. Who is Deboney?

A. He used to be a kind of actor there.

Q. Deboney called him, and told him Booth wanted him?

A. Yes, sir.

Q. How long was it after that that Spangler called you?

A. I do not know how long : not very long ; about six or seven or eight minutes.

Q. What were you doing when Spangler called you?

A. I was sitting at the first entrance on the left.

Q. What business were you doing?

A. I was attending to the stage-door there.

Q. What had you to do at the stage-door there?

A. I keep strangers out, and prevent those coming in who do not belong there.

Q. You told him that you could not hold the horse ; that you had to attend that door?

A. Yes, sir.

Q. And he said what?

A. If there was any thing wrong, to blame it on him.

Q. Were-you round in front of the theatre that night?

A. I was out there while the curtain was down. I go out between every act while the curtain is down : when the curtain is up, I go inside.

Q. Did you see Booth in front of the theatre?

A. No, sir : I did not.

Q. Did you see Spangler in front of the theatre?

A. No, sir.

Q. Did you ever see Spangler wear a mustache?

A. No, sir.

Q. Do you know whether Spangler wore any whiskers of any kind that night?

A. I did not see him wear any.

Q. Was not Spangler in the habit of hitching up Booth's horse?

A. He wanted to take the bridle off, and Booth would not let him.

Q. When was that?

A. Between five and six that evening. At first he wanted to take the saddle off, but Booth would not let him ; then he wanted to take the bridle off, but he would not agree to it ; and he just put a halter round the horse's neck. He took the saddle off afterwards, though.

Q. Was not Spangler in the habit of bridling and saddling, and hitching up Booth's horse?

A. When I was not there, he used to hitch him up.

Q. Was he not in the habit of holding him, too, when you were not about?

A. Yes, sir ; and he used to feed him when I was not about.

Q. Then you and Spangler together attended to Booth's horse?

A. Sometimes. Mr. Gifford gave me the job to attend to. He asked me if I knew any thing about horses ; and I told him I knew a little about them. Then he asked me if I would not attend to Booth's horse ; and he gave me the job.

Q. And Spangler used to help you about it?

A. Yes, sir.

Q. And when you were not there, Spangler did it himself?

A. Yes, sir; and Spangler used to go after feed sometimes.

Q. Do you know the way Booth went out after he jumped out of the President's box?

A. No, sir: I was not in the alley.

Q. Do you know the passage between the green-room and the scenes, through which Booth ran, which leads right out to the door?

A. Yes, sir: that is on the other side of the stage.

Q. The one that Booth ran through when he went out into the alley?

A. I do not know what entrance he ran through.

Q. Was Booth about the theatre a great deal?

A. He was not about there much: he used to go there sometimes.

Q. Which way would he enter the theatre generally?

A. On Tenth Street.

Q. Did he sometimes enter back?

A. Sometimes.

Q. How far was the stable where Booth kept his horse from the back entrance of the theatre?

A. About two hundred yards.

Q. Do you recollect what act was being played when you first went out to hold Booth's horse?

A. I think it was the first scene of the third act. The scene had curtains on the door.

Q. Was that scene being played when you went out to hold the horse?

A. Yes, sir: they had just been closing in.

By the JUDGE ADVOCATE:

Q. You have the nickname of "Peanuts" about there?

A. Yes, sir: I used to stay at a stand in front of the theatre; and they call me "John Peanuts" about there.

Q. Was there more than one horse in the stable that evening?

A. Only one: that is all I saw; and Booth brought that there.

Q. Do I understand you to say that there was only one horse in the stable that afternoon?

A. That was all I saw when I was there between five and six.

Q. You were not in the stable afterwards?

A. No.

By Mr. Ewing :

Q. Do you know on what side of the theatre Spangler worked ?

A. Always on the left side.

Q. Is that the side the President's box was on ?

A. Yes, sir.

Q. Was that the side you attended the door on ?

A. Yes, sir.

Q. When you were away, did he not attend the door for you ?

A. Yes, sir : when I was away, he used to attend the door.

Q. His position, then, was near to where your position was ?

A. Yes, sir.

Q. What door was that ? the door that went into the little alley ?

A. Yes, sir : from Tenth Street.

Q. You attended there to see that nobody came in that was not authorized to come ?

A. Yes, sir : when the curtain was down, I used to go outside and stay until the curtain was up.

Q. When the play was going on, who was there on that side to shove the scenes, except Spangler ? Anybody ?

A. There was another man there on that side : two men worked on this side, and three on the other.

Q. Who was the man that worked with Spangler on that side ?

A. I think his name is Simmons.

Q. Who are the men that worked on the other side ?

A. One of them is Skeggy ; another is Jake ; and I do not know the other fellow's name.

Q. While the play was going on, did these men always stay there ?

A. Yes, sir : they are always about there.

Q. They had to stay there in order to shove the scenes, had they not ?

A. Yes, they always have to be there when the whistle blows, and shove them.

Q. Did they usually stay there on their sides ?

A. Yes, sir ; but sometimes, when a scene would stand a whole act, they would go around on the other side, and those on the other side would come on their side.

Q. But did not go out?

A. Sometimes they used to go out; not very often, though.

By the JUDGE ADVOCATE:

Q. Was there another horse in that stable some days before, or not?

A. Yes: there was one other horse there, — two horses there one day.

Q. How long before?

A. Booth brought a horse and buggy there. I cannot tell you when it was.

Q. Do you remember the color or appearance of the horse?

A. It was a little horse: I do not remember the color.

Q. Do you remember whether he was blind of one eye?

A. No, sir. The fellow that brought the horse there used to go with Booth very often.

Q. Do you see among the prisoners here the man who brought the horse?

A. No, sir: I do not see him there [pointing to the dock of the prisoners]. It was the fellow who lived at the Navy Yard, I think. I saw him going in a house down there one day, when I was carrying bills there. I do not know whether he lived there or not.

Q. Do you remember his name?

A. No, sir: I never heard his name.

By the COURT:

Q. Did you see Booth at the instant he left the back door of the theatre after the assassination of the President?

A. He rode off.

Q. Did you see him when he came out of the door?

A. Yes, sir.

Q. What door did he come out of, the small one or the large one?

A. The small one.

Q. Was there anybody else at that door?

A. No, sir: I did not see anybody else.

Q. Did Spangler pass through that door leading into the passage at any time while you were sitting at the door, — the passage towards the street?

A. I did not take notice.

Q. You did not see him go out or come in while you were there?

A. No, sir.

Q. You said that you were in the President's box on the day of the murder?

A. Yes, sir.

Q. What time in the day was that?

A. About three o'clock.

Q. Did all the *employés* in the theatre know that the President was to be there that night?

A. I heard Harry Ford say so.

Q. Anybody else? Did you hear Spangler speak of it?

A. No: I told him the President was coming there.

Q. What time did you say you were there?

A. It was about three o'clock when we went up to take out the partition.

Q. Who were in the box at the time the partition was taken out?

A. Spangler, Jake, and myself.

Q. Who is Jake?

A. All I know is that his name is Jake.

Q. A black man or a white man?

A. A white man.

Q. Employed there?

A. Yes: he used to be a stage-carpenter there.

Q. Was he regularly employed in that theatre at that time?

A. He worked there day and night.

Q. Had he been working there for some time?

A. He had been working there about three weeks.

Q. When they were there, how long did they stay in the box?

A. I staid there until they took the partition out, and sat down in the box.

Q. Did you observe what else they did in the box?

A. No, sir. Spangler said it would be a nice place to sleep in after the partition was down. That is all I recollect.

20*

Mrs. Mary Ann Turner,

a witness called for the prosecution, being duly sworn, testified as follows : —

By the Judge Advocate :

Q. State to the Court where you reside in this city.

A. I reside in the rear of Ford's Theatre.

Q. How far from it ?

A. As far as from here to where that gentleman sits over there, or may be a little farther [pointing to one of the counsel for the accused, a distance of about eight feet].

Q. Did you know John Wilkes Booth ?

A. I knew him when I saw him.

Q. Will you state what you saw of him on the afternoon of the 14th of April last ?

A. That afternoon I saw him, I think, to the best of my recollection, between three and four o'clock, standing in the back door of Ford's Theatre, with a lady by his side. I did not take any particular notice of him at that time ; but I turned from the door, and I saw no more of him, until, to the best of my recollection, between seven and eight, or near about eight o'clock that night, when he brought a horse up to the back door, opened the door, and called for a man by the name of " Ned " three times, — to the best of my recollection, not more than three times. This " Ned " came to him ; and I heard him say to " Ned " in a low voice, " Tell Maddox to come here." I then saw Maddox come. He [Booth] said something in a very low voice to this Maddox ; and I saw Maddox reach out his hand and take the horse, but where " Ned " went I cannot tell. This Booth went on into the theatre.

Q. Did you see him or hear him when he came out after the assassination of the President ?

A. I only heard the horse going very rapidly out of the alley ; and I ran immediately to my door and opened it, but he was gone : I did not see him at all.

Q. Did you see the man named " Ned," of whom you speak ?

A. Yes, sir.

Q. At what time did you see him ?

A. I rushed to the door immediately : the crowd came out, and this time this man "Ned" came out of the theatre.

Q. Which of those men in the dock is it ?

A. There he sits, with dark shirt and dark coat on [pointing to the accused, Edward Spangler].

Q. Spangler, you mean?

A. Yes, sir : Ned Spangler. And said I to him, "Mr. Ned, you know that man Booth called you ?" Said he, "No, I know nothing about it ;" and then he went down the alley.

Q. Was that all that occurred between you and him ?

A. That was all that was said between me and him.

Cross-examined by Mr. Ewing :

Q. How far is your house from the back door of the theatre ?

A. My front door fronts to the back of the theatre. It comes out into the open alley, which leads up to the door. There is another house between mine and the theatre. The two houses are adjoining ; and my house stands as far from the door of the theatre as from here to the post [about twenty-two feet]. I think it would allow that space for the two houses.

Q. Did you see where Spangler went after he called Maddox ?

A. No, sir : I did not see where Spangler went after he called Maddox.

Q. Did he go off ?

A. I do not remember whether he went off or not. I did not see him any more.

Q. Did you see him go in to call Maddox ?

A. Yes, sir : he turned from the door to call Maddox.

Q. Did you hear him call him ?

A. No, sir : I did not hear him call Maddox.

Q. Did you see Spangler come out again ?

A. I do not remember whether he came out or not : I do not think I did see him come out.

MRS. MARY JANE ANDERSON,

a witness called for the prosecution, being duly sworn, testified as follows : —

By the JUDGE ADVOCATE:

Q. Will you state where you live in this city?

A. I live between E and F and Ninth and Tenth Streets.

Q. Do you live near Ford's Theatre?

A. Yes, sir: right back of the theatre.

Q. Does your house adjoin that of Mrs. Turner, who has just testified?

A. Yes, sir: my house and hers are adjoining

Q. Did you know John Wilkes Booth?

A. Yes, sir: I knew him by sight.

Q. Did you see him on the afternoon or night of the 14th of April last?

A. Yes, sir: I saw him in the morning.

Q. State what you saw.

A. I saw him down there by the stable; and he went out of the alley, and I did not see him again until between two and three o'clock in the afternoon, when I saw him standing in the back theatre-door, in the alley that leads out back. He and a lady were standing together, talking. I stood in my gate, and I looked right wishful at him. He and this lady were pointing up and down the alley as if they were talking in their conversation about the alley, as it seemed to me; and they stood there a considerable while. After that, they both turned into the theatre together. I never saw any more until at night. I went up stairs pretty early; and, when I went up stairs, there was a carriage drove up the alley, and after that I heard a horse step down in the alley again. I looked out of the window; and it seemed as if the gentleman was leading this horse down the alley. He did not get any farther than the end of the alley, and in a few minutes he returned back again. I still looked out to see who it was. He came up to the theatre-door, this gentleman did, with the horse by the bridle. He pushed the door open, and said something in a low tone; and then in a loud voice he called, "Ned," four times. There was a colored man up at the window; and he said, "Mr. Ned, Mr. Booth calls you." That is the way I came to know it was Mr. Booth. It was dark, and I could not see his face. When Mr. Ned came, Booth said to him in a low tone, "Tell Maddox to come here." Then Mr. Ned went back, and

Maddox came out. They said something to each other; but I could not understand from my window what the words were. After that, Mr. Maddox took hold of this horse. It seems it was between him and Mr. Ned. He had this horse. He carried it from before my door, right at the corner of my house, around to where the work-bench was: that stood at the right side of the house. I could not see the horse; but they both returned back into the theatre again. This man that carried the horse up went in the door too. The horse stood out there a considerable while. It kept up a great deal of stamping on the stones; and I said, "I wonder what is the matter with that horse," it kept stamping so. After a while I saw this person have a hold of the horse, and he kept the horse walking backwards and forwards. I suppose the horse was there completely an hour and a half altogether: then I saw the door open; I did not see any person passing backwards and forwards; and, in about ten minutes after that, I saw this man [Booth] come out of the door with something in his hand glittering. I did not know what it was; but still I thought some person ran out of the theatre, and jumped on the horse. He had come out of the theatre-door so quick, that it seemed like as if he but touched that horse, and it was gone like a flash of lightning. I thought to myself "That horse must surely have run off with that gentleman." Presently I saw a rush out of that door, and heard the people saying, "Which way did he go?" and "Which way did he go?" and still I did not know what was the matter. I asked a gentleman what was the matter; and he said the President was shot. "Why!" said I: "who shot him?" Said he, "That man who went out on the horse: did you see him?" I said I saw him when he first came out. That was the last time I saw him to know him.

Q. Did you see the prisoner Spangler at that time?

A. Yes, sir. I saw Mr. Spangler after that. After that I came down stairs, and was at the door talking. I went up to the theatre-door; and I saw Mr. Spangler when he came out of the door. Some one said, "Did you see that man?" I said to Mr. Spangler, "Mr. Spangler, that gentleman called you." Said he, "No, he did not." Said I, "Yes, he did: he called you." He said, "No, he did not: he did not call me." I said, "He did call you;" and

I kept on saying so. With that he walked down towards the alley, and I did not see him any more until Sunday; but I did not say any thing to him at all then : I had no other conversation with him.

Cross-examined by Mr. EWING :

Q. Did you know Mr. Maddox ?

A. Yes, sir.

Q. What kind of a looking man is he ?

A. He has a kind of a reddish skin, and sometimes a kind of palish and light hair.

Q. How old a man is he ?

A. I suppose he is about twenty-five or twenty-six.

Q. Have you seen him often ?

A. Yes, sir : I have seen him very often. I live close by there. I used to work for him right smart. I used to wash some pieces for him, and used to go there to the door and bring them. I know him very well by sight.

Q. Was it he who held this horse during all the time it was in the alley there ?

A. No, sir : it did not seem like as if he held it all the time ; but he took hold of the horse, and it seemed as if he had him a little while, and he moved him out of my sight; and then I saw him return, and go into the theatre. This gentleman had on a light coat.

Q. Then who held the horse when he went in the theatre ?

A. I did not see, because it was carried around from my door; and I could not see it out of my window. It was carried around the house like, out of sight : but then, when it was in a commotion, it seemed as if there was a man had it, but I could not tell who he was.

Q. When the horse was moving up and down, it seemed as if a man had it ?

A. Yes : as if a man was keeping it in motion all the time.

Q. Marching it up and down to keep it from fretting and stamping ?

A. Yes, sir : it was making a great deal of noise, stamping its feet ; and it seemed as if a man was carrying it backward and forward all the time.

Q. Mr. Spangler just came to the door; and Booth said to him, "Tell Mr. Maddox to come out"?

A. Yes, sir.

Q. And then Spangler went in, did he?

A. Yes, sir: he went in; and then it seemed as if he came out again.

Q. Are you sure he came out again?

A. It seems to me like as if he came out again. Whether he came out or not, I am not certain; but I know he came to the door when Mr. Booth called.

Q. But you are not certain that he came out again?

A. No, sir: I am not certain whether he came out again or no; but I know he came out to the door when Booth called him, and he told him to tell Maddox to come out; and Maddox came out to this Mr. Booth, and had some conversation with him; but I could not hear what it was.

Q. How long was it from the time that Booth rode up there until the people said he had shot the President?

A. I suppose it was about an hour — not quite an hour — from the time he came up there to the time they said the President was shot. I think it was almost an hour; but I do not think it was quite an hour.

Q. Did you see the man who held the horse at the time Booth ran out and rode away on him?

A. Yes, sir: I saw the man, but I could not tell who the man was. I know a man had hold of the horse when Booth came out, because, when he came out, he was walking the horse up and down; and it seemed as if, the minute he touched the horse, the horse was gone. I was looking down the alley to see which way he went; and when I looked back again, I did not see anybody.

Q. Did that man look like Mr. Maddox?

A. He looked very much like Mr. Maddox to me. I know Mr. Maddox. He wears a light coat, and this man seemed as if he had a light coat on. It was pretty dark there that night: I could not see distinctly from my window; but the coat he had on seemed as if it was light.

Q. How far was he from you when you say you thought it was Mr. Maddox?

A. He was right near the door.

Q. How far from where you were?

A. About as far as from here to that window, or a little farther [about fifteen feet].

Q. Whereabouts was the horse just at the time when Booth ran out the door?

A. Standing right at the door.

Q. And this man with the light coat on was standing right by him?

A. I cannot say whether he was standing by him, because I was looking at the man when he rushed out the door so; and every thing was in such a twinkling of an eye, that I could not say distinctly that it was the man with the light coat on : but I know there was a man holding the horse all the time, as far as I could see.

Q. It was not Mr. Spangler that was holding him?

A. I do not know. It seems to me, it was between all three of them. They all three seemed to be out there with the horse apparently. I knew Mr. Ned came out to the door, and then Mr. Maddox came out, and then it seemed as if Mr. Ned came out again.

Q. But you are not certain that he did come out again?

A. No, sir : I am not very certain of that ; but I know there were three men in it altogether.

Q. That is, three men connected with it in some way?

A. Yes, sir : three men connected with it in some way.

Q. But you cannot say that you saw Mr. Spangler except when he came out of the door, and Booth told him to call Maddox?

A. No, sir : I cannot say for certain ; but I know one of the men had on a light coat.

Q. That was the one that was holding the horse?

A. Yes, sir.

WILLIAM A. BROWNING,

a witness called for the prosecution, being duly sworn, testified as follows : —

By the JUDGE ADVOCATE:

Q. Will you state if you are the private secretary of the President?

A. Yes, sir: I am.

Q. Were you with him on the 14th of April last?

A. I was.

Q. [Exhibiting a card to the witness.] What knowledge, if any, have you of that card having been sent to him by John Wilkes Booth?

A. Between the hours of four and five o'clock in the afternoon, I left Vice-President Johnson's room in the Capitol, and went to the Kirkwood House, where I was boarding with him. Upon entering, I went up to the office, as was my custom; and I saw a card in my box. Vice-President Johnson's box and mine were adjoining: mine was 67, his was 68. In 67 I noticed a card. The clerk of the hotel, Mr. Jones, handed it to me. This I recognize as the card.

Q. Will you read what is on it?

A. "Don't wish to disturb you. Are you at home? J. Wilkes Booth." It was in my box.

[The card was offered in evidence without objection.]

Q. You do not know any thing about the handwriting of Booth?

A. No, sir.

Q. You had no acquaintance whatever with J. Wilkes Booth, had you?

A. Yes, sir: I had known him when he was playing in Nashville, Tenn. I met him there several times. That was the only acquaintance that I had with him.

Q. Did you understand the card as sent to the President, or to yourself?

A. At the time, I attached no importance to it. I had known him in Nashville; and, seeing the card, I made the remark, when it was handed to me by the clerk, "It is from Booth: is he playing here?" I had some idea of going to see him. I thought, perhaps, he might have called upon me, having known me; but, when his name was connected with this affair, I looked upon it differently. It was a very common mistake in the office to put the cards intended for me in the Vice-President's box; and his would find their way into mine, they being together.

Cross-examined by Mr. Doster:

Q. Will you state, if you know, at what hour the Vice-President was in his room that day?

A. I cannot do so with accuracy. I really do not know at what hours he was there. He was at the Capitol, I think, for the greater part of the forenoon of that day, — that is my impression, — and was at dinner at five o'clock. I do not think he was out afterwards. I was out myself, and did not return till after this occurrence at the theatre.

Q. Do you know at what time he left his room in the morning?

A. I do not.

Q. You know he returned about five o'clock?

A. He was there at five o'clock; but I cannot state at what hour he returned. He was there at dinner; and we generally dined at about five o'clock.

Q. You say he was in his room for the balance of the evening?

A. Yes, sir: that is my impression.

Q. Were you in his room in the course of the evening?

A. I was there, I think, up to six or seven o'clock; and I was not there afterwards until about eleven o'clock. It was after the assassination that I returned. I was out that evening.

MAJOR KILBURN KNOX,

a witness called for the prosecution, being duly sworn, testified as follows: —

By the JUDGE ADVOCATE:

Q. Will you state whether or not, on the evening of the 13th of April last, you were at the house of the Secretary of War, in this city?

A. Yes, sir: I was.

Q. Do you see among the prisoners here any person whom you saw there on that occasion?

A. Yes, sir.

Q. Which one is it?

A. There he is [pointing to Michael O'Laughlin].

Q. Can you state under what circumstances you saw him, and at what hour, and what occurred?

A. I was at the house of the Secretary of War about half-past ten o'clock, I should judge. I had been on duty at the War Department, and left there at ten o'clock, after the illumination was over, and walked up to the Secretary's house. On the steps were General Grant, Mrs. Grant, the Secretary, General Barnes and his wife, Mr. Knapp and his wife, Miss Lucy Stanton, Mr. David Stanton, and two or three small children. There was a band there playing at the house. I was talking to Mrs. Grant and to the General. They were standing on the upper steps. They set off some fireworks in the square opposite; and I stepped down a little to allow the children to see them. I got down on the step, I think, next to the last one, leaning against the railing; and this man [O'Laughlin] came up to me, I suppose after I had been there ten minutes, probably, and he said, "Is Stanton in?" Said I, "I suppose you mean the Secretary?" He said, "Yes." I think he made the remark, "I am a lawyer in town: I know him very well." I was under the impression he was under the influence of liquor. I told him I did not think he could see him then; and he walked to the other side of the steps, and stood there probably five minutes. I still staid there, I suppose, for about five minutes; and he walked over to me again, and said, "Is Mr. Stanton in?" and then he said, "Excuse me: I thought you were the officer on duty here." Said I, "There is no officer on duty here." He then walked on to the other side of the steps, and walked inside of the hall, the alcove, and stood on the inside step. I saw him standing there; and I walked over to Mr. David Stanton, and said, "Do you know that man?" He said he did not. I said to him, "He says he knows the Secretary very well; but he is under the influence of liquor, and you had better bring him out." Mr. David Stanton walked up to him, talked to him a few moments, and then took him down the steps. He went off, and I did not notice him again.

Q. Did he say any thing about General Grant?

A. He did not. General Grant, I think, had gone into the

parlor at the time. I am not certain about that; but that is my impression.

Q. He was looking in to see the Secretary from his position, was he?

A. I think the Secretary stood on the steps outside, and this man stood behind the Secretary; and from where he stood he could see into the parlor. On the left-hand side of the hall, going in, is the library; on the other side is the parlor-door. He stood on the side next to the library; and, in that position, he could have looked into the parlor, and seen who was in there, through the door. The whole house was illuminated and lighted up.

Q. Do you feel perfectly certain, or not, that the prisoner O'Laughlin is the man you saw?

A. I feel perfectly certain.

Cross-examined by Mr. Cox:

Q. Was it moonlight or dark on that evening?

A. I cannot tell: I do not recollect.

Q. Was there a crowd there surrounding the Secretary's house at the time?

A. Yes, sir: quite a large crowd.

Q. Close up to the steps?

A. Yes, sir: all around.

Q. And he mingled with the crowd, or close to them?

A. I did not notice any thing at all about him until he walked up on the steps and spoke to me. I paid no attention to it whatever; and, after he went out again, I saw him no more.

Q. You did not go inside of the hall while he was there?

A. Not while he was there.

Q. I understand you to say that Secretary Stanton was on the upper step at that time?

A. I think so.

Q. Did he pass by him?

A. Yes, sir: he went to the right of them. I am certain that Secretary Stanton was on the upper side at the time, talking to Mrs. Grant.

Q. He walked by the Secretary, did he?

A. Secretary Stanton was on the left-hand side; and the man went up on the right-hand side, and went in, and took a place on the step on the left-hand side.

Q. How was he dressed?

A. He had on a black slouch hat, a black frock-coat, and a black pair of pants: as to his vest I cannot say.

Q. That was while the fireworks were going on, you stated?

A. Yes, sir: there were fireworks after that.

Q. Had you ever seen that man before?

A. I never had.

Q. Have you seen him since?

A. I have.

Q. When?

A. A week ago last Sunday.

Q. Here?

A. In this prison.

Q. You came here for the purpose of identifying him?

A. Yes, sir.

Q. Did you come in company with any one else?

A. Yes, sir.

Q. With Mr. Stanton?

A. No, sir.

Q. It was the hour of half-past ten, I think you said?

A. Yes, sir, it was half-past ten. I was on duty at the War Department that night; and, after the lights were put out, I walked up to the house. I suppose I had been there ten or fifteen minutes.

Q. You cannot remember whether it was a dark night or moonlight?

A. I cannot. It is my impression that it was a moonlight night; but I did not take any particular notice.

John C. Hatter,

a witness called for the prosecution, being duly sworn, testified as follows: —

By the JUDGE ADVOCATE:

Q. Will you state whether or not you know the prisoner O'Laughlin?

A. I know a man by that name.

Q. Do you recognize him here?

A. It is that man sitting back there [pointing to the prisoner O'Laughlin].

Q. Will you state whether you saw him on the 13th of April last? and if so, where, and under what circumstances?

A. I saw him on the night of the illumination — I suppose it was the night General Grant came from the front — at Secretary Stanton's house.

Q. What occurred there between you and him? What was said?

A. I was standing on the steps, looking at the illumination; and this man [O'Laughlin] approached me, and asked me if General Grant was in. I told him he was. He said he wished to see him. Said I, " This is no occasion for you to see him. If you wish to see him, step out on the pavement, or on the stone where the carriage stops, and you can see him."

Q. What time of night was it?

A. I should judge it was about nine o'clock: it may have been a little after nine.

Q. Was that all that occurred between you?

A. Yes, sir.

Q. He did not go in the house, or attempt to go in?

A. No, sir.

Q. Was he on the steps of Mr. Stanton's house?

A. Yes, sir: I was standing on the top step.

Q. Was he on the top step also?

A. Yes, sir: he was on the steps, I should judge about two steps below me; which brought him, I believe, about the third step from the pavement.

Q. Did he leave the steps while you were there?

A. He left the step after I spoke to him. He was talking; but I did not understand what he was saying. He walked off away from the step towards the tree-box. He seemed to reflect over something, and came back, and walked off; and then I turned my eyes off him, and did not see him any more.

Q. Was the house illuminated?

A. Yes, sir: the house was lit up from the inside; and it was pretty light outside too.

Cross-examined by Mr. Cox:

Q. What is your business.

A. I am employed at the War Department: I am a sergeant in the Adjutant-General's service.

Q. Were you on duty at Mr. Stanton's?

A. Yes, sir: I am on duty at the Secretary's room.

Q. Had you ever seen this man before that evening?

A. I do not think I had: not to my knowledge.

Q. When did you see him the next time?

A. I next saw him in prison; I think, in this building, or the one adjoining.

Q. How long ago?

A. That was last Sunday week.

Q. You came here to see if it was the same man?

A. When I first started to come down here, I did not know the object of my coming down.

Q. Who did you come with?

A. I was accompanied by Major Eckert and Major Knox. When I came down here, I did not know what I had to come down for. I inquired of Major Eckert if I had to come in the building, when in front of the house; and the major told me to come in. Then, when I was inside the building, I was told to stop a moment at the door. I was up, I should judge, about two steps in the second story; and even then I did not know what I came down for, until Major Eckert called me in: but, the moment I looked around the room and saw the man, I thought to myself, "I see the object of my coming down."

Q. Those are the only two occasions on which you recollect ever having seen him?

A. Those are the only times with the exception of this time.

Q. What made you think it was the same man? Was there any thing peculiar about his appearance?

A. The first time I saw him it was very light, and he had on a dark suit of clothes, with a heavy mustache, black, and an imperial;

and the way I took so much notice of him was, while I was speaking to him he was standing a little lower down, and I was looking right in his face at the time.

Q. What kind of a hat had he on?

A. A black hat.

Q. What kind?

A. A dark slouch hat, not very high, a little low, something like the one on the table there.

Q. How was he dressed?

A. In dark clothes.

Q. What sort of a coat had he on, — a dress-coat or a frock-coat?

A. A dress-coat.

Q. What was the color of his pantaloons?

A. They were dark: I could not say exactly whether they were black or dark-brown. They were dark, though.

Q. What size was he?

A. I should judge he was my size. While he was standing there, he might seem to be a little lower, because he was standing about two steps below me. I should judge him to be about five feet four or five inches.

Q. That you think was at nine o'clock?

A. I should think it was about nine o'clock: it might have been after.

Q. Had a crowd come to serenade the Secretary?

A. Yes, sir: there were four or five bands there at the time.

Q. Was the Secretary on the steps at the time?

A. No, sir: the Secretary was inside in the parlor with General Grant.

Q. They had not come out then?

A. No, sir: they had not been out then.

Q. There was nobody on the steps but you?

A. Nobody but myself.

Q. Was the crowd close up to the steps?

A. The crowd was pretty close; right up to the lower step.

Q. Was the front door open at the time?

A. Yes, sir; both doors were open: the front door was open,

and then there was another door like a front entry open too ; and the gas was full lit all around.

DR. ROBERT KING STONE,

a witness called for the prosecution, being duly sworn, testified as follows : —

By the JUDGE ADVOCATE :

Q. State to the Court if you are a practising physician in this city.

A. I am.

Q. Were you or not the physician of the late President of the United States ?

A. I was his family physician.

Q. State whether or not you were called to see him on the evening of his assassination, and the examination which you made, and the result.

A. I was sent for by Mrs. Lincoln immediately after the assassination. I arrived there in a very few moments, and found that the President had been removed from the theatre to the house of a gentleman living directly opposite the theatre ; had been carried into the back room of the residence, and was there placed upon a bed : found a number of gentlemen, citizens, around him ; and, among others, two assistant surgeons of the army, who had brought him over from the theatre, and had attended to him. They immediately gave over the case to my care, knowing my relations to the family. I proceeded then to examine him, and instantly found that the President had received a gun-shot wound in the back part of the left side of his head, into which I carried immediately my finger. I at once informed those around that the case was a hopeless one ; that the President would die ; that there was no positive limit to the duration of his life ; that his vital tenacity was very strong, and he would resist as long as any man could ; but that death certainly would soon close the scene. I remained with him, doing whatever was in my power, assisted by my friends, to aid him : but, of course, nothing could be done ; and he died the next morning at about half-past seven o'clock.   It was about a quarter-past ten that I reached him.

Q. He died from that wound?

A. Yes, sir.

Q. Did you extract the ball?

A. Yes, sir.   The next day, previous to the process of embalm-ment, with some medical friends, Dr. Curtis and Dr. Woodward of the army, and in the presence, also, of Surgeon-General Dr. Barnes, the examination was made.   We traced the wound through the brain; and the ball was found in the anterior part of the same side of the brain, the left side, — a large ball, resembling those balls which are shot from the pistol known as the Derringer, — an unusu-ally large ball; that is, a larger ball than those used in the ordi-nary pocket revolvers.

Q. Was it a leaden ball?

A. Yes, sir: a hand-made ball, from which the top on the little end had been cut by hand.   The ball was flattened somewhat, im-pressed in its passage through the skull; and a portion had been cut off in going through the bone.   I marked the ball with the initials of the late President, and sealed it in the presence of the Secretary of War in his office, — sealed it with my private seal, and indorsed it with my name.   The Secretary enclosed it in another envelope, which he indorsed in like manner, and sealed with his private seal.   It is still in his custody; and he ordered it to be placed among the archives of his department.

Q. Was the ball slightly flattened?

A. Yes, sir.

Q. Did you see the pistol?

A. No, sir: I did not.   I may state that I marked the ball with the initials of the President, "A. L.," so that I could recog-nize it instantly.

Q. [Exhibiting a ball to the witness.]   Look at that ball, and tell the Court whether it is the one which you extracted from the head of the President.

A. It is.   I recognize the mark I put upon it with my penknife, — "A. L.," — and the shape of the ball.   This is the fragment of which I spoke, which was cut off in its passage through the skull. The ball was flattened, as I described it to the Court.

[The ball was offered in evidence without objection.]

Q. You know nothing in regard to the pistol?

A. No, sir: I never saw it.

SERGEANT SILAS T. COBB,

a witness for the prosecution, being duly sworn, testified as follows: —

By the JUDGE ADVOCATE:

Q. Will you state whether or not, on the night of the assassination of the President, you were on duty at what is called, I believe, the Navy-Yard Bridge?

A. I was.

Q. Do you remember to have seen two men passing rapidly on horseback that night? and if you did so, at what hour was it?

A. There were three men approached me rapidly on horseback; and two of them passed.

Q. At what hour?

A. Between half-past ten and eleven o'clock in the evening.

Q. Did you challenge them?

A. The sentry challenged them; and I advanced then to recognize them.

Q. Did you recognize them?

A. I satisfied myself that two of them were proper persons to pass, and passed them.

Q. Do you recognize either of those persons among the prisoners here?

A. No, sir.

Q. Could you describe either of those men, or both of them?

A. Yes, sir: I could describe them.

Q. Do you think you would recognize them, or either of them, by a photograph?

A. I think I would.

[The photograph of J. Wilkes Booth, Exhibit No. 1, was shown to the witness.]

The WITNESS. That man passed first.

Q. Alone?

A. Yes, sir.

Q. I thought you said the three were together?

A. No, sir: I did not. I said that two of them passed me; but they were not together.

Q. Did you have any conversation with him as he passed?

A. I had, for some three or four minutes.

Q. What name did he give?

A. He gave me his name as Booth.

Q. What did he say? Any thing special beyond the desire to pass?

A. I asked him, "Who are you, sir?" He said, "My name is Booth." Then I asked him where from; and he made answer from the city. Said I, "Where are you going?" and said he, "I am going home." I asked him where his home was. He said it was in Charles. I understood, by that, that he meant Charles County. I asked him what town, and he said he did not live in any town. Said I, "You must live in some town." Said he, "I live close to Beantown; but I do not live in the town." I asked him why he was out so late; if he did not know the rules, that persons were not allowed to pass after nine o'clock. He said it was new to him; that he had somewhere to go, and it was a dark night, and he thought he would have the moon. The moon rose that night about that time. I thought he was a proper person to pass, and I passed him.

Q. How long after him was it that the other two men came?

A. The next one came, I should think, in from five to seven, or perhaps ten minutes at the outside, not later.

Q. Did they seem to be riding rapidly or leisurely?

A. The second one that came did not seem to be riding so rapidly, or his horse did not show signs of it so much, as the first one.

Q. What did he say to you?

A. I asked him who he was, and he said his name was Smith, and that he was going home; that he lived at White Plains. I asked him how it was that he was out so late. He made use of a rather indelicate expression, and said he had been in bad company.

Q. Was that a large or small man?

A. He was a small-sized man, not a large man.

Q. Did you have a good view of his face? Was there a light?

A. I did. I brought him up before the guard-house door, so that the light shone full in his face and on his horse.

Q. How would he compare in size with the last man on the row in the prisoner's dock? [David E. Herold, who stood up for identification.]

A. He is very near the size, but I should think taller, although I could not tell it on the horse; and he had a lighter complexion than that man.

Q. Did you allow him to pass after that explanation?

A. Yes, sir.

Q. What became of the other man?

A. The other man I turned back. He did not seem to have any business on the other side that I considered sufficient to pass him.

Q. Was he on horseback also?

A. Yes, sir.

Q. Did he seem to be the companion of these other men?

A. No, sir.

Q. Did they come up together?

A. No, sir: they were some distance apart.

Q. Did this man make any inquiry as to Booth?

A. He made inquiry after a roan horse, — not after Booth, — a man passing on a roan horse.

Q. Which man did? the small man that you describe, or the one that you turned back?

A. The one I turned back.

Q. Did the small man make any inquiry in regard to another horseman that had passed?

A. No, sir: none whatever.

Q. What was the color of the horse of the second one?

A. The second one was a roan horse.

Q. At what gait was he travelling?

A. I could not tell.

Q. Was he trotting?

A. No; he did not seem to be trotting: I should think a kind of half racking, or something like that. The horse did not move like a trotting horse.

Q. Did you notice the horse of Booth, his size and color?

A. Yes, sir.

Q. Can you describe the animal?

A. He was a small-sized horse; rather an undersized horse, I should think; a very bright bay, smooth, shiny skin; and looked as though he had just had a short burst, — a short push, — and seemed restive and uneasy, much more so than the rider.

Q. Was it a horse or a mare?

A. I could not tell: I did not take particular notice.

By the COURT:

Q. Did the rider have any spurs on?

A. I did not notice particularly about his spurs. I did not notice that he had spurs. I confined my attention more to his face and general appearance.

By the JUDGE ADVOCATE:

Q. Did you say that the first one had spurs on?

A. I do not know that he had: I could not swear to it.

By the COURT:

Q. I understood you to say that the second man that passed was on a light horse?

A. A roan horse.

Q. Was he not taken as a light-colored horse, nearly white? Did he not appear so?

A. No, sir: I think it was a roan.

Q. A light roan?

A. He was a light roan. He had some dark spots on him; but he was easily distinguished as a roan horse in the light.

Q. Was he a large-sized horse?

A. No, sir; about a medium-sized horse: he carried his head down; he did not carry his head up.

Q. Do you think he would be easily distinguished as a roan horse by moonlight?

A. Yes, sir.

Q. Was the moon up at this time?

A. I think it was not.

Q. What time did the moon rise that night?

A. I do not recollect the exact time, but somewhere between eleven and twelve o'clock, I think.

Q. The moon rose after the horsemen had gone forward?

A. Yes, sir: I think it did.

POLK GARDNER,

a witness called for the prosecution, being duly sworn, testified as follows: —

By the JUDGE ADVOCATE:

Q. Will you state whether you were on the road between Washington and Bryantown on the night of the 14th of April last, coming to Washington?

A. Yes, sir.

Q. Will you state if you met one or more horsemen, and at what hour, and under what circumstances?

A. I met two, about eleven o'clock, riding very fast.

Q. In what direction?

A. They were going towards Marlboro'. I met them at Good-Hope Hill. The first one was alone; and then there was one about half a mile behind him, I suppose.

Q. Both riding rapidly?

A. Very fast.

Q. Did they say any thing to you?

A. The first one stopped me, and asked me the road to Marlboro'. He first asked me if there was a horseman passed ahead; and then he asked me the road to Marlboro', if it did not turn to the right. I told him to keep the straight road.

Q. Was it light enough for you to see his horse and its color?

A. The first one was a dark horse; I think, a bay.

Q. What did the other one say?

A. The other one said nothing to me. I think I heard him ask whether there was a horseman passed; but there was a lot of teamsters passing at the time, and I did not know whether he asked me or them. I never answered him.

Q. How far was he behind the other?

A. About half a mile, I reckon : I suppose it was that.

Q. What was the appearance of his horse? Did you notice the color?

A. It was a roan horse; a light horse, a roan, or an iron-gray.

Q. Was the man a large or small one?

A. I never noticed the man particularly.

Cross-examined by Mr. Cox:

Q. How far from this city was it that you met them?

A. It was on Good-Hope Hill; I suppose, two and a half miles or three miles from the city; half-way up the hill.

Q. That was the one that inquired the way to Marlboro'?

A. Yes, sir.

Q. What did you say was the color of his horse?

A. It was a bay; a dark-bay, it seemed to be.

Q. How long was it before the other one came along?

A. I do not suppose it was over five or ten minutes: I do not know exactly.

Q. What did you say the second one inquired of you?

A. I do not know whether he inquired of me or the teamsters; but I heard him ask whether a horseman had passed ahead or not. I did not answer, though.

Q. The road forks at Good Hope,—one turning to the right, and the other to the left. Were you this side of the forks?

A. I think I was. I do not know where they fork. I am not acquainted with the road much. I have never travelled it but two or three times, and the first time was in the night.

Q. Was the foremost man riding at a rapid gait?

A. Yes, sir: he was riding very fast. Both of them were riding very fast.

Q. Was it on the top of the hill?

A. No, sir: it was about middle-way up, I suppose.

Q. Had you got down to the bottom when you met the other man?

A. Oh, yes, sir! I had got off the bill entirely.

Q. You could not give the first man the direction he asked for?

A. No, sir. He asked me the road to Marlboro'. He asked me if it did not turn to the right. I told him no; it kept a straight road.

WILLIAM T. KENT,

a witness called for the prosecution, being duly sworn, testified as follows: —

By the JUDGE ADVOCATE:

Q. [Exhibiting a pistol to the witness.] Will you state whether or not the pistol which you now have before you was picked up by you in the box of the President on the night of his assassination?

A. Yes, sir: this is the pistol.

Q. What is it, — a Derringer pistol?

A. A Derringer I believe is the name of it. I know that was the name of it, because it is marked on it.

[The pistol was offered in evidence without objection.]

Q. How long after the President was shot did you pick it up?

A. I do not know exactly how long. About three minutes after the President was shot, I went into the box. There were two other persons there then; and a surgeon, apparently, asked me for a knife to cut open the President's clothes. I handed him mine, and with it he cut the President's clothes open. I then went out of the theatre, and went down to call my room-mate; and I missed my night-key, and, thinking that I had dropped my night-key in pulling out my knife, I hurried back to the theatre; and when I went into the box, and was searching around for it on the floor, I knocked my foot against the pistol, and, stooping down, I picked it up. I held it up, and cried out, "I have found the pistol!" Some persons told me to give it to the police; but a gentleman, representing himself as the agent of the Associated Press, came to me, and told me he was the agent of the Associated Press; and I handed it to him, and gave him my name at the same time. The next morning, I went round to the police station, and I identified it there.

Q. You recognize the pistol as the same?

A. Yes, sir.

a witness called for the prosecution, being duly sworn, testified as follows : —

By the JUDGE ADVOCATE :

Q. Will you state whether or not, the day after the assassination of the President, you with others were engaged in the pursuit of the murderers ?

A. Yes, sir.

Q. What route did you take ?

A. The route by Surrattsville.

Q. Will you state whether or not, in pursuing the route, you came to the house of the prisoner Dr. Samuel Mudd ?

A. Yes, sir.

Q. Do you recognize him ?

A. Yes, sir.

Q. Did you stop there ?

A. Yes, sir.

Q. And make inquiries of him in regard to it ?

A. I made inquiries of his wife first, as he was out at the time.

Q. State all the inquiries which were addressed to him by yourself or other members of your party, and what he said.

A. We first asked whether there had been any strangers at his house, and he said there were. In the first place, he did not seem to care about giving any satisfaction ; and then he went on to state that on Saturday morning, at daybreak, two strangers had come to his place : one of them rapped at the door, and the other sat on a horse ; and he went down and opened the door, and went out with the young man, and helped the other off the horse into the house ; that one of them had a broken leg, and he went to work to set the leg. I asked him who the man was. He said he did not know. He said he was a stranger to him. I asked him what kind of looking man the other was. He said he was a young man about seventeen or eighteen.

Q. How long did he say they remained there ?

A. He said they remained there for a short time. This was the first conversation that I had with him.

Q. You say a short time. Do you mean, by that, that they went away in the course of the morning? What did he state as to that?

A. That is what I understood him.

Q. On what day was this?

A. This was on Tuesday, the 18th of April.

Q. Did he state to you whether, at the time of their visit, he heard any thing in regard to the assassination of the President? What did he say on that subject?

A. He said he had heard that the President was assassinated on Sunday, I think; that he had heard it at church.

Q. What distance is his house from Washington?

A. By the way of Bryantown, it would be about thirty miles, I suppose.

Q. Is it upon one of the highways of the country, an open road?

A. No, sir: it is off the road, I suppose, a quarter of a mile.

Q. A quarter of a mile from one of the principal roads and thoroughfares?

A. Yes, sir: the road runs from Bryantown.

Q. Did you have any considerable conversation with him in regard to the assassination of the President?

A. We did not talk much about that: I was making inquiries about these men more than any thing else.

Q. How long were you at his house?

A. Probably an hour.

Q. Did he continue to the last, until you left, to make the same representation, that those men were entire strangers to him?

A. Yes, sir.

Q. That he knew nothing of them?

A. He said he knew nothing of them: he said that one of them called for a razor; and he furnished him with a razor and some soap and water, and he shaved his mustache off there. I asked him if he had any other beard: he said yes; he had a long pair of whiskers.

Q. And that they both left there on that morning?

A. I understood that in that conversation.

Q. Did he state that they both left on horseback?

A. He said that one of them went on crutches, — he had a pair of crutches made for him.

Q. Did you understand him to say they were both mounted when they left his house?

A. I asked that question; and he said the injured man went off on crutches. He showed them the way across the swamp.

Q. Did he state what the injured man did with his horse?

A. No, sir: now I recollect, he said the other led the horse.

Q. And that the lame man went off on the crutches?

A. Yes, sir: he said he had had a pair of crutches made for him.

Q. Did he say that he showed him across or into the swamp?

A. He said he showed him across the swamp, so I understood. I was perfectly satisfied, then, that this party was Booth and Herold.

Q. Did you arrive at that conclusion from the description given of the men?

A. Yes, sir.

Q. Did he state to you for what purpose these men had gone into the swamp?

A. He said that they were going towards Allen's Fresh.

Q. Did he state for what purpose he supposed the lame man had shaved off his mustache?

A. No, sir. He said it looked suspicious. Some of the men that were along with me made a remark that it looked suspicious, and Mr. Mudd also said then that it did look suspicious.

Q. Will you state whether you had a subsequent interview with the prisoner Dr. Mudd?

A. I had.

Q. How long after the one of which you have spoken?

A. At the time of that first interview, I had my mind made up to arrest him when the proper time should come.

Q. When did the second interview occur?

A. I think, on Friday, the 21st of April. I went there for the purpose of arresting him.

Q. Will you state to the Court what he then said in regard to those two men?

A. When he found that we were going to search the house, he said something to his wife; and she brought down a boot, and handed me the boot.

Q. What did he say in regard to the boot?

A. He said he had to cut it off the man's leg in order to set the leg. I turned down the top of the boot, and saw some writing on the inside, — saw the name "J. Wilkes" written in it. I called his attention to it; and he said he had not taken notice of that before.

Q. [Exhibiting a boot.] Is that the boot?

A. It is.

[The boot was offered in evidence without objection.]

Q. Did he at that time still insist that they were strangers to him? or did he profess now to know either of them?

A. No, sir: not at that time. He still said they were strangers.

Q. Did he at any subsequent time admit to you that he knew Booth?

A. Yes, sir: he subsequently said he was satisfied that it was Booth.

Q. Did he state why he was so satisfied?

A. No, sir.

Q. When was that?

A. That was on Friday, the same day. I made the remark to him that his wife said she had not seen their whiskers back disconnected from the face. I suppose he was satisfied then.

Q. I understood you that he said quite distinctly, and insisted on it, that he had not known this man Booth before?

A. Yes, sir.

Q. Did he or not, in any subsequent conversation in regard to this man Booth, admit that he knew him?

A. After I left, we got our horses; and, going on the main road, I told one of the men to show him Booth's photograph. The man held it up to him; and he said that it did not look like Booth.

Q. [Exhibiting to the witness Booth's photograph, Exhibit No. 1.] Is that the same kind of photograph you exhibited?

A. The same. The photograph we showed may have had Booth's name written or printed on it.

Q. Did Dr. Mudd say it was not like him, or was like him?

A. He said it looked a little like him across the eyes. Shortly after that, he said he had had an introduction to Booth last fall, in November or December. He said a man named Johnson had given him the introduction.

Q. Where?

A. At church, I think he said.

Q. He did not state that he had ever met Booth in this city?

A. No, sir. On being questioned by one of the other men, he stated that he was along with Booth in the country, looking up some land; and that he was along with him when he bought a horse of Squire Gardner.

Q. Did he state the time?

A. Last fall, I think he said.

Q. Did he make any remark about the character of the horse, or his description?

A. He said he had bought a good riding-horse or farm-horse. I have inquired of Dr. Graham since about the horse.

Cross-examined by Mr. EWING:

Q. You say that Dr. Mudd gave you a description of those two persons?

A. Yes, sir: he said one was quite a young man.

Q. What further did he say?

A. He said the other one had whiskers on, — large chin-whiskers.

Q. What did he say about the resemblance between the photograph and this other one? Did he not say the upper part of the face resembled the photograph?

A. He said, in the first place, it did not look like Booth; and then he said it looked like him across the eyes.

Q. Did you tell him about your tracking Booth from Washington?

A. I do not think, that, up to that time, I had mentioned Booth's name at all. It was not my business to tell him who I was after.

Q. The second time you went, Dr. Mudd was where?

A. He was out to some place: his wife sent after him.

Q. Did you not meet him before he got to his house?

A. I walked down and met him.

Q. Did you not say to him that you wanted the razor that the man shaved with that was at his house?

A. Yes, sir: we demanded that after we went into the house.

Q. Did not Dr. Mudd tell you, that, since you had been there before, the boot had been found?

A. Not until we were in there a few minutes.

Q. But he volunteered the statement, that the boot had been found since you were there before?

A. Yes, sir : he said something to his wife ; and she went up and brought it down.

Q. But did he not say, that, since you were there before, the boot had been found?

A. He said that after one of the men told him that we would have to search the house : one of the special officers said that.

Q. Are you sure he did not state what I have asked you until after that was said?

A. Yes, sir.

Q. He said he had shown these men the way across the swamp?

A. So I understood.

Q. To what swamp was he alluding?

A. The swamp in the rear of his house, I believe.

Q. Is there a swamp immediately in the rear of his house?

A. It is down, I suppose, about a thousand yards below the house.

Q. State, if you please, what else he said in describing those persons.

A. I asked him if that might not have been a false whisker? He said he did not know. The reason I asked him was, his wife had said that the whisker became detached when he got down to the foot of the stairs. It seemed Booth had been up stairs. The doctor never told me he had Booth up stairs.

Q. He did not say where he had been?

A. He told me he was on the sofa and lounge.

Q. And when you asked the doctor how long these two men had staid, he said they did not stay long?

A. He said the first time I spoke to him, at the first interview I had with him, that they staid but a short time. Afterwards his wife told me they had staid until about three or four o'clock on Saturday afternoon.

Q. You need not state what his wife said.

A. I think he told me that himself afterwards.

Q. Did you ask Dr. Mudd whether he charged any thing for setting the leg?

A. Yes, sir.

Q. What did he say?

A. I did not ask him if he had charged any thing. I asked him if the men had much money about them. He said they had considerable greenbacks. I then asked him if they had arms about them. He said, "This injured man"— he did not say Booth — "had a pair of revolvers."

Q. Did he say any thing about being paid for setting the leg?

A. I did not ask him that. I did not ask him what he charged, nor any thing else; but he went on to say it was customary for men to make a charge to strangers.

Q. He spoke in that connection of the fact of their having money?

A. Yes, sir: after I asked him if they had much money about.

Q. Did he not say that these men arrived at his house before daylight?

A. About daybreak.

Q. Who went with you to his house the second time you went?

A. There were three special officers, besides some cavalry.

Q. What special officers were those?

A. There were Simon Callaghan, Joshua Lloyd, and William Williams.

Q. What citizen went with you the first time?

A. It was a Dr. George Mudd, the first time.

Q. Was he present when you conversed with this Dr. Mudd?

A. He was present part of the time.

Q. When you were there the second time, do you not recollect that he told you that they went to the Rev. Mr. Wilmer's; that they started to his house?

A. Yes, sir; but I paid no attention to that. I thought it was a blind to throw us off our track.

Q. But he said it?

A. Yes, sir He said they went to Parson Wilmer's, or inquired after Parson Wilmer's, and were on their way to Allen's Fresh.

Q. Did he mention that the second time?

A. I do not think I asked him both times.

Q. You only asked him the first time?

A. The first time, I believe.

Q. Are you sure that it was not out of doors that you asked Dr. Mudd first for the razor?

A. I might have spoken to him out of doors; but I demanded it in the house.

Q. Are you sure it was not before he got to the house that he told you, that, since you were there before, a boot had been found up stairs?

A. Yes, sir: he told me that in the house, — not outside.

Q. He did not tell you there?

A. No, sir.

Q. Was there not a citizen with him at that time, — Mr. Hardy?

A. No, sir: no citizen that I know of.

Q. Was there not one with him?

A. There was a citizen stood in the door after he went in the house; went in the front room: I did not pay any attention much to the citizen.

Q. You do not know who that was?

A. No, sir.

Q. Did Dr. Mudd come to the house alone? Was he alone when you met him first as he was coming to the house?

A. There was a citizen walking with him, I think.

Q. Was it this man you spoke of who subsequently stood up by the door?

A. Yes.

Cross-examined by Mr. STONE:

Q. When you went to Dr. Mudd the first time, did you have any conversation before you went into the house?

A. No, sir: I think not. I had a conversation with his wife.

Q. As soon as you asked if two strangers had been there, he told you they had?

A. Yes, sir: he was made aware, I suppose, of what we were after, by a friend of his.

Q. What friend?

A. Dr. Mudd. They compelled him to go from Bryantown along with us.

Q. When you asked him the question, he told you at once that there had been two strangers there?

A. Yes, sir: he seemed very much excited, and got as pale as a sheet of paper when he was asked about it, but admitted it, — that there had been two strangers there.

Q. Then you asked him to describe them, and he did give you the description?

A. Yes, sir: he gave the description.

Q. Was Dr. Mudd present then, sir?

A. He was present part of the time?

Q. Between the time, though, of your asking him if two strangers had been there, and his reply to you, he had not left your presence at all, had he?

A. No, sir: he had spoken to the other doctor previous to that, though.

Q. Who did he say introduced Booth to him at church last fall?

A. A man named Johnson, I think.

Q. He told you he was introduced to Booth at church by this man Johnson?

A. Yes, sir. He did not tell me that in the first place. He didn't know Booth at all.

Q. This was in the interview on Friday?

A. Yes, sir.

Q. Did you ask him at the first interview, on Tuesday, whether he knew Booth or not?

A. No, sir: I did not mention Booth to him on Tuesday.

Q. But when, on the second interview, you mentioned Booth, he told you he had been introduced to Booth last fall?

A. He did not mention it until we were on horseback. I do not think he mentioned it until I had arrested him. I had mentioned Booth's name to the other doctor, though.

Q. You say that the doctor seemed to be very much excited and alarmed?

A. He seemed to turn very pale, and blue about the lips, like a man that is frightened at something.

Q. Like what?

A. Like a man that might be frightened at something he had done. I do not mean to say that he was afraid of us.

Q. I suppose all you can say is, that he looked frightened and alarmed. Did he mention, in connection with his acquaintance with Booth, or the introduction he received to Booth last fall, a man by the name of Thompson?

A. Not that I am aware. Perhaps it might have been Thompson, and not Johnson, that gave him the introduction. I might have been that much mistaken in the name. I understood it to be Johnson: it might have been Thompson.

By the JUDGE ADVOCATE:

Q. You state that Dr. Mudd appeared very much frightened. Had you or not addressed any threat to him of any kind?

A. No, sir. I was in citizen's clothes at the time. I addressed no threat to him.

Q. The alarm, then, was not in consequence of any thing you said or did to him?

A. No, sir. He seemed very anxious also. I got the boot out. Some of the other men said the name of Booth was scratched out; and I insisted upon it the name of Booth had never been written.

By ASSISTANT JUDGE ADVOCATE BINGHAM:

Q. Who insisted that the name of Booth had never been written?

A. I merely suggested that it had never been written there.

By the JUDGE ADVOCATE:

Q. Who were with you in the pursuit on that occasion?

A. Three special officers — Simon Callaghan, Joshua Lloyd, and William Williams — and some cavalry.

Q. You say Dr. Mudd stated, when you asked if the men were armed, that one of them, the man with a broken leg, had a brace of revolvers?

A. Yes, sir.

Q. Did he say any thing about the other having a carbine?

A. No, sir.

Q. Did he say any thing about either of them having a knife?

A. No, sir.

Q. Did you understand him to say that this brace of revolvers were the only weapons they had? — the party?

A. The injured man had a pair of revolvers. I had more conversation with other parties in this house than I had with him (Dr. Mudd), because he seemed reserved. He did not seem to care much about giving me information.

Q. State what his manner was. Was it frank or evasive?

A. Very evasive. He seemed reserved in every thing.

Q. Did he not speak of these men having any other weapons than the brace of pistols of which you have spoken?

A. Not to me: because, when he answered that question, I turned around, and spoke to his wife; and one of the others, one of the special officers, spoke to him about the other [weapons].

Q. Which of the special officers?

A. I think it was William Williams, if I am not mistaken.

Q. Did I understand you to say that Dr. Mudd stated that he did not hear the news of the assassination of the President until Sunday, at church?

A. It was on Sunday morning, at church, as I understood him.

Q. At the time he spoke of having heard of the assassination of the President on Sunday, did he mention the name of the assassin?

A. No, sir.

By Mr. Ewing:

Q. Did not Dr. Mudd say that he only heard the circumstances of the assassination on Sunday?

A. I understood him to say that he only heard it on Sunday morning.

Q. Who was present when he said that?

A. I think these other officers were present.

Q. At what interview was that?—the last one, or the first one?

A. That was the first one, on Tuesday.

Q. Did he not speak about his having been at church, and heard the details of the assassination on Sunday morning?

A. I do not recollect that he did. There was very little talk about the details. We held very little conversation about the matter of the President; in fact, I was thinking about what I was attending to at the time.

Q. You did not very closely attend to what he did say in regard to that?

A. Not in regard to that. I know I made the remark at the time to one of the officers, that he must have known it, because the cavalry was close to his house on Saturday; and everybody in that neighborhood knew it on Saturday.

Q. Are you certain that Dr. Mudd said any thing himself about those men going in the direction of Allen's Fresh?

A. Yes, sir: I am positive of that.

Q. Did he mention it in connection with their going to the Rev. Mr. Wilmer's?

A. He said they inquired for Mr. Wilmer's, and he took them to the swamp; and they were going across the swamp towards Mr. Wilmer's.

Q. They inquired for Wilmer's?

A. Yes, sir. I went to Mr. Wilmer's, and searched his house, —a thing I did not like to do. I was satisfied before I searched it that there was nothing there, because I knew the man by reputation. I was satisfied it was only a blind to throw us that way.

Q. Do you know whether, in going from Dr. Mudd's to Mr. Wilmer's by the shortest route, you would or would not cross the swamp?

A. Yes, sir: you can get that way across the swamp, because I went through it half a dozen times after that. It is not a very nice job, though.

23*

Q. Did you follow the track of these men, — Booth and this man who was with him?

A. I tracked them as far as I could.

Q. Did you track them into the swamp and across it?

A. We went into the swamp, and scoured the swamp all over and across it.

Q. Did you find the tracks on the other side?

A. We found some tracks, — not any track that would lead us to think it was this party.

By the COURT:

Q. When you reached Mudd's house on Tuesday morning after the assassination, was it generally understood there that Booth was the man who assassinated the President?

A. Every person understood so around Bryantown, and along the way; even the darkies knew it.

Q. That was the common understanding along there, — that Booth was the man?

A. Yes, sir: I was told by the darkies afterwards that they heard a gentleman say it was Booth was there, and that he had his leg broken.

Q. Is there a telegraph down in that region of country?

A. The only telegraph there that I know is the one that runs to Point Lookout. I do not know the exact distance to that place.

Q. You do not know the telegraph-office nearest to that place?

A. No, sir. There was one established to Port Tobacco, went all the way down through. That is in connection with Port Tobacco. But if any person had seen these men, and wanted to give information, he had not far to go: they could have gone out to the road, and seen the cavalry all along the road.

Q. What is the distance from Washington to Surrattsville?

A. About ten miles, I should judge.

Q. What is the distance from Surrattsville to Dr. Mudd's?

A. The way we first went, it is about twenty miles. It is about sixteen miles to Bryantown, and about four or four and a half miles from Bryantown to Dr. Mudd's. But, going back the second time, I went across the country.

Q. In going to Dr. Mudd's, did you go through Surrattsville?

A. Yes, sir : there is a road runs from Port Tobacco. You can go to it in that way, — two or three different roads.

Q. It is about twenty miles, then, beyond Surrattsville to Dr. Mudd's?

A. Yes, sir; that is, by way of Bryantown. I did not inquire the distances. I just found where the places were, and pitched ahead.

Mr. Aiken. I would ask permission of the Court to ask the witness a few questions, but not in reference to any thing asked in the examination in chief. I do this simply to economize the time of the Court, and save calling him again.

The Court having granted the permission requested, —

By Mr. Aiken:

Q. Are you acquainted with Mr. Lloyd, who keeps a hotel at Surrattsville?

A. I arrested him on the 18th of April. That was the first acquaintance I had with him.

Q. Did he make any statement to you at that time?

A. No, sir : not at that time.

Q. Did he subsequently?

A. Yes, sir.

Q. At what time did you arrest him?

A. On Tuesday, the 18th.

Q. Where did you take him?

A. I sent him back under a guard of cavalry to Roby's Post Office, where I had established a prison or guard-house.

Q. Was there an examination made of Mr. Lloyd at that time?

A. No, sir.

Q. Were you present at any subsequent period when an examination was made?

A. Yes, sir.

Q. Did Mr. Lloyd make any statement, in that examination, of his connection with the affair?

The JUDGE ADVOCATE objected to the question. To lay a proper foundation for such a question, which is evidently designed to impeach or contradict the witness Lloyd, that witness must first be interrogated as to the time, the place, and the words used. No such questions had been put to Lloyd; and this question was therefore incompetent.

MR. AIKEN responded, that while there was no foundation for impeachment, yet, as the witness Lloyd had testified to having made remarks to Lieutenant Lovett and others on the occasion referred to, those remarks were part of a transaction that occurred there; and this witness was asked for his knowledge of that part of what occurred, but without any reference to what Mr. Lloyd has said.

ASSISTANT JUDGE ADVOCATE BINGHAM. The declarations of Lloyd are inadmissible for any purpose whatever at the instance of anybody, save for impeachment; and they cannot be introduced to impeach, except under the rule stated by the Judge Advocate General; to wit, he must first be asked if he said what is proposed to be proved, what he said, and where and why he said it. There is no such foundation laid here.

MR. AIKEN waived the question.

By MR. EWING:

Q. From whom did you first hear that there were two men who staid at Dr. Mudd's house?

A. I heard it from a soldier.

Q. Do you know his name?

A. Yes, sir: Lieutenant Dana.

Q. Did Dr. Mudd say any thing to you about it?

A. When I sent for him, he did.

Q. Then you heard it from Dr. George Mudd?

A. I took him up into a room in the hotel, and asked him to make a statement of what he heard. He stated that two — a party — had been at Dr. Samuel Mudd's.

JOSHUA LLOYD,

a witness called for the prosecution, being duly sworn, testified as follows : —

By the JUDGE ADVOCATE :

Q. Will you state whether or not, some days after the assassination of the President, you engaged with others in pursuing the murderer ?

A. Yes, sir.

Q. What direction did you take ?

A. The direction to Surrattsville.

Q. Did you or not, in the course of your pursuit, go to the house of the prisoner, Dr. Samuel Mudd ?

A. Yes, sir.

Q. On what day did you get there ?

A. On Tuesday, the 18th.

Q. State what reply he made to your inquiry in regard to the matter.

A. We asked him did he know these parties. He denied it : he denied ever having seen them.

Q. What was your inquiry of him ?

A. I asked if he did not hear of the President being assassinated. He said, " Yes." I asked him if he ever saw any of the parties, — Mr. Booth, Mr. Herold, and Mr. Surratt. He said he never had seen them.

Q. Did you ask him if parties had passed at a given time ?

A. Yes, sir.

Q. What time did you name ?

A. I asked if a party passed there on Saturday, about four o'clock in the morning.

Q. State what he said.

A He said at first there had not; and then owned it, — that there was a man came there with a leg broken. At the first interview, he denied every thing.

Q. Denied having seen anybody?

A. Yes, sir.

Q. When did you have the second interview with him ?

A. On Friday, the day he was arrested, — the 21st.

Q. What did he say?

A. He owned up that two men had passed there : he set the limb of one man. We showed him the likenesses. He said he had seen them before. Then I asked him if he was introduced to Mr. Booth last fall. He said he was. I had very little conversation with him after that.

Q. How long did he represent that these men remained at his house?

A. I think he said they remained there from about four o'clock in the morning until about four o'clock in the afternoon.

Q. Did he say they were on horseback, or on foot?

A. On horseback.

Q. How did he say they left the house?

A. He said one was riding; and the other was walking, leading his horse.

Q. You had the photograph of Booth with you?

A. Yes: Lieutenant Lovett had.

Q. [The photograph, Exhibit No. 1, is submitted to the witness.] Look at that, and see if that is the one exhibited to him then, — to Dr. Mudd.

A. Yes, sir.

Q. Will you describe the doctor's manner?

A. He appeared to be very much excited when we went there the last time. He was not in. In fact. his lady sent for him. She appeared to be very much worried, and likewise he did. We had the boot when he came back.

Q. What did you say to him on your second visit?

A. I had very little conversation with him at all that time. I was not well, and was sitting in the room. Lieutenant Lovett and Mr. Williams did most of the talking to him at the time.

Q. Did he make the statement to you, or all of you?

A. To all of us. We were sitting in his parlor. He appeared to be very much excited.

Q. Did he make any reference to his previous denial of having ever seen these men?

A. No, sir: I do not know that he did. The first time he denied ever having seen them.

Q. On the second occasion, did he profess to have any knowledge of Booth other than the introduction last fall?

A. After the boot was presented to him by his lady, he said he had been in company with him; that he had been introduced to him by a man named Thompson. Colonel Wells sent me that night to arrest him.

Q. Where did he say he was introduced?

A. I think he said at church.

Q. Did he speak of having been in company with him in Washington City?

A. No, sir.

Q. He did not speak of having any acquaintance with the man who accompanied Booth?

A. No, sir.

Q. Did he describe him to you?

A. No, sir.

Q. He offered no explanation, I understood you, of his previous denial?

A. No, sir. I asked a very few questions the second time we went there. I was not well, and I asked him very few questions.

Q. Did he state to you what direction they took when they left there?

A. He said they went up the hill towards Parson Wilmer's.

Q. Did he speak of having conducted them any part of the way?

A. I think he said he showed them the road; which road, I shall not be certain.

Cross-examined by MR. STONE:

Q. What time on Tuesday were you there, — Tuesday morning, or Tuesday evening?

A. It was late on Tuesday evening.

Q. That was the first time you saw him?

A. Yes, sir.

Q. Did you ride to the house in company with Lieutenant Lovett?

A. Yes, sir.

Q. Was the doctor in the house when you got there?

A. No, sir. He was not at home either time. He was out. It was not very far; for he was not very long coming.

Q. Do you know where he was?

A. No, sir.

Q. Was he sent for?

A. Yes, sir.

Q. He returned with the messenger?

A. Yes, sir.

Q. Did you ask him, as soon as he returned, if two men had been there?

A. No, sir: Lieutenant Lovett asked him these questions. He said they had, after we had the boot. The first time, he did not.

Q. I am asking entirely about the Tuesday interview.

A. He denied every thing.

Q. Did you ask him any questions at all yourself on Tuesday?

A. Yes, sir.

Q. What did you ask him?

A. I asked him about these parties coming that way. He said he had not seen them, and knew nothing of them.

Q. When you say "These parties," do you mean that you asked him if Booth and Herold had passed that way?

A. Yes, sir: any strangers. I described them to him, and the horses.

Q. Did you ask him if Booth or Herold or any strangers had passed?

A. I asked him, first, if any strangers had; and then if Booth and Herold had. He said he did not know them at all.

Q. He denied that either strangers or Booth and Herold had passed?

A. Yes, sir.

Q. That was Tuesday evening?

A. Yes, sir.

Q. How long did that interview last?

A. A very few minutes.

Q. Did you remain there as long as Lieutenant Lovett did?

A. Yes, sir.

Q. The boot had not been produced then?

A. No, sir.

Q. Did he tell you on that occasion of his setting the man's leg?

A. No, sir: not the first time.

Q. Nothing was said about his having a crutch made for him?

A. No, sir, not at the first interview: in fact, I did not hear the conversation about the crutch at any time.

Q. Did you and Lieutenant Lovett leave the house together?

A. Yes, sir: we went there together and left together.

Q. All the conversation with Dr. Mudd was in your presence?

A. Yes, sir; but I was at one time searching the stable during the conversation,—looking through the stables and out-houses.

Q. That was the first interview on Tuesday?

A. Yes, sir.

Q. You say the doctor seemed to be a good deal excited?

A. No, sir: he did not the first time.

Q. What time of day on Friday did you go there?

A. It was about between one and two o'clock. It was somewhere about noon. None of us had a watch with us; and I could not tell exactly the time.

Q. It was on that day that he told you he had been introduced to Booth by Thompson last fall?

A. No, sir: not that time.

Q. Did he say to you he had seen him at any other time?

A. No, sir: he said he was introduced to him last fall. He was there to buy some property. It was something about some property.

Q. He said he came there to buy some property?

A. I think he said so, if I am not mistaken.

Q. He did not say whether he had seen him between last fall and the time you were there or not?

A. No, sir.

Q. He did not say to you that he went across the swamp with them, but only showed them the direction?

A. ˙No, sir: he did not say he went across the swamp with them at all; he only showed them the road.

Q. They did go across the swamp?

A. That is more than I can say.

Q. Did you examine any tracks?

A. No, sir: not by his house. I saw some tracks up across the swamp. I do not know whose tracks they were. I could not say.

Q. What did he say, when asked if he had heard that the President had been assassinated, on Tuesday when you saw him?

A. He said he had heard it on Sunday at church. He was like pretty much all the rest of the people. He appeared to be sorry, I thought, from the way the gentleman spoke. It did not appear that he was glad of it, or any thing of the kind.

Q. Was the question asked him directly on Tuesday, at the first interview, whether he knew Booth?

A. Yes, sir.

Q. By whom was it asked?

A. I do not remember which one of the party it was. Four of us were in company; and I disremember which it was.

Q. Was that question asked by yourself?

A. Yes, sir: I asked him once, and he denied it; and some of the rest asked him.

Q. Was Dr. George Mudd there then?

A. Yes, sir.

Q. He was present at this interview?

A. Yes, sir.

Q. How many of you were in the room at this time?

A. I think, four or five; I am not certain which. He came in with the other Mr. Mudd, and he had some conversation out of doors before we spoke to him. But this conversation took place in the presence of four officers and Dr. George Mudd and Dr. Samuel Mudd.

Q. Name the officers.

A. Lieutenant Lovett, Mr. Callaghan, Mr. Williams, and myself.

Q. You say the question was repeated by another officer present?

A. Yes, sir: I think I asked him, I think every one asked him, the same question.

Q. If he knew Booth?

A. Yes, sir.

Q. And he denied knowing him?

A. He denied it.

Q. Who was present on Friday when he was asked the question?

A. The same party.

Q. You say on Friday he did admit it?

A. Yes, sir; after he saw we had the boot. Before he came into the house, his lady brought us the boot.

Q. You say he was away from home both times when you went there?

A. Yes, sir.

Q. Was the boot brought down by Mrs. Mudd before he returned home?

A. I think it was, sir.

Q. So that you had the boot there when he arrived?

A. Yes, sir.

Q. Do you recollect on that occasion who it was that asked him whether he knew Booth or not?

A. I cannot answer that question.

Q. Did you ask him on that day?

A. Yes, sir. He said he did not know him. I showed him the likeness Mr. Callaghan had in his pocket; and he said he had seen it before.

Q. Did he say that the likeness had been shown him on the Tuesday before?

A. I do not think he did. I know it was shown to him.

Q. You are positive in your recollection that he denied on Tuesday that there had been two strangers at his house at all?

A. Yes, sir.

Q. You are equally positive that Dr. Mudd, the prisoner, told you on Friday the likeness of Booth had been shown to him before?

A. I cannot say that.

Q. Did Dr. Mudd tell you that it had been shown to him before?

A. No, sir.

Q. Do you know whether he was shown the likeness on Tuesday or not?

A. Yes, sir: he was shown the likeness on Tuesday.

Q. By whom?

A. I could not say. I think it was Mr. Callaghan or Mr. Williams: I am certain it was one of them.

Q. It was some one of the party?

A. Yes, sir.

Q. When you showed it to him on Friday, he said he had been shown it before?

A. This was on Friday that I spoke of.

Q. Did you accompany Lieutenant Lovett from Washington on the search for Booth?

A. No, sir.

Q. Where did you join them?

A. At Surrattsville, what they call Roby's Post Office now, sir.

Q. Are you any connection of Mr. Lloyd that lives there?

A. No, sir : no relation to him at all.

Q. On which day did Dr. Mudd seem to be most excited, — Tuesday or Friday?

A. Friday, sir.

Q. He did, though, seem to be excited and alarmed on Tuesday; did he not?

A. I do not think he was much alarmed on Tuesday, sir. He did not appear to be much excited.

Q. Was he under arrest while this conversation took place? Had he been actually arrested on Friday?

A. Yes, sir : he was arrested directly that he came to the house.

Q. Who made the arrest?

A. I do not know that any one in particular made it, — Lieutenant Lovett, I suppose : he being a commisioned officer, we submitted to him.

Q. You are sure that the arrest was made before this conversation was held on Friday?

A. I cannot say as it was made before the conversation ; because, directly that we got hold of the boot, we made up our minds to arrest him.

Q. But the actual arrest of him was after the conversation?

A. Not exactly after the conversation. We had some conversation before he was arrested, no doubt.

Q. Can you speak positively on that point, — whether he was notified that he was arrested before or afterwards?

A. I cannot speak positively of the lieutenant. I cannot say what Lieutenant Lovett said; for I was out of the house part of the time, searching out-houses.

Q. Were you present when any one arrested him, and notified him that he was under arrest?

A. I cannot say which one it was; but I think it was Lieutenant Lovett.

Q. Were you present?

A. I think I was. I was sitting on the steps, I think, at that time.

Q. Do you remember what the terms of the arrest were; whether he was ordered to report to Bryantown or not?

A. I cannot state exactly what.

Q. Was he placed under guard?

A. No, sir: we did not place him under any guard. He rode in between two detective officers, sometimes between me and another, and sometimes between the others.

Q. Was any thing said about the razor on that Friday?

A. He brought the razor down himself, sir, and gave it to Lieutenant Lovett: that is all I can say about the razor. I cannot say that I would know it if I saw it now. I paid no attention to it.

By the COURT:

Q. Did you hear any thing said by the doctor about how Booth's leg was broken?

A. No, sir. I think he said, if I am not mistaken, it was by the fall of a horse; that a horse fell upon him. I had very little conversation with him at all.

By the JUDGE ADVOCATE:

Q. I understand you to say that he stated that he had crutches made for him?

A. I do not think I heard any conversation about that.

COLONEL H. H. WELLS,

a witness called for the prosecution, being duly sworn, testified as follows: —

By the JUDGE ADVOCATE:

Q. State to the Court whether or not, some time during the week

24*

subsequent to the assassination of the President, you had an interview with the prisoner Dr. Mudd.

A. Yes, sir: I had an interview with him, I think, on the 21st of April; which was Friday.

Q. State what he then said in regard to the men who called at his house on the Saturday morning after the assassination.

A. I had three definite conversations with him.

Q. State them, if you please.

A. The first conversation, I think, occurred about noon, or a little after noon, on Friday. I sent and had the doctor brought to my headquarters, and took his statement. It was taken in writing. He said to me —

Mr. EWING objected to any oral statement of what Dr. Mudd said, if the writing could be produced.

The JUDGE ADVOCATE exhibited to the witness a written paper, and asked, —

Q. Look at that paper, and see if it contains the statement which he then made.

A. This is a copy of one of the statements he made.

Q. Which one?

A. My impression is that this is the statement made at the second interview.

Q. Have you a copy of the first statement?

A. No, sir. I should state, that, in the first interview, the statement he made was not put in writing: but I think the second one was put in writing; and the third one, I think, was not put in writing.

Q. Now state what he said on the first occasion, which was not reduced to writing.

A. He commenced by remarking, that on Saturday morning, about four o'clock, he was aroused by a loud knock at his door: he was surprised at the loudness of the knock, and inquired who could be there. Receiving some answer, he looked, I think, from the window, or went to the door, and saw standing in his front yard one person holding two horses, and a second person sitting on one of the horses that he was holding. He described the appearance of the person; said that he seemed to be a young man, very talkative, and fluent in his speech. He said that the person on horseback had broken his leg, and desired medical attendance. He [the doctor] assisted in bringing the person that was on horseback into his house, and laying him upon the sofa in the parlor; that after he had taken him in, and he had lain on the sofa for some time, he was then carried up stairs, and put on a bed in what he called his front room; that he then proceeded to examine the leg, and discovered that the front bone, the outer bone, was broken nearly at right angles across the limb, about two inches above the instep. It was not a compound fracture: it seemed as slight a breaking as could possibly be, in his judgment. He said that the patient complained of pain in his back. He examined, and found no apparent cause for the pain, unless it might have been from his falling from a horse, as he said he had fallen. He said that he then dressed the limb as well as he was able to do it with the limited facilities he had, and called a young man, a hired servant, — a white servant, I think, — to make a crutch for him. The crutch was made. Breakfast was then prepared; and the younger of the two persons, the one who was not injured, was invited to breakfast, and took breakfast with them. He said, that, after breakfast, he observed the condition of his patient; that he seemed much debilitated; pale to such an extent that ho was unable to tell what his complexion might have been, and hesitated whether to say that the skin was light or dark. After breakfast, the young man made some remark in relation to procuring a conveyance to take his friend away. He said, that, in the mean time, he had been about giving some directions to his farm servants. I think he said they remained about the house until after dinner; and some time after dinner he started with the young man to go down and see if a carriage could be procured at his father's house; that, on the way, the young man did not stop at his [Dr. Mudd's] father's house, but he called his brother, the younger Mudd, found that tho carriage could not be procured, and then rode on to join the young man who had gone ahead, and overtook him, and rode into the pines, a mile or a mile and a half beyond the elder Mudd's house. The young man remarked that he believed he would not go any farther to get a carriage, but would go back to the house and see if he could not get his friend off in some way. The doctor said that he then went to the town, or near the town, I think; saw some friends or some patients. and returned to his house; that, as he came back to the house. he saw the person that he afterwards supposed to be Herold passing to the left of the house, and towards the barn or the stable; that he did not see the other person at all after he left him at the house, which was about one o'clock, I think. I should say here that he said he thought he returned to the house about four o'clock in the afternoon. I asked him then if he knew who the person was. He said that he did not recognize him. Speaking of the wounded man, he said he did not recognize him. I then exhibited what was said to be a photograph of Booth; and he said, that, from the photograph, he could not recognize him. He said, however, in answer to another question, that he met Booth some time in November. I think he said he was introduced by Mr. Thompson, a son-in-law of Dr. Queen, to Booth. I think he said the introduction took place first at the chapel or church on Sunday morning; that, after the introduction had passed between them, Thompson said, " Booth wants to buy farming-lands;" and they had some little conversation on the subject of lands; and then Booth asked the question, whether there were any desirable horses that could be bought in that neighborhood cheaply; that he mentioned the name of a neighbor of his who had some horses that were good travellers; and that he remained with him that night, I think, and next morning purchased one of those horses.

I asked him in that connection if he could now recognize the person that he had treated as the same person to whom he was introduced as Booth. He said he could. I asked him if he had seen Booth at any time after the introduction in November, and prior to his arriving there the Saturday morning; and he said he had not. I asked him if he knew Herold; and he said he did not, and did not know that he had ever seen him; that Herold mentioned the names of several persons living in that neighborhood whose acquaintance he had made, — a merchant by the name of Moore, and some other persons there. I asked him then, if he had any suspicion of the character of either of these persons. He said he had not, but that he first thought there was something strange about them, when, shortly after breakfast, the younger man came down and asked for a razor, and said his friend wished to shave himself; and that he went up stairs shortly afterwards, and noticed that the person he supposed to be Booth had shaved off his mustache. He said, in answer to the question whether the man had a beard or not, that his impression was that he had a long, heavy beard, and, referring to my own, said that he thought it was longer than mine, but that he could not observe him accurately enough to determine whether it was a natural or artificial beard; that he kept a shawl about his neck, and seemed to conceal intentionally the lower part of his face. I asked him then, if he at this time had heard of the murder of the President. He said he had not. I think, however, he remarked to me in one of these interviews, that he heard of that for the first time either on Sunday morning, or late in the evening of Saturday. I think — so my impression is — that in any event it was after the persons had left his house.

I then, getting the best description I could of the locality from him, went to the house of the doctor myself; and I asked him what these persons said in relation to the route they were to take. He said that Herold, the younger of them, — he passed by that name after the first explanations were over, — asked him the direct route to Piney Chapel, Dr. Wilmer's, saying that he was acquainted with Dr. Wilmer. He described the main travelled road, which leads to the right of his house, and was then asked if there was not a shorter or nearer road. He said, "Yes: there is a road across the swamp that is about a mile nearer, I think." He said it was five miles from his house to Piney Chapel by the direct road, and four miles by the marsh, and undertook to give him (as he said) a description by which they could go by the nearer route. He said that the directions were these: They were to pass down by his barn, inclining to the left, and then pass straight forward in a new direction across the marsh; and that, on passing across the marsh, they would come to a hill. Keeping over the hill, they would come in sight of the roof of a barn; and, letting down one or two fences, they would reach the direct road. I went to the premises, and made him point out to me the location, point out the position where they stood, and the direction that they took, and followed the direction that he pointed out. I then went with Dr. Mudd ; asked him if he could show me the tracks of the horses, the bay mare that he described more particularly. He pointed the track out to me : I took that track with him, and followed it for a long way into the marsh, across the marsh on to a hill, where they turned square to the left, instead of going straight over the hill on to a piece of ploughed ground, and across the ploughed ground ; and there the trail was lost, because the ground had been ploughed around it. I believe that embraces the substance of the conversation between Dr Mudd and myself.

Q. That embraces all that occurred in the several interviews ?

A. There are other detached things that occurred. For instance, the first time that I saw him, I did not know that a boot had been left at his house ; but the boot was brought in, and he then said to me that his attention had been that morning called to the fact that the boot was left there; and he described the boot, and undertook to tell me how he had cut it to take the foot out.

Q. I understand you to say that Dr. Mudd stated distinctly that he had not seen Booth since that introduction in November last?

A. Yes, sir : until the Saturday morning when he arrived at his house.

Q. And that he did not recognize him?

A. No, sir : he said he did not recognize him at first; but, on reflection, he knew it was the same person.

Cross-examined by Mr. Ewing :

Q. Did Dr. Mudd seem unwilling to give you this information ?

A. Dr. Mudd's manner was so very extraordinary, that I scarcely know how to describe it. I will undertake, if you desire me, to do it as well as I can.

Q. I wish you would.

A. He did not seem unwilling to answer a direct question that I asked ; but I discovered almost immediately, that, unless I did ask the direct question, important facts were omitted.

Q. Was he alarmed ?

A. He did seem very much embarrassed.

Q. And alarmed ?

A. I should think, not alarmed at the first or second interview; but I think, that, at the third interview, he was, from some statements that I made to him.

Q. At what time on Friday was the first interview?

A. It was not far from mid-day : it might have been a little before or after noon.

Q. How long was it after Lieutenant Lovett had gone for Dr. Mudd?

A. I cannot remember that : I am not quite certain. I do not think I sent Lieutenant Lovett to Dr. Mudd. Lieutenant Lovett had come from Washington by one route, and I had taken another one; and, as soon as I arrived at Bryantown, I sent for Dr. Mudd. I am not quite certain whether Lieutenant Lovett was sent by me at that time or not.

Q. That was about noon on the Friday after the assassination?

A. I think the day was Friday. I am a little indistinct as to the day ; but I think it was Friday. I think it was the 21st.

Q. At that interview, there was no written statement made?

A. Not at the first interview. I should say here that we kept talking for several hours. I deemed it of so much importance, that I kept talking with him for a long time, — tried to get the facts ; and, after I thought I had a general statement of facts, I had it taken down in writing.

Q. Then you had him state it over?

A. There were at least a dozen interviews between us. I had him state it over.

Q. When was the last interview?

A. The last interview was on Sunday, I think.

Q. Did you have more than one interview on Friday?

A. Oh, yes, sir! He was in my presence almost the entire time for five or six hours, talking here and talking there from time to time.

Q. You said, that, at the last interview, he was very much alarmed from some statements that you made to him. What were the statements you made to him?

A. I said that it seemed to me he was concealing the facts, and that I did not know whether he understood that that was the strongest evidence of his guilt that could he produced at that time, and might endanger his safety.

Q. When was it that you went off with Dr. Mudd, and he took you along the route that those two men took from his house?

A. One Sunday morning. I am quite confident of that.

Q. You spoke of their going the direct route toward Parson Wilmer's, or Piney Chapel?

A. Yes, sir.

Q. Parson Wilmer's is at Piney Chapel?

A. Yes, sir : within three or four hundred yards of the chapel.

Q. You spoke of the tracks leading in the direct route towards Piney Chapel until they abruptly turned off?

A. There is no road. They took the direction pointed out by the doctor until they came to the hill, with this exception : the marsh there is filled full of holes and bad places. I discovered from the tracks, as I thought, that they had got lost there ; and the reason was, that they had gone to the right to avoid a bad place, and then come back, and changed directions in that way until they had lost the general direction.

Q. You say that the doctor said to you that he heard of the assassination of the President either on Sunday morning, or late on the evening of Saturday.

A. My impression is that he told me he had not heard of it before Saturday evening or Sunday morning. I am rather inclined to the opinion that it was Saturday evening.

Q. You think he said " Saturday evening "?

A. I think he did.

Q. Did he mention how he heard it, and where?

A. No, sir : I cannot say that he did. I have an indistinct impression on the subject, though it is not worth much. It is that somebody brought the news from town, — from Bryantown ; but I am not sure of that.

Q. Or was it that he heard it at the town?

A. I am not sure whether he said that he heard it at the town, or that somebody from the town brought the news to him : I am inclined to think, the latter ; because I was told what expressions he made at church the next Sunday morning.

Q. Did he say when it was that Thompson introduced him to Booth, — in what month ?

A. He said it was in the fall; and I think he said it was about November.

Q. Did he say whether it was before daybreak that those two persons came to his house ?

A. He said it was about daybreak, — about four o'clock.

Q. Did you ask him whether they paid him any thing for setting the leg ?

A. I did not ask him that question myself; but it was asked, I remember, by some person.

Q. What statement did he make ?

A. I think he said twenty-five dollars.

Q. That they paid him twenty-five dollars for setting the leg?

A. Yes, sir, I think so. I think that statement was made to one of the men who were with me, but not to me directly.

Q. Did not Dr. Samuel Mudd say to you that he told Dr. George Mudd that there had been two suspicious men at his house ?

A. Yes, sir.

Q. Did he not say to you that he told that on Saturday evening?

A. I cannot remember. I think not.

Q. On Sunday morning ?

A. No, sir. I think it was later than that ; but it is possible it was on Sunday, though I am not at all distinct as to it.

Q. I mean to ask if he did not, in some one of your interviews, tell you that he had told that on Sunday to Dr. George Mudd ?

A. My impression is that he said he told it to Dr. George Mudd on Monday; though I am not sure but that it was on Sunday.

Q. You recollect distinctly his having said that he told Dr. George Mudd ?

A. Yes : he said that he told Dr. George Mudd ; and he said it in this connection : I said to him, "One of the strongest circumstances against you is, that you have failed to give early information, as you might have done, in this matter ;" and he mentioned then to whom he told it first, and I think he said it was Dr. George Mudd.

Q. Did he examine the likeness of Booth in your presence?

A. Yes, sir: the photograph.

Q. He recognized that as a likeness of the man to whom he had been introduced?

A. My impression is, that he said, that, from the photograph, he could not recognize him.

Q. As the man to whom he had been introduced?

A. Yes, sir.

Q. Did he not say, that, from the photograph, he could not recognize it as the man who had his leg broken?

A. No, sir: I think he said he would not have known Mr. Booth from the photograph. I think that was what he said; and he said also, I think, that he did not recognize the man when he first saw him; but, on reflection, he knew it was Mr. Booth, the person to whom he had been introduced.

Q. Did he not say to you that that was like a likeness which he had already seen of Booth, with his name marked under it?

A. I do not remember that.

Q. Was there not intense excitement in the town among the soldiers and the people?

A. The soldiers were not particularly excited. The people were generally excited. The soldiers were very active. The town was full of soldiers and people coming and going all the while.

Q. There was a state of angry and excited feeling, was there not?

A. I do not know that there was any angry feeling exhibited; but there was an excited state of feeling undoubtedly.

By the JUDGE ADVOCATE:

Q. Can you state what time Dr. Mudd professed to have recognized Booth as the man to whom he had been introduced? Was it during their stay at his house, or after they left?

A. It was during their stay at the house.

Q. You understood him to admit that he recognized him as Booth before he left.

A. Yes, sir: his expression was, that he did not recognize him at first; but, on reflecting, he remembered him as the person. I think that was about the expression.

By the COURT:

Q. Did you say that Dr. Mudd's statement was, that, when he went to the door, there was a man standing, holding two horses, one of which had a man sitting on him?

A. I am not quite sure whether he said there was a man holding two horses, or whether there was one horse there, and he was holding one horse with the man on it. He was certainly holding one horse; but, whether he said the man was holding the other horse too, I cannot be positive.

Q. Were you at his house?

A. I was.

Q. Could he ride near enough to the door to knock?

A. No. The doctor pointed out to me a cedar-tree at which they were standing; and I should say it was certainly twenty paces.

Q. Did he speak to you of one of the parties leaving on foot on crutches?

A. He said, that, as he came up, — he was going away from the house toward his farm-hands, — he saw one of them hobbling through the yard. I think that was his expression.

Q. What did he say became of the other horse?

A. Herold had been riding the bay horse; and Herold was going off on the bay horse: the roan horse was in the stable, as he supposed.

Q. Did he find the horse at his house?

A. Not at that time, but subsequently. Both horses were at his house, and put into the stable.

Q. But did those two men go away, and leave one horse?

A. Oh, no! Booth was hobbling around from the house to the stable, which was perhaps a hundred yards from the house; and, as you get to the stable, you are lost to view from the house.

Q. Where they took Booth's horse away?

A. That was the impression, though he said he did not see them there; and in point of fact, from the position he described them as being in, he could not see them the moment after they left his stable.

By Mr. Ewing:

Q. Please state, as near as you can, Dr. Mudd's exact words when he spoke of the reflection and recollecting, believing it was Booth who had been at his house.

A. Do you wish me to state all that he said?

Q. All relating to that point.

A. On showing him the photograph, he said that he should not have recollected the man from the photograph; and he said that he did not know him or remember him when he first saw him; but that, on reflection, he remembered that he was the man who was introduced to him in November last, or in the fall.

Q. Those were the words?

A. I will not quite say that they were the exact words, but as nearly as I can give them.

Q. There was nothing but that in his conversation on that point, was there?

A. That was the substance of it. Of course it was said many times over, and varied somewhat; but that was the general tenor of what he said on that subject.

Q. He did not say whether this reflection, on which he would recognize the man with the broken leg as the one to whom he had been formerly introduced, was reflection after the man left or not?

A. It was, as I understood.

Q. But he did not say?

A. I think he did say. He left the impression very clearly on my mind that it was before the man left.

Q. But you are unable to say that he said that?

A. Certainly. I am not able to say that he mentioned the precise time when the reflection occurred to him, in so many words; but I know what impression the general scope and tenor of his language left on that subject. He gave as a reason for not remembering him at first, that the man was very much worn and debilitated; and he said that he seemed to make an effort to keep the lower part of his face disguised; and that when he came to think, reflect, he remembered that it was the man to whom he was introduced. He did not, however, I think, say to me that that reflection or that memory came to him at any particular moment.

Q. Did he speak of this disguise as having been thrown off or discontinued during the man's stay in the house?

A. No, sir; not as having been discontinued. Of course the opening light of the day, the shaving of the face, and the fact that he sometimes slept and then woke, gave the doctor, as he passed into the room, better opportunities. That was the impression left on my mind. I do not think he said any thing to indicate that he, at any time, entirely threw off his attempt to disguise.

Q. He did not say that he reflected that it was Booth during the time Booth was at his house?

A. No, sir: I think I have said that he did not say that in so many words.

By the COURT:

Q. Did he, in any of his conversation, attempt to account to you for the fact that he had denied, in the first instance, any persons having been at his house?

A. I do not remember that it was ever brought to my notice that he did deny that a person had been to his house. He did not deny it to me, certainly.

The Commission then adjourned until to-morrow (Wednesday) morning, May 17, at ten o'clock, A.M.

WEDNESDAY, May 17, 1865.

The Commission again assembled; and, when the record of yesterday had been read and approved, General Harris rose, and said, —

I have in my hand a letter of the Hon. Reverdy Johnson, on which my objection to him as counsel before this Court was founded; and whilst I think the honorable gentleman ought to be very thankful to me for having made an occasion for him to disclaim before the country any obliquity of intention in writing that letter, yet in view of his age, and public relations to the country and to his State, I feel that it is due to myself and the Court that I should ask to have this letter made a part of the records of this Court.

The PRESIDENT. There is no objection in my mind; and I think it would be well for the Judge Advocate to read it.

25*

The letter of Mr. Johnson, dated "Baltimore, Oct. 7, 1864," was read, and ordered to be recorded.

WILLIAM WILLIAMS,

a witness called for the prosecution, having been duly sworn, testified as follows : —

By the JUDGE ADVOCATE :

Q. Will you state to the Court whether or not, after the assassination of the President, you were, with others, engaged in making pursuit after the assassin ?

A. Yes, sir. We went on the 17th of April. We proceeded to Surrattsville, in company with some cavalry.

Q. Will you state whether or not, in the course of that pursuit, you went to the residence of the prisoner, Dr. Mudd ?

A. Yes, sir.

Q. State what occurred there.

A. We went there on Tuesday, the 18th of April. On arriving there, Dr. Mudd was not at home ; but Mrs. Mudd told us she would send for him where he was in the neighborhood. She sent for him, and the doctor arrived. We asked him if any strangers had been that way, and he said there had not been. On questioning him about two men being at his house, one with a broken leg, he denied that any persons had been there. Some of the officers then spoke to him ; and I could not hear all. I merely asked him if any strangers had been there at that time.

Q. Did you mention the time when you supposed the strangers had been there, — the day ?

A. We did in the first visit.

Q. Did you have any further conversation with him at a later period ?

A. No, sir : not on our first visit.

Q. Did you say that he denied altogether that there had been any strangers there ?

A. Yes, sir.

Q. Did you, or did some one with you, make a remark about the man with the broken leg ?

A. I believe it was one of the other officers.

Q. Did you hear Dr. Mudd reply to that remark?

A. I am not positive what his reply was. I know he made a reply to it; but I am not positive what it was.

Q. Did he, on that occasion, state to you when he learned for the first time of the assassination of the President?

A. Yes, sir. To the best of my knowledge, he stated that he learned it at church on Sunday morning.

Q. Did he converse freely with you? Was his manner frank, or was it evasive?

A. He seemed to be a little uneasy. He did not seem to be willing to give us any information, without being asked directly.

Q. When did you see him the second time?

A. On Friday, the 21st.

Q. State what occurred then.

A. We went there for the purpose of arresting Dr. Mudd. On arriving there, Mrs. Mudd was there. She said the doctor was not at home; but he was in the neighborhood, and she would send for him. She sent for him. On his arriving in the house, Lieutenant Lovett, I believe, asked him a question first. I then asked him concerning those two men who had been at his house previously, one with a broken leg. He then said they had been there. Some of the other officers then asked him questions. I asked him also if the men at his house were not Booth and Herold. He said they were not. He said that he knew Booth; that he was introduced to Booth last fall, by a man by the name of Thompson, I believe.

Q. And that was not Booth who was at his house?

A. He said so. After we arrested him, on our way to Bryantown, I showed him Booth's picture, and asked him if that looked like the man who had his leg broken. After looking at the picture a little while, he first said it did not; he did not remember the features: but, after a while, he said it looked something like Booth across the eyes. I informed Mrs. Mudd that we had to search the house. That was on the second visit. She then said —

Mr. Ewing: You will not say what Mrs. Mudd said.

By the Judge Advocate: Any thing that was said in Dr. Mudd's presence is admissible.

A. This was said in Dr. Mudd's presence, to the best of my knowledge: I believe he was in the parlor. She said that one of the men, the man with the broken leg, had left the boot in bed. This was when I informed her we had to search the house. She then went and brought the boot down. It was a long riding-boot, with the maker's name, Broadway, N.Y., marked inside, and "J. Wilkes." The boot was cut some ten inches from the instep.

Q. Did the prisoner, Dr. Mudd, state to you that he had set the leg of that man?

A. Yes, sir.

Q. How long did he say they remained at his house?

A. He stated to me that they left about between three and four in the afternoon of Saturday.

Q. Did he state at what hour they arrived?

A. Before daybreak.

Q. Did he state how they left, — whether on horseback or en foot?

A. He said that they went away afoot.

Q. Did you understand her to say that in his presence?

A. Yes, sir.

Q. Did you understand her as speaking of one or both of them?

A. I believe it was Dr. Mudd who said the wounded man went away on crutches he had made for him by one of his men.

Cross-examined by MR. STONE:

Q. Was Lieutenant Lovett present?

A. Yes, sir.

Q. He was there both on Tuesday and Friday?

A. Yes, sir.

Q. He was present at all the conversations you had with Dr. Mudd?

A. Yes, sir; but I might have had some little conversation with Dr. Mudd going towards Bryantown, concerning the doctor, that Lieutenant Lovett did not hear.

Q. But I alluded to the interviews at the house.

A. Yes: Lieutenant Lovett was at the house both times.

Q. Mrs. Mudd was in the parlor when she made these declarations about the boot ?

A. She was standing in the door of the parlor and hall-way, I believe.

Q. Where was Dr. Mudd then ? — in the parlor ?

A. Yes, sir : to the best of my knowledge, he was sitting in the parlor on a chair.

Q. Could he hear what Mrs. Mudd said ?

A. I judged he could : he was not farther from her than where you are sitting. [About nine feet.]

Q. She was the first one who mentioned about the boot to you ?

A. Yes, sir : I told her we were compelled to search the house. She then said that the man who had his leg broken left a boot in bed.

Q. And she went up stairs, and brought it down to you ?

A. Yes, sir : we requested her to bring it down ; and she went up stairs and brought it down.

Q. Was it on the Tuesday or the Friday that he told you that the first knowledge he had of the assassination of the President he derived at church on the Sunday before ?

A. It was on Friday, I think.

Q. Was any question asked him whether he had, or had not, heard of the assassination of the President on Tuesday ?

A. I did not ; and it was not asked, unless some of the other officers did.

Q. Do you remember that any one asked him that in your presence ?

A. I do not.

Q. You were all together in one room ?

A. Yes, sir.

Q. Did you or Lieutenant Lovett ask him whether two strangers had been at his house at any time previous ?

A. I asked him ; and Lieutenant Lovett asked him also, I believe. I know that I asked Dr. Mudd that question.

Q. Do you remember which of you asked him first ?

A. I would not be positive as to that.

Q. Was the reply that he made to you the same that he made to Lieutenant Lovett ?

A. I think it was.

Q. You feel confident of that?

A. His reply on Tuesday to me was, that there had not been; and I think it was the same reply he made to Lieutenant Lovett.

Q. If his reply to Lieutenant Lovett had been different, as you were all together, you would have noticed the difference, would you not?

A. I do not know that I would, because I did not hear the reply that he made to Lieutenant Lovett.

Q. Do you remember, on the Friday examination, who asked him first, yourself or Lieutenant Lovett?

A. I think it was Lieutenant Lovett.

Q. Do you remember whether he asked him whether two strangers had been there, or whether Booth and Herold had been there?

A. "Two strangers," I think he said.

Q. What did he answer to that on Friday?

A. The question that I asked him was, if two strangers had been there, one with a broken leg. That was on Friday. Dr. Mudd then said that they had been; that he had set a man's leg; that two men came there at daybreak, one a young man apparently seventeen or eighteen years of age; and that they came to his door, and knocked at the door, and the doctor looked out of the window up stairs, and asked them who they were. I believe their reply was, that they were friends, and they wanted to get in. Dr. Mudd then came down stairs, and, with the assistance of the young man, got the wounded man off his horse into the parlor, and examined his leg on the sofa.

Q. Did you ask him on Friday to describe the two strangers?

A. Yes, sir.

Q. What description did he give?

A. He said one of them was about seventeen or eighteen years of age, — quite a young man. The other had a mustache and whiskers; pretty long chin-whiskers. I asked him if he thought the whiskers were natural whiskers. He said he could not tell.

Q. Did he tell you the color of the other man's hair?

A. Not that I remember.

Q. Did he tell you his height?

A. I will not be positive now whether he did or not.

Q. Did he describe to you his dress?

A. I think he said that the injured man had a shawl around his shoulders : I will not be positive ; but I think he did.

Q. Did he describe to you the younger man?

A. I do not remember his saying any thing about his dress.

Q. His height or general appearance?

A He said that he was a smooth-faced young man, about seventeen or eighteen years of age, as far as I can remember.

Q. Did he, on that occasion, point out to you the direction by which they had left his house?

A. He said, that, on leaving there, they asked him the road to Parson Wilmer's, and that he had shown them the way down to the swamp. There is a swamp, situated, I should judge, a thousand yards back of his house.

Q. Did you examine for the horses' tracks? Did he point out to you the road they had travelled away from his house?

A. Yes : we examined the swamp all through from there to Parson Wilmer's.

Q. And did you find horses' tracks in the direction he pointed out to you?

A. We found horses' tracks ; but there were teams going that way. We found a road, and horses' tracks on the road ; but I did not come to any conclusion that they were the tracks of the horses these men had. I did not pay any attention to going to Parson Wilmer's in the first place, because I thought it was to throw us off the track. The men did not go to Parson Wilmer's.

Q. But did you find horses' tracks on the road he pointed out to you?

A. Yes, sir.

Q. This road across the swamp is not a much travelled road?

A. I judge not.

Q. Did any of you, or you yourself, go immediately from his house across the swamp?

A. After leaving Dr. Mudd at Bryantown, — it was on Friday, — we came right back, and then went to go through the swamp from there to Parson Wilmer's.

Q. Did you not go across the swamp on Tuesday also?

A. Yes, sir.

Q. You followed that road?

A. We followed the road as far as we could, and through the swamp there. We did not exactly keep to the road altogther. Wo looked all through the swamp.

Q. You followed the road that Dr. Mudd pointed out to you on Tuesday also, did you not?

A. Yes, sir: we went down that road. We did not keep on the road, though: we divided ourselves in the swamp, and went through the swamp different roads.

Q. Were you one of the party that went to Rev. Mr. Wilmer's house?

A. Yes, sir.

Q. What time did you get there?

A. I think it was on Thursday, or Tuesday night: I will not be positive. I think it was late in the evening we got there.

Q. You are positive it was one or the other of those times?

A. I think it was.

Q. This was in pursuance of what Dr. Mudd told you? You went to Wilmer's in consequence of his having told you that they inquired the way there?

A. Yes, sir.

Q. What time in the day did you say you got to Mr. Wilmer's?

A. I think it was in the evening. It was very late in the evening, or early in the morning. I think it was Wednesday evening, to the best of my recollection.

Q. Did you hear any thing of them on the road?

A. No, sir: I did not.

Q. This was before Dr. Mudd was carried to Bryantown?

A. Yes, sir.

Q. Were you and Mr. Lloyd acting under Lieutenant Lovett's orders?

A. We were acting under the orders of Major O'Beirne.

Q. Was Major O'Beirne present?

A. No, sir.

Q. Were you not subordinate, in this business, to Lieutenant Lovett's orders?

A. Yes, sir : he had charge of the squad.

Q. Mr. Lloyd was with you ?

A. Yes, sir.

Q. Were you in court this morning when the testimony was read ?

A. No, sir.

SIMON GAVACAN,

a witness called for the prosecution, being duly sworn, testified as follows : —

By the JUDGE ADVOCATE:

Q. State to the Court whether or not you are acquainted with the prisoner Dr. Mudd.

A. Yes, sir.

Q. Were you or not at his house on the Tuesday following the assassination of the President ?

A. Yes, sir.

Q. Will you state what inquiries were made of him there connected with your pursuit of the murderers, and what his replies were ?

A. We went there, I think, on the forenoon of Tuesday, the 18th. We went through Bryantown to his house. We went there, and we made inquiries if there were any two men passed there on Saturday morning : that was the Saturday after the assassination. He said, "No." Then we asked him more particularly if there were two men came there, one of them having his leg fractured. He said, "Yes." We asked him about what time. He said at four or half-past four o'clock on Saturday morning; that they came to his door, and made a rap at the door; that he was a little alarmed at the noise, and he came down stairs and let them in. I believe I understood him to say that he and the other person assisted the man with the fractured leg into the house ; and he attended to the fracture as well as he possibly could. He said he did not have much facilities for doing so ; but he did it as well as he could. Then I believe he said the person who had the fractured leg staid on the sofa for a while, and, after that, was taken into one of the rooms up stairs, and remained there until between three and five o'clock in the afternoon of Saturday, and then they left there; and I believe he said that he went part of the way with them; but, previous to this, he went looking for a buggy with the other man to have him taken away, and could not find any. He then went with them, I believe, part of the way, I understood him to say, on the road where they were going to; that they first inquired the road to Allen's Fresh, and also inquired the way to the Rev. Dr. Wilmer's; and Dr. Mudd went with them a part of the way, I believe he said, to show them the road. That is what I understood him to say.

Q. Did you ask him whether he knew these persons, or either of them?

A. We asked him first if he knew them. He said, " No : he did not know them at all."

Q. Did you, on a subsequent day, have an interview with him? and if so, when?

A. Yes, sir : on Friday, the 21st of April.

Q. State what occurred then.

A. We went there for the purpose of arresting him, and searching his house. When we went there, he was not in ; and his wife sent for him. When he came there, we informed him that we would have to search his house. His wife then went up stairs, and brought a boot down stairs. We examined the boot, and found the words, " J. Wilkes " marked on the inside of the leg of it. She also brought a razor down stairs, which one of our party took in charge.

Q. Did you again repeat the inquiry then, whether he knew who these persons were?

A. Yes, sir.

Q. What did he say?

A. We asked him if he thought that was Booth. He said ho thought not.

Q. Did he give any reason why he thought so?

A. We made inquiries about his face. He said he had whiskers on, and spoke also of his having his mustache shaved off. He said ho thought he shaved his mustache off up stairs.

Q. Did he speak of having known him before?

A. Yes, sir: when we made inquiries if he knew Booth, he said he was introduced to him last fall by a man by the name of Thompson.

Q. But that he thought this man was not Booth?

A. But he thought it was not Booth.

Cross-examined by Mr. Ewing:

Q. Who was the chief of the party who went to Mudd's house with you on Tuesday?

A. We did not have any chief in particular.

Q. Who was in charge of the party?

A. Lieutenant Lovett went out in charge of a squad of cavalry with us. We went out under orders from Major O'Beirne.

Q. In the absence of Major O'Beirne, were you not under the orders of Lieutenant Lovett?

A. Yes, sir: partly.

Q. Who commenced the conversation with Dr. Mudd on Tuesday?

A. That I am not able to say.

Q. How long did the conversation last?

A. Probably an hour.

Q. Was it in your presence?

A. Yes, sir.

Q. You heard what he said?

A. Yes, sir.

Q. Did not Lieutenant Lovett conduct the inquiry chiefly?

A. No, sir: the doctor was asked questions by the whole of us.

Q. He was asked questions by all of you?

A. Yes, sir.

Q. But in the presence of Lieutenant Lovett and yourself?

A. Yes, sir.

Q. Did not Dr. Mudd himself produce the boot?

A. No, sir; his wife produced it: his wife went up stairs and brought it down.

Q. Whom was it given to?

A. It was given to one of our party: I don't know which one

exactly,—tho one who was nearest to the stairs coming down stairs.

Q. Was the boot given up before Dr. Mudd got to the house, or afterwards?

A. After he got to the house.

Q. Did you, in point of fact, make a search of the house?

A. No, sir: we did not; we did not go up stairs. When wo found the boot and razor, we thought we had satisfactory evidence that it was Booth and Herold that went through there.

Q. Did you go out to meet Dr. Mudd on Friday, as he was coming to the house?

A. No, sir: I did not.

Q. Did Lieutenant Lovett?

A. Lovett, I believe, did.

Q. Did anybody else?

A. There might be one or two of the officers: I am not sure.

Q. Did you ask him on Tuesday for a description of the parties?

A. No, sir: we did not; but I believe there was a photograph of Booth shown to him, and he said he did not recognize it as any of the parties.

Q. That he did not recognize it?

A. Only that there was something about the forehead or the eyes that resembled one of the parties.

Q. That was in your conversation on Tuesday?

A. Yes, sir.

Q. Did he point you the route they took across the swamp?

A. No, sir: he did not point out the route; but he said they had made inquiries how they would get to the Rev. Dr. Wilmer's.

Q. He mentioned that on Tuesday?

A. Yes, sir.

Q. Did he tell you how you would go to go to Dr. Wilmer's by the route he had directed them?

A. Yes, sir.

Mrs. Emma Offutt,

a witness called for the prosecution, being duly sworn, testified as follows:—

By the JUDGE ADVOCATE:

Q. Will you state to the Court whether or not you are the sister-in-law of John M. Lloyd?

A. I am.

Q. State whether or not, on Tuesday, the 11th of April, you were with him.

A. I was in the carriage with Mr. Lloyd.

Q. Did you on that occasion meet Mrs. Surratt?

A. Yes, sir.

Q. Can you state where the meeting took place?

A. Somewhere about Uniontown, — I believe the place is called.

Q. Will you state whether or not a conversation took place between Mr. Lloyd and Mrs. Surratt on that occasion?

A. Yes, sir: I saw them talking together.

Q. Did you or not hear that conversation?

A. I did not.

Q. Under what circumstances did the conversation take place?

A. Indeed, I do not know. Our carriage passed before we recognized that it was her; and then Mr. Lloyd got out of the carriage. I do not know exactly whether she called him or not; but he went to the carriage. I was some distance off.

Q. The conversation took place at her carriage?

A. Yes, sir: not at ours.

Q. Were you at Mr. Lloyd's house on Friday, the 14th?

A. Yes, sir.

Q. Will you state whether you saw the prisoner Mrs. Surratt there?

A. Yes, sir: I saw her.

Q. Did you observe any conversation on that occasion between her and him?

A. I saw them conversing together. I did not hear it. She came into the parlor. After that, I had occasion to go through the back part of the house, and she came with me; and I noticed them talking together.

Q. Did you or not hear what was said on that occasion?

A. I did not. I could not tell a word that passed between

them. I paid no attention to them at all. I was engaged on that day.

Q. Did the conversation take place in the house or yard?

A. In the yard. I saw them talking together in the yard

Q. Had Mr. Lloyd been to town that day, — on Friday?

A. He had been to Marlboro' that day, attending court.

Q. Had he just returned?

A. Yes, sir.

Q. Do you know what he brought with him?

A. He brought some oysters and fresh fish with him on that day; and that is the reason why he drove around to the back part of the yard.

Q. Was there anybody else in the house besides yourself, Mrs. Surratt, and Mr. Lloyd, at the time of this conversation?

A. No, sir.

Cross-examined by Mr. AIKEN:

Q. How far apart were the two carriages at Uniontown on the 11th?

A. I cannot tell you: I suppose, some two or three yards. I never looked out of the carriage at all after he left the carriage. It was misty, and raining a little; and I was in a hurry to get to Washington. They were not talking together more than a very few moments.

Q. Did Mr. Lloyd make any statement to you about what the conversations were?

A. No, sir: not on that day.

Q. Did he make any statements about what the conversation was that occurred between himself and Mrs. Surratt in the yard on the 14th?

A. No, sir: he did not.

Q. Have you been acquainted with Mrs. Surratt for some time?

A. Only since December or January.

Q. At what time in the day did she arrive at Mr. Lloyd's on Friday, the 14th?

A. I think, about four o'clock; four or five.

Q. Did you have conversation with her previous to Mr. Lloyd's coming home?

A. Yes: I had a conversation with her in the parlor before Mr. Lloyd came in.

Q. Did you learn any thing of her business there that day?

ASSISTANT JUDGE ADVOCATE BINGHAM objected to the question. Statements of Mrs. Surratt, in the absence of Mr. Lloyd, were not admissible.

MR. AIKEN varied his question so as to read, —

Q. Did Mr. Lloyd make any statement to you with reference to his conversation or business with Mrs. Surratt?

A. He did not.

Q. Did Mrs. Surratt have any business with you there that day?

A. No, sir: when I went into the parlor, she told me her business concerned —

ASSISTANT JUDGE ADVOCATE BINGHAM objected to any statement of what Mrs. Surratt told the witness in the absence of Mr. Lloyd; and the Commission sustained the objection.

By MR. AIKEN:

Q. Did you see certain other parties at the house that day?

A. I did not.

Q. Did Mrs. Surratt give you any charges that day with reference to any of her business?

A. No, sir: she did not; only concerning her farm; that is all.

Q. Did she place in your hands any packages?

A. No, sir.

Q. During your visit to Mr. Lloyd's, did you ever hear any conversation there with reference to "shooting-irons"?

ASSISTANT JUDGE ADVOCATE BINGHAM objected to the question. The witness had already stated that she did not hear the conversation between Mr. Lloyd and Mrs. Surratt.

MR. AIKEN claimed the right to ask the question, in order to impeach the credibility of the previous witness (Lloyd).

The Commission sustained the objection.

WILLIE S. JETT,

a witness called for the prosecution, being duly sworn, testified as follows : —

By the JUDGE ADVOCATE:

Q. Will you look at the prisoners at the bar, and see if you recognize any of them?

A. Only one of them.

Q. Which one?

A. Herold.

Q. Will you state on what occasion you first saw him, and all the circumstances attending your meeting?

A. Since the 25th of last October, I had been stationed in Caroline County, as Commissary Agent of the Confederate-States Government. I was formerly a member of the Ninth Virginia Cavalry, Company C. On the 29th of June last, I was wounded; and I remained out of service until the 25th of October. I went before the Medical Board in Richmond, was assigned to light duty, and appointed Commissary Agent, and was stationed in Caroline County on duty. I remained there as Commissary Agent until —

Q. You need not go through all your services: just commence where you left Herold.

A. I was on my way from Fauquier County, Va., over into Caroline County. Having been stationed there, I had a great many friends, and was going over on a visit. I got right at Port Conway; and, about one hundred yards from the wharf, I saw a wagon down on the wharf, — no uncommon occurrence, as it was a regular ferry.

Q. What day was that?

A. That was on Monday.

Q. What day of the month?

A. The 18th of April, as near as I can come to it.

Q. It was the Monday following the assassination of the President?

A. No, the Monday week following that we saw the wagon there. There were three of us together, — Lieutenant Ruggles, a

young man named Bainbridge, and myself, — all on our way to
Caroline County. We rode down to the wharf: but, just before we
got to the wagon, we saw a man get out of the wagon, — apparently
a young man; and it seemed to us as if he put his hand in his
bosom. We rode on down, did not pay any attention to it, passed
by him, and went down on the wharf. I do not remember whether
we hailed the ferry-boat or not. Anyhow, while standing there,
this young man got out of the wagon, and came towards where we
were, and asked us what command we belonged to. Lieutenant
Ruggles spoke up, and said, "We belong to Mosby's command."
I made no reply then myself at all. I do not remember whether
there was any thing else said or not. Anyhow, he said, "If I am
not inquisitive, can I ask where you are going?" I spoke up, and
replied, "That is a secret where we are going." I did not say
any thing more then, that I remember. We went back on the
wharf again; and then a man got out of the wagon, and one of us
(which one it was I do not know) asked him what command he
belonged to. He said he belonged to A. P. Hill's corps; that
there were two of them by the name of Boyd. He said his brother
had been wounded down below Petersburg, and asked if we would
take him out of the lines. We did not say then where we were
going. I do not remember now what was said then, if any thing
was. Anyhow, Herold asked us to go and take a drink. None
of our boys drank any thing; and we declined. We rode up towards the house there. I got down, carried my horse in the stable,
and tied him; and the other two boys tied their horses near the
shed. We all sat down there; and Herold, after sitting down there,
talking some time or a little while, — it was a very short time, —
touched me on the shoulder, and said he wanted to speak to me;
carried me down to the wharf, and he said, "I suppose you are
raising a command to go South?" I did not know why he thought
that. He said he would like to go along with us. I did not say
any thing. After talking a little while, I said, "I cannot go with
any man that I do not know any thing about." He seemed very
much agitated; and then remarked, when we got down on the wharf,
"We are the assassinators of the President." I was so much confounded, that I did not make any reply then, that I remember.

Lieutenant Ruggles was very near, watering his horse; and I called to him, and he came there; and either Herold or myself remarked to Lieutenant Ruggles that they were the assassinators of the President. Booth then came up; and Herold introduced himself to us, and then introduced Booth. Booth, I remember, had on his hand "J. W. B." We went back then to the house, and sat there some time on the steps. Then we went across the river. Booth was riding Ruggles's horse. Herold was walking. When we got on the other side of the river, before they got out of the boat, I got out on my horse, and rode up to Port Royal, went into a house, and saw a lady. He passed his name off to us first as Boyd, and said he wanted to pass under that assumed name. I asked her if she could take in a wounded Confederate soldier — just as he represented himself to me — for two or three days. She at first consented. Then afterwards she said she could not. I walked across the street to Mr. Catlitt's; but he was not at home. We then went on up to Mr. Garrett's; and there we left Booth. Herold and all of us went on up the road then to within a few miles of Bowling Green. Bainbridge and Herold went to Mrs. Clark's; and Ruggles and myself, to Bowling Green. The next day Herold returned to Garrett's, or that way; and that was the last I saw of him.

Q. Herold introduced Booth to you as his brother, by the name of Boyd, did he?

A. Yes, sir.

Q. Did he afterwards change the name?

A. He afterwards told us that his name was Herold, and Booth's name was Booth. They kept the same name, Boyd, though.

Q. Do I understand you to say that both these men, Herold and Booth, went to Garrett's?

A. No, sir. Herold did not go in; but Bainbridge and Herold staid at the gate, and Ruggles and Booth and myself rode up together. We left Booth there, and then came out to the gate, and met Herold and Bainbridge, and went up the road together.

Q. You did not meet either of them afterwards?

A. I met with Herold afterwards; with Booth I did not. Herold came up to Bowling Green the next day, and spent the day, and had dinner, and came down that evening; and that was the last I saw of them.

Q. Do you know where Herold went from Bowling Green?

A. I do not know. That was the last I saw of him. The next day, on Wednesday, he left at, I suppose, half-past two or three o'clock. That was the last I saw of him, except the night they were caught, when I went down there; and I saw him the next morning.

Q. When you saw Herold the next morning, he was in the custody of the officers; was he not?

A. He was.

Q. Did you or not, before this declaration that they were the assassinators of the President, make known that you were in the Confederate service?

A. They saw that, because we were all dressed in Confederate uniform. I had just returned from Fauquier County, where I had been with Mosby's command in hopes of getting to my own regiment after the fall of Richmond. We had not then heard of the surrender of General Lee.

Cross-examined by Mr. STONE:

Q. This young man Herold wanted to aid Booth in getting farther South?

A. Yes, sir. That of course we could not do, because we had no facilities: at least, we did not do it.

Q. Did he not seem to be a good deal disappointed when you could not do it?

A. Yes, sir: I think he seemed to be disappointed after we made known to him what our object was, — that we were going over on a visit.

Q. Was Booth present when you were talking with Herold?

A. Not when Herold first told me that they were the assassinators of the President: Booth was not present then. Booth came up a few moments afterwards with Bainbridge, I think, or probably a little ahead of him, perhaps behind him; I do not remember which.

Q. Did not Herold appear to be a good deal agitated?

A. Yes, sir: his voice trembled very much.

Q. He was not very self-possessed?

A. No, sir : I do not think he was.

Q. How did Booth seem to be?

A. Booth remarked that he would not have done it.

Q. Would not have done what?

A. Would not have told. Booth said he did not intend telling.

Q. Herold did tell?

A. Herold had told when Booth came up.

Q. Herold did not tell you that he had killed the President?

A. No. He said, "We are the assassinators of the President;" and then I think he said, "Yonder is the assassinator!" pointing back to where Booth was standing.

Q. You think he may have used the word "we;" but that he pointed back, and said, "Yonder is the assassin"?

A. No: he said first, "We are the assassinators of the President;" and then in a few moments he said, "Yonder is J. Wilkes Booth, the man who killed the President;" or he may have said "Lincoln" instead of the "President."

By Mr. AIKEN :

Q. Have you ever taken the oath of allegiance?

A. No, sir. I am perfectly willing to do it, though.

EVERTON J. CONGER,

a witness called for the prosecution, being duly sworn, testified as follows : —

By the JUDGE ADVOCATE :

Q. Were you, with others, engaged in the pursuit of the murderers of the President after his assassination?

A. I was.

Q. Will you please take up the narrative of that pursuit at the point where you met with Willie Jett, who has just given his testimony here, and state what occurred afterwards until the pursuit closed?

A. I found him in a room at a hotel in Bowling Green. It will be necessary to premise a little to make myself intelligible. I expected to find somebody else.

Q. Go on, and tell your story in your own way.

A. I went into a room in a hotel at Bowling Green, and found these two men in bed. As I went in, one of them began to get up in the bed. I said to him, " Is your name Jett?" He said, " Yes, sir." Said I, " Get up: I want you!" He got up, and I told him to put on his clothes. He put on his pants, and came out to where I was in the front part of the room. I asked him, " Where are the two men who came with you across the river at Port Royal?" I was sitting on a chair. He came up towards me, and said, " Can I see you alone?" I said, " Yes, sir: you can." Lieutenant Baker and Lieutenant Doherty were with me. I asked them to go out of the room. After they were gone, he reached out his hand to me, and said, " I know who you want ; and I will tell you where they can be found." Said I, " That's what I want to know." Said he, " They are on the road to Port Royal, about three miles this side of that." " At whose house are they?" I asked. " Mr. Garrett's," he replied: " I will go there with you, and show where they are now; and you can get them." I said, " Have you a horse?" — " Yes, sir." — " Get it, and get ready to go!" I said to him, " You say they are on the road to Port Royal?" — " Yes, sir." I said to him, " I have just come from there." He stopped a moment, and seemed to be considerably embarrassed. Said he, " I thought you came from Richmond: if you have come that way, you have come past them. I cannot tell you whether they are there now or not." I said it did not make any difference : we would go back and see. He got up; had his horse saddled. We gathered the party around the house together; went back to Mr. Garrett's house. Just before we got to the house, Jett, riding with me, said, " We are very near now to where we go through : let us stop here, and look around." He and I rode on together. I rode, in the first place, alone forward to find the gate that went through to the house, and rode about as far as I understood him to say it was, and did not see any opening. There was a hedge, or rather a bushy fence, along the side of the road. I turned around, and went back to him; and I told him I did not see any gate,— at any rate, within the distance he named. Then we rode on, I should think three hundred yards farther, and then stopped again. Then we went — Lieutenant Baker and myself — to find it. We opened that gate, and went through. I sent Lieutenant Baker to open another, and I went back for the cavalry ; and we rode rapidly up to the house and barn, and stationed the men around the house and quarters.   I went to the house, and found Lieutenant Baker at the door, telling somebody to strike a light, and come out.   I think the door was open when I got there.   The first individual we saw was an old man, whose name was said to be Garrett.   I said to him, " Where are the two men who stopped here at your house ? " — " They have gone." — " Gone where ? " — " Gone to the woods." — " Well, sir, whereabouts in the woods have they gone ? "   He then commenced to tell me that they came there without his consent ; that he did not want them to stay.   I said to him, " I do not want any long story out of you : I just want to know where these men have gone."   He commenced over again to tell me ; and I turned to the door, and said to one of the men, " Bring in a lariat rope here, and I will put that man up to the top of one of those locust-trees."   He did not seem inclined to tell.   One of his sons then came in, and said, " Don't hurt the old man : he is scared.   I will tell you where the men are you want to find."   Said I, " That is what I want to know : where are they ? "   He said, " In the barn."   We then left the house immediately, and went to the barn, and stationed the remaining part of the men.   As soon as I went to the barn, I heard somebody walking around inside on the hay.   I stationed the men around it.   There were two Garretts : by that time another one had come from somewhere ; and Lieutenant Baker said to one of the Garretts, " You must go in the barn, and get the arms from those men."   I think he made some objection to it : I do not know certainly.   Baker said, " They know you, and you can go in."   Baker said to the men inside, " We are going to send this man, on whose premises you are, in to get your arms ; and you must come out, and deliver yourselves up."   I do not think there was any thing more said.   Garrett went in ; and he came out very soon, and said, " This man says, ' Damn you ! you have betrayed me ! ' and threatened to shoot me."   I said to him, " How do you know he was going to shoot you ? "   Said he, " He reached down to the hay behind him to get his revolver, and I came out."   I then directed Lieutenant Baker to tell them, that, if they would come out and deliver themselves up, very well ; if not, in five minutes we would set the barn on fire.   Booth replied, " Who are you? what do you want? whom do you want?" Lieutenant Baker said, "We want you, and we know who you are. Give up your arms, and come out!" I say Booth: I presume it was him. He replied, "Let us have a little time to consider it." Lieutenant Baker said, "Very well;" and some ten or fifteen minutes probably intervened between that time and any thing further being said. He asked again, "Who are you? and what do you want?" I said to Lieutenant Baker, "Do not by any remark made to him allow him to know who we are: you need not tell him who we are. If he thinks we are rebels, or thinks we are his friends, we will take advantage of it. We will not lie to him about it; but we need not answer any question that has any reference to that subject, but simply insist on his coming out, if he will." The reply was made to him, "It don't make any difference who we are: we know who you are, and we want you. We want to take you prisoners." Said he, "This is a hard case: it may be I am to be taken by my friends." Some time in the conversation he said, "Captain, I know you to be a brave man, and I believe you to be honorable: I am a cripple. I have got but one leg: if you will withdraw your men in 'line' one hundred yards from the door, I will come out and fight you." Lieutenant Baker replied, that we did not come there to fight; we simply came there to make him a prisoner: we did not want any fight with him. Once more after this he said, "If you'll take your men fifty yards from the door, I'll come out and fight you. Give me a chance for my life!" The same reply was made to him. His answer to that was, in a singularly theatrical voice, "Well, my brave boys, prepare a stretcher for me!"

Some time passed before any further conversation was held with him. In the mean time, I requested one of the Garretts to pile some brush up against the corner of the barn,—pine-boughs. He put some up there, and after a while came to me, and said, "This man inside says, that, if I put any more brush in there, he will put a ball through me."—"Very well," said I: "you need not go there again." After a while, Booth said, "There's a man in here wants to come out." Lieutenant Baker said, "Very well: let him hand his arms out, and come out." Some talk, considerable, passed in the barn: some of it was heard, some not. One of the expressions made use of by Booth to Herold, who was in the barn, was, " You damned coward! will you leave me now? Go, go! I would not have you stay with me." Some conversation ensued between them, which I supposed had reference to the bringing-out of the arms, which was one of the conditions on which Herold was to come out. It was not heard: we could simply hear them talking. He came to the door, and said, " Let me out!" Lieutenant Baker said to him, " Hand out your arms!" The reply was, " I have none." He said, " You carried a carbine; and you must hand it out." Booth replied, " The arms are mine; and I have got them." Lieutenant Baker said, " This man carried a carbine; and he must hand it out." Booth said, " Upon the word and honor of a gentleman, he has no arms: the arms are mine, and I have got them." I stood by the side of the lieutenant, and said to him, " Never mind the arms: if we can get one of the men out, let us do it, and wait no longer." The door was opened. He stuck out his hands: Lieutenant Baker took hold of him, brought him out, and passed him to the rear. I went around to the corner of the barn, pulled some hay out, twisted up a little rope about six inches long, set fire to it, and stuck it back through on top of the hay. It was loose, broken-up hay, that had been — I thought so from seeing it afterwards when I went in the barn — trodden upon the barn-floor. It was trodden down; was very light; and it blazed very rapidly, — lit right up at once. I put my eye up to the crack next to the one the fire was put through, and looked in; and I heard something drop on the floor, which I supposed to be Booth's crutch. He turned around towards me. When I first got a glimpse of him, he stood with his back partly to me, turning towards the front door. He came back within five feet of the corner of the barn. The only thing I noticed he had in his hands when he came was a carbine. He came back, and looked along the cracks one after another rapidly. He could not see any thing. He looked at the fire; and, from the expression of his face, I am satisfied he looked to see if he could put it out, and was satisfied that he could not do it, it was burning so much. He dropped his arm, relaxed his muscles, and turned around, and started for the door for the front of the barn. I ran around to the other side; and, when about half round, I heard the report of a pistol. I went right to the door and went in, and found Lieutenant Baker looking at him, or holding him, raising him up, I do not know which. I said to him, "He shot himself." Said he, "No, he did not, either." Said I, "Whereabout is he shot?—in the head or neck?" I raised him then, and looked on the right side of the neck. I saw a place where the blood was running out. Said I, "Yes, sir: he shot himself." Lieutenant Baker replied very earnestly, that he did not. I said to him, "Let us carry him out of here: this will soon be burning." We took him up, and carried him out on to the grass underneath the locust-trees, a little way from the door. I went back into the barn immediately to see if the fire could be put down, and tried somewhat myself to put it down; but I could not, it was burning so fast; and there was no water, and nothing to help with. I turned around, and went back. Before this, I supposed him to be dead. He had all the appearance of a dead man; but, when I got back to him, his eyes and mouth were moving. I called immediately for some water, and put it on his face; and he somewhat revived, and attempted to speak. I put my ear down close to his mouth, and he made several efforts; and finally I understood him to say, "Tell mother, I die for my country." I said to him, "Is that what you say?" repeating it to him. He said, "Yes." They carried him from up there to the porch of Mr. Garrett's house, and laid him on an old straw bed or tick or something. At that time he revived considerably. He could then talk so as to be intelligibly understood, in a whisper: he could not speak above a whisper. He wanted water: we gave it to him. He wanted to be turned on his face. I said to him, "You cannot lie on your face;" and he wanted to be turned on his side. We turned him upon his side three times, I think; but he could not lie with any comfort, and wanted to be turned immediately back. He asked me to put my hand on his throat, and press down, which I did; and he said "Harder." And I pressed down as hard as I thought necessary; and he made very strong exertions to cough, but was unable to do so,—no muscular exertion could be made. I supposed he thought something was in his throat; and I said to him, "Open your mouth, and put out your tongue, and I will see if it bleeds;" which he did. I said to him, "There is no blood in your throat: it has not gone through any part of it there." He repeated two or

27*

three times, "Kill me, kill me!" The reply was made to him, "We don't want to kill you : we want you to get well." I then took what things were in his pockets, and tied them up in a piece of paper. He was not then quite dead. He would — once, perhaps, in five minutes — gasp: his heart would almost die out; and then it would commence, and, by a few rapid beats, would make a slight motion again. I left the body and the prisoner Herold in charge of Lieutenant Baker. I told him to wait an hour if he was not dead ; if he recovered, to wait there, and send over to Belle Plain for a surgeon from one of the gunships ; and, if he died in the space of an hour, to get the best conveyance he could, and bring him on, dead or alive.

Q. You left before he died ?

A. No : I staid there some ten minutes after this was said ; and the doctor who was there said he was dead.

Q. I suppose you have seen the dead body since ?

A. Yes, sir.

Q. [Exhibiting to the witness a knife numbered 28.] State if that is the weapon you took from him.

A. I did not take it from him myself ; but that is the knife. I saw it taken.

Q. It was taken by others with you ?

A. Yes, sir.

Q. [Exhibiting to the witness a pair of pistols.] Do you recognize these pistols as having been taken from him ?

A. I did not examine the pistols with any care. I have no means of knowing that these are the identical ones ; but they were similar to these.

Q. [Exhibiting to the witness a belt, a holster, and a knife.] Do you recognize these ?

A. That is the belt and holster, and that is the knife taken from Booth.

[The pistols were offered in evidence without objection.]

Q. [Exhibiting a file with a cork attached to one end.] Was that taken out of his pocket ?

A. Yes, sir ; and also the spur and the pipe, and the cartridges now in your hand ; but I am not so positive in regard to the cartridges.

Q. [Exhibiting a spur.] Is that the spur?

A. I cannot swear that it is positively: I turned the spur over to Mr. Stanton; and, if that is the spur that has been in his department, its history can be easily traced.

Q. There was a spur?

A. There was a spur very similar to that: I judge that to be the one; but I cannot say so with certainty.

[These articles were offered in evidence without objection.]

Q. [Exhibiting a carbine to the witness.] Is that the carbine you took there?

A. Yes, sir.

Q. Is that what is called a Spencer rifle?

A. A Spencer carbine. It is a cavalry weapon; and it has a mark on the breech by which I know it.

Q. Were these weapons loaded?

A. The carbine was loaded at the time, and the pistols were loaded. In Mr. Secretary Stanton's office, I unloaded this carbine myself. Here are the cartridges that were taken out of it.

Q. How many balls were in it?

A. I did not count them.

Q. Was it fully charged?

A. I should think it was. I believe there was one in the barrel, and the chamber was full.

Q. [Exhibiting bills of exchange.] Examine these bills of exchange, and see whether they are the same that you took from the person of Booth or not.

A. Yes, sir: they are. I put the initials of my name on them at the time; but they are partly rubbed out: still they can be seen.

[The bill of exchange in triplicate was offered in evidence without objection. The first of the set was read, as follows:—

No. 1492.

(Stamp)   The Ontario Bank,

Montreal Branch.

Exchange for £61 12s. 10d.

Montreal, 27 Oct'r, 1864.

Sixty days after sight of this first of exchange (second and third of the same tenor and date unpaid), pay to the order of J. Wilkes Booth sixty-one pounds, twelve shillings, and ten pence sterling. Value received, and charge to acct. of this office.

To Messrs. Glynn Mills & Co.,

    London.   Sgd   H. Stanus,

                                                      Manager.]

Q. In what State and county was the house of Garrett, where Booth was captured and killed?

A. I think, Caroline County. It is in the State of Virginia, three miles south, or nearly so, from Port Royal, on the road to Bowling Green.

Q. Do you or not recognize the prisoner Herold as the man that you took out of the barn on that occasion?

A. I do. [Pointing out David E. Herold.]

Q. What articles did you take from Herold? Any thing?

A. A little piece of a map of the State of Virginia, and a part of the Chesapeake Bay on it.

Q. Do you remember whether that map embraced the region of country where they were?

A. It did. It embraced that region of country known in Virginia as the "Northern Neck."

Q. Was it a map prepared in pencil?

A. No, sir.

Q. Was it a regular map?

A. Part of an old school map; a map that had originally been five or six inches square.

Q. [Exhibiting a map.] Is that it?

A. Yes, sir: that is it.

Q. That embraces the region of country in which they were captured?

A. Yes, sir. That is the only property I found on Herold.

Q. Look at this pocket-compass. [Exhibiting a pocket-compass.]

A. That was taken from Booth's pocket, just as it is now, with the candle-grease on it and all.

[The map and compass were offered in evidence without objection, and are marked Exhibit No. 38.]

· Cross-examined by Mr. STONE :

Q. You did not find any arms on Herold ?

A. No, sir.

Q. He seemed to have some conversation in the barn with Booth before he came out?

A. Yes, sir.

Q. Could you judge the nature of that conversation ?   Did Herold seem to be willing to surrender himself?

A. I do not know any thing about it ; only the remark made by Booth to Herold.

Q. You did not hear any other part of the conversation ?

A. I did not.

Q. In that remark, Booth spoke harshly to Herold, — called him a coward ?

A. Yes, sir.

Q. When the question was raised about Herold's delivering up the arms before he came out, I understood you to say that Booth replied that the arms were all his ?

A. Yes, sir.

Q. What was the interval that they were together there in the barn, after you first notified them, before Herold came and surrendered himself?   What time do you suppose elapsed ?

A. I think I looked as soon as I could conveniently ; and I believe we got to the barn about two o'clock in the morning. Booth was shot, and carried out on the grass ; so that there was time to look at the watch, — about fifteen minutes after three : that would have been an hour and a quarter.

Q. He was carried out almost immediately after he was shot, I presume ?

A. Yes, sir : there was no time between it scarcely.

Q. Did you hear Booth say any thing about Herold, besides what you have already stated ?   Do you remember hearing him say that Herold was not to blame ?   Can you remember any thing ?

A. I have an indistinct recollection of something of that kind.

I will tell you, as nearly as I can, what it was. He said, "Here is a man in here who wants to go out," and I think he added, "who had nothing to do with it."

Q. That was, as near as you could remember, about the substance of his remark?

A. Yes, sir: I think that is, as near as I can recollect now, what was said.

Q. And, after that, Herold did come out?

A. Yes, sir.

Q. Can you remember any thing else?

A. I cannot.

By the JUDGE ADVOCATE:

Q. Had you ever seen Booth before?

A. I had seen him.

Q. Were you able from any knowledge thus acquired to recognize him as the same person?

A. Yes, sir. I think that I saw him, and remarked his resemblance to his brother; and inquired who it was. I had often seen his brother, Edwin Booth, play in the theatre, and was told this was a brother of his.

Q. Had you seen him in this city?

A. Yes, sir.

Q. And you were satisfied it was the same man?

A. Yes, sir.

SERGEANT BOSTON CORBETT,

a witness called for the prosecution, being duly sworn, testified as follows:—

By the JUDGE ADVOCATE:

Q. Lieutenant-Colonel Conger has just detailed to the Court all the circumstances connected with the pursuit and capture and killing of Booth, in which, I believe, you were engaged. I will ask you what part you took, not in the pursuit, but in the capture and killing of Booth, taking up the narrative at the point when you arrived at the house.

A. When we rode up to the house, my commanding officer, Lieutenant Doherty, as we were standing in the road, rode up to me, and told me that Booth was in that house, saying, " I want you to deploy the men right and left around the house, and see that no one escapes." That was done : the men were deployed around the house. After making inquiries at the house, it was found that Booth was not in the house, but in the barn. A guard was then left upon the house, and the main portion of the men thrown around the barn, closely investing it, with orders to allow no one to escape, but previously being cautioned to see that our arms were in readiness for use. After being ordered to surrender, and told that the barn would be fired in five minutes if he did not do so, Booth made many replies. In the first place, he wanted to know who we took him for. He said that his leg was broken, and what did we want with him? and he was told that it made no difference. His name was not mentioned at all in the whole affair; not giving them satisfaction to know whether we knew who they were or not, any further than he was told that they must surrender, and give themselves up as prisoners. He wanted to know where we would take them if they would give themselves up as prisoners. He received no satisfaction, but was told that he must surrender unconditionally, or else the barn would be fired. The parley lasted much longer than the time first set ; probably, I should think, a full half-hour. I could not say whether it was exactly that time, more or less ; but it was time for many words to and fro : he was positively declaring that he would not surrender. At one time he made the remark, " Well, my brave boys, you can prepare a stretcher for me ; " and at another time, " Well, captain, make quick work of it; shoot me through the heart ! " or words to that effect ; and thereby I knew that he was perfectly desperate, and did not expect that he would surrender. After a while, we heard the whispering of another person, — although he [Booth] had previously declared that there was but one there, himself, — who proved to be the prisoner Herold. Although we could not distinguish the words, his object seemed to be to persuade Booth to surrender. After hearing him, probably, a while, he sang out, " Certainly ! " seeming to disdain to do it himself. Said he, " Cap., there

is a man in here who wants to surrender mighty bad." Then I
suppose words followed inside that we could not hear.   Perhaps
Herold thought he had better stand by him, or something to that
effect.   Then Booth said, "Oh! go out, and save yourself, my boy,
if you can:" and then he said, "I declare before my Maker that
this man here is innocent of any crime whatever;" seeming willing
to take all the blame on himself, and trying to clear Herold.   They
were then told, that, if both would not surrender, the surrender of
one of them would be accepted; and he was told to hand out
his arms.   Herold declared that he had no arms; and Booth declared that the arms all belonged to him; that the other man was
unarmed.   He was finally taken out without his arms.   Immediately after Herold being taken out, the detective, Mr. Conger, came
from that side of the barn where he had been taken out, around to
the side where I was, and, passing me, set fire to the hay through
one of the cracks of the boards, at the end of the same side of the
barn where I was, a little to my right.   I had previously said to
Mr. Conger, though, and also to my commanding officer, that the
position in which I stood left me in front of a large crack, — you
might put your hand through it; and I knew that Booth could
distinguish me and others through these cracks in the barn, and
could pick us off if he chose to do so.   In fact, he made a remark
to that effect at one time.   Said he, "Cap., I could have picked
off three or four of your men already if I wished to do so.   Draw
your men off fifty yards, and I will come out," or such words.
He used such words many times.   When the fire was first lit, which
was almost immediately after Herold was taken out of the barn,
as the flame rose, he was seen.   We could then distinguish him,
apparently, I think, about the middle of the barn, turning towards
the fire, either to put the fire out, or else to shoot the one who
started it, I did not know which; but he was then coming right
towards me, as it were, a little to my right, — a full front breast
view.   I could have shot him then much easier than the time I
afterwards did; but as long as he was there, making no demonstra-
tion to hurt any one, I did not shoot him, but kept my eye upon
him steadily.   Finding the fire gaining upon him, he turned to the
other side of the barn, and got towards where the door was; and,

as he got there, I saw him make a movement towards the floor. I supposed he was going to fight his way out. One of the men who was watching told me that he aimed the carbine at him. He was taking aim with the carbine, but at whom I could not say. My mind was upon him attentively to see that he did no harm; and, when I became impressed that it was time, I shot him. I took steady aim on my arm, and shot him through a large crack in the barn. When he was brought out, I found that the wound was made in the neck a little back of the ear, and came out a little higher up on the other side of the head. He lived, I should think, until about seven o'clock that morning: I could not say whether after or before, but near seven o'clock, one way or the other; perhaps two or three hours after he was shot. I did not myself hear him speak a word after he was shot, except a cry or shout as he fell. Others, who were near him, and watching him constantly, said that he did utter the words which were published. I did not hear him speak a word audibly after I shot him.

Q. What time did he die?

A. I think it was about seven o'clock.

Q. Will you state whether or not you recognize the prisoner Herold as the man you took out of the barn?

A. That is the man. [Pointing to David E. Herold, one of the prisoners.]

Q. Did you know Booth before?

A. No, sir: I had never seen him before; but I was perfectly satisfied from his first remarks that it was him; for my commanding officer told me, while on the boat coming down to Belle Plain, that his leg was broken; and, when he was summoned to surrender, his first reply was that his leg was broken, and he was alone. I knew also from his desperate replies that he would not be taken alive, and such remarks, that it was Booth. I knew that no other man would act in such a way.

Cross-examined by MR. STONE:

Q. You say you judged from the conversation in the barn that Herold at first was anxious to surrender?

A. Yes, sir.

Q. And upon Booth refusing to surrender, he seemed, you judged, to desire to stay with him?

A. I rather thought so.

Q. It was after that that Booth made the declaration that you have mentioned?

A. I cannot certainly say whether it was after or before; but I I am very positive that he made the declaration that the man with him was innocent of any crime whatever; that he declared it before his Maker, using those words. I wish to state here, as improper motives have been imputed to me for the act I did, that I twice offered to my commanding officer, Lieutenant Doherty, and once to Mr. Conger, to go in the barn and take the man, saying that I was not afraid to go in and take him; it was less dangerous to go in and fight him than to stand before a crack, exposed to his fire, where I could not see him, although he could see me: but I was not sent in. Immediately when the fire was lit, our positions were reversed: I could see him, but he could not see me. It was not through fear at all that I shot him, but because it was my impression that it was time the man was shot; for I thought he would do harm to our men in trying to fight his way through that den if I did not.

John Fletcher,

a witness called for the prosecution, being duly sworn, testified as follows: —

By the Judge Advocate:

Q. Do you live in the city?

A. Yes, sir.

Q. What business have you been engaged in?

A. I am foreman at T. Naylor's livery-stable.

Q. Do you know the prisoner Atzerodt?

A. Yes, sir.

Q. Will you state whether or not you saw him in the month of April, — say the 3d of April?

A. Yes, sir.

Q. What was he doing at the stable then?

A. He came to the stable with another gentleman, on the 3d of

April, between six and seven o'clock, with two horses, and inquired for Mr. Naylor. I told him that Mr. Naylor was out, and asked him what did they want particular. He said they wanted to put up the horses there at the stable. I told him I attended to that business. They came in; and I ordered the horses down into the stable to be put in. The other gentleman that was with Atzerodt told me that he was going to Philadelphia, and that he would leave the sale of his horse to Atzerodt. I have never seen that man since. Atzerodt kept the horses at the stable. He sold one of them to Thompson, the stage-contractor. He kept the brown horse at the stable until the 12th of the month. On the 12th of April, he took the horse away. I did not see them afterwards until one o'clock on the 14th of April, when he came into the stable with a dark-bay mare. I asked him what he had done with the brown horse; and he told me that he had sold him in Montgomery County, with the saddle and bridle, and had bought this mare, saddle, and bridle. He then told me to put up that mare in the stable; and I did so.

Q. Will you describe the appearance of that horse? Was he blind of one eye?

A. Yes, sir. He was a very heavy, common work-horse, blind of one eye.

Q. What color?

A. A dark-brown horse, with a heavy tail, — the mane was not very heavy, — and with heavy fetlocks down to the feet.

Q. Was that the horse he brought back with the mare on the 12th of April?

A. No, sir: that was the horse he took away on the 12th.

Q. Proceed with your statement.

A. I went to supper at half-past six o'clock on the 14th; and, when I came back from supper, the colored boys had this mare right at the carriage-house door, with a saddle and bridle on her. He paid the colored boys fifty cents for her keeping. He said that was right, and I told him yes. Said he, "If I stay until morning, how much are you going to charge me again?" — "Only fifty cents more," said I. He went out, and staid out about three-quarters of an hour, and returned back again with the same mare. He told me not to take the saddle or bridle off that mare until ten o'clock, and to keep the stable open for him. I told him yes : I would be there at that time myself. At ten o'clock, he came after the mare. He asked me to have something to drink with him. I told him I had no objection ; and he and I went down to the Union Hotel, at the corner of Thirteen and a Half and E Streets. He asked me what I would have. I told him I would have a glass of beer. He took some whiskey. Returning to the stable again, he said to me, " If this thing happens to-night, you will hear of a present." He seemed to me as if he was about half tight ; and I did not pay much attention to him.

Q. Did he say that you would hear of a present, or hear of the President ?

A. Of a present.

Q. That is, that you would get a present ?

A. Yes, sir : something that way. I was not paying much attention to him. We then went back to the stable together, and he mounted the mare. I said, " I would not like to ride that mare through the city in the night ; for she looks so skittish-looking." " Well," said he, " she is good upon the retreat." I then said to him, " Your acequaintance is staying out very late with our horse." That was Herold. " Oh ! " said he, " he will be back after a while." I watched him then until he went down E Street, passed Thirteen and a Half Street ; and I followed him down. I saw him go in the Kirkwood House. I watched until he came out, and mounted the mare again. He went along D Street, and turned on Tenth Street, to the left of D Street and Tenth. I returned back to the stable again. I did not go into the office, but staid at the carriage-house door. I was thinking about him living so far away, and the horse I had hired to Herold ; and I had a suspicion of the party, that they were taking the horse away. I went across E Street again, and went up Fourteenth Street until I came upon Pennsylvania Avenue close to Willard's ; and then I saw Herold riding the roan horse belonging to Mr. Naylor that I had hired him. The horse seemed as if he wanted to go to the stable. I thought, if I could get close enough to him, that I would take the horse from him ; but I expect he knew me by the light of the gas, — the lamp at Willard's corner. He began to move the horse away a little. Said I, " You

get off that horse now! you have had that horse out long enough."
He put spurs into the horse, and went up Fourteenth Street. I
kept sight of him until he turned to the east of F Street. I then
returned to the stable for a saddle and bridle and horse myself. I
got a horse, and went along the avenue until I came to Thirteenth
Street; went up Thirteenth Street to E, along E until I came to
Ninth, and turned down Ninth Street to Pennsylvania Avenue
again. I went along the avenue to the south side of the Capitol. . I
there met a gentleman coming down; and I asked him if he saw
any men going up there, riding on horseback. He said yes, and
that they were riding very fast. I did not ask him any more questions. I followed on until I got to the Navy-Yard Bridge; and the
guard there halted me, and called for the sergeant of the guard of
the heavy artillery, and he came out. I asked him if a roan horse
had crossed that bridge, giving him a description of the horse, saddle, and bridle, and the man that was riding the horse. He said,
" Yes: he has gone across the bridge." Said I, " Did he stay
long here?" He replied, " He said that he was waiting for an
acquaintance of his that was coming on; but he did not wait; and
another man came riding a bay horse or a bay mare, I do not know
which, right after him." Said I to the sergeant, " Did he tell you
his name?" — " Yes," said he: " he said his name was Smith."
I asked the sergeant if I could cross the bridge after them. He
said, " Yes: you can cross the bridge; but you cannot return back."
I said, " If that is so, I will not go." So I turned around, and
came back to the city again. When I came to Third Street, I
looked at my watch, and it wanted ten minutes to twelve. I rode
pretty fast going down to the Navy Yard; but I rode slow coming
back. I went along E Street until I got to Fourteenth Street, and
inquired of the foreman at Murphy's stable, by the name of Dor-
sey, whether this roan horse had been put up there. He said, " No."
But said he, " You had better keep in; for President Lincoln is
shot, and Secretary Seward is almost dead." I then returned to
the stable, put up the horse, came outside of the office-window, and
sat down there: it was half-past one o'clock. There were people
passing on the sidewalk, and they were saying that it was men riding
on horseback that had shot President Lincoln. Then, on account

of Atzerodt leaving the stable so late at night, and Herold having the horse, I had a suspicion of the party. I went across E Street, again into Fourteenth Street, and asked a cavalry sergeant if they had picked up any horses. He told me that they had picked up some horses, and for me to go down to the police-office on Tenth Street. So I went down Tenth Street to the police-office, and met with a detective there by the name of Charley Stone, and called him to one side, and asked him if they had picked up any horses of such a description. He told me there were some horses up at General Augur's headquarters, and asked me who I hired the horse to; and I told him. I told him the time he left the stable. He then asked me to go along with him to General Augur's office. We went there together; and, when we went into the office, General Augur asked me if I knew the man that I hired the horse to. I told him I did. I gave him the name of Herold, his description, and his age, as far as I could judge, and told him that I had pursued him to the Navy-Yard Bridge. There was a saddle and bridle lying right close to his desk in the office, and that was Atzerodt's saddle and bridle; for he came for his horse many days while the colored boys were at dinner, and I would saddle and bridle the horse for him. General Augur asked what kind of a horse had that saddle and bridle on. I told him a big, brown horse, blind of one eye; a heavy horse, with a heavy tail; a kind of a pacing horse. He asked me did I know that man's [Atzerodt's] name. I told him that I did not know his name, but I had it at the office. He sent the detective, Charley Stone, with me down to the office; and I went into the office, and got his name right upon one of our cards, and brought it up, and gave it to the general.

Q. [Exhibiting a saddle and bridle to the witness.] Will you look at that saddle and bridle, and see if they are the same that belonged to the horse that Atzerodt rode on that night?

A. This is not the saddle and bridle that belonged to the horse he rode out of the stable that night; but this is the saddle and bridle that he told me he sold in Montgomery County.

Q. With the one-eyed horse?

A. Yes, sir.

Q. They are the saddle and bridle that you spoke of as having seen at General Augur's headquarters?

A. Yes, sir.

[The saddle and bridle were offered in evidence without objection.]

Q. Did he call that night precisely at ten?

A. Yes, sir: he came to the minute of ten.

Q. You kept the horse, saddle, and bridle waiting for him?

A. Yes, sir.

Q. Do you remember whether he made any remark about something strange or wonderful likely to happen that night, — if he said any thing on that subject?

A. He told me, "If this thing happens to-night, you will hear of a present."

Q. Had you been talking about any thing before that?

A. No, sir; but he seemed very excited-looking: nothing more than that.

Q. When you last saw him, was he going up Tenth Street?

A. Yes, sir.

Q. Was it in the direction of Ford's Theatre?

A. Yes, sir.

Q. You spoke of Herold having a horse from your stable?

A. Yes, sir: he hired a horse from me.

Q. When did he hire that horse?

A. On the 14th of April.

Q. At what time in the day?

A. I guess it wanted about a quarter to one o'clock.

Q. Did he hire it for any given time?

A. Yes, sir: he engaged the horse, and told me to keep it for him; that he would be after it at four o'clock. He did not come for the horse until a quarter-past four; and he asked me how much I would charge for the hire of the horse. I told him five dollars. He wanted him for four dollars. I told him he could not have it for that. He knew this horse, and inquired for it. I went down to the stable with him; and I told him to take a mare that was in the stable, but he would not have her. I then told him I would give him the other horse. He then wanted to see the saddles and bridles. I showed him a saddle, and he said it was too small.

Then I showed him another saddle. That suited very well, only that it had not the kind of stirrups he wanted. The stirrups were covered with leather ; and he wanted a pair of English steel stirrups. He then wanted to see the bridles. I took him into the office, and showed him the bridles ; and he picked out a double-reined bridle. Before he mounted the horse, he asked me how late he could stay out with the horse. I told him he could stay out no later than eight o'clock, or nine at the farthest. Afterwards I became very uneasy about the horse, and wanted to see about it before I closed up the stable ; and that is how I got to see Atzerodt and Herold.

Q. At what hour did you see Herold riding that night ?

A. It was about twenty-five minutes past ten o'clock.

Q. From what direction was he moving ?

A. He seemed as if he was coming down from the Treasury upon the avenue ; and I met him close to Willard's, on the avenue.

Q. And he was going what way ?

A. He was passing Fourteenth Street. The horse was pulling to get to the stable ; for he was a horse very well acquainted with the stable. I suppose Herold knew me ; and he turned the horse round, and I hallooed to him to get off that horse.

Q. Did he move off pretty rapidly ?

A. He put spurs to the horse, and went, as fast as the horse could go, up Fourteenth Street.

Q. Do you mean North ?

A. Yes, sir : North Fourteenth Street.

Q. You say he knew that horse ?

A. Yes, sir.

Q. Was he a fast horse ?

A. He was not a very fast horse. He was a lady's saddle-horse. He was all the time used as a lady's saddle-horse ; and any one could ride him, he was so gentle and nice.

Q. Did he trot, or pace ?

A. A single foot-rack. He would trot if you would let the bridle-rein go slack.

Q. He made no reply when you called to him ?

A. No, sir : not the slightest.

Q. Had you not separated then from Atzerodt ?

A. Yes, sir: it was after returning back from him.

Q. You had not then heard any thing of the assassination of the President?

A. No, sir: not a word.

Q. Have you seen the horse that Herold rode, since?

A. No, sir.

Q. Describe that horse.

A. He was a light roan horse; black tail, black legs, black mane, and close on fifteen hands high.

Q. When did you say you saw that saddle and bridle at General Augur's office?

A. At two o'clock on the night of the 14th of April.

Q. You mean the morning of the 15th?

A. Yes, sir: I count that the night.

Q. Have you seen the one-eyed horse since?

A. No, sir: I have not seen him since.

Cross-examined by Mr. STONE:

Q. At what time did you say that Herold hired this horse from you?

A. He engaged it at a quarter to one o'clock.

Q. Was he to take it at that hour?

A. No, sir: he was to take it at four o'clock.

Q. Was it at a quarter to one, or when he did take the horse at four o'clock, that he tried to Jew you down about the price?

A. When he engaged the horse at a quarter to one.

Q. You charged him five dollars, and he wanted to get it for four?

A. Yes, sir.

Q. You told him he could keep it until eight o'clock?

A. Until eight o'clock, or nine at the farthest.

Q. In which direction did he ride away from the stable?

A. He rode out E Street, and down Thirteenth Street to the avenue. E Street runs along the stable.

Q. You did not see him any more until you saw him opposite Willard's?

A. No, sir.

Q. Did the horse seem then to be tired?

A. Not very.

Q. But still he seemed to be somewhat tired.

A. Yes, sir: he seemed as if he kind of wanted to go to the stable.

Q. He seemed as if he had been ridden a right smart distance?

A. Yes, sir.

Q. How near were you to him, do you think, when you first saw him?

A. I was not fifteen yards from him.

Q. At what gait was he going then?

A. He was going kind of easy,—letting the horse go slow. The horse was pulling; and he would almost bring him up standing.

Q. Was he on a gallop, or a trot?

A. He was neither galloping nor trotting.

Q. But a kind of pace?

A. He was in a kind of pace.

Q. Did you call him by name?

A. No, sir: I did not.

Q. What did you say?

A. I said, "Get off that horse! you have had him out long enough."

Q. The man that you saw, and supposed to be Herold, took no notice of what you said to him at all?

A. No, sir.

Q. Fourteenth Street is the street that runs by Willard's, is it not?

A. Yes, sir.

Q. He turned up that street?

A. Yes, sir.

Q. And increased the speed of the horse?

A. Yes, sir.

Q. Did I understand you to say it was Herold that examined the saddles in your stable, and was a little hard to please about a saddle?

A. Yes, sir.

Q. You showed him two or three before he could get one to suit him ?

A. Yes, sir.

Q. Was it about a quarter-past four that he came to the stable ?

A. Yes, sir: when he left the stable with the horse.

Q. And you think it was about a quarter-past ten when you saw him at Willard's ?

A. About twenty-five minutes past ten, to the best of my belief.

Q. Are you satisfied that it was the same man now in the box ?

A. Yes, sir: I am very well satisfied it was Herold.

Q. Were you acquainted with him before ?

A. I got acquainted with Herold in this way : He came one day to the stable — I believe it was the 5th or 6th of April — inquiring for this man Atzerodt, but did not inquire for him by name. He inquired for the man that kept the horse in the side-stable, and wanted to know if he had been there that day.

Q. Did you ever see him except that ?

A. Never, to my knowledge.

Q. So that you never saw him but twice ; once on the 5th or 6th of April, and then when he came to the stable for that horse ?

A. He was coming there every day from about the 6th of April until the 12th, inquiring for Atzerodt ; and I saw him riding with Atzerodt. One day, Atzerodt went out riding himself, and sent the horse back with Herold ; and, the next day, Atzerodt asked me how did he bring the horse ? did he ride him fast ?

Q. Was he near the sidewalk, or near the middle of the street, when you saw him ?

A. He was not in the middle of the street ; but he was very near it. He was to the south side of Fourteenth Street and Pennsylvania Avenue. He was near to that side.

Q. Did you notice the horse or the man particularly, or both ?

A. I noticed the horse and the man both together.

Cross-examined by MR. DOSTER :

Q. What time in the evening of the 14th was it when Atzerodt came to your stable ?

A. We left there at seven o'clock, and came back at a quarter to eight.

Q. What was the last time he came there?

A. At ten o'clock.

Q. Did you notice the time particularly?

A. Yes, sir: I always keep a timepiece in my pocket.

Q. It was about ten o'clock?

A. Yes, sir.

Q. How long did you stay with him until you parted with him?

A. Only while he and I went together to the Union Hotel; and I stopped there while he was taking a drink of whiskey, and I a drink of beer; and, on coming back to the stable, the colored boy did not bring up the right horse to him, and I went down to the stable myself and brought up the right horse. There was a horse in the stable, belonging to him, with a saddle and bridle on him.

Q. How long did you judge all that took?

A. Close on ten minutes between all of them.

Q. How far is the Union House from your stable?

A. About a hundred yards, as near as I can judge.

Q. You went down there and came back, and then you say you saddled up another horse for him?

A. No, sir: I did not saddle up another horse. The colored boy, in mistake, brought up another horse to the front of the carriage-house; and I took that horse down again, and brought up the right horse to him.

Q. Was Atzerodt's horse saddled then?

A. Yes, sir.

Q. It was ready saddled?

A. Yes, sir.

Q. You say all that only took ten minutes?

A. No more.

Q. It was ten minutes from the time you reached the stable until he went away?

A. I cannot say about that. It was ten minutes from the time we went to the Union Hotel and back again, and the horse was brought up to the carriage-door in mistake, and I returned the horse back, put him into the stable, and brought up the other horse.

Q. You say you took a drink together?

A. Yes, sir.

Q. Did you take but one?

A. That is all.

Q. Did Atzerodt say that he had been taking a good many more?

A. Yes, sir.

Q. What conversation had you immediately preceding this remark you have mentioned?

A. We had not a word: we were just going along together.

Q. And did not say any thing?

A. No, sir: I made no remark to him, nor he to me.

Q. Did you reply to that remark?

A. I did not pay much attention to it.

Q. You have mentioned that Atzerodt kept a brown horse at your stable until the 12th day of April, to which that saddle used to belong?

A. Yes, sir.

Q. I understand you to say, that, when he returned, he told you that he had sold the horse and the saddle?

A. Yes, sir : in Montgomery County.

Q. Did you ask him to whom he sold it?

A. No, sir: I did not.

Q. Do you remember what day it was that he told you he had sold the saddle?

A. On the 14th of April.

Q. The same day as the assassination?

A. Yes, sir.

Q. He told you that he had sold the saddle?

A. He told me that he had sold the horse, saddle, and bridle in Montgomery County.

Q. What made you follow Atzerodt that night?

A. On account of his acquaintance with Herold, who had another horse out so late. He told me he would be in at eight or nine o'clock at the farthest.

Q. But what had Atzerodt to do with Herold, that you knew of?

A. They were acquaintances together.

Q. Did you suppose that Atzerodt was going to where Herold was? Was that your idea?

A. He was so far away from home; and I supposed that he was going home that time of night, knowing he lived down in T. B., in Maryland.

Q. Your purpose in following Atzerodt was to find Herold?

A. Yes, sir.

Q. You never saw the horse that Herold rode in the hands of Atzerodt?

A. No, sir.

Q. Were you called upon to identify a horse at General Augur's stable?

A. No, sir.

Q. How long was it between the time you saw this saddle at General Augur's headquarters and the time you had seen it before?

A. It was from the 12th to the 14th of April, at two o'clock in the night.

Q. I understood you to say a few moments ago that he told you he had sold that horse and saddle and bridle on the 14th.

A. No, sir: on the 12th. He came back on the 14th.

Q. What did Herold tell you when he engaged the horse on the 14th?

A. He told me that he wanted to go riding with a lady.

Q. Where to?

A. I did not ask him.

Q. Did he not tell you without your asking?

A. No, sir.

Q. Did he not say at all where he was going?

A. No, sir: I did not ask him where he was going, and he did not tell me.

Q. You say that you think you saw Atzerodt going into the Kirkwood House on the night of the 14th of April?

A. Yes, sir.

Q. Will you state how long he staid there?

A. Not more than five minutes, I think, to the best of my recollection.

Q. Did you see him come out again?

A. Yes, sir.

Q. What were you doing all the time? — watching for him?

A. I was watching the horse he rode, that was outside.

Q. You say that Atzerodt rode away from the stable, and you followed him?

A. Yes, sir.

Q. Did you follow him on foot?

A. Yes, sir.

Q. Did you not state before that he rode at great speed? How did you manage to keep up with him?

A. He rode the horse fast from the stable; but, when he got out about thirty yards, he began to walk the horse slow, and I kept up with him walking.

Q. Did you keep up with him up to the time he entered the Kirkwood House?

A. When he went into the Kirkwood House, I stopped on the south side of the avenue, close to the curbstone.

Q. You came, then, about the same time he did?

A. I went right after him.

Q. How long after?

A. Just as he dismounted from the horse.

Q. Now far is it from the stable to the Kirkwood House the way you went?

A. The stable is at Thirteen and a Half and E Streets.

Q. How far is it, do you judge, from where you started to the Kirkwood House, by the way you went?

A. You may say it is two squares.

Q. Did you keep up with Atzerodt afterwards?

A. No, sir: I did not.

Q. What did you do?

A. I kept in sight of him: that was all.

Q. At what pace was he riding?

A. He was going on a walk.

Q. How far did you follow him?

A. I only just kept in sight of him until I saw him turning Tenth Street, and did not go any farther.

Q. Then you quit him?

A. Yes, sir.

Q. And you never saw him again until you saw him here to-day?

A. No, sir.

Q. Which way did he seem to be moving when you left, in Tenth Street?

A. He was moving in the way of Tenth Street.

Q. Which direction in Tenth Street?

A. Turning to his left in Tenth Street, off D.

The JUDGE ADVOCATE requested the witness to visit the stable at Seventeenth and I Streets, and examine a horse there to see if he could identify him; and, on his return, his examination was continued as follows:—

By the JUDGE ADVOCATE:

Q. Now state to the Court whether, since you left here, you have visited the stable, and examined the horse of which we were speaking?

A. Yes, sir.

Q. Where did you find the animal?

A. I found him right in the middle of the stable, the first stall, at General Augur's headquarters' stable, corner of Seventeenth and I Streets.

Q. Did you examine him?

A. Yes, sir.

Q. Do you, or do you not, recognize that as the horse spoken of in your testimony, that Atzerodt had at your stable, and took away, — a one-eyed horse, the one he said he had sold?

A. Yes, sir: the same one. The right eye of the horse is blind.

By MR. DOSTER:

Q. How long was that horse kept in your stable?

A. He was kept there from the 3d to the 12th of April.

Q. Did you have the grooming of him?

A. No: I had not.

Q. What is your exact business in the stable?

A. I have saddled the horse, I believe, three or four times.

John Greenawalt,

a witness called for the prosecution, being duly sworn, testified as follows : —

By the Judge Advocate :

Q. Will you state whether or not you are the keeper of the Pennsylvania House in this city?

A. I am.

Q. Where is that house situated?

A. At Nos. 357 and 359, C Street, between Four and a Half and Sixth Streets.

Q. Are you acquainted with the prisoner Atzerodt?

A. I am.

Q. Were you or not acquainted with J. Wilkes Booth in his lifetime?

A. I was never acquainted with him?

Q. Did you know him by sight?

A. I never knew him. A man came to the house : from the description I had of him afterwards, it was Booth. He has been there to see Atzerodt.

Q. Did you see him?

A. I did.

Q. Look at that photograph, and see if you recognize it as the photograph of that man? [Exhibit No. 1.]

A. That is the person.

Q. State whether or not that person, Booth, had frequent interviews with the prisoner Atzerodt at the Pennsylvania House.

A. He had.

Q. What was the character of those interviews?

A. Atzerodt generally sat in the sitting-room, and Booth would come in through the hall. Sometimes he would not enter the room at all : he would walk in and walk back. Atzerodt would get up and follow him out. They frequently had interviews in front of my house. Several times that I walked on the steps, they walked off down by the livery-stable, towards the National Hotel, and stood and had interviews there.

Q. Did you or not at any time hear the prisoner Atzerodt speak of expecting to have plenty of gold soon? State what he said on that subject.

A. Once, he and some more, — there was a number of young men from Port Tobacco met him there, and they had been drinking. He asked me to take a drink. I took a drink, and he said, "Greenawalt, I am pretty near broke; but I have always got friends enough to give me as much money as will see me through; though," said he, "I am going away some of these days, but I will return with as much gold as will keep me all my lifetime."

Q. When was it that he made that declaration?

A. It must have been nine or ten days after he first came to my house.

Q. What month was that?

A. He came there on the 18th of March last, I believe. I think it must have been about the 30th or 31st of March, or the 1st of April, when this happened, as near as I can remember.

Q. Was he or not in the habit, when in the city, of stopping at your house?

A. He stopped there before this last time. He stopped over night: he never stopped any length of time.

Q. Will you state how long before the assassination he left your house?

A. I think, on Wednesday morning.

Q. Had he any baggage with him?

A. No, sir.

Q. Will you state when you next saw him again?

A. I saw him next on Saturday morning, between two and three o'clock, after the assassination.

Q. Did he come to your home and ask for a room at that hour?

A. I had just come in the house myself, and went to my room. About five minutes afterwards, a servant came up with a five-dollar bill, and told me, "There is a man come in with Atzerodt, who wants lodging, and wants to pay for it." So I went down, and gave the man his change. I had an uneasiness about the thing myself, — thought there was something wrong.

Q. Did they take a room together?

A. Yes, sir. Atzerodt asked for his old room; and I told him it was occupied. I told him he would have to go with this gentleman. So I gave the man his change, — this Thomas, — and told the servant to show him to his room; and Atzerodt was going to follow him. Said I, "Atzerodt, you have not registered." Said he, "Do you want my name?" Said I, "Certainly." He hesitated some, but stepped back and registered, and went to his room. That was the last I saw of him.

Q. Will you describe the appearance of that man who was with him?

A. He was a man about five feet seven or eight inches high; and his weight was about one hundred and forty pounds, I should judge.

Q. How was he dressed?

A. Poorly dressed, and in dark. His pants were worn through at the back, near the heels. I took notice of that as he walked out of the door to go to his room. He was quite dark-complexioned, and very much weather-beaten. He had dark hair.

Q. Had he the appearance of a laboring man?

A. Yes, sir: the appearance of a laboring man.

Q. Could you express an opinion as to whether the clothes in which he was dressed were such as he would probably ordinarily wear, or were assumed as a disguise? Have you an opinion on that subject?

A. I judged them to be more of a disguise. I think it was a broadcloth coat he had on; very much worn, though.

Q. The whole appearance, you say, was shabby?

A. Yes, sir.

Q. What name did he assume?

A. Sam Thomas.

Q. What became of that man the next morning?

A. He got up about five o'clock, I think, and left the house. That was what the servant told me. There was a lady stopping there, and I had given the servant orders to get her a carriage to take her to the railroad depot for the 6.15 train. She had left before I got up; and, as the servant was going out of the door, this man Thomas went out, and asked the way to the railway depot.

Q. He had no baggage?

A. No, sir: not any.

Q. He came between two and three, you say, and left at five?

A. Yes, sir.

Q. Did Atzerodt remain?

A. Atzerodt left shortly afterwards, and he walked towards Sixth Street. As the servant came back from getting the carriage, he met Atzerodt, and said to him, " Atzerodt, what brings you out so early this morning?"—" Well," said he, " I have got business." These were all the words.

Q. In what direction was he going?

A. Towards Sixth Street; that is, west from my house.

Q. Had he paid his bill?

A. No, sir.

Q. He left without paying?

A. Yes, sir.

Q. When did you see him again?

A. I have not seen him since.

Q. Do you recognize him among these prisoners?

A. Yes, sir: there he sits [pointing to George A. Atzerodt].

Q. Is this the first time you have seen him since?

A. It is.

Q. What was the manner of these men that night? Did you observe any thing unusual, — any excitement about them?

A. No, sir: there was no excitement about them. This man Thomas stared at me. He kept a close eye on me as I came in.

Q. Did they have any conversation with each other in your presence?

A. No, sir.

Q. Which of them asked for the room?

A. Thomas asked for it.

Q. Did he ask for both? How did they happen to have the same room?

A. He just asked for himself. Atzerodt was lying on the settee in the corner of the room as I came in; and Thomas was standing at the counter, at the register.

Q. How did it happen, then, that they went to the same room?

A. Atzerodt asked for his old room. I told him that was occupied, and he would have to go in with this man. The room that he was in was a large room, — a room with six beds in. There were other parties in it before these men went there.

Q. Do you know the prisoner O'Laughlin?

A. No, sir.

Q. You do not remember to have seen him?

A. No.

Q. Did you observe whether either of these parties was armed?

A. I have seen Atzerodt have a revolver.

Q. On the occasion spoken of?

A. There are others in the party who said he had a knife; but I did not see that.

Q. Did you observe whether the other man, Thomas as he called himself, was armed?

A. I did not.

Q. You say he stared at you very much. Did he make any remark to you?

A. All that he said to me was that he was a poor writer.

Q. Did he enter his name himself?

A. I did not see that; but I judge that his name was entered when I came into the room.

Q. You say Atzerodt was in the habit of stopping at your hotel. Had he, on any previous occasion, hesitated to register his name when taking rooms there?

A. No, sir.

Q. You say that he did hesitate on this occasion?

A. On this occasion, he hesitated somewhat.

Q. You speak of having seen Atzerodt armed. When was that?

A. That must have been in March, when I first saw his revolver. He had just bought it; and he came in, and made the remark that he had just bought it; and I told him I wished I had known that he wanted one, for I could have sold him one that I had, — a new one, which I had traded a small one for, and I had no use for it.

Q. Did he exhibit the revolver to you?

A. It was put in my care, — handed in to the office.

Q. Do you think you would recognize it if you saw it again?

A. I think I would.

Q. [Exhibiting the revolver identified by John Lee, as found in a room at the Kirkwood House.] Is that it?

A. I would not be certain. I do not think it is the same one; but it is something similar.

Cross-examined by MR. DOSTER:

Q. Will you be kind enough to state on what day, before the 14th of April, Atzerodt left your house?

A. It must have been on Wednesday, the 12th.

Q. How long had he staid at your house at that time?

A. He staid from the 18th of March, until, I think, the 27th. If I had my register, I could tell.

Q. I only want to know about the last visit before the 14th of April. How long was he at your house then?

A. He was away for several days, — from Wednesday until Saturday morning between two and three o'clock.

Q. You say he left on Wednesday, the 12th. How long had he been there before he left on that Wednesday? Do you remember?

A. He had been there from the 18th of March. He had been away but once, and then he told me that he was going to the country; and he staid over night, and returned the next day with a man named Bailey, when he came to the house.

Q. You say that you know of Atzerodt having had interviews with Booth. Can you tell about how many they had?

A. I cannot tell exactly, but quite a number.

Q. Were you present at any of them?

A. No, sir.

Q. Where were these interviews?

A. In front of my house.

Q. On the street?

A. Sometimes on the pavement; sometimes below my house, down towards the National, I have seen them stand.

Q. Were their interviews held in secret in any room?

A. No, sir: I never saw Booth in any room.

Q. You mentioned before that Atzerodt had, previous to this last visit, had arms in his possession?

A. I saw them once: that was when he handed them into the office there.

Q. And you kept them for him?

A. Yes, until he called for them.

Q. Could you or could you not recognize them again?

A. I could not swear to them.

Q. What were the arms?

A. A large revolver, — something similar to the one shown me.

Q. What else?

A. Nothing else that I saw.

Q. Did he have a knife?

A. Other persons there say they have seen him with a knife; but I never saw it.

Q. You have mentioned that Atzerodt boasted, that, on some day, he would have enough gold and silver to keep him all his life. What led to that remark? Do you remember the conversation that preceded it?

A. I came into the room. He was drinking at the time. He asked me to take a drink. I took a drink. He paid the bill; and then he said, "Greenawalt, I am pretty near broke; but I have always got friends enough to give me as much money as will see me through."

Q. Did you not have gold and silver in your hand, and shake it in his face?

A. No, sir.

Q. Did any one of the company have gold and silver there?

A. Not that I remember, and not that I saw. I have had half

a dollar in my pocket, and I might have had that out; but I do not remember having it out.

Q. Do you not remember saying that you had bought some gold that morning?

A. No, sir.

Q. Had you also been drinking?

A. I had taken a drink : I was not in liquor.

Q. Do I understand you to say that you do not remember saying that you had bought gold and silver that morning?

A. I do not remember that I did. When Mr. Bailey left my house, he wanted to pay his stage-fare; and I bought some eight or nine two and a half dollar gold-pieces ; and I do not remember the exact amount of silver, but some seven dollars, I think.

Q. What brought the conversation to gold and silver?

A. I do not know that I ever had any conversation about gold and silver. There was only the remark of Atzerodt: there was no other conversation about it.

Q. Had you not before been talking about money in some shape?

A. No, sir : I had not been talking with him at all until I entered the room. He asked me to drink.

Q. Had any one else, to your knowledge, been talking with him about money?

A. No, sir.

Q. You mentioned a man by the name of Thomas as having come to your house on the morning of this Saturday, between two and three o'clock, in company with Atzerodt. Did they seem to be intimate ?

A. No, sir.

Q. Did you take them to be previously acquainted?

A. I could not tell in regard to that. They came to my house.

Q. You can tell what you took them to be. Did you take them to be acquaintances, or strangers ?

A. I thought they were in company by the way they came there.

Q. Did they look as though they had known one another previously? or had met one another on the street, and just happened to come to your house together?

A. I judged that they were acquainted.

Q. You say this man exhibited signs of disguise. What were they ?

A. He had on broadcloth clothing. It did not look like working clothing; and it was well worn;—not laboring man's clothing.

Q. His clothing was well worn and broadcloth; and that made you think he was in disguise ?

A. Yes, sir.

Q. You have also mentioned that Atzerodt hesitated to register his name. In what shape did he hesitate ?

A. " Well," said he, " do you wish my name ?" I said, " Certainly." He stood back ; and then he walked forward and stopped, and then followed it up, and put down his name.

Q. Is it an unusual thing for men to hesitate, when they come there at two or three o'clock in the morning, to register their names ?

A. I have not been receiving any guests at that hour. I never had any one to hesitate about registering.

Q. Did he say he would not like to do it ?

A. No, sir.

Q. Did he seem sleepy ?

A. No, he did not, to my knowledge.

Q. Did he seem in liquor ?

A. No : he was not in liquor.

Q. Did he seem wide awake ?

A. He did.

Q. Do you recognize among the prisoners at the bar the stranger by the name of Thomas ?

A. There [pointing to Edward Spangler] is a man who resembles him somewhat. It appears to me he is not as dark. He has not got the beard on he had then. His hair was longer, and, I think, darker. I could not be positive as to that man.

Q. His hair was longer and darker ?

A. Yes, sir; and cut down half over his ears. I think he was heavier.

Q. Still you would not swear this was the man ?

A. No, sir.

Q. That man staid with you until five o'clock in the morning ?

A. He left about that time, as I understand

Q. Did you have a conversation with Atzerodt about where he was going in the morning?

A. No, sir: I did not have any conversation with him that morning, no more than I asked him whether he had got back. That was all the conversation that I passed with him, except that I asked him to register.

Q. After he registered, and while he was registering, he remarked that he was a poor writer?

A. No, sir: Thomas made that remark.

Q. [Exhibiting to the witness the coat identified by John Lee as having been found in the room at the Kirkwood House.] Look at that coat. Do you remember ever having seen that in the possession of Atzerodt?

A. I never did.

Cross-examined by Mr. Ewing:

Q. Describe the color of the mustache that the man had on, who, you say, resembled Spangler.

A. Dark, black.

Q. Heavy mustache?

A. Yes, sir.

Q. Had no other whisker?

A. Yes, sir: I think his beard was cut down at the sides.

Q. Was the beard on the side of the face close?

A. His beard came front, and was cut down from the mustache up; but it was either that way or whiskers all around. I know he had whiskers in front.

Q. What sort of a hat did he wear?

A. A dark slouch hat.

Q. Worn?

A. Yes, sir.

By the Judge Advocate:

Q. Do I understand you to say that you are certain you have not seen the prisoner O'Laughlin at your house?

A. I am. I do not know the man.

Q. Did I understand you to say that Thomas came in company with Atzerodt?

A. I did not see them come in. When I first saw them, Atzerodt was lying on the settee, and Thomas standing at the counter at the register.

Q. What made you think they belonged together?

A. The servant told me they came in together.

Q. That is the only ground of your believing they were intimate?

A. That is all I had.

Q. Will you state, if you please, the exact color of the hair and beard of Thomas?

A. As near as I can tell, his hair was black, black eyebrows, and black whiskers. He had a mustache cut off from sides rather close, and beard in front.

Q. Did either the hair or mustache appear to be dyed?

A. No, sir.

Q. What was the color?

A. Black.

Q. Did not Atzerodt refuse or object to this stranger going into his room?

A. No, sir.

Q. Did he ask that he should come in?

A. No, sir.

Q. He simply acceded to it when you told him that there was no other room?

A. Yes, sir. I told him he would have to room with that man.

Q. You forced them together, in short?

A. I told him he would have to. That was my work. I would not force him: he could have taken that, or left the house: that was the best I could do for him.

By the Court:

Q. Do you know whether they got up at the same time in the morning?

A. I do not.

Q. Did they occupy the same bed?

A. No.

Q. You said that the last time Atzerodt left your house before the assassination was on Wednesday?

A. I think so. He told me, going away. "Greenawalt, I owe you a couple of days' board: will it make any difference to you whether I pay for it now, or when I come back?" I said, "No." Then he remarked, "It will be more convenient for me to pay when I come back." He said he was going to Montgomery County.

Q. Do you know the man that they call O'Laughlin, here.

A. No, sir.

Q. Do you know the man with the black mustache, there in the centre of the prisoners' dock [referring to O'Laughlin].

A. I do not know him.

Q. You say the man Thomas stared at you at one time?

A. Yes, sir: when I entered the room, he did.

Q. Was that in the light?

A. Rather a dim light, — about half the jet of gas burning, — one burner.

Q. Did you have a distinct view of his face then?

A. I had a fair view of him.

Q. Do you recognize that face among the prisoners at the bar?

A. I do not, — not that I could swear to.

Q. Did you see the color of his eyes, his hair, his complexion?

A. He had dark eyes, dark complexion.

Q. What was his beard?

A. Black.

John F. Coyle,

a witness called for the prosecution, being duly sworn, testified as follows: —

By the JUDGE ADVOCATE:

Q. Will you please state to the Court whether you were acquainted with J. Wilkes Booth in his lifetime?

A. I knew him.

Q. Did you know him somewhat intimately?

A. Not at all.

Q. J. Wilkes Booth, before he died, made this statement, —

that, on the night before the assassination of the President, he wrote a long article, and left it for one of the editors of the "National Intelligencer," in which he fully set forth the reasons for the crime. Will you state whether such a paper was received?

A. I never heard of any such thing. This is the first I ever heard of it.

Q. Are you quite certain that no such paper was received at the office of the "Intelligencer"?

A. Not that I heard of.

HEZEKIAH METZ,

a witness called for the prosecution, being duly sworn, testified as follows : —

By the JUDGE ADVOCATE:

Q. Where do you reside?

A. In Montgomery County, Md., Clarksburg District.

Q. Will you state whether you have ever met the prisoner Atzerodt before? and if so, under what circumstances, and where?

A. I met a man by the name of Atwood at my house on Sunday.

Q. Look at these prisoners, and see if you recognize the man you were going to speak of.

A. Yes, sir: there he is [pointing out George A. Atzerodt]. That is the man.

Q. Proceed with your narrative.

A. On Sunday, after the death of Mr. Lincoln, he was at my house; and he ate his dinner there. He was just from Washington, and we were inquiring about the news: and a conversation came up about General Grant's being shot, — we had understood that he was shot, on the cars; and he said, if the man that was to follow him had followed him, it was likely to be so. That is the way I understood it.

Q. That if the man who was to have followed him had followed him, it would have been so?

A. It might have been so. That is the way I understood him.

30*

Q. What did he say further? Did he speak of the assassination of the President?

A. Not that I recollect. I do not recollect any more that passed there.

Q. How far is that from Washington City where you live?

A. About twenty-two or twenty-three miles.

Q. In what direction did he seem to be going?

A. In the direction of Barnsville, on the Barnsville Road.

Q. Was he travelling in that direction?

A. Yes, sir.

Q. Did he represent himself as having come from Washington?

A. Yes, sir.

Q. Did he not speak at all of the assassination which had just occurred here?

A. I do not recollect. We were inquiring; but I do not recollect any particulars that he said about it. The conversation turned to General Grant; and he used the words I have stated.

Q. Did you pursue the matter? Did you make any remark or any inquiry after he made that statement?

A. Not at the time. We talked about it afterwards.

Q. What occurred afterwards between you and him?

A. Not between him and me; but we talked the matter over among ourselves after he left. He did not stay long after that.

Q. Did he make that remark at the table, or where?

A. It was in the room before dinner came on.

Q. What was his manner? Was it excited, or calm?

A. I could not say it was excited.

Q. Where did he represent himself to be going?

A. He did not tell me where he was going.

Q. By what name did he call himself, then?

A. He passed in the neighborhood by the name of **Andrew Atwood**. That was the name I understood always.

Q. You say a rumor had reached you of the assassination of General Grant. Where was it said he had been assassinated?

A. I do not recollect any particulars about it. It was talked about in the neighborhood. I cannot say any thing about how it was said to have occurred. We had just heard it.

Cross-examined by MR. DOSTER:

Q. What is your business. Are you a hotel-keeper?

A. No: my business is farming.

Q. How long had you known Atzerodt before he came to see you the other day?

A. I think it is two or three years since I first got acquainted with him in that neighborhood. He was there, and I had a small acquaintance with him. I saw him three or four times, perhaps: I do not recollect how many. I merely knew him when I saw him. I do not recollect, really, that I ever saw him but once before this Sunday he came there.

Q. You say he went by the name of Andrew Atwood all around the country there?

A. Yes: all around my neighborhood.

Q. That is the name he has gone by for two years, — ever since you knew him?

A. It is the only name I ever knew for him. In two years, I think, I have seen him but twice.

Q. Is your house near the road?

A. Yes, sir: about half a mile from it.

Q. Where does the road lead to?

A. It leads to Barnsville.

Q. How many miles is it from Washington to your house?

A. I suppose, between twenty-two and twenty-three.

Q. What time of day was it when Atzerodt got there on this Sunday that you speak of?

A. I suppose it was between ten and eleven o'clock; somewhere thereabout: I disremember exactly.

Q. What did he say when he came there? What did he come for?

A. I did not hear any business.

Q. How long did he stay?

A. As well as I recollect, some two or three hours.

Q. Did he recognize you as an old acquaintance?

A. He knew me.

Q. Had you heard of the assassination of the President?

A. Yes, sir.

Q. Did you speak about the assassination, the first thing, yourself?

A. I do not recollect any thing of that. I do not recollect of his saying any thing about the assassination of the President

Q. You do not know who began the conversation?

A. I do not.

Q. Was anybody else talking with you when he made the remark which you mentioned about somebody following General Grant?

A. There was a couple of young men in the room at the time.

Q. How far were you from Atzerodt at the time he made this answer, as you say?

A. We were all in the room together.

Q. How far were you away from him?

A. I cannot say exactly.

Q. Were you sitting within one foot of him, or at the other end of the room?

A. Perhaps three yards. I disremember. I think I was sitting near the middle of the room; and he was sitting on one side of the room, as well as I recollect.

Q. You said, as I understood you, that you had heard that General Grant had been killed.

A. Yes, sir: we had heard that.

Q. And that he then answered? What was his precise answer?

A. We heard it, and we got to talking about it.

Q. Was not this the answer: "A man must have followed General Grant to have killed him"?

A. Not exactly; it was not spoken in that way: but, if the man who was to follow him had followed him, it was likely he might have killed him.

Q. His evident meaning, as far as you understand it, was, that General Grant, to have been killed, must have been followed?

A. To be sure: I should suppose so.

By the COURT.

Q. You say there were two young men at your house when Atzerodt came there?

A. Yes, sir.

Q. Who were they?

A. Two young men named Lemon.

Q. Do they belong to the neighborhood?

A. Yes, sir: their names are James Lemon and Somerset Lemon.

Q. Are you well acquainted with them?

A. Yes, sir.

Q. Was there nothing said about the assassination of the President?

A. There might have been; but I do not recollect. They might have been talking before I came into the room. The conversation about General Grant occurred after I came into the room. That is all I recollect hearing.

Q. Did or did not the prisoner Atzerodt appear to be pleased at what had taken place?

A. I could not say. I do not know that I saw any change in him as to that.

Q. Did he express himself gratified at what had taken place?

A. I do not know that he did.

By the JUDGE ADVOCATE:

Q. Were other persons present when this remark of his was made about General Grant?

A. Two others.

Q. The two young men of whom you have spoken?

A. Yes, sir.

SERGEANT Z. W. GEMMILL,

a witness called for the prosecution, being duly sworn, testified as follows:—

By the JUDGE ADVOCATE:

Q. Do you not recognize the prisoner Atzerodt as a man you have seen before?

A. Yes, sir.

Q. Which is he? Point him out.

A. That is the man [pointing to George A. Atzerodt].

Q. State whether or not you arrested him after the assassination of the President, where, and all the circumstances.

A. I arrested him in Montgomery County, Md.

Q. At what house?

A. At the house of a man by the name of Richter, near a place called Germantown.

Q. On what day?

A. On the 20th of April, about four o'clock in the morning. I left camp on the 19th, — the day before.

Q. State the circumstances of the arrest.

A. On the 19th, I was sent for to camp by Captain Townsend, and reported to him. He told me to detail six men to go out on a scout. I detailed them; and we got ready, and left camp about fifteen minutes before ten. I proceeded to Mr. Purdon's house to take him as a guide to Mr. Richter's house. He went with me to the house, stopping a short piece in the rear until I saw the prisoner was there. I knocked at the door; and Richter asked me twice there who came, before he would let me in. I told him to come and see. When he came to the door, I asked him if there was a man there by the name of Atwood. He said no; that there was no one there; that he had been there, but had gone to Frederick, or the neighborhood of Frederick. I then told him that I was going to search the house. He then told me that his cousin was up stairs in bed. His wife spoke up, and said, that, as for that, there were three there. He got a light, and I took two men with me, and went up to the room, where he was lying on the front of the bed. I asked him his name, and he gave me a fictitious name, — a name that I did not understand.

Q. Can you recall it now?

A. No, sir. I told him to get up and dress himself, and then took him to Mr. Lemon, a loyal man, to prove his name; and he told me it was the man.

Q. Did he ask you why you were arresting him?

A. No, sir.

Q. Made no inquiry?

A. No, sir.

Q. Did he persist in denying his name?

A. No : he said he did not give me a fictitious name.

Q. Denied having done it ?

A. Yes, sir. The time I went to the house, he hallooed to Mr. Lemon ; and Mr. Lemon put his head out of the window, and asked him if he did not know him. He said no. When he came down and went to the door, he knew him.

Q. This is the man ?

A. Yes, sir.

Q. Did you bring him immediately to Washington ?

A. I took him from Germantown to camp, to Captain Townsend ; and there he was examined by Major E. R. Artman.

Q. Did he ask you on the way why you had arrested him ?

A. No, sir : I asked him, just before I left Germantown, if he had left Washington shortly, and he told me no ; and then I asked him if he had not something to do with the assassination. He said no. After the major examined him, he ordered me to go to the Relay House with them, and report him there to General Tyler ; and then he sent me to Washington with him.

Q. When you asked him about having had any thing to do with the assassination, it was some time after the arrest ? Had you taken him before the officer at that time ?

A. No, sir.

Q. What time did you ask that question ?

A. As near as I can remember, between the hours of seven and eight o'clock, — just as I was going to leave Germantown to start for camp.

Q. You arrested him about four o'clock ?

A. Yes, sir.

Q. And, up to that time, he had made no inquiry as to the cause of his arrest ?

A. No, sir.

Cross-examined by Mr. DOSTER :

Q. What made you go in search of Atzerodt ? Did you have orders to arrest a man corresponding to him ?

A. Yes, sir.

Q. From whom did you get those orders ?

A. From Captain Townsend.

Q. Were the orders to arrest a man by the name of Atzerodt, and answering to his description?

A. No : a man by the name of Atwood.

Q. Did you have a description?

A. No, sir : I had no description in the orders. Mr. Purdon gave me a description of him.

Q. What were your orders in substance?

A. The orders were, to proceed to James Purdon's, and press him for guide to the house of a man named Richter, and to arrest a man there of the name of Atwood. That is all I remember of it.

Q. I understood you to say that you did not understand the name the man gave you first?

A. No, sir : I did not.

Q. You do not know what it was?

A. No, sir.

Q. You could not absolutely swear that it was not Atzerodt?

A. No, sir.

Q. And he afterwards insisted upon it that he had given you the name of Atzerodt?

A. Yes, sir.

Q. He never admitted any thing to you of the assassination?

A. No, sir. He never said any thing about it, except when I asked him the question.

Q. You did not examine him on that subject at all?

A. No, sir.

Q. Did he go along with you?

A. Yes, sir.

By the JUDGE ADVOCATE :

Q. You say that he denied that he had given you a fictitious name?

A. Yes, sir.

Q. Can you undertake to state now whether the name he actually gave was Atzerodt, or some other name?

A. I cannot say. He spoke in German, and I could not understand his language well at all. That is the reason why I did not understand the name he gave me.

Q. You are certain, however, that he said he had not come from Washington?

A. Yes, sir.

Thomas L. Gardiner,

a witness called for the prosecution, being duly sworn, testified as follows : —

By the Judge Advocate :

Q. Have you a knowledge of a dark-bay, one-eyed horse, now in General Augur's stables in this city, at Seventeenth and I Streets?

A. Yes, sir.

Q. When did you see the animal last?

A. I saw him on the 8th of this month, Monday.

Q. Have you any knowledge of that horse having been sold by your uncle? and if so, to whom?

A. It was sold by my uncle to a man of the name of Booth.

Q. When?

A. Some time in the latter part of November last, I think.

Q. Do you mean J. Wilkes Booth?

A. I do not know: I only knew him as Booth.

Q. What is your uncle's name?

A. George Gardiner.

Q. How near does he live to the prisoner Dr. Mudd?

A. Very near ; not over a quarter of a mile, I should judge.

Q. Do you know under what circumstances the animal was bought by Booth?

A. There were no special circumstances, I think. I knew of none. My uncle had three horses for sale ; and Booth selected this horse of the three.

Q. Do you know whether he did it on recommendation of the prisoner Dr. Mudd?

A. I do not know.

Q. Did he go there alone, or with others?

A. He came there with Dr. Samuel A. Mudd.

Q. Describe the color of the horse, and which eye is blind.

A. A dark-bay horse, blind in the right eye.

Cross-examined by Mr. Stone:

Q. When was that sale made?

A. In the latter part of November: I cannot arrive at the day exactly.

Q. How far is your uncle's from Dr. Mudd's?

A. A very short distance: I do not think it is over a quarter of a mile. I cannot state the distance positively; but it is very short.

By the Court:

Q. Were you present at your uncle's when Dr. Mudd came with Booth to buy that horse?

A. Yes, sir.

Q. Did you see them come?

A. Yes, sir.

Q. Did they come in a carriage, or on horseback?

A. I think they were on horseback.

Q. Did they both leave together after the horse was purchased?

A. I think they did.

Q. Who purchased the horse, and made the agreement for him?

A. Booth.

Q. Did Dr. Mudd take any part in that purchase?

A. None whatever that I know of.

Q. Did he look at the horse before the purchase was made?

A. Yes, sir: I think he did.

Q. Did he give his opinion and advice on the horse to Booth?

A. Not that I know of.

Q. Did he seem to take an interest in that purchase?

A. No, sir: I think not. I did not notice any thing of the sort.

Q. Was it your impression that he came there as a friend of Booth, or that he happened along accidentally with him?

A. Indeed, I am not able to say.

Q. The question is, What is your impression?

A. Dr. Mudd was aware that my uncle had horses for sale; and perhaps he brought him there, thinking that he could purchase a horse there.

Q. Was that your impression, that Dr. Mudd brought Booth there to purchase the horse?

A. I never formed any opinion in regard to that. It is a thing I never thought of.

Q. He looked at the horse, and examined him with Booth, did he?

A. Yes, sir. Dr. Mudd knew the horse well; had known him for some years previous: he was a very old horse.

By Mr. STONE:

Q. And did Booth take away the horse then?

A. Booth requested my uncle to send the horse to Bryantown the next morning; and I took the horse myself the next morning to Bryantown. He requested him to be sent to Montgomery's stable, in Bryantown.

Q. Did you hear Booth describe what sort of a horse he wanted, — a farming-horse, or a saddle-horse?

A. I think he said something about looking at lands in the lower part of Maryland, and said he wanted a horse to run in a light buggy. I recollect that distinctly. My uncle told him he had but one horse that he could recommend as a buggy horse, and that he could not spare it, as he wanted it for his own use. He told him then that he would send him a young mare. Booth said a mare would not suit him. Then my uncle told him that he had an old saddle-horse that he would sell him, if the horse would suit him. Booth examined the horse, and said he thought that horse would suit him; that he only wanted a horse for one year; and he bought the horse, and paid for him, and requested him to be sent to Montgomery's stables, at Bryantown, the next morning; and I took the horse down myself the next morning to him.

Q. Dr. Mudd took no more interest in the purchase of the horse than any other spectator, I suppose?

A. None whatever. I did not perceive that Dr. Mudd took any interest whatever in the purchase of the horse.

Q. I understand you to say your uncle had three horses for sale at that time?

A. Yes, sir: two of them were mares. Booth selected this one out of the three.

Q. I understood you to say that Booth spoke of buying land in the lower part of Maryland?

A. I think, if I am not mistaken, he said he wanted a horse to run in a light buggy, to travel over the lower counties of Maryland, to look at the lands; that he desired to buy some land.

By the JUDGE ADVOCATE:

Q. Do you know where Booth staid that night?

A. I do not.

Q. Where did you find him next morning?

A. At Montgomery's tavern, in Bryantown; where I delivered the horse to him.

Q. Did he and Dr. Mudd go away together from your uncle's?

A. Yes, sir.

Q. Did they go in the direction of Dr. Mudd's home?

A. I think they did.

By MR. STONE:

Q. Do you remember what day of the week this was?

A. If I am not mistaken, it was on Monday; but I will not be positive.

Q. Had you been at church the preceding Sunday?

A. Yes, sir.

Q. Did you see Booth at church there?

A. No, sir.

By the COURT:

Q. Was Booth in the habit of staying at Dr. Mudd's when he was in that neighborhood?

A. I do not know that he was ever in the neighborhood before. It was the last time I ever saw Booth.

By MR. STONE:

Q. Did you ever see or hear of his being in the neighborhood before or since?

A. I think I did hear that he was in the neighborhood of Bryantown some time before that.

Q. How long before that?

A. Really, I do not know. I am one of the worst hands in

the world to keep dates: it was some time previous to that, though, I think.

Q. You never saw or heard of his being there since?

A. No, sir: I never saw or heard of the man since, until I saw his name in the papers after the assassination.

Q. Did you ever hear of his being at Dr. Mudd's before or since?

A. No, sir.

Q. Do you live with your uncle?

A. Yes, sir.

Q. And you say that is about a quarter of a mile from Dr. Mudd's house?

A. Within half a mile: I suppose hardly more than a quarter of a mile. The farms are adjoining.

Q. I suppose, then, you see Dr. Mudd almost every day?

A. I very often see Dr. Mudd; sometimes every day, sometimes two or three times a week.

LIEUTENANT JOHN J. TAFFEY,

a witness called for the prosecution, being duly sworn, testified as follows: —

By the JUDGE ADVOCATE:

Q. Have you or not knowledge of a dark-bay horse, blind of one eye, now at Major-General Augur's stables, in this city, at the corner of Seventeenth and I Streets?

A. I do not know about its being there; but a horse answering to the description was seen by me on the night of the 14th or the morning of the 15th of April last. I was going to the hospital, where I am on duty. I saw a horse standing at Lincoln Branch Barracks, about three-quarters of a mile east of the Capitol. I ordered the guard to stop it; and I put a guard around it, and kept it there until a cavalry picket was thrown out, and I reported at the office of the picket. He requested me to take it down to the old Capitol Prison, where the headquarters of this picket were. I then reported to Captain Lord, having the horse; and he requested me to take it to General Augur's headquarters. I

31*

took it there with Captain Lansing, of the Thirteenth New-York Cavalry. They took the saddle off, and took the horse away.

Q. Would you recognize the saddle now?

A. I think I should. I rode on it.

Q. [Submitting to the witness the saddle, which is Exhibit No. 39.] Look at that saddle, and say if it is the one.

A. I should think that was the saddle : I know the stirrups.

Q. Describe the horse.

A. A large brown horse. About the blindness of the eye, I did not notice that until I got to General Augur's headquarters, when the men spoke of it. I then found the horse to be blind of one eye.

Q. Had the horse saddle and bridle on when you saw him?

A. Yes, sir: the sweat was pouring off him, and the sweat was on the ground, — a regular puddle of water.

Q. Was he standing still?

A. Yes, sir: the sentinel at the hospital had stopped him.

Q. And that was between twelve and one'clock?

A. About that time : it may have been a little after one.

Q. In what direction is that from here?

A. Directly east of the Capitol, abut three-fourths of a mile.

Q. Were there any indications from the horse that he had probably fallen in the flight?

A. When I rode him down, he seemed to be a little lame : that was all I noticed.

Cross-examined by Mr. Doster :

Q. State where that road leads to out of Washington.

A. It is a sort of by-road that leads to Camp Barry : it turns north after it gets to the branch barracks towards Camp Barry to the Bladensburg Road.

Q. Is it on the main Bladensburg Road?

A. No: not on the main road. I do not know the name of the street; but it is between East Capitol Street and the Bladensburg Road.

Q. And did you find the horse on the road?

A. Just outside of the road by the dispensary of the hospital.

Q. Did you look at your watch at the exact time you found him?

A. I did not.

Q. Was he standing or running when you got him?

A. He was standing then. The guard had him.

Q. Did you understand that the horse had come running there?

A. Yes, sir. He had stopped running then.

Q. From what direction had the horse come?

A. I do not know.

By the JUDGE ADVOCATE:

Q. How far is it from the heart of the city to where the horse was picked up, — say from the Treasury Building?

A. From the Treasury Building it is about a mile and a half.

By the COURT:

Q. What is the distance from the Lincoln Hospital to the Navy-Yard Bridge?

A. There is a bridge nearer than the Navy-Yard Bridge, — the Anacostia, about three-quarters of a mile: the Navy-Yard Bridge is fully a mile.

The Commission then adjourned until to-morrow, Thursday morning May 18, 1865, at ten o'clock.

THURSDAY, May 18, 1865.

The Commission met this morning, and proceeded to business at the usual hour. The following testimony was taken: —

A. R. REEVE,

a witness called for the prosecution, being duly sworn, testified as follows: —

By the JUDGE ADVOCATE:

Q. Will you state where you reside?

A. In Brooklyn, Long Island, N.Y.

Q. In what business were you engaged there in March la. \ ?

A. In the telegraph business.

Q. [Handing the witness a telegraphic despatch.] Will you look at this despatch, and state what you know in regard to it?

A. It was handed to me at the St. Nicholas Hotel, New York, to be sent to Washington, by John Wilkes Booth.

Q. Read it.

A. " To WEICHMANN, Esq., No. 541, H Street, Washington : —
" Tell John, telegraph number and street at once.

"J. BOOTH."

Q. That was John Wilkes Booth?

A. Yes.

Q. Was it or was it not sent on its date to this city?

A. It was sent on the 23d of March.

[The despatch was offered in evidence without objection.]

Cross-examined by MR. AIKEN :

Q. How is it that you identify that telegram?

A. I remember his signing " J. Booth," instead of " John Wilkes Booth," knowing his name to be that.

Q. Were any remarks made to you by the gentleman who gave you that despatch at the time?

A. No, sir. I was very busy at the time ; but, on sending it, — I transmitted the despatch myself, — I noticed that " Wilkes " was left out.

Q. Are you in the habit of keeping all the despatches you receive for transmission?

A. Yes, sir.

By the JUDGE ADVOCATE :

Q. Is this the original despatch?

A. Yes, sir : it is.

By MR. AIKEN :

Q. What sort of a looking person was the one that handed you that despatch?

A. If I saw his likeness, I could tell you.

Q. Could you tell from a photograph?

A. Yes, sir: I could.

Q. [Exhibiting to the witness Booth's photograph, Exhibit No. 1.] Is that the man?

A. That is the gentleman.

Louis J. Weichmann

recalled for the prosecution.

By the Judge Advocate:

Q. [Exhibiting the telegraphic despatch identified by the witness Reeve.] Look at that telegram, and say whether you received it.

A. Yes, sir: I did.

Q. On the day of its date?

A. I cannot say that I received this particular paper on March 23; but I received a telegram, which is of the exact nature of this, about the 17th of March, or after that.

Q. Who is the person referred to there as John?

A. John Surratt: he was in the habit of being called John.

Q. Did you or not deliver to him the message contained in the despatch?

A. I delivered it to him the same day.

Q. What did he say?

A. I asked him what particular number and street was meant; and he said, "Don't be so damned inquisitive!"

Q. [Exhibiting a telegraphic despatch.] Is this the one you received?

A. This is the one I received and delivered.

NEW YORK, March 23, 1865.

"To Weichmann, Esq., 541 H Street:—

"Tell John telegraph number and street at once.

[Signed]   "J. Booth."

[This telegraphic despatch was offered in evidence without objection.]

Q. Do you know the handwriting of J. Wilkes Booth?

A. I have seen his handwriting, and I could recognize his autograph.

Q. Look at the original despatch, and see whose writing it is. Is it Booth's handwriting?

A. It is.

Q. Will you state whether on or about, or probably a little after, the 4th of March last, you had an interview in your room with J. Wilkes Booth, John H. Surratt, and Payne, the prisoner at the bar?

A. I will state, that, as near as I recollect, it was after the 4th of March: it was the second time that Payne visited the house. I returned from my office one day at half-past four o'clock: I went to my room, and rang the bell for Dan, the negro servant, and told him to bring me some water, and inquired at the same time where John had gone. He told me Massa John had ridden out about two o'clock in the afternoon, with six others, on horseback; that he had left the front of the house with six others on horseback about half-past two o'clock. On going down to dinner, I found Mrs. Surratt in the passage. She was weeping bitterly, and I was endeavoring to console her. She said, "John is gone away: go down to dinner, and make the best of your dinner you can." She went out. After dinner, I went to my room, sat down, and commenced reading: and about half-past six o'clock Surratt came again, and was very much excited; in fact, rushed into the room. He had a revolver in his hand, — one of Sharpe's revolvers, a four-barrelled revolver, a small one; you could carry it in your vest-pocket, — and he appeared to be very much excited. I said, "John, what is the matter? why are you so much excited?" Said he, "I will shoot any one that comes into this room; my prospect is gone, my hopes are blighted; I want something to do; can you get me a clerkship?" In about ten minutes after, the prisoner Payne came into the room. He was also very much excited; and I noticed he had a pistol. About fifteen minutes afterwards, Booth came into the room; and Booth was so excited, that he walked around the room three or four times very frantically, and did not notice me. He had a whip in his hand, and I spoke to him; and he recognized me, and said, "I did not see you." The three then went up stairs into the back room, in what I call the third story, and must have remained there about thirty minutes, when they left the house together. On Surratt's returning home, I asked him where he had left his friend Payne. He said Payne had gone to Baltimore. I asked him where John Wilkes Booth had gone. He said Booth had gone to New York. This is all that I remember of that circumstance ; and some two weeks after, Surratt, when passing the post-office, went to the post-office, and inquired for a letter that was sent to him under the name of James Sturdey; and I asked him why a letter was sent to him under a false name, and he said he had particular reasons for it.

Q. What day was that ?

A. It must have been about two weeks after that affair.

Q. The latter end of March ?

A. Yes, sir : it must have been before the 20th of March. The letter was signed " Wood ; " and the writer stated that he was at the Revere House in New York, and that he was looking for something to do, and that he would probably go to some boarding-house in Grand Street : I think it was West Grand Street. That was the whole substance of the letter.

Q. Do you say you were familiar with Booth's handwriting, or simply with his signature ?

A. I have seen his autograph on the hotel register and also at the house.

Q. [Exhibiting a note.] Here is a note signed by R. D. Watson. Will you look at it, and see whether that is Booth's handwriting or not ?

A. No, sir. I would not recognize that as Booth's handwriting.

Q. Was there any remark made at all in their excited conversation as to where they had all been riding ?

A. No, sir : they were very guarded indeed. Payne made no remark at all. The only remarks that were made were those excited remarks by Surratt.

Q. Surratt had been riding, and you say Booth had a whip in his hand ?

A. Yes, sir.

Q. Did Payne appear to have gone with them also ?

A. Yes, sir : he was much excited. In fact, I asked the negro servant that afternoon to tell me who the seven were. He said one was Massa John, the other Booth ; and then he said Port Tobacco, and then that man who was stopping at the house, whom I recognized as Payne.

Q. Do you mean by Port Tobacco the prisoner Atzerodt?

A. Yes, sir.

Cross-examined by MR. AIKEN:

Q. What time in the day did you meet Mr. Lloyd on his way to Washington at Uniontown?

A. It must have been about ten o'clock in the morning.

Q. Did you hear any of the conversation that passed at that time between him and Mrs. Surratt?

A. No, sir. I leaned back in my buggy; and Mrs. Surratt leaned sideways in the buggy, and whispered, as it were, in Mr. Lloyd's ear.

Q. Did she state any thing to you afterwards of what the conversation was about?

A. No, sir. The only conversation that I heard at that particular time was between her and Mrs. Offutt. She was talking about the man Howell.

ASSISTANT JUDGE ADVOCTE BINGHAM. I object. There is nothing of that in the case.

By MR. JOHNSON:

Q. Was it at the time?

A. No, sir: after the conversation between Lloyd and herself.

Q. On the same spot? Had she moved off?

A. No: Mrs. Offutt was in the carriage; and of course, Mrs. Offutt being in the carriage, she was obliged to speak much louder to her.

By MR. AIKEN:

Q. You stated, I think, that you did not learn any thing of the contents of those packages?

A. No, sir: they were wrapped up in paper, and appeared to me three or four saucers rolled up; and the package was deposited in the bottom of the carriage. I took it at that time to be a package of saucers.

Q. Were there several articles in that paper?

A. That I did not know. I did not know of the contents of the paper.

By Mr. Ewing:

Q. Do you recollect when Booth played in the " Apostate " the part of Pescara ?

A. Yes, sir : he played at that time for the benefit of John Mc-Cullough. It must have been about the 24th of March, I think.

Q. Was not this occasion of their return from the ride the day before or the day after he played in the " Apostate " ?

A. That I cannot say. It must have been after the 4th of March. This man Payne was stopping at the house at the time ; and, when he came to the house, he made some excuse to Mrs. Surratt, saying he would have liked to have been here before the 4th of March, but he could not get here by the 4th of March ; and, by that circumstance, I recollect that it was after the 4th of March. Whether it was before or after the day that Booth played Pescara in the " Apostate " I could not say, because I am not positive as to the date.

Q. Did you go to see that play ?

A. Yes, sir. Booth gave a pass to Surratt for two ; and he asked Surratt whether I would go. Surratt said he thought not ; but, when Surratt asked me, I did go. It was a written pass ; and the doorkeeper at first refused admission on the pass.

Q. State, to the best of your recollection, whether this occasion was before or after Booth played in the " Apostate."

A. To the best of my recollection, it was before.

Q. About how long before ?

A. As near as I can recollect, two weeks before that time.

Q. Did you have any means of ascertaining ?

A. No : only I know that it was after the 4th of March, from the remark Payne made when he visited the house the second time.

Q. You cannot state positively whether it was before or after he played in the " Apostate " ?

A. I should not like to state positively.

By Mr. Dorster :

Q. You have stated that Payne came to the house of Mrs. Surratt in company with John Surratt : will you state what time that was ?

A. I stated that when these circumstances happened, of their ride, Surratt came home first, and in about ten minutes Payne came into the room. Surratt came into my room first, and had his conversation ; and then Payne came in, and was much excited.

Q. What date was that ?

A. It was after the 4th of March. I could not give the precise date.

Q. Is that visit of Payne exclusive of the other two visits you mentioned in your testimony the other day ?

A. It was during the last, — the second visit of Payne.

Q. During the time, he claimed to be, as you say, a Baptist preacher ?

A. Yes, sir : it was during his long stay in the house, when he stopped three days.

By Mr. AIKEN :

Q. How did you learn any thing with reference to the antecedents of Mrs. Slater ?

A. It was told to me by Mrs. Surratt herself.

Q. What did Mrs. Surratt tell you ?

A. Mrs. Surratt told me that she came to the house in company with this man Howell ; that she was a North-Carolinian, I believe, and that she spoke French ; and that she was a blockade-runner, or bearer of despatches.

Q. Where were you at the time Mrs. Surratt told you this ?

A. I was in the house, in the dining-room.

Q. Are you certain, beyond all doubt, that Mrs. Surratt ever told you Mrs. Slater was a blockade-runner ?

A. Yes, sir.

Q. Had you ever seen Mrs. Slater at the house of Mrs. Surratt before that time ?

A. I myself saw Mrs. Slater at the house only once. I learned she had been to the house twice.

Q. You never saw her but once ?

A. I saw her only once.

Q. How long was she there?

A. She remained there one night.

Q. Did you have any conversation with her yourself?

A. She drove up to the door in a buggy: the bell rang, and there was a young man in the buggy with her. Mrs. Surratt told me to go out and take her trunk. That is all the conversation I had with her. She had a mask down,—one of the short masks ladies wear. They call them masks, I believe: they are not veils.

Q. Do you mean to say Mrs. Slater wore a mask?

A. What ladies call a mask.

Q. What was it made of?

A. Crape. They do not cover the entire face: they come down to the chin, and I believe the ladies call them masks.

By the COURT:

Q. Are they of this texture?

A. Yes, sir.

Q. A thin, short veil, that just covers the face?

A. Yes, sir. I believe the name for them is masks.

By MR. AIKEN:

Q. There is nothing peculiar about them from ordinary veils?

A. No, sir.

Q. At the time you say she told you she was a blockade-runner, did she tell you of her being a North-Carolinian, and speaking French?

A. Yes, sir.

Q. Were you in the house at that time?

A. I was in the house at that time.

Q. Was any one present besides yourself?

A. Not that I remember.

Q. What day was that?

A. It was some time in the month of February.

Q. What day?

A. I do not remember the precise day.

Q. Did you hear any thing said about Mrs. Slater afterwards?

A. No, sir.

Q. What was the exact language Mrs. Surratt used to you in giving you this information?

A. She stated that this woman was from North Carolina, and that, if she got into any trouble, there was no danger, because she could immediately apply to the French consul, speaking French as she did. That is about the only language that I remember.

By Mr. Clampitt:

Q. When John Surratt returned to the house in a state of excitement, did he tell you the occasion of it?

A. No, sir: he showed me his pistol, and said he would shoot any man that came into the room. I said, "John, why are you so excited? why don't you settle down like a sensible young man?" Said he, "My hopes are gone, my prospects blighted: can't you get me something to do? can't you get me a clerkship?" These were his precise words. I looked at him, and laughed at him, and told him he was foolish.

Q. You remarked that Mrs. Surratt was weeping bitterly: did she state the cause?

A. She merely said, "Go down, and make the best of the dinner you can. John is gone away." John, when he returned to me, said he had three pairs of drawers. From that I thought he was going to take a long ride.

By Mr. Aiken:

Q. By whom were you called on first to give your testimony in this case?

A. I was called on by the War Department.

Q. What member of the War Department?

A. I was called on by Judge Advocate Burnett, I believe.

Q. Were you arrested?

A. I surrendered myself up on Saturday morning at eight o'clock to Superintendent Richards, of the Metropolitan Police force. I stated to him what I knew of Payne, Atzerodt, and Herold visiting the house. I stated also what I knew of John Surratt; that I saw these men in private conversation.

Q. What was your object in being so swift to give all this information?

A. My object was to assist the Government.

Q. Were any threats ever made to you by any officer of the Government in case you did not divulge?

A. No, sir: no threats at all.

Q. Any inducements?

A. No, sir: no inducements at all. I read in the paper that morning the description of the assassin of Secretary Seward. He was described as a man who wore a long gray coat. I had seen Atzerodt wear a long gray coat; and I went to a stable on G Street, and told the man there I thought it was Atzerodt. We went down towards Tenth Street, and I met a gentleman by the name of Holahan, and he also communicated his suspicions to me. The gentleman and I returned to breakfast, and took breakfast; but, at half-past eight o'clock, we gave ourselves up to Superintendent Richards, of the Metropolitan Police force. I told Officer McDevitt about this man Payne, and where he had been stopping. I also told him of Atzerodt, and I also told of Herold. Officer McDevitt put me in his charge, and said, "You will go with me." We then went to General Rucker's office; and General Rucker gave us an order for a horse. We went to Captain Tompkins; and there I met a man who has something to do with a stable at the corner of Thirteenth and E Streets, and he said to me that a man had been to him that afternoon hiring a horse. I asked him if he would give me his description. He described him as small, black eyebrows, and with a laugh on his face all the time; and I asked him his name, and he said Herold. Then I told Officer McDevitt we should go for the horse; and we went, and we searched Mr. Herold's house, and procured photographs; and Officer McDevitt also procured a photograph of Booth at that time; and Mr. Holahan, who was in our company, went and procured a photograph of Surratt. I also stated to Officer McDevitt that I knew that Herold had been in the habit of riding in Maryland; he had great many acquaintances there; and that I thought, if they would take any road, they would probably take this road through Maryland; that, after the deed had been committed, there was no train for them to leave; and that we should go over into Maryland.

Q. Did you ever say to any one, about the time or previous to your surrendering yourself to Superintendent Richards and going to the office of Colonel Burnett, that you were fearful of an arrest?

A. I myself had a great deal to fear. Being in this house where these people were, I knew that I would be brought into public notice.

Q. I am not asking what you had to fear —

Assistant Judge Advocate Bingham. You have asked him the question : you must allow him to answer it.

The Witness. But as far as myself was concerned, as being cognizant of any thing of this kind, I had no fears at all; for I was not cognizant. When I surrendered myself to the Government, I surrendered myself because I thought it was my duty. It was hard for me to do so, situated as I was with Mrs. Surratt and her family, and with John Surratt ; but it was my duty, and my duty I have always regarded it since.

Q. Did you, at any time during the year 1863, board at a hotel called the Reynolds House?

A. I did.

Q. Did you become acquainted there with a gentleman who went by the name of St. Marie?

A. I became acquainted with that gentleman, Henry de St. Marie. I will state that some time in 1863, about Easter, I met St. Marie at a village in Maryland called Ellangowan. This Marie was introduced to me there by a clergyman by the name of William Mahony. He was teaching school at that time. He was a gentleman that spoke French, Italian, and English fluently ; and his manners were very fascinating indeed. He said that he had come from Montreal, and that he had been unfortunate in this country ; that he had lost some five or six thousand dollars, the proceeds of his farm. He stated that he had sold his farm in Canada. He stated that he had come to New York, and that he had embarked on a vessel for the purpose of going to South America. He said this vessel was captured, and he was thrown into Fort McHenry. He was released from Fort McHenry, so he said, by the agency of the French consul. Destitute of means at that time, he was obliged to seek some occupation ; and he met with a farmer in Baltimore, who told him to go on his farm, and he would give him employment. The farmer took him to his place; and his occupation, he said, for three weeks, was to feed the horses and cows morning and evening. There was a young lady I knew at that time who was travelling through that portion of the country for the purpose of collecting money enough for the purchase of a melodeon for the church at Ellangowan; and she met this man St. Marie, was introduced to him, and she saw that he was a person of education; and she, in her turn, had him introduced to the Rev. Mr. Mahony. Mr. Mahony took him as his teacher; but St. Marie stated that he did not receive sufficient compensation, and that he would like to leave the place. I told him I would do for him all I could as soon as I returned to Washington. I was engaged at that time in teaching myself. On my return to Washington, — I had been back hardly two weeks, — when returning to my room one day, I found St. Marie seated there. He stated that he was determined to remain in Washington, and I should get him something to do anyhow. I applied to Father Wiget, President of Gonzaga College, on F Street, between Ninth and Tenth; and I recommended this gentleman as a good, honest man. I told him he was educated, and that he would be of service to him. Father Wiget employed him; and he had hardly been there two weeks before a vacancy occurred in my school, and St. Marie —

ASSISTANT JUDGE ADVOCATE BINGHAM. There is no occasion for any further statement on that matter.

By MR. AIKEN:

Q. Did you pay his board at the Reynolds House, or become responsible for it?

ASSISTANT JUDGE ADVOCATE BINGHAM objected to the question, and it was waived.

By MR. AIKEN:

Q. Did he state to you at any time that there was no aristocracy at the North, and that he wished to go South?

ASSISTANT JUDGE ADVOCATE BINGHAM. I object to that. It is of no sort of consequence whether he did or not.

MR. AIKEN. I will vary my question.

Q. Did he state, that, if he could not get there in any other way, he would join a Federal regiment, and desert?

ASSISTANT JUDGE ADVOCATE BINGHAM objected to the question, and it was waived.

Q. Do you know whether Reynolds reported any of his treasonable talk and language at that time to the War Department?

ASSISTANT JUDGE ADVOCATE BINGHAM objected to the question.

MR. AIKEN stated that this question was but the prelude to a series of questions which he proposed to put to the witness for the purpose of extracting from his own lips certain treasonable practices, sayings, and professions of his own, for the purpose of impairing his credibility as a witness, and relieving much of the weight of his testimony against his [MR. AIKEN's] client.

ASSISTANT JUDGE ADVOCATE BINGHAM replied, that, if the counsel chose to put a question to the witness about his own conduct, that would be another thing; but the question now asked was, whether Reynolds, whom he understood to be a police-officer, had reported treasonable practices of St. Marie to the War Department. That was a wholly immaterial issue in every way: it was not evidence, and therefore should not be admitted before the Court. If the counsel chose to ask the witness whether he himself was guilty of any treason against his country and Government, nobody would object to it.

The Court sustained the objection.

MR. AIKEN. As long as the Judge Advocate has informed us that he will not object to any questions that may be asked the witness as to his own treasonable conduct, I will ask this question: —

Q. Did you give notice to St. Marie that he would probably be arrested by the Government?

A. No, sir: I had no time to give notice to St. Marie. St. Marie taught school for me for two weeks; and he rose one morning early, and left. I will state that he afterwards enlisted in a Delaware regiment as a soldier, and was taken prisoner, and was lodged in Castle Thunder. I saw that myself in a paper.

Q. Are you a clerk in the War Department?

A. I have been.

Q. Did you agree, while a clerk in the War Department, to communicate to any one of the prisoners at the bar any information you might obtain from that department?

A. No, sir.

Q. Or any of the secrets of the department?

A. No, sir.

Q. Are you acquainted with a Mr. Howell?

A. I have met him at Mrs. Surratt's house.

Q. What was Howell's first name?

A. When he was at the house, he gave the name of Spencer. They refused to tell me his right name when he was at the house. I afterwards learned from John Surratt that his name was Augustus Howell.

Q. Were you intimate with him while at Mrs. Surratt's house?

A. I was introduced to him. I never spoke about giving him any information at all: on the contrary, I spoke with a clerk in our office, Captain Gleason; and I said to him, "There is a blockade-runner at Mrs. Surratt's house: shall I have him delivered up?" I agitated the question myself for three days, and decided in favor of Surratt. I thought it would be the only time the man might be there, and let him go in God's name.

Q. Did you ever have any conversation with Howell with reference to going South yourself?

A. I told him that I would like to be South. I had been a student of divinity myself; and I was studying for the diocese of Richmond. I told him I would like to be in Richmond for that purpose, — for the purpose of continuing my studies.

Q. Did he offer to make any arrangements for you in Richmond to get you a place there?

A. No, sir.

Q. Was it your purpose, in wishing to go to Richmond, to continue your theological studies?

A. Yes, sir.

By Mr. CLAMPITT:

Q. Why had you a greater desire to continue your studies in Richmond than in the North?

ASSISTANT JUDGE ADVOCATE BINGHAM. I object to that question. It is wholly immaterial what reasons he had for that.

MR. CLAMPITT. It is important, and concerns the *res gestæ* of the case.

ASSISTANT JUDGE ADVOCATE BINGHAM. Supposing he should give an answer, how would you dispose of it?

MR. CLAMPITT. By further testimony that we may adduce hereafter. It may be a connecting link.

ASSISTANT JUDGE ADVOCATE BINGHAM. You cannot do that in that way, as you understand very well. If you had asked him for his declarations, I could understand it; but this is an attempt to get at the interior motive of the witness, which you cannot do unless you can obtain the power of Omnipotence.

The question was waived.

By MR. AIKEN:

Q. Did this man Howell, while you were a clerk in the War Department, teach you a cipher?

A. Yes, sir: he showed me an alphabet.

Q. What was the purpose of his showing you that cipher, as you understood it at the time?

A. He had no particular purpose at all: he stated no particular purpose.

Q. Was it not for the purpose of corresponding with you from Richmond?

A. No, sir: we made no arrangements about corresponding at all. The cipher-alphabet was in my box, and no doubt was found there. I once wrote a poem of Longfellow's in it; and that was the only use I made of it. I showed that poem, written in that particular cipher, to Mr. Cruikshank, a clerk in the War Department. He was in the habit of making puns and enigmas himself; and I told him that I would give him an enigma which he could not make out.

Q. Was that all the use you ever made of the cipher?

A. Yes, sir. I never had a word of correspondence with Howell; and I never saw him a second time until I saw him a prisoner.

Q. Was any objection ever made by any of these prisoners at the bar to your being present at any of their conversations?

A. Not any objection that I heard; but they always withdrew themselves. When Surratt was in the parlor, and Booth would call, Surratt and Booth would perhaps converse with me five or ten minutes; and then I noticed that John would tap or nudge Booth, or else Booth would nudge Surratt; and then they would go out of the parlor, and stay up stairs for two or three hours. I had not a word of private conversation with them which I would not be willing to have the world hear.

Q. Had not Howell just returned from Richmond when he taught you that cipher?

A. No, sir: I believe he came from New York.

ASSISTANT JUDGE ADVOCATE BURNETT. Will the counsel not assume what has not been testified to? The testimony of the witness was, not that he taught him the cipher, but that he showed him the cipher. Whether the witness figured it out himself afterwards, or learned it from somebody else, is another question.

Q. Did Howell give you the key of that cipher, or teach it to you?

A. He showed me the cipher: he showed me the alphabet, and showed me how to use it.

Q. Then he taught it to you, did he not?

A. I made no use of it whatever, except in that particular case, when I showed it to Mr. Cruikshank, in the War Department.

Q. That is hardly an answer to my question. He taught you the cipher, did he not?

A. Yes, sir.

Q. According to the best of your recollection, how soon was that after his return to Richmond?

A. He had returned from New York; and he did not tell me when he had come from Richmond, because it was the first and only time I ever saw the man in my life. He was well acquainted with Mrs. Surratt; and his nickname around the house was Spencer. He had been in the house a day and a half before I ever met him.

Q. Did he tell you that that was a cipher used in Richmond?

A. No, sir.

Q. You state that all the prisoners at the bar were free and unreserved in your presence in their conversation?

A. They spoke in my presence on general topics, and so on; but, on their private business, they never spoke to me.

Q. Do I understand you as stating to the Court, that, in all your conversation with them, you never learned of any intended treasonable purpose or act or conspiracy of theirs?

A. No, sir.

Q. You never did?

A. No, sir.

Q. And you were not suspicious of any thing of the sort?

A. I would have been the last man in the world to suspect John Surratt, my schoolmate, of the murder of the President of the United States.

Q. You state that your suspicions were aroused at one time by something you saw at Mrs. Surratt's?

A. My suspicions were aroused by John Surratt and this man Payne and Booth coming to the house. My suspicions again were aroused by their frequent private conversations. My suspicions were aroused by seeing Payne and Surratt playing on the bed with bowie-knives. My suspicions were again aroused by finding a false mustache in my room.

Q. Your suspicions were not aroused by the fact that Payne came back with three pairs of drawers on, as you stated?

A. No, sir: that was Surratt. I thought he was going to take a long ride into the country, and that, perhaps, he was going South.

Q. Then, if your suspicions were aroused on all these different occasions which you have mentioned, and you had reason to believe that something was in the wind that was improper, did you communicate any of them to the War Department?

A. My suspicions were not of a fixed or settled character. I did not know what they intended to do. I made a confidant of Captain Gleason, in the War Department. I told him that Booth was a secesh sympathizer: I mentioned snatches of conversation that I would hear from these parties; and I asked him, "Captain, what do you think of all this?" We even talked over several things which they could do. I asked him whether they could be bearers of despatches or blockade-runners. At one time I saw in the paper the capture of President Lincoln fully discussed; and I remarked to Captain Gleason, "Captain, do you think any party could attempt the capture of President Lincoln?" He laughed and hooted at the idea.

Q. You did hear, then, that the capture of President Lincoln was contemplated?

A. I did not hear it: it was a casual remark of mine. I saw the thing freely discussed in the papers. If you will read the "New-York Tribune" of March 19, you will find the details mentioned there. It was merely a casual remark that I mentioned to Captain Gleason at the time. This happened before this horseback ride; and, after these parties had been out riding, I remarked to Captain Gleason, the next morning, that Surratt had come back; and I told him the very expressions Surratt had used; and I told him, that, to all appearances, what they had been after had been a failure, and that I was glad, and that I thought Surratt would be recalled to a sense of his duties.

Q. You stated that what you thought they had been after had failed?

A. Not what I thought they had been after. I did not think, even, that the capture of President Lincoln was contemplated. It was a casual remark of mine. I had been seeing the subject freely discussed in the papers; and, as I said before, I would have thought John Surratt the last man in the world to have contemplated such a thing.

Q. How came you to connect the discussion which you read in the papers with any of these parties, and have your suspicions aroused against them?

ASSISTANT JUDGE ADVOCATE BINGHAM. I object to the question. It is no matter how the man's mental processes worked. We cannot inquire into that.

MR. AIKEN. It will be recollected that yesterday, in the questions from the Court to one of the witnesses, he was asked what his impressions were, and it was not objected to.

ASSISTANT JUDGE ADVOCATE BINGHAM. The question is now, how he came to form certain conclusions. We cannot try a question of that sort. No court on earth could do it. It is a thing we cannot understand, nor anybody else; and perhaps the witness himself, at this time of day, would not be able to state what controlled his mental operations at that time.

MR. AIKEN. I insist on my question.

ASSISTANT JUDGE ADVOCATE BINGHAM. The witness has already gone on and told all he can tell, and given declarations; and now he is asked to state how he came to connect them with the newspaper article. Of what use is that to anybody? I object to it as a wholly immaterial and irrelevant question. No matter how the witness answers, it can throw no light on the subject in favor of or against the prisoners.

MR. AIKEN. But the Judge Advocate is aware that the witness did not tell all he wished to know in the examination in chief, and, in his re-examination, went into matter not brought out in the examination in chief, or in the cross-examination, which was not objected to either by us.

The COURT sustained the objection.

Q. Did you understand yourself as being on intimate personal relations with the prisoners at the bar?

A. Not intimate personal relations. I met them merely because I was boarding at Mrs. Surratt's house. I have never been on personal relations with the man Payne, nor have I been on personal relations with Atzerodt. I never had a word of correspondence with either of them. I met Atzerodt and Payne, and went to the theatre with him [Atzerodt]. I looked upon him, as every one in the house looked upon him, in fact, as a good-hearted countryman.

Q. But you were a room-mate of Surratt's?

A. John Surratt has been my companion for seven years now.

Q. And did you still profess to be a friend and confidant of his at the time you were giving this information to the War Department that you speak of?

A. I was a friend so far as he himself was concerned ; but, when my suspicions were aroused as to the danger to the Government in any particular, I preferred the Government to John Surratt. I did not know what he was contemplating. He said he was going to engage in cotton speculations ; he was going to engage in oil.

Q. If you did not know what he was contemplating, how could you forfeit your friendship to him? What is the rationale of that proceeding?

A. I never forfeited my friendship to him : he forfeited his friendship to me.

Q. Not by engaging in the cotton speculation?

A. No, sir : by placing me in the position in which I now am, — testifying against him.

Q. But you could not, of course, have been aware that you would be placed in any such position?

A. I think I was more of a friend to him than he was to me. I knew that he permitted a blockade-runner at the house without informing upon him, because I was his friend. I thought of it for three days.

MR. AIKEN. I do not know that we have any thing further to ask from the witness in cross-examination. We propose to make him our own witness at a subsequent stage of the trial. We are not very tender of him, at any rate.

A member of the Court desiring an explanation of the last remark, —

MR. AIKEN said, The remark, so far as the witness is concerned, in the way in which it was made, was made simply with reference to his time that we were occupying, and the physical fatigue which he may be undergoing, — no more in the world.

Cross-examined by MR. EWING :

Q. You spoke of a publication in the "Tribune" of March 19 in regard to a plot to capture the President?

A. Yes, sir.

Q. Cannot you, by connecting that publication with this ride which you said these parties had in the country, fix more closely the time?

A. I do not know where they rode to.

Q. I do not ask that. Cannot you, by connecting that publication in the "Tribune," which you saw, with the parties coming in on that occasion from the ride, now inform the Court whether it was before or after that publication of March 19?

A. I think it was after.

Q. It was after the publication of March 19?

A. Yes, sir.

Q. Then it must have been about the time of Booth's playing Pescara in the "Apostate"?

A. Yes, sir. I will also state that I saw in the "Republican," some time in February, that the assassination of President Lincoln was contemplated; and Surratt once made the remark to me, that, if he succeeded in his cotton speculation, his country would love him forever, and that his name would go down green to posterity.

Q. You think this occasion, when they appeared to have come in from a ride in the country, was after the publication of March 19 in the "New-York Tribune"?

A. Yes, sir.

Q. Was it very shortly after?

A. It was between March 19 and the time Booth played.

Q. The understanding is that Booth played on the 18th of March?

A. I think he played Pescara on the 26th of March. It was after this publication that I saw it. I did not connect the capture of President Lincoln with these parties at all. When I made that remark to Captain Gleason at the War Department, it was merely a casual remark. I said to him, " Captain, do you suppose anybody — could capture President Lincoln?" or, "Do you suppose President Lincoln could be captured?" He laughed at the idea; he hooted it; and he said, not in a city guarded as Washington was. It was merely a casual remark of mine; it was merely a thought.

Q. Was that remark to Captain Gleason after these parties came in apparently from a ride in the country?

A. Yes, sir: it was the morning after I stated to Captain Gleason that Surratt's mysterious and incomprehensible business had failed ; and I said, " Captain, let us think it over, and let us think of something that it could have been." We mentioned a variety of things, — blockade-running, bearing despatches ; and we then thought of breaking open the old Capitol Prison : but all those ideas vanished ; we struck nothing ; and so the thing has rested. I will state, that, since that ride, my suspicions were not so much aroused as before, because Payne has not been to the house since ; and Atzerodt, to my knowledge, had not been to the house since the 2d of April. The only one that visited the house during that time was this man Booth.

Q. Have you ever seen the prisoner Arnold ?

A. No, sir : I never saw him.

Q. Will you state to the Court where St. Charles College is ?

A. St. Charles College is in Howard County, Md., about five miles from Ellicott's Mills.

Q. Is it not in Charles County ?

A. No, sir : it is in Howard County.

Q. You have stated that you first met the prisoner, Dr. Samuel Mudd, on Seventh Street, opposite Odd Fellows Hall ?

A. Yes, sir.

Q. State to the Court whereabouts on H Street Mrs. Surratt lived. Was it nearer Seventh Street, or nearer to Sixth Street ?

A. It was next to Sixth.

Q. The next door to Sixth Street ?

A. Yes, sir : it was the first house on H Street from Sixth Street.

Q. State to the Court whether or not the Pennsylvania House, at which Dr. Mudd stopped, and the National Hotel, at which Booth stopped, are not both between Four and a Half and Sixth Streets.

A. Yes, sir.

Q. Then the point where you met Dr. Samuel Mudd on Seventh Street would not be in the route between either the National Hotel or the Pennsylvania House and Mrs. Surratt's residence ?

A. I stated, that, on meeting Dr. Mudd on Seventh Street —

Q. I am not asking you what you stated. I wish you to state to the Court whether the point on Seventh Street, at which you met Dr. Samuel Mudd, was on the most direct route between either the

National Hotel or the Pennsylvania Hotel, and Mrs. Surratt's residence.

A. I should think it was the most direct route to the National Hotel.

Q. You do not understand my question. Is the point on Seventh Street, at which you met Dr. Mudd that morning, on the direct route between the Pennsylvania Hotel and Mrs. Surratt's?

A. No, sir.

Q. Is it on the direct route between the National Hotel and Mrs. Surratt's?

A. No, sir.

JOHN GREENAWALT

recalled.

By the JUDGE ADVOCATE:

Q. Yesterday, in describing the poorly-dressed, dark, weather-beaten-complexioned man, who, with the prisoner Atzerodt, passed the night of the 14th of April at the Pennsylvania House, you said that he had black hair : you omitted to state the color of his mustache. Will you state it now?

A. That was black.

Q. Were the whiskers black?

A. Yes, sir.

Q. I believe you stated that he wore a slouch hat?

A. Yes, sir.

JAMES WALKER (colored),

a witness called for the prosecution, being duly sworn, testified as follows :—

By the JUDGE ADVOCATE:

Q. Will you state to the Court whether or not, on the 14th and 15th of April last, you were living at the Pennsylvania House in this city?

A. Yes, sir : I was there.

Q. What were you doing there? what was your business?

A. My business has been, stopping there since the 4th of last April, say twelve months. I have been making fires, carrying water, and waiting on gentlemen late and early, whenever they come in.

Q. Have you ever seen the prisoner Atzerodt?

A. I have seen him at the house.

Q. Do you recognize him now?

A. Yes, sir: that is him [pointing to George A. Atzerodt].

Q. Will you state whether or not on the 14th of April, or the morning of the 15th, he came to that house? and under what circumstances?

A. He came there about two o'clock in the night.

Q. Do you mean at two o'clock on the morning of Saturday, the 15th?

A. Yes, sir. Saturday morning, before day, he came in about two o'clock, or it may have been a few minutes after; and he left there between five and six in the morning.

Q. Did he come there on foot, or horseback, first?

A. The first time he came there, he came on horseback; and I held the horse for him at the door.

Q. What hour was that?

A. Between twelve and one o'clock, I think.

Q. What did he do while you were holding his horse?

A. He went in to the bar: I did not know what he did in there. When he came out, he mounted the horse, and asked me to give him a stick or switch, as the horse was shy of the light; and I gave him a piece of hoop, and he went off.

Q. Did you notice that he had arms with him?

A. I knew not what he had. I did not see any thing in his hand.

Q. When he came back again at two o'clock, was he on horseback, or on foot?

A. He came on foot. He came on foot; and I was lying down, and had to get up, and let him in.

Q. How long did he stay?

A. It was between five and six that he left.

Q. Had he a room, or not?

A. He desired to go to 51, which he had been commonly staying in. I told him the room was taken up, and he went to 53.

Q. Did he stay in 53?

A. He stopped in 53 that night.

Q. At what hour did he leave in the morning?

A. Between five and six.

Q. Where did you see him at that hour?

A. I started for a hack to take a lady to the 6.15 train. I overtook him just about thirty strides from my door: he had come out while I was up stairs talking to the lady about getting a hack.

Q. What direction did he seem to be going?

A. Right towards the National.

Q. Did he make any remark to you, or you to him?

A. No, sir: I overtook him. He was walking along slowly.

Q. Did you see another man who came there about the same time that night, and staid also?

A. He came out before Atzerodt.

Q. How long before?

A. It might have been five minutes, for all I know; or it might have been more than that.

Q. Did he occupy the same room with Atzerodt?

A. He stopped in 53.

Q. What time did he go away in the morning?

A. He went to take the 6.15 train.

Q. Did you see him going to it?

A. Yes, sir: I opened the door, and let him out.

Q. Did he have any baggage?

A. None that I saw.

Q. Do you remember that man's appearance and dress? Could you give a description of him?

A. He seemed to have dark clothes on, a slouch hat; and, when he came in, it was dark: the gas was put down pretty low. I did not raise the gas high to examine the persons that came in. They came in, took a room, and staid there.

Q. Did he go to the room immediately?

A. Yes, sir: straight on to the room.

Q. Did he pay for his room in advance?

A. Yes, sir.

Q. Do you think you would know that man, — the poorly-dressed man, — if you should see him again?

A. I do not know that I would: I was not so well acquainted

with him as I was with Mr. Atzerodt. Mr. Atzerodt had been stopping there a couple of weeks.

Q. Look at all these prisoners, and see if any of them resemble him.

A. I cannot say that.

Cross-examined by Mr. Doster :

Q [Exhibiting the coat identified by John Lee as found at the Kirkwood House.] Take that coat, and say whether you ever saw it in the possession of Atzerodt.

A. I do not recollect of seeing it with him.

Q. Did you use to brush off his clothes?

A. Mr. Atzerodt has got me to clean off his clothes and his boots.

Q. You never saw that coat?

A. No, sir.

Q. What time do you generally go to bed?

A. We generally close up at half-past twelve or one o'clock; and sometimes it is two or three o'clock before I get to sleep, because people oftentimes come in.

Q. What time of night was it when Atzerodt came the first time in the evening of Friday, the 14th of April?

A. We had not shut up then.

Q. What time of night was it?

A. Between twelve and one o'clock.

Q. Are you sure of that?

A. I think it was somewhere about that time.

Q. Did you close up right after he went away?

A. No, sir : a few minutes after, we closed.

Q. You say you held his horse the first time?

A. I did.

Q. What kind of a looking horse had he?

A. A kind of a bay ; a small bay.

Q. Describe the horse.

A. He seemed to be a kind of light-bay horse, small.

Q. Any particular marks about him?

A. I was not near enough to see that.

Q. Young?

A. Yes: had plenty of spirit.

Q. Would you recognize the horse again if you saw him?

A. I do not know that I would.

Q. Did you ever see any arms in the possession of Mr. Atzerodt?

A. I have seen him have a belt with a pistol and a knife.

Q. When?

A. Some four or five days, probably, before this occurrence.

Q. Did you see any on that night or Saturday morning?

A. No, sir: nothing like it.

Q. Could you identify the arms that you saw?

A. No, sir: I could not. I never saw the knife out of the sheath.

Q. Did you open the door for Atzerodt on the second visit?

A. Yes, sir.

Q. Did he seem to know the man he was with?

A. I do not know whether he seemed to know him or not. They had no conversation in my presence.

Q. You were there with them all the time until they went to bed?

A. I was there, took them to the room, and staid no longer.

Q. They had no conversation together as long as you saw them together?

A. No, sir.

By the JUDGE ADVOCATE:

Q. Was the knife of which you spoke any thing like that? [Exhibiting the knife identified by John Lee as found at the Kirkwood House.]

A. I cannot tell: it had a belt and a sheath over it.

Q. It was done up in that way?

A. Yes, sir.

Q. [Exhibiting a knife marked F. 1.] Is that the knife?

A. It looks something more like that.

Q. Now take it out of the sheath.

A. That looks more like the knife than the other one.

[The knife was offered in evidence without objection.]

By Mr. DOSTER:

Q. Did you ever have that knife in your hand before?

A. No, sir.

Q. Where did you see it before ?

A. I saw a knife something like that in the belt he had on around a pistol.

Q. You never saw it out of the sheath ?

A. No, sir.

WILLIAM CLENDENIN,

a witness called for the prosecution, being duly sworn, testified as follows : —

By the JUDGE ADVOCATE :

Q. [Handing to the witness a knife.] Look at that knife, and say whether you have had it in your hand before, and under what circumstances.

A. I have had it before.

Q. State what you know about it.

A. In passing down F Street on the morning after the assassination, I had just crossed Eighth Street, going towards Ninth, when I saw a colored woman pick up something in the gutter. She was about ten feet from me ; and, when I got to her, I asked her what it was ; and she gave a knife to me in a sheath. I examined it. A lady in the third-story window of the house next to where Creaser keeps a shoe-store said she saw this in the gutter, and sent the colored woman down to get it ; but she did not want it to come into the house. I told her then that I would take it, and give it to the chief of police ; and I took it, and gave it to him.

Q. That was the Saturday morning after the assassination ?

A. Yes, sir.

Cross-examined by MR. DOSTER :

Q. What time in the morning was it when you found it ?

A. About six o'clock.

Q. You say a colored woman found it there, and handed it to you ?

A. Yes, sir.

Q. Did you see the colored woman pick it up ?

A. Yes, sir.

Q. Whereabouts was it in the street, precisely ?

A. The knife lay in the gutter on F Street, in front of Creaser's house, as if thrown under the carriage-step.

Q. Under the carriage-step?

A. As if it was thrown under the carriage-step, — as if the intention were to throw it there : it may not have been exactly under the carriage-step.

Q. Whereabouts is Creaser's house situated?

A. About the middle of the square, I should judge.

Q. What square?

A. Between Eighth and Ninth, on F Street, opposite the Patent Office.

James L. McPhail,

a witness called for the prosecution, being duly sworn, testified as follows : —

By the Judge Advocate :

Q. State to the Court whether or not, in a conversation you had with the prisoner Atzerodt, he said, that, on the night of the assassination of the President, he had thrown his knife away in the streets of Washington.

A. Yes, sir : he did.

Mr. Doster. I object to that question.

The Judge Advocate. What is the objection?

Mr. Doster. The objection is, that it will involve a confession made (if made at all) under duress.

The Judge Advocate (to the witness). I ask you, then, under what circumstances the statement was made ; and the Court will determine whether it was under duress or not.

A. I received an intimation, coming from Mr. Atzerodt, that he desired to see me : that was all.

Q. You went to see him accordingly?

A. Yes, sir.

Q. Did you make any promise or any threat to him in connection with that confession of his?

A. None whatever.

By Mr. Doster :

Q. Was he not in irons at the time ?

A. Yes, sir : he was in a cell in the prison, and in irons.

Mr. Doster. I respectfully submit that a confession made under such circumstances is not admissible ; because it was made under duress, which put the mind of the prisoner in a state of fear.

The Judge Advocate. I think nothing is clearer than that, if there was neither threat nor promise, the fact that the man was in prison, or even in irons, does not affect the question of his mental liberty. A man's limbs may be chained, and his mind be perfectly free to speak the truth, or to conceal it, if he chooses.

Mr. Doster, in support of his objection, quoted from the case of Commonwealth *vs.* Mosler (4 Barr's Reports, 265), to the effect that a confession to an officer, as well as to a private person, must be unattended with any inducement of hope or fear, and must be founded on no question calculated to entrap the prisoner ; and referred also to 1 Leech, 263 ; 2 East's Pleas of the Crown ; 2 Russell on Crimes, 644 ; 1 Washington's Circuit-Court Reports, 625 ; 1 Chitty's Criminal Law, 85 ; 1 Greenleaf on Evidence, 214 ; 2 Starkie, 36.

The Judge Advocate admitted the law to be as stated in the authorities cited.

Mr. Doster. Is not a statement made by a man in irons one made under duress ? I claim that the prisoner was under the influence of fear when he made that confession, and, without that influence, would not have made it.

The Judge Advocate. I think it is due to the witness that he should be allowed to state precisely under what circumstances this confession was made ; and, if there is a trace of fear or hope or incitement of that kind, I shall not insist for a moment on the answer being heard.

Gen. Wallace (to the witness). Do I understand that the statement was made wholly without inducement or promise of any kind ?

The Witness. Certainly. I had no disposition or desire to

visit the prison. It was repeatedly stated to me that Atzerodt wished to see me, and that another prisoner did; and I visited the prison after consultation with the Secretary of War, who gave me a pass, for the purpose of gratifying the prisoner. There was no threat: on the contrary, I told him I could make no promises to him; I had nothing to say to him whatever; if he had any thing to say to me, say it. That was all; and I tried to get away from him.

By the COURT:

Q. What is your profession or business?

A. I am acting under the War Department in Maryland. I have been during the war.

Q. In what capacity?

A. Provost-marshal of the State. My commission reads, "The police and loyalty of the State."

Q. Did he know that you were provost-marshal?

A. I think he did.

By MR. DOSTER:

Q. Was not this conversation on a gunboat?

A. No, sir. I saw him on the gunboat.

Q. Where was it?

A. In the cell of this prison. I saw him first on the gunboat. I will further state that the brother-in-law of Atzerodt is on my force, and the brother of Atzerodt has been temporarily on it; and they were repeatedly after me to go to see Atzerodt, and the Secretary of War was acquainted with the same fact. I had no desire, as I said before, to see him: I merely went to accommodate them. I asked him not a single question as to a confession. I said simply, "What you have to say, say it; for I want to go: I cannot stay."

The COMMISSION overruled the objection.

The JUDGE ADVOCATE. The question was answered, and the answer will stand as recorded.

By MR. DOSTER:

Q. Was his statement, that he had thrown away his knife, all he said?

A. He did say more. I answered the question that was put to me.

Q. Did he describe the knife to you?

A. A knife. He said he threw the knife he had away in the streets of Washington. He named the place he threw it.

By the JUDGE ADVOCATE:

Q. Where did he mention?

A. Near the Herndon House, — just above the Herndon House. I think that is at Ninth and F Streets.

By MR. DOSTER:

Q. Did he not state to you where his pistol was?

A. He did.

Q. Where did he say it was?

A. At Matthew & Company's, Georgetown, in the possession of a young man by the name of Caldwell.

Q. Did he tell you how it got there?

A. Yes, sir.

Q. How was it?

A. He had got ten dollars upon it.

Q. He had pawned it?

A. He had gone there and borrowed ten dollars upon the pistol, and left the pistol.

Q. On what day?

A. On Saturday morning, the 15th of April.

Q. Did he not mention to you a certain coat, containing a pistol, bowie-knife, and other articles, hanging in a room at the Kirkwood House, and say to whom it belonged?

A. Yes, sir.

Q. To whom did he say that it belonged?

A. He stated that the coat at the hotel belonged to Herold.

Q. And the arms?

A. That the arms belonged to Herold.

MR. STONE. I must object to that.

MR. DOSTER. The answer has been obtained. I do not wish to press it any further.

LIEUTENANT W. R. KEIM,

a witness called for the prosecution, being duly sworn, testified as follows : —

By the JUDGE ADVOCATE:

Q. State whether or not you passed the night of the 14th of April last in the Pennsylvania House, in this city.

A. I did.

Q. Did you or not see the prisoner Atzerodt there?

A. I did.

Q. State under what circumstances you saw him.

A. I came into the hotel about four o'clock on Saturday morning; and I should think he was lying in bed when I came into the room. I asked him whether he had heard of the assassination of the President. He said that he had; that it was an awful affair. I went to bed then after talking a few minutes. I woke up, I should judge, about seven o'clock; and I found that he was gone. He slept in the bed opposite to that in which I was.

Q. Did you see his arms?

A. Not that time. When we had room No. 51, I saw him have a knife and revolver.

Q. You say you saw them in another room?

A. Yes, sir: in room No. 51.

Q. How long before the day you now mention?

A. I think, either the Sunday before or the Sunday week: I would not be positive.

Q. What were the arms?

A. A large bowie-knife in a sheath.

Q. [Submitting to the witness the knife offered in evidence, as Exhibit No. 41.] Was it a knife resembling that?

A. About that sized knife. I would not swear that was the knife: a knife about that size, though.

Q. State under what circumstances you saw it.

A. Atzerodt went out, and left the knife in his bed. I got up and took the knife, and put it under my pillow. He came back in a few minutes, and went over to his bed, and looked about, and then said to me, "Have you seen my knife?" I said, "Yes: here

it is." Then he said, " I want that : if one fails, I want the other."
I gave it to him.

Q. Did he have a pistol then ?

A. Yes : he always carried it around his waist.

Cross-examined by MR. DOSTER :

Q. Did you know the prisoner Atzerodt before your meeting him
at the Pennsylvania House ?

A. No, sir.

Q. What time of night was it when you were shown to his room?

A. I would not be positive. It was nearly four o'clock in the
morning.

Q. What day was that?

A. That was the next morning after the assassination, — Saturday morning.

Q. Did you speak to him immediately when you entered the
room ?

A. Not immediately, but in a few minutes. My bed was right
opposite to his. I went and saw him in bed five or ten minutes before I spoke to him.

Q. You mentioned the assassination of the President, and he said
it was an awful thing ?

A. Yes, sir.

Q. Did he say any thing more about it ?

A. No : I think that was about all he said.

Q. Was he undressed ?

A. He was in bed. I do not know whether he was undressed or
not. I could not see that.

Q. You mentioned that Atzerodt called you " Lieut." Were
you on intimate terms ?

A. No : he always called me " Lieut." He always addressed
me by that name.

Q. Did you see him again after that ?

A. No, sir.

Q. Will you repeat what you mentioned just now about the knife
failing ?

A. He went out of the room. The knife was in the bed. I went over and got the knife, and put it under my pillow.

Q. I want the words he used.

A. He said, if this would fail, the other would not.

Q. What other?

A. I do not know.

Q. That was after the assassination?

A. No: that was a week or ten days before the assassination.

Q. That was on another occasion?

A. Yes, sir.

Q. What time was that?

A. As I say, it was a week or ten days before; but I am not positive as to the time exactly.

Q. At the time he used those words, had you been drinking with him?

A. Yes, sir: we had two or three drinks.

Q. Where did you drink?

A. In bed, I think, — while we were lying in bed.

Q. Were those remarks made after you had taken those drinks?

A. Yes, sir: he dressed, and went out of the room, and did not come back.

Q. What kind of drinks were they.

A. Whiskey cocktails, if I am not mistaken.

Q. Three apiece?

A. Two or three: I am not positive.

Q. Do you remember any thing else that passed in that interview?

A. No, sir.

Q. Did you stay in your room after you had taken these drinks?

A. Yes sir: it was an hour or two, I judge, before I got up.

WASHINGTON BRISCOE,

a witness called for the prosecution, being duly sworn, testified as follows: —

By the JUDGE ADVOCATE:

Q. State to the Court whether or not, on the night of the 14th of April, you saw the prisoner Atzerodt.

A. I did.

Q. State where, and at what hour, and under what circumstances.

A. He got on the car at Sixth Street, Navy Yard, east, between half-past eleven and twelve.

Q. Did he get a car going to the Navy Yard?

A. Yes, sir.

Q. What did he say?

A. He did not recognize me when he got in till I spoke to him.

Q. What occurred then?

A. I asked him if he had heard the news. He said he had. Then he asked me to let him sleep in the store with me.

Q. Where was your store? — down at the Navy Yard?

A. Yes, sir.

Q. What did you say?

A. I told him he could not.

Q. What was his manner?

A. I judged that he was excited : he seemed to be. He did not recognize me when he came in.

Q. Did he urge you, and seem very anxious to sleep with you?

A. He asked me three times.

Q. And when you refused, what became of him?

A. He rode down as far as I did, and then got out, and asked me again ; and I told him he could not; that the gentleman I was with was there, and he did not ask him, and I had no right to ask him.

Q. What hour was that?

A. Between half-past eleven and twelve o'clock.

Q. How long have you known him?

A. I have known him for several years, — seven or eight years.

Q. Did he express any determination to go anywhere else to sleep that night?

A. He said he was going back to the Kimmel House, on C Street ; that he was stopping at the house.

Q. Is that the Pennsylvania House?

A. Yes, sir.

Q. He said that when he left you?

A. Yes, sir.

Cross-examined by Mr. Doster:

Q. Did you notice the precise time when you met Atzerodt that evening?

A. I did not. I think it was between half-past eleven and twelve o'clock.

Q. What was the time he left you, as near as you know?

A. Near twelve o'clock.

Q. So he was with you not quite half an hour?

A. He was in the car and with me together. He stopped on the corner, and waited until the car came back.

Q. Where was he standing with you?

A. On the corner of I Street and Garrison Street.

Q. That is near the Navy Yard?

A. Yes, sir.

Q. Were you going towards the Capitol?

A. No: I was going towards the Navy Yard, my home, where I am stopping.

Q. Did he ride down with you, then, in the same car to your house?

A. He rode as far as I Street, near my store, and got out where I did.

Q. What was his manner during that time? Did he appear to be disturbed?

A. I judged from his manner that he was a little excited.

Q. Did he look as though he had been drinking?

A. I hardly know. I did not notice him very particularly.

Q. You saw him take the car again?

A. Yes, sir.

W. H. RYDER,

a witness called for the prosecution, being duly sworn, testified as follows: —

By the Judge Advocate:

Q. Where do you reside?

A. At Chicago, Ill.

Q. What is your profession?

A. Clergyman.

Q. Will you state to the Court whether, recently, you visited Richmond, Va., and at what time?

A. I left Chicago on the 9th of April, and arrived in Richmond on the 14th of April, and remained in Richmond until the 21st of April.

Q. While there, did you go into the State Capitol?

A. Yes, sir.

Q. Did you find the archives of the so-called Confederate States there? and in what condition?

A. Generally confused.

Q. Scattered about the floor?

A. Yes: scattered.

Q. Did you, in common with others, pick up as many of these papers as you chose?

A. Yes, sir.

Q. [Submitting to witness a paper.] Will you state whether or not the paper which you now hold in your hand was picked up in the Capitol at Richmond under the circumstances you mentioned?

A. It was picked up either in the building or immediately about the building, or was handed me by some soldier, who had picked it up among the rubbish, as I went about the rooms. There were one or two persons with me. We would stoop down, and handle over the papers, and, as we judged any thing important, put it in the pocket; and in some instances the orderly in attendance — for I had a permit from the provost-marshal — would say, "This is something good;" put it in my pocket: and, having thus collected quite a number of things, they were thrown into a common receptacle, which finally became a box. We transferred the papers to a box, and they were forwarded to Chicago.

Q. Is that one of the papers?

A. This is one of the papers so found.

[The paper was offered in evidence without objection, and read as follows: —

RICHMOND, Feb. 11, 1865.

His Excellency Jefferson Davis, President C. S. A.

SIR, — When Senator Johnson of Missouri and myself waited on you a few days since in relation to the prospect of annoying and harassing the enemy by means of burning their shipping, towns, &c., &c., there were several remarks made by you upon the subject, that I was not fully prepared to answer, but which, upon subsequent conference with parties proposing the enterprise, I find cannot apply as objections to the scheme.

1. The combustible material consists of several preparations, and not one alone; and can be used without exposing the party using them to the least danger of detection whatever. The preparations are not in the hands of McDaniel, but are in the hands of Professor McCullough, and are known but to him and one other party, as I understand.

2. There is no necessity for sending persons in the military service into the enemy's country; but the work may be done by agents, and, in most cases, by persons ignorant of the facts, and therefore innocent agents.

I have seen enough of the effects that can be produced to satisfy me that in most cases, without any danger to the parties engaged, and in others but very slight, we can, 1. Burn every vessel that leaves a foreign port for the United States. 2. We can burn every transport that leaves the harbor of New York or other Northern port with supplies for the armies of the enemy in the South. 3. Burn every transport and gunboat on the Mississippi River, as well as devastate the country of the enemy, and fill his people with terror and consternation. I am not alone in this opinion; but many other gentlemen are as fully and thoroughly impressed with the conviction as I am. I believe we have the means at our command, if promptly appropriated and energetically applied, to demoralize the Northern people in a very short time. For the purpose of satisfying your mind upon the subject, I respectfully but earnestly request that you will have an interview with General Harris, formerly a member of Congress from Missouri, who, I think, is able, from conclusive proofs, to convince you that what I have suggested is perfectly feasible and practicable.

The deep interest I feel for the success of our cause in this struggle, and the conviction of the importance of availing ourselves of every element of defence, must be my excuse for writing you, and requesting you to invite General Harris to see you. If you should see proper to do so, please signify the time when it will be convenient for you to see him.

I am, respectfully, your obedient servant,

W. S. OLDHAM.

[Indorsement.]

Hon. W. S. Oldham. Richmond, Feb. 12, 1865. In relation to plans and means for burning the enemy's shipping, towns, &c., &c. Preparations are in the hands of Professor McCullough, and are known to only one other party. Asks the President to have an interview with General Harris, formerly M.C. from Missouri, on the subject. Secretary of State at his convenience please see General Harris, and learn what plan he has for overcoming the difficulty heretofore experienced.

20 Feb'y, '65.   J. D.

Rec'd Feb'y 17, 1865.]

JOHN POTTS,

a witness called for the prosecution, being duly sworn, testified as follows : —

By the JUDGE ADVOCATE :

Q. Will you state to the Court what position you occupy in the public service here ?

A. Chief Clerk of the War Department.

Q. How long have you been in the War Department ?

A. Upwards of twenty years.

Q. Were you or not perfectly familiar with the handwriting of Jefferson Davis ?

A. I have been, of course.

Q. Look at the indorsement on that paper, and state whether it is in his handwriting [exhibiting to the witness the letter].

A. In my belief, it is.

Q. While he was Secretary of War, I suppose you had abundant opportunities of becoming acquainted with his handwriting ?

A. Of course.

Q. In order that there may be no mistake, I will ask you to

read, if you please, the indorsement which you regard as in his handwriting.

A. "Sect'y of State at his convenience please see Gen'l Harris, and hear what plan he has for overcoming the difficulty heretofore experienced." [Sgd] J. D., 20 Feb., '65. That is the indorsement to which I referred.

NATHAN RICE,

a witness called for the prosecution, being duly sworn, testified as follows : —

By the JUDGE ADVOCATE :

Q. State to the Court whether or not you are acquainted with the handwriting of Jefferson Davis.

A. I was, eight years ago, when he was Secretary of War. I was requisition-clerk; and he had to sign all the requisitions that came before me every day.

Q. Will you look at the indorsement upon the paper signed "J. D.," and just read by Mr. Potts, and state whether or not you regard it as in the handwriting of Jefferson Davis ?

A. I should think it was.

Q. You had ample opportunities of becoming acquainted with his handwriting ?

A. Very good : I had from ten to twenty-five signatures of his before me every day, sometimes signed in my presence, but not always so.

JOSHUA T. OWEN,

a witness called for the prosecution, being duly sworn, testified as follows : —

By the JUDGE ADVOCATE :

Q. [Submitting to the witness Exhibit No. 42.] Do you know Professor McCullough ?

A. I have known a gentleman who has been designated Professor McCullough, I suppose, for twenty years.

Q. Professor of what is he ?

A. He was professor of chemistry at Princeton College ; he was a professor of mathematics at Jefferson College, Penn., where I graduated ; and about 1839 or 1840, if my recollection serves me, he was assayer of the mint at Philadelphia.

Q. Do you know where he has been during the present Rebellion ?

A. From information that I consider reliable, he has been at Richmond, in the service of the Confederates. I may say that his father was one of the comptrollers of the Treasury in Washington. I think name was Hugh McCullough ; the same name as the present secretary.

Q. This McCullough had some distinction as a chemist ?

A. Yes, sir ; considerable. Perhaps more in that than any thing else.

Q. Is it in that capacity that he has been in the service of the Confederates, as you understand ?

A. I do not know.

A. B. OLIN,

a witness called for the prosecution, being duly sworn, testified as follows : —

By the JUDGE ADVOCATE :

Q. Judge, will you state to the Court whether or not, on the morning of the 15th of April, you visited Ford's Theatre, and inspected the President's box, as it is called there ?

A. Sunday following, the 16th, I first visited the theatre. The assassination was on the evening of the 14th ; and on the 15th I was engaged in taking depositions.

Q. Will you state the examination which you made, and the condition in which you found the box and doors and locks ?

A. My attention was called to the incision into the wall that was prepared to receive the brace that fitted into the corner of the panel of the door. The brace was not there.

Q. That is the outer door you speak of ?

A. The door entering the alley-way into the box which crossed the alley at an angle with the wall ; and a brace fitted against the wall to the corner of the door fastens the door very securely. I discovered that, and looked for the remains of the plastering that had been cut from the wall to make this incision. That was all, so far as I could observe, carefully removed from a little carpet, where it must have fallen as it was cut by some sharp instrument. That plastering was all carefully removed.

It was said to me that the pistol was discharged through the panel of the door. The passage-way is somewhat dark ; and I procured a light, and examined very carefully the hole bored through the door. I discovered at once that that hole was made by some small instrument in the first place, and was, as I supposed, cut out then by a sharp instrument like a penknife ; and you can see, by placing a light near the door, — if I am not very much mistaken, I thought I saw, — marks of a sharp-cutting knife, cleaning out every obstacle to looking through that hole in the door. I then discovered also that the clasp that fastens the bolt of the first door, — this would be a double box on some occasions, there is a movable partition fitted to it, — on the clasp that receives the lock of that door, the upper screw holding the clasp had been loosened in such a way, that when the door was locked, by putting my forefinger against the door, and pushing it, I could push the door open.

I seated myself as near as I could ascertain the position of the chair in which the President sat that evening ; for I procured, to accompany me, Miss Harris, who, I understood, was in the box on that occasion ; and she located the chair as nearly as she recollected it to have been placed on the evening. And in seating myself in the chair, closing that door, and letting a person place his eye very near that hole, close to the door, the range would be about from one to the other, striking my head about midway from the base to the crown.

I directed my attention principally, at that early stage of the investigation, to ascertaining more particularly the precise period of the occurrence, as there was some uncertainty at that time whether the attack upon Mr. Seward's family, and the assassination of the President, was the result of the act of some one person or more persons ; and I directed my attention in the first place more particularly to ascertaining the precise period of time as nearly as I could when this occurred. I continued to make some examinations.

Q. Did you examine the conditions of the locks on the doors ?

A. I did. I examined the condition of the locks. The lock played readily.

Q. A hasp, or catch?

A. As I before observed, the catch of one door, the first door that would enter into the first box as you passed into the box from this alley-way, the upper screw holding the hasp was loosened in such a way, that it could be pressed upon with the finger when the door was locked, and the hasp would fall back. I also examined to see if I could discover the chips that must have been made by boring and cutting out this small hole; but they had apparently been removed. I discovered nothing of them.

Q. Did you see the bar? or had it been lost?

A. It had been removed by some one. You could see the indentation upon the door, in the panel of the door, where some brace might have been made from the wall to the door. That indentation there is perceptible; and the brace was so fixed in, that it would be very difficult to remove it from the outside. I do not think it could be done without breaking the door down. The more pressure that was made from the dress-circle of the theatre upon that bar, the firmer it would have been held in its place: but it was securely fastened in its place; for it rested on that hole in the wall and the panel of the door.

Q. Did it bear the appearance of having been recently made?

A. Yes, sir. It was a freshly cut hole. The wood was as fresh as it would have been the instant it was cut, apparently, to the observation.

Q. Can you describe the chair?

A. It is a large, high-backed arm-chair, and satin cushions.

Q. A rocking-chair?

A. I think, not a rocking-chair. From nearly opposite the place where the President's head might have rested against the chair, I think I could discover, although it was red, the marks of several drops of blood.

By Mr. Aiken:

Q. Are the civil courts of this District in full and free operation?

A. They are in operation; at least, they were before I adjourned one to-day.

By Mr. Doster:

Q. Will you be kind enough to state whether the civil courts are supposed to sit by the consent of, and in order to carry out the will of, General Grant?

A. I really do not know how anybody supposes that. He has given me no information on that subject.

MAJOR HENRY R. RATHBONE
recalled.

By the Judge Advocate:

Q. After the shot had been fired, did you go to the outer door of the President's box, and examine how it was closed?

A. I did, sir, for the purpose of calling medical aid.

Q. In what condition did you find it?

A. I found the door barred, so that the people who were knocking on the outside could not gain an entrance.

Q. Did you make an attempt to remove the bar?

A. I did, sir; and removed it with difficulty.

Q. Was that after you had received the stab from the assassin?

A. Yes, sir.

Q. [Exhibiting a bar to the witness.] Is that blood on that wooden bar from your arm?

A. I am not able to say that; but my wound was bleeding freely at the time.

Q. In what condition did you find the bar?

A. The bar was securely fastened in the wall, and appeared to be resting against the moulding of the door. I think it could not have been jostled out by any pushing from the outside.

Q. Did you notice particularly the chair in which the President sat? What was its character?

A. Nothing, except that it was a large, easy-chair, covered with damask cloth.

Q. You do not know whether it had rockers or not?

A. My impression was that it had: I am not sure.

By the COURT :

Q. Is that the bar the door was closed with ?

A. I am not able to say.

Q. Was it similar to that ?

A. My impression was that it was a different piece of wood.

ISAAC JAQUETTE,

a witness called for the prosecution, being duly sworn, testified as follows : —

By the JUDGE ADVOCATE:

Q. [Exhibiting a bar to the witness.] Will you please state to the Court whether or not you found that bar in Ford's Theatre, and under what circumstances, and where ?

A. Yes, sir. Soon after the President was carried out, I went to the box with several others; and this bar was lying inside of the first door going into the box, — lying on the floor. I picked it up. I staid around there some time, and then carried it out.

Q. Did you take it home with you ?

A. Yes, sir.

Q. There has been a piece sawed off, has there not ?

A. Yes, sir. There was an officer stopping at the same boarding-house where I was ; and he wanted a piece of it. I sawed a piece off ; but he concluded not to take it afterwards.

Q. These spots upon it are blood ?

A. Yes, sir.

Q. Were they fresh at the time ?

A. They looked fresh at the time.

[The bar was offered in evidence without objection.]

JOE SIMMS (colored)

recalled for the prosecution.

By the JUDGE ADVOCATE:

Q. Will you state whether or not you have been working at Ford's Theatre ?

A. Yes, sir. I have worked at Mr. Ford's Theatre for two years.

35*

Q. Were you there on the evening of the day on the night of which the President was assassinated?

A. Yes, sir.

Q. Did you see the persons engaged in decorating the President's box that afternoon?

A. Mr. Harry Ford and another gentleman, I do not know his name exactly, were up there fixing up the box. Mr. Harry Ford told me to go up to his bed-room, and get a rocking-chair out, and bring it down, and put it in the President's box. I did so, according to his orders. When I carried the chair into the private box, and set it down, Mr. Harry Ford said, "You can go down; that is all I want;" and I immediately passed down the stairs.

Q. You carried it into the box yourself, did you?

A. Yes, sir. He told me to bring it out of his sleeping-room, and put it into the private box.

Q. Had it ever been there before?

A. Not this season.

Q. Was it a rocking-chair?

A. Yes, sir.

Q. How was the back, high or low?

A. It was a chair with a high back to it.

Q. And cushioned?

A. Yes, sir.

Q. Did you see the prisoner, Edward Spangler, there on that occasion?

A. Not at that time. There was no one in the box at that time but Mr. Harry Ford and the other gentleman that was helping to fix it. He had started to go down when he told me to go after the chair.

Q. Was Spangler on the stage that afternoon when you were bringing the chair?

A. Mr. Spangler was obliged to be there: he was there all the time.

Q. Was he there that afternoon?

A. He was there that afternoon. He was obliged to be there. There was no other place for him. He worked there altogether, the same as I did ; and had no calling away, only when he went to his boarding-house.

Q. I understood you to say that he was in there when the chair was put in the box ?

A. I did not see Mr. Spangler in the private box. I carried it up ; but I did not say Mr. Spangler was in there.

Q. Was he on the stage at the time, do you know ?

A. He might have been on the stage, or somewhere about the building.

Cross-examined by Mr. Ewing :

Q. You say Mr. Spangler might have been on the stage then ?

A. Yes, sir.

Q. You did not see him then ?

A. No, sir : I did not see him. I did not notice particular. When Mr. Harry Ford told me to go up in his room, and bring down the chair, of course I went, not noticing particular, which I hardly ever did. I have been there so long at work, that I hardly ever notice persons so particular ; but this Mr. Spangler had no other calling away in the week, only right at the theatre, on the stage, except when called up to his boarding-house.

Q. You say he had no "other calling away." You mean that was all the business he was engaged in ?

A. Yes, sir : that was his business.

Q. You do not know whether he might not have had something to call him away from the theatre just at that time, do you ?

A. No, sir : I do not.

Q. Who was this other gentleman that was in the box with Mr. Harry Ford ?

A. I think his name is Mr. Buckingham : I may be mistaken.

Q. Was he employed about the theatre ?

A. He stood at the door at nights to take the tickets when the people came in. He was doorkeeper in front of the house.

Q. You think it was Mr. Buckingham that was there then with Mr. Harry Ford ?

A. I think it was Mr. Buckingham that was helping Mr. Harry Ford to fix up the private box.

Q. What hour in the afternoon was it?

A. It was a little after three o'clock, I think. I did not notice the time particularly : it might have been later, and it might have been sooner.

Q. Mr. Ford called you to come up to the box, did he?

A. Yes, sir. I was doing something somewhere around the building; and he called me, and told me to go to his room, and bring down that large rocking-chair out of his sleeping-room, and put it in the private box. I did so, according to his order.

Q. Where were you when he called you?

A. I do not know exactly where I was, — whether I was out in the alley, or whether I was up on the flies; but I was somewhere about the building, I know, when he called me.

Q. You were near enough to hear when called?

A. I had come in from carrying bills. I carried the bills out every day, so that the people could see what was going to be played ; and I came back that evening, and was about to take my meal, — was going to eat up on the flies, — when he called me. He called me down, and told me to go up to his room, and get the chair.

Q. You took your meals up on the flies, did you?

A. Yes, sir : I used to take my meals there, of course.

Q. At what time did you generally take that meal?

A. I generally took it whenever I could. When I came in the mornings, I would take out the bills; and that would keep me sometimes until three o'clock, and sometimes longer ; and, whenever I would come back, I would eat.

Q. And you were eating when he called you?

A. When he called me to bring the chair, I put down my meal, and went and got the chair for him, and put it in the private box.

Q. Did you see Mr. Spangler as you went to the box at all?

A. No, sir : I did not see Mr. Spangler. I did not see him when I went to the box, neither did I see him when I came away from the private box.

Q. Describe that chair.

A. There is not a chair in here like it ; but it was one of those high-backed rocking-chairs, with a high cushion on it, — a red cushion.

Q. What kind of material was the cushion made of, — cloth or satin?

A. A kind of satin.

Q. Do you know that the chair never was in the private box before this season?

A. Not this season, that I know of.

Q. When was it in?

A. Last season. When they got it last season, it was in tho private box; and Mr. Harry Ford told me to take it out of the private box, and carry it up in his room. That was the only one up in his room.

Q. It was bought last season?

A. Last season.

Q. Was there any other furniture for the box, of the same character?

A. Yes, sir.

Q. What other pieces?

A. There was a sofa, and some more other chairs.

Q. Any other big chair?

A. Not in that box, that I know of. I did not notice particularly. It was not my business to be looking into this place; and therefore I did not notice particularly. I never went in there only when I was sent: for there were persons to clean it up, and go all about; and I just attended to the outside work.

Q. Was the sofa covered with the same material?

A. Yes, sir: it was covered with the same material.

Q. Was that furniture bought for the private box?

A. I do not know whether it was bought for the private box, or whether it was bought for the properties, to be used on the stage.

Q. Was it bought for the theatre?

A. Yes, sir.

Q. And it was in the private box last season?

A. Yes, sir: last season.

Q. With the rest of the set that it belonged to?

A. With the rest of the furniture that was in there.

Q. The rest of the furniture you spoke of was covered with the same sort of cloth?

A. Yes, sir.

By the JUDGE ADVOCATE:

Q. Did you take a large chair out of that box at the time you put this one in?

A. No, sir: I did not take one in and one out.

Q. You do not know what kind of a chair was there before?

A. No, sir: I do not. I just brought that chair in, and set it down. Mr. Ford said, "That is all I want with you;" and I went down immediately.

JOHN J. TOFFEY

recalled for the prosecution.

By the JUDGE ADVOCATE:

Q. Since you were on the stand yesterday, will you state whether you have been to the stable, and seen the horse of which you were speaking?

A. I was.

Q. Where did you find him?

A. In the stables at Seventeenth and I Streets

Q. General Augur's stables?

A. Yes, sir.

Q. Do you or not recognize him as the horse you found standing with a saddle and bridle on, under the circumstances mentioned in your testimony?

A. I do, sir.

Q. You have no doubt of his being the same horse?

A. No, sir.

By the COURT:

Q. Is there any thing peculiar about that horse by which you would be able to recognize him readily?

A. Being blind in the right eye.

Q. The right eye is gone?

A. Yes, sir.

WILLIAM EATON,

a witness called for the prosecution, being duly sworn, testified as follows : —

By the JUDGE ADVOCATE :

Q. Will you state whether or not, after the assassination of the President, you went to the room of J. Wilkes Booth at the National Hotel, and opened his trunk ?

A. I did go there that same evening.

Q. You went there under the authority of the War Department ?

A. Yes, sir : from the provost-marshal's office.

Q. What did you do on arriving there ? Did you ask for J. Wilkes Booth's room ?

A. Yes, sir.

Q. Were you shown to it ?

A. Yes, sir ; by the book-keeper.

Q. What did you do then ?

A. I went to his room, and took charge of his trunk ; that is, I took charge of what was in it. I took charge of the papers, and took those papers to the provost-marshal's office ; and they were examined that evening in the office.

Q. You took all the papers which you found in his trunk to what officer of the provost-marshal's office ?

A. To Lieutenant Terry.

Q. You placed them in his hands ?

A. Yes, sir.

LIEUTENANT WILLIAM H. TERRY

a witness called for the prosecution, being duly sworn, testified as follows : —

By the JUDGE ADVOCATE :

Q. Will you state whether you are attached to the office of the provost-marshal of this city ?

A. Yes, sir ; Colonel Ingraham's office.

Q. Will you state whether or not, on the night after the assassination of the President, the witness who has just been examined here (Mr. Eaton) placed in your hands certain papers which he represented to have taken from the trunk of **J. Wilkes Booth**?

A. Yes, sir.

Q. [Exhibiting a letter to the witness.] Will you state to the Court whether that letter, with the envelope, was one of those papers?

A. Yes, sir: this is one of the papers; and it was in that envelope. Colonel Taylor marked the envelope "Important," and signed his initials to it.

The letter was read, as follows: —

HOOKSTOWN, BALTO. Co., March 27, 1865.

DEAR JOHN, — Was business so important that you could not remain in Balto. till I saw you? I came in as soon as I could, but found you had gone to W——n. I called also to see Mike, but learned from his mother he had gone out with you, and had not returned. I concluded, therefore, he had gone with you. How inconsiderate you have been! When I left you, you stated we would not meet in a month or so: therefore I made application for employment, an answer to which I shall receive during week. I told my parents I had ceased with you. Can I, then, under existing circumstances, come as you request? You know full well that the G——t suspicions something is going on there: therefore the undertaking is becoming more complicated. Why not, for the present, desist, for various reasons, which, if you look into, you can readily see, without my making any mention thereof? You nor any one can censure me for my present course. You have been its cause; for how can I now come after telling them I had left you? Suspicion rests upon me now from my whole family, and even parties in the county. I will be compelled to leave home anyhow, and how soon I care not. None, no, not one, were more in for the enterprise than myself, and to-day would be there, had you not done as you have, — by this I mean manner of proceeding. I am, as you well know, in need. I am, you may say, in rags; whereas to-day I ought to be well clothed. I do not feel right stalking about with means, and more from appearances a beggar. I feel my dependence : but even all this would and was forgotten ; for I was one with you. Time more propitious will arrive yet. Do not act rashly or in haste. I would prefer your first query, "Go and see how it will be taken at R——d ; " and ere long I shall be better prepared to again be with you. I dislike writing ; would sooner verbally make known my views : yet your non-writing causes me thus to proceed.

Do not in anger peruse this. Weigh all I have said ; and, as a rational man and a *friend,* you cannot censure or upbraid my conduct. I sincerely trust this, nor aught else that shall or may occur, will ever be an obstacle to obliterate our former friendship and attachment. Write me to Balto., as I expect to be in about Wednesday or Thursday ; or, if you can possibly come on, I will Tuesday meet you in Balto., at B——. Ever I subscribe myself,

Your friend,   SAM.

WILLIAM McPHAIL,

a witness called for the prosecution, being duly sworn, testified as follows : —

By the JUDGE ADVOCATE :

Q. Are you acquainted with the handwriting of the prisoner Samuel Arnold ?

A. I am.

Q. [Exhibiting to the witness the letter.] Will you look at this letter, and state to the Court whether it is in his handwriting or not ?

MR. COX. Before you look at that letter, I will ask you how you became acquainted with the handwriting of Mr. Arnold ?

A. I am acquainted with it from the fact of his having made an instrument, and placed it in my hands.

The witness, after examining the letter, said, "That has somewhat the appearance of it ; rather a little heavier, I think, in some parts of it. I should say it was his handwriting.

Cross-examined by MR. EWING :

Q. What instrument did he write, and place in your hands ?

A. An instrument purporting to be a confession of his connection with this transaction.

Q. When did he write it?

A. On Tuesday, the 18th of April.

Q. Where did he write it?

A. He wrote it in the back-room, in Marshal McPhail's office.

Q. Where?

A. Fayette Street, No. 40, between North and Holliday.

Q. What became of the paper?

A. The paper was handed by me to the marshal, on his arriving from Washington. I do not know what became of it afterwards, other than that I was informed that it was delivered to the Secretary of War.

Q. To what marshal?

A. To Marshal James L. McPhail.

Q. That was a paper purporting to state all that he knew in regard to this affair?

A. Yes, sir.

James L. McPhail

recalled for the prosecution.

By the Judge Advocate:

Q. [Exhibiting to the witness the letter.] Will you state whether or not you are acquainted with the handwriting of the prisoner Samuel Arnold?

A. Only by receiving a letter of his from his father, dated the 12th. This looks similar to the writing of that letter.

Q. Did that letter purport to be written by him?

A. Yes, sir; written and dated the 12th of April, at Fortress Monroe. That letter was in the hands of Mr. Wharton.

Q. In whose handwriting is the indorsement on the back of that envelope?

A. This direction, "J. Wilkes Booth," I should think, was in M. Samuel Arnold's handwriting.

Q. You mean the prisoner at the bar?

A. Yes, sir.

Q. Have you looked at the body of the letter itself?

A. No, sir: I did not. I merely looked over the letter: I did not read it.

Q. You looked at the handwriting?

A. Yes, sir.

Q. Whose do you think it is?

A. I think it is the writing of Mr. Arnold.

LITTLETON P. D. NEWMAN,

a witness called for the prosecution, being duly sworn, testified as follows: —

By the JUDGE ADVOCATE:

Q. Are you acquainted with the handwriting of the prisoner Samuel Arnold?

A. No, sir: I am not. I never saw it.

Q. Do you know him?

A. Yes, sir.

Q. Will you state whether or not, some time last fall, you were present when he received a letter in which money was enclosed? and, if the letter was exhibited to you, state its character, as far as you know.

A. On the 9th, 10th, or 12th of September, Mr. Arnold had been helping us to thresh wheat at a neighbor's; and there was a letter brought to him. In that letter there was either a twenty or a fifty dollar note: I am not positive which. He read the letter, and remarked that he was flush, or had money, or something of that character. After having read the letter, he handed it over to me; and I read some half a dozen lines, possibly, — not more. I did not understand it; it was very ambiguous in its language; and I handed it back to him, and asked him what it meant. He remarked that something big would take place one of these days, or be seen in the paper, or something to that effect. That was about all that occurred.

Q. Did you see the name signed to the letter?

A. I do not remember whether I looked at that at all.

EATON G. HORNER,

a witness called for the prosecution, being duly sworn, testified as follows: —

By the JUDGE ADVOCATE:

Q. Will you state whether or not, some days after the assassination of the President, you arrested the prisoner Samuel Arnold, and where?

A. On the morning of the 17th of April, Mr. Voltaire Russell and myself arrested him at Fortress Monroe.

Q. Did you find any arms in his possession?

A. Yes, sir. We took him in the room back of the store, where he slept. We there searched his person and his carpet-bag. Out of the carpet-bag we got a pistol. He said he had another pistol, and a knife also, at his father's place in the country, near the Hookstown Road.

Q. What kind of pistol did you find in his possession?

A. Something like a Colt's pistol.

Q. He said he had left another pistol and a knife at his father's?

A. Yes, sir.

Cross-examined by MR. EWING:

Q. Did he not say he had left the pistol and the knife at Hookstown?

A. At his father's place.

Q. At Hookstown?

A. Near Hookstown.

Q. What else did he say to you at that time?

A. He made a statement verbally to us at Fortress Monroe. Before we left Baltimore, a letter was given to us by his father to give him when we should arrest him. We handed him the letter, and he read it. I inquired of him if he was going to do as they asked him to do; and he said he was. He then gave us a statement and the names of certain men connected with a plan for the abduction of Abraham Lincoln.

ASSISTANT JUDGE ADVOCATE BINGHAM. I think we did not ask for any thing of this sort. What is this question about?

The JUDGE ADVOCATE. We have obtained from the witness a statement that Arnold left a pistol and a knife at his father's; and, as a part of that confession relative to the pistol and knife, I understand Mr. Ewing to insist on these statements.

Mr. Cox. I presume any thing relating to the other prisoners will not be allowed to be given in evidence.

The Judge Advocate [to the counsel for the accused]. That is a question which you must adjust among yourselves, gentlemen.

Mr. Ewing. I will ask the witness the question, what else Arnold stated in that conversation. Does the Judge Advocate object to the question ?

The Judge Advocate. I do not.

Mr. Stone. We object, may it please the Court, to the confession of any one of the accused being offered in evidence as against either of the other accused ; to allowing the declarations of one of the accused to be used against any of the other accused, when he himself is not a competent witness to be placed in the box. In other words, we object that the declarations of Arnold cannot be used to convict the other seven, or any of them. Mere declarations made by him — and made, perhaps, for the purpose of shoving the responsibility off his own shoulders on the shoulders of others — are not, properly, evidence against us or any of the others who stand here accused, and now on their trial.

Mr. Ewing. The objection having just been formally presented, I should like to make a remark or two to the Court on the subject. The Judge Advocate asked what Arnold said about arms ; and the witness said that he answered, that he had another pistol and a knife at his father's house near Hookstown. I asked what further he said ; and think the whole of his statement then made is admissible, as it goes to account for his possession of the arms, and explains the possession. It is very true, that the confession of one of the accused in a conspiracy or alleged conspiracy, after the conspiracy has been either executed or abandoned, is not admissible, — that is, will not be considered by the Court in weighing the question of the guilt or innocence of those who are associated with him in the charge ; but that is a rule of law which should not be so applied as to cut off one of the accused from giving in evidence any statement which he made accompanying such an incident as his confession of the possession of arms, which statement would be admissible by way of explanation if he were the only person implicated in the charges ; and the objection which the counsel takes is an objection which I admit to be well taken to that extent, but not to the extent of excluding his confession from being given in evidence in vindication of Arnold. It is well taken to exclude whatever confession Arnold made at the time from being weighed by the Court when they come to consider the case of those who are associated with him in the charges: that is, counsel should state their objection when they come to argue the case as presented, and ask the Court, in making up its judgment from the evidence as to the guilt or innocence of the others who are included with Arnold in the charge, to exclude Arnold's confession, and not allow it to have any weight in their minds as against others. That I conceive to be the true law of the case.

Mr. Cox. If it please the Court, I do not suppose anybody objects to any explanation, any additional statement made by the accused, Arnold, which may tend to explain his possession of the arms found on his person, or in his possession, to exonerate himself. I think that is proper testimony, and is fairly admissible; but that may be admitted without admitting any thing which refers to other parties. It is admitted by the counsel who has just resumed his seat, that any confession made after the termination of a conspiracy, or its execution or abandonment by one of the original conspirators, would not be competent evidence against any other of the parties accused. That is conceded to be the law. He maintains, however, that this Court ought to admit the evidence, and exclude it from their consideration; but I take it, that is not the rule which governs courts-martial, as it certainly does not govern any other courts in the consideration of evidence. Whatever is not competent evidence is not allowed to go to a jury at all; it is excluded from their consideration entirely: and I take it for granted that this Court, having to determine both the law (under the guidance and advice of the learned Judge Advocate) and the facts of the case, will discard entirely from the record all evidence which is clearly inadmissible, and which ought not to be weighed adversely to a prisoner; because it is impossible for any man, in the nature of things, to discard from his consideration, and prevent his judgment from being biassed by, evidence which is once submitted to him, and which may be in its nature adverse to the prisoner, although it may be incompetent and illegal evidence. I submit therefore to the Court, with great confidence, that this evidence, so far as it relates to any other or others of the accused, ought to bo entirely excluded. It can be done without depriving the accused, Arnold, of the benefit of any exculpatory explanation which accompanies his admission of the possession of these arms.

ASSISTANT JUDGE ADVOCATE BINGHAM. I desire to say in connection with this matter, that, while there can be no dispute about the law on the hypothesis assumed by the gentleman who first spoke here, the evidence before this Court already in the case — I do not desire to say any thing particularly about the letter of Herold in this connection, but to speak generally of the evidence — shows very well that it is an open question, at all events, whether this conspiracy was executed on the day of this man's arrest; and therefore, in settling this point now of the admission of this man's declarations, the Court cannot be expected to decide that the conspiracy had been either executed or abandoned on that day. There is testimony here as to certain other persons that were to be the victims of this conspiracy; and it had not yet executed its declared purpose. There is evidence tending to show that certain of the conspirators attempted to execute their purposes, but have not yet succeeded; and what further evidence may be disclosed hereafter, touching their pursuit of this same conspiracy after the date of this arrest, it is not necessary now for me to speak of. I make this remark at this time to notify the Court, that, in this stage of the cause, they cannot assume any such thing as is assumed here, — that this conspiracy has been either abandoned on the one hand, or executed on the other; and therefore this question, as it stands before the Court, is simply this: Whether the declaration of this party, made at the same time, — for his declaration at any other time cannot be admitted, — whether the declaration made at the same time — a portion of which, it seems, was called out by the Judge Advocate General — shall be wholly given to the Court. The Judge Advocate General himself, as I think, very properly suggested that the whole of that declaration may go to the Court without objection from him; and I ask the Court in ruling it to confine itself to the admissibility or non-admissibility of the whole of the declaration of Arnold made at that conversation, and at that one time and place.

Mr. Cox. The Court will allow me a single word. I think the learned Judge Advocate will agree with me, that it is only declarations made by a conspirator in the course of the prosecution of the conspiracy, and accompanying acts which are prosecuted in pursuance of the conspiracy, which are admitted in evidence against alleged co-conspirators. If a conspiracy be once proved, or sufficient *primâ-facie* evidence of that be allowed once to go to the Court, on which they might found judgment that the conspiracy was proven, then the declarations of any one of these conspirators, made accompanying an act done in the prosecution of the conspiracy, would be receivable as evidence against his co-conspirators; but whether the conspiracy be abandoned or executed, or whether a confession be made not in the prosecution of the conspiracy, and accompanying any act, but independently of that, it is clearly not admissible against others of the accused parties.

Assistant Judge Advocate Bingham. That is true, as a general thing : but the difficulty about it is, that the conversation may disclose something further in connection with the conspiracy, on which the others may have acted ; and, in that way, it becomes evidence. Their very action on it afterwards is a confirmation of the whole thing ; so that, any way you view it, I see no objection to the question.

Mr. Ewing. I asked what he said at that time with the expectation of eliciting from the witness a statement made by Arnold, either a partial or a full statement, as to the connection with the alleged conspiracy ; and I claim that that properly comes in if the statement was made at that time, because the Judge Advocate, in the charges and by the evidence, has sought to associate him with the conspiracy ; and one of the links of the association is these arms there. Therefore it seemed to me that any statement he made at that time and place with reference to his connection with the conspiracy is legitimate. If the Court will allow me, I will read a short paragraph from Roscoe's Criminal Evidence, page 53 : —

   " Where a confession by one prisoner is given in evidence which implicates the other prisoners by name, a doubt arises as to the propriety of suffering those names to be mentioned to the jury. On one circuit, the practice has been to omit their names (Fletcher's Case, 4 C. & P., 250); but it has been ruled by Littledale, J., in several cases, that the names must be given. Where it was objected, on behalf of a prisoner whose name was thus introduced, that the witness ought to be directed to omit his name, and merely say another person, Littledale, J., said, 'The witness must mention the name. He is to tell us what the prisoner said; and, if he left out the name, he would not do so. He did not say another person; and the witness must give us the conversation just as it occurred: but I shall tell the jury that it is not evidence against the other prisoner.' (Hearne's Case, 4 C. & P., 215; Clewe's Case, *id.* 255.)"

This paragraph evidently contemplates only confessions introduced by the prosecution; but if the course of the examination has been such as to make it the right of a prisoner to introduce a confession or statement, made at a particular moment, on his own behalf, he has just as much right to introduce the confession, even though there be others associated with him in the charge, as the prosecution would have the right to introduce his confession if the prosecution saw fit to do so.

The PRESIDENT, after consultation with the members of the Commission, announced that the objection was overruled.

The question was repeated to the witness; and he answered as follows:—

A. About three or four weeks previous to his going to Fortress Monroe, three weeks say, he was at a meeting held at the Lichau House in this city.

Q. I understand you to say it is the same conversation, and the same time, that he told you about the pistols on his father's farm?

A. Yes, sir. He stated that there was a meeting held there. I asked him who attended. He gave me the names of them; he gave the names of J. W. Booth, M. O'Laughlin, G. W. Atzerodt, John Surratt, and a man with an *alias* of Mosby, and another, a small man, that he did not know the name of: he could not recollect it.

By Assistant Judge Advocate Burnett :

Q. Did he say whether he was present at that meeting, — he and these other men ?

A. Yes, sir. I asked him if he ever corresponded with Booth ? At first, he said he did not. Then I mentioned the letter that was in the " Sunday American " of the 16th of April, published in Baltimore, where it gave a statement of a letter captured in Mr. Booth's trunk, or found in Mr. Booth's trunk. Then I mentioned over to him how that letter read, and that it was dated Hookstown, and mailed at Hookstown ; and then he said that he wrote that letter. We imprisoned him there that day until evening, when we brought him into Baltimore.

By Mr. Ewing :

Q. What else did he say ?

A. I asked him in the conversation if Wilkes Booth was acquainted in St. Mary's or Charles County. He said that he had letters of introduction to Dr. Mudd and Dr. Queen. I asked him who he got the letters from. He said he did not know. We proceeded to Baltimore with him, and took him to the office of Mr. McPhail, Provost Marshal. There he asked for a pen and ink and paper.

The Assistant Judge Advocate Bingham. You need not state any thing about that : that was at another time.

By Mr. Ewing :

Q. Did he not state to you a discussion that took place at the meeting, — an angry discussion ?

A. Yes, sir : he did.

By Assistant Judge Advocate Bingham :

Q. Was that at the same time that he told you about the pistol ?

A. Yes, sir.

By Mr. Ewing :

Q. What did he say about that discussion ?

A. I cannot recollect every thing. I recollect his saying that Booth got angry at him at something he said. Mr. Arnold said, if the thing was not done that week that he was there, he would withdraw; and Wilkes Booth got angry at him, and said he ought to be shot for expressing himself in that way; and he observed that two could play at that game. That was about the substance of it.

Q. Did he not say that Booth threatened to shoot him?

A. He said he had said enough for him to shoot him, or something like that. I do not remember the words exactly.

Q. Did he not say that he withdrew from the arrangement?

A. He said he withdrew then, and went and accepted a position at Fortress Monroe with John W. Wharton.

Q. Did he state to you the exact date when the meeting at Washington was held?

A. He may have. I do not remember that he did.

Q. Did he state to you whether he had seen Booth since or not?

A. I do not recollect that he did state to me when he last saw him, or whether he had seen him since that last meeting.

Q. But he stated that he had nothing more to do with the conspiracy?

ASSISTANT JUDGE ADVOCTE BINGHAM objected to the question.

A. He stated, as I said before, that he would withdraw, or would not have any connection with the business, if it was not done that week.

Q. And that Booth said he would be justified in shooting him for expressing himself in that way?

A. Yes, sir.

Q. And then he said he would withdraw?

A. I do not remember whether he said that or not.

Q. Did not Arnold after that say to you, that, after Booth said that in reply to him, he did withdraw?

A. I will state again, he may have said so; but I do not remember it.

Q. He said to you, then, that, after that time, he had nothing further to do with the conspiracy?

A. Yes, sir: he said that.

Q. Did he say where he went?

A. Yes, sir: he went and accepted this position under Mr. Wharton, as I have said.

Q. Did he say at what time he accepted it?

A. I think it was on the first of April, or last day of March: I am not certain.

Q. Did he not say that this interview was at Gautier's, instead of the Lichau House?

A. It was a singular name to me; and I might be mistaken as to the name. I thought it was the Lichau House. He spoke of the Lichau House in our conversation; and I think he said it was at the Lichau House. It happened on Pennsylvania Avenue, between Sixth and Four and a Half Streets, as well as I recollect.

Q. Did he say any thing to you as to what had been the purpose of the parties up to the time he withdrew from the arrangement, the conspiracy?

A. Yes, sir: he said the purpose, when he was a member of it, was to abduct or kidnap the President, and to take him South for the purpose of making this Government have an exchange of prisoners, or something to that amount. I asked him also what he was to do in it; what his part was. I think he said he was to catch him when he was thrown out of the box.

By Assistant Judge Advocate Bingham:

Q. At the theatre?

A. Yes, sir.

By Mr. Ewing:

Q. Did he say any thing to you as to the cause of his writing that letter to Booth, as to Booth's importuning him to continue in the plot?

A. There was a good deal of talk between us; and I cannot recollect every thing.

Q. Can you recollect of his telling you that? Do you not recollect of his saying that Booth went to his father's house twice, in Baltimore, to find him after that, in order to get him to go on with the conspiracy?

A. No, sir: I do not recollect any thing about that.

Q. Did he say any thing to you as to whose arms those were in the country?

A. I asked Arnold where he got the arms.   He said that Booth furnished the arms for all the men.

Q. Did he not say to you, that, when he left the conspiracy, Booth finally told him to sell the arms?

A. Yes, sir.

Q. He was alluding then to what arms?

A. Arnold told me he asked Booth what he should do with the arms.   Booth told him to take them and do any thing with them, — sell them if he chose.

Q. What arms was he speaking of then?

A. I have not seen the pistol yet.   The pistol and knife were in the carpet-sack; and, when he went down to Fortress Monroe, he said he took the pistol down there to sell.   The other arms I did not see until they were brought to the office.

Q. Did you not understand him as referring to the arms out at his father's house as well as to this pistol?

A. No.   He said that Booth told him to sell the arms if he chose; and he told me that the one we got in his carpet-bag he took to Fortress Monroe to sell.

Q. And that there was a knife and pistol of the same arms at his father's?

A. Yes, sir.

Q. You understood that the knife and pistol at his father's belonged to the same lot of arms that Booth told him to sell?

A. Yes, sir.

By Mr. Cox:

Q. Did he tell you that that was the first and only meeting he ever attended to consider the subject of abducting the President?

A. That was not the first meeting, I did not think, from what he told me.

Q. Did he tell you he had never met these same men there before?

A. There was some new men he had not met: there was one man that he did not think of the name of; he had to hear it; he was brought from the North or New York.

Q. Did he tell you, that, after discussing that scheme, the meeting came to the conclusion that it was impracticable?

A. Yes, sir: he made use of that word, "impracticable."

Q. Did he tell you they had abandoned that scheme at that time?

A. He told me he had.

Q. That they, the meeting, considered it impracticable, and that, in consequence of that, the scheme fell through entirely?

A. I do not remember that.

Q. He told you that these parties who were met there considered the scheme, after discussion, impracticable?

A. He made use of the word "impracticable."

Q. Did he make use of it as expressing the conclusion of the meeting?

A. He said he, individually, as I understood him, considered it impracticable; and he wished to withdraw from having any thing to do with it.

By the JUDGE ADVOCATE:

Q. I did not understand you to say that he conveyed to you the idea that the meeting itself had determined to abandon their contemplated attack on the President?

A. No, sir: I only understood him to say he himself had withdrawn; that he thought that plan or mode of kidnapping him impracticable, and he himself withdrew.

Q. State whether or not you found a rope in his carpet-sack at Fortess Monroe.

A. I do not recollect.

By MR. COX:

Q. You say you do not recollect the date of the meeting. Did he tell you what the date was?

A. He may have. I do not remember. It was previous to his going to Fortress Monroe; some week or two, perhaps: I would not be certain, sir, about the date.

Q. It was a week or two before he went to Fortress Monroe?

A. Yes, sir.

Q. You think that was the time he fixed as the date of this meeting?

A. He may have said two or three weeks. I do not remember exactly the date.

Q. He went there about the 1st of April, or last of March?

A. I think that was the time he said he went there to work there with Mr. Wharton.

By Mr. AIKEN:

Q. Was the name of Mrs. Surratt mentioned to you by Mr. Arnold?

A. No, sir: not that I recollect.

By Mr. EWING:

Q. Did you examine the carpet-bag of Arnold at Fortress Monroe?

A. I assisted, sir.

Q. You found no rope there?

A. I do not remember, sir, of seeing any rope there.

Q. Did he not say to you that Booth had a letter of introduction to Mr. Queen *or* Dr. Mudd?

A. I understood him to say *and* Dr. Mudd.

By the JUDGE ADVOCATE:

Q. Which Dr. Mudd did you understand him to refer to?

A. I do not remember to have heard him say. It was a physician in Charles County, I understood.

By Mr. STONE:

Q. Did he tell you that? Did he speak of Mr. Queen or Dr. Queen?

A. Dr. Queen.

Q. Dr. Queen and Dr. Mudd?

A. Yes, sir.

DANIEL J. THOMAS,

a witness called for the prosecution, being duly sworn, testified as follows:—

By the JUDGE ADVOCATE:

Q. State whether or not you are acquainted with the prisoner Dr. Mudd.

A. I am.

Q. State whether or not, some weeks before the assassination of the President, you saw him, and had a conversation with him.

A. Yes, sir: some time in March.

Q. What was the time in March?

A. I think it was in the latter part of March. It has now been nearly two months, I think.

Q. Where did that conversation occur?

A. At John S. Downing's.

Q. Where is that?

A. Close by where I live.

Q. Where is that? Near Dr. Mudd's?

A. It is a mile and a quarter from Dr. Mudd's, I think.

Q. In that conversation, did he speak of the President of the United States?

A. He said that the President, or Abraham Lincoln, was an abolitionist; that the whole Cabinet were such; and that he thought the South would never be subjugated under abolition doctrine; and he went on stating that all the Cabinet, and every Union man in the State of Maryland besides that, would be killed in six or seven weeks.

Q. Did he speak of the President as embraced in that?

A. He said that the President was an abolitionist, and the whole Cabinet were such.

Q. Did he speak about the President being killed?

A. Yes, sir: he said the President and the whole Cabinet were abolitionists, and that the whole would be killed in six or seven weeks, and every Union man in the State of Maryland; and then he remarked to me that I was no better.

Q. Was he very violent and excited in the declaration?

A. From his conversation, I would not think he was excited much.

Q. You were engaged in a conversation about the politics of the day?

A. Yes, sir. I made a remark to Dr. Mudd, that the war would soon be over; that South Carolina was taken, and also, I thought, Richmond would be, from what I understood; and that would be the ending of the war; and that we would soon have peace. Then he went on, stating 'that the South would never be subjugated under those principles; that the President, or that Mr. Lincoln, was an abolitionist, and also the whole Cabinet.

Q. And then added what you have stated, that they would be killed in six or seven weeks?

A. Yes, sir; and also every Union man in the State of Maryland.

By Mr. Stone:

Q. How far do you live from Dr. Mudd?

A. My place is not more than a mile and a half from his.

Q. Did you see him frequently?

A. Not very, sir.

Q. Was Mr. Downing at home the day you had this conversation?

A. He was at home : yes, sir.

Q. Was he there present?

A. I believe he had gone out. I believe he was out at the time.

Q. He had gone out where?

A. He went out in the kitchen, I think, somewhere, or out at the wood-pile, or somewhere else.

Q. How long did he remain out?

A. It is impossible for me to say.

Q. You do not remember how long he remained out?

A. No, sir : I do not precisely.

Q. Had you any conversation with Dr. Mudd before Mr. Downing left the house?

A. I believe I had.

Q. Mr. Downing left while you were conversing?

A. Yes, sir.

Q. How did that conversation commence?

A. It commenced about the war. I told him the war would be soon over, and that I was glad to see it.

Q. Had you been discussing with Dr. Mudd the question of exempting persons from military service?

A. Not at all.

Q. Had the doctor said nothing to you about that matter?

A. Not a word.

Q. What time do you say this conversation occurred, as well as you can recollect?

A. About some time in March.

Q. You cannot fix the precise date?

A. No, sir; not precisely: it is impossible. I am convinced that it was in March. I think it was some time in the latter part of March.

Q. You say the doctor did not seem to be angry or excited?

A. No, sir: at the time, I did not think so.

Q. What was said after Mr. Downing's return?

A. I had made a proposition to Mr. Downing. I asked him, if he had taken the oath of allegiance, would he consider it binding. He said he would not consider such an oath as that binding on himself; but he was loyal to the Government as he had taken it, but he did not consider it binding upon him.

Q. Was that all that occurred after that?

A. No, sir.

Q. Had you met Dr. Mudd at Mr. Downing's at any other time during this year?

A. No, sir: that is the only time.

Q. How long did you remain there that day?

A. I do not think, more than half an hour or three-quarters of an hour.

Q. Was not Dr. Mudd's manner and conversation with you jocose?

A. No, sir.

Q. Did he seem to be in earnest in the suggestion?

A. It is impossible for me to say.

Q. How did it appear to you?

A. From the way he said it, I considered that — He did not look mad or in malice at all. He did not look like he was angry at the time.

Q. Did he look like he was in earnest?

A. It is impossible for me to say. I cannot judge of a man whether he is in earnest or not: from the language he used, I should think so, — to talk of the President being assassinated.

Q. Did you think at the time that he was in earnest?

A. No, sir: I did not think any such thing could ever come to pass. I thought the President was well guarded. I thought it was a want of sense on his part saying it.

Q. It made no particular impression on you at the time?

A. When he remarked that every Union man in the State of Maryland would be killed, I remarked that I was not the least afraid of Jeff. Davis and the whole Confederate army combined together, for my part.

Q. It made no serious impression upon you at the time, did it? You never supposed such a thing was coming to pass?

A. No, sir: I never did.

Q. You did not dream of it?

A. No, sir: I never dreamed of such a thing coming to pass; and I was really surprised when I first heard it after that.

Q. Will you repeat what you last said?

A. After Dr. Mudd said this, I went home, and remarked there what Dr. Mudd had said; and they all laughed at the idea of such a thing. The thing was what everybody said would never come to pass, and that it was a want of sense on his part in saying such a thing.

Q. You laughed when you heard it?

A. Yes, sir: I laughed at it, to think the man had no more sense. I did not think any thing of it at the time at all of ever seeing it come to pass.

Q. Did Dr. Mudd, when he said that, look to you as if he really thought so himself?

A. I could not say whether he thought so.

Q. What impression did he make upon you?

A. At first, when he commenced, when he first said it, I thought he meant it.

Q. When he first said it, you really thought he meant, that, in six or seven weeks, the President, and all the Cabinet, and every Union man in all Maryland, would be killed.

A. When he first said that, I thought he meant it; but after a day or two I thought, if Dr. Mudd said that, he certainly could not have meant it at the time; but after the President was killed, after

Mr. Lincoln was really assassinated, I thought he really meant it, after hearing of Booth being at his house.

Q. He did not tell you how the President and Cabinet and these Union men were to be killed?

A. No, sir: he did not.

Q. If you had ever supposed that there was any conspiracy to kill the President, or to kill any Union man in reality, would you not have given immediate information of it?

A. Certainly; and I did give information of what Dr. Mudd said; but everybody laughed at the idea of such a thing.

Q. Who did you give that information to?

A. Most everybody I saw. But everybody laughed at the idea of such a thing, and at his saying it.

Q. Can you name any one that you gave the information to?

A. Yes, sir.

Q. Who?

A. I told my brother, Dr. John C. Thomas; I told several others about it, — Mr. Watson, — good Union men; and I told a good many persons in Woodville.

Q. Will you mention one in Woodville to whom you told it?

A. Yes, sir: I told old Mr. Peter Wood. He said it was not the words of a man of sense; but, after the President was killed, he said —

Q. Did you give any information of this declaration to any one in authority?

A. I wrote to Colonel Holland about it, but never received any answer from him.

Q. When did you write to Colonel Holland?

A. About a week after he said it.

Q. Did you get no answer from the colonel?

A. No, sir; and I came to the conclusion that Colonel Holland never received my letter. If he had, he would have answered it.

Q. You are satisfied that you never were at Mr. Downing's with Dr. Mudd but on that one occasion?

A. I do not think I ever met him there besides that time.

Q. I speak of this year.

A. No, sir: only that once.

Q. You are satisfied that nothing was said between Dr. Mudd and yourself about exempting drafted men ?

A. No, sir : never.

Q. You are positive on that question ?

A. Yes, sir.

Q. And that the conversation that you have detailed is all that occurred substantially?

A. Yes, sir.

Q. Who left the house first, — you or Dr. Mudd ?

A. I believe we both left principally at the same time.

Q. You both went away together ?

A. No, sir : I went home ; and he went to his house, I guess.

Q. Why did you come to the conclusion that Colonel Holland never received your letter?

A. I had written to him several times, and never received any answer ; and I concluded they must have miscarried in some way.

Q. Had you ever written to him before ?

A. Yes, sir.

Q. Had you never got answers before ?

A. No, sir.

Q. Had you not been speaking with Dr. Mudd of desertions from the rebel army ?

A. Never, sir.

Q. Had you been speaking to him of desertions from the Union army ?

A. Never, sir.

Q. Had you not been speaking to him on the subject of desertions at all ?

A. No, sir : never.

Q. When Mr. Downing returned into the room after this short absence, did not Dr. Mudd say to Mr. Downing that you had been calling the Southern army *" our army "* ?

A. No, sir.

Q. Nothing of that sort ?

A. Never, sir. [To Mr. Stone.] Mr. Stone, I will call your attention for one minute to a fact : My principles were made known to the public when I announced myself as a candidate for a seat in the House of Delegates of the State of Maryland in a card published in the " Times." You may have seen the card.

Q. A card in the " Times " ?

A. Yes, sir: in the " Port-Tobacco Times."

By Mr. Ewing:

Q. How long was Mr. Downing out of the room during this conversation ?

A. I do not know, sir, precisely the date.

Q. Do you know what he went out for ?

A. I do not.

Q. Do you know what he brought in ?

A. I think, to the best of my knowledge, he brought in some wood, sir.

Q. Was not he out about long enough to get some wood ?

A. Yes, sir: as soon as he came in, we started.

Q. You did not have any further conversation ?

A. No, sir, not at all : only I asked him there if he was a man that had taken the oath. I said, "You are a man who took the oath : do you not consider it binding ? " He said no ; he did not consider it binding : if a man was compelled to take an oath, it was not binding. I told him no man was going to kill him : there was no compulsion to make him take the oath. He said he thought it was compulsion.

By Mr. Stone:

Q. You say you mentioned this occurrence to Mr. Peter Wood, of Woodville, within a week ?

A. Yes, sir. I cannot say precisely the time : I think, about a week or more. He laughed at the idea. I know I mentioned it to him, and to my brother, and several parties.

Q. You mentioned it to Mr. Wood before the President's death ?

A. No, sir: after the President was assassinated.

Q. Did you mention it to your brother before the President was assassinated ?

A. Before, sir.

Q. When did you mention it to Mr. Watson ?

A. Before the President was assassinated.

Q. What is Mr. Watson's first name?

A. Lemuel Watson. I mentioned it to several other gentlemen too.

Q. Can you recollect any others now besides those three?

A. Yes, sir. I mentioned it to several men in Bryantown during the time they were looking for Booth.

Q. After the assassination?

A. Yes, sir.

Q. But, before the assassination actually occurred, did you?

A. No, sir: I do not think I did, because I never paid much attention to it until the President was assassinated.

Q. Are you satisfied that you mentioned it to Mr. Watson before the assassination?

A. Yes, sir; and to my brother also, before the assassination.

Q. Which one of your brothers?

A. I mentioned it to several of them.

Q. Which one did you mention it to?

A. I mentioned it to my brother Dr. John C. Thomas, of Woodville.

Q. Was it Mr. Peter Wood saw you with them?

A. It was old Mr. Wood.

Q. You mentioned it to him after the transaction had actually occurred?

A. Yes, sir. He asked me what I knew about Dr. Mudd. I told him I did not know any thing about Mr. Booth being with Dr. Mudd, but only the conversation I had with Mr. Mudd. I do not know whether Mr. Booth was at Dr. Mudd's or not. It is impossible for me to say.

Q. You cannot remember the names of any others that you mentioned it to, except those three, before the assassination?

A. No, sir.

Q. Your brother Dr. John C. Thomas, and Mr. Watson, — those two?

A. Yes, sir.

Q. Can you recollect the name of any other brother of yours that you mentioned it to?

A. No, sir; but I might have mentioned it to all of them in the family there : I do not know whether I did or not; but I did not take particular much account of it.

Q. You thought it was a mere joke at the time from the way he said it ?

A. He was laughing at the time, or something like.

Q. If the President had not actually been assassinated, you would likely never have thought of it any more ?

A. No, sir : after I wrote to Colonel Holland about it, I thought to myself he could not have got my letter, and afterwards he might have not answered it ; but I do not know whether he ever got it or not.

Q. Was that letter to Colonel Holland written before the assassination ?

A. Yes, sir.

Q. Colonel Holland is the Provost Marshal ?

A. Colonel John C. Holland is Provost Marshal of the Fifth Congressional District of the State of Maryland.

Q. Where did you direct your letter to Colonel Holland ?

A. I mailed it at Horsehead. I directed it to Ellicott's Mills, Md.

Q. You say Dr. Mudd was smiling at the time he made the remark to you ?

A. Yes, sir. I have never heard of Booth being there. I went over to Mr. Gardiner's last fall. I had never heard of Mr. Booth but at Mr. Gardiner's last fall with a Mr. Turner to buy a horse; and Mr. Gardiner told me he had sold his horse to a man named Booth. He did not say where he was from ; but, to the best of my knowledge, he said he came there with Dr. Mudd.

Q. This declaration of Dr. Mudd did not seem to make any impression on Mr. Downing, did it ? Mr. Downing did not seem to think much of all this talk of Dr. Mudd about killing all the Union men in the State, the President and his Cabinet ?

A. He said he did not hear it. I mentioned it to him. He said he was not listening to it: he was not in there. I mentioned it to him about it two or three weeks afterwards. He said he did not know any thing about it, and "I am glad I don't."

Q. You mentioned it two or three weeks after that, and he said he was glad he did not hear any thing about it?

A. Yes, sir: if he had, he would not have said any thing about it.

Q. It was after the assassination of the President that you had this conversation with Mr. Downing about this?

A. I mentioned the conversation that Dr. Mudd used; and he laughed at the idea of such a thing. He also said he would not consider the oath binding upon himself: he had taken the oath, and he did not consider the oath binding.

Q. You said you mentioned it to Mr. Downing about two or three weeks after?

A. Yes, sir.

Q. Was not that after the assassination of the President?

A. No, sir: I do not think it was.

Q. It was before?

A. Yes, sir: before.

Q. But Mr. Downing said, when you mentioned it to him, which was before the assassination, that he did not hear any thing of it, and was glad he did not hear it?

A. He said he did not hear it. I told him I thought he had been in there. When I told him what Dr. Mudd said, he said, "Well, if that be the case, I am glad I was not in there."

Q. Why was he glad?

A. I do not know: perhaps he thought I would have him up as a witness.

Q. When did you meet Mr. Downing when you were talking to him?

A. I met him on the road.

Q. On what road?

A. On the road leading from his house to Horsehead. But he said then that he did not think Dr. Mudd — or that it was a joke; that Dr. Mudd was always running on his joking ways; that this was one of his jokes. I know Dr. Mudd myself. We went to school together; and he was a boy full of fun, joking men.

Q. You know him very well, and know he is full of fun and jokes?

A. Yes, sir: he used to be when we went to school together.

By Mr. Ewing:

Q. Please state what conversation you can recollect that occurred before this declaration of Dr. Mudd and at that interview.

A. I spoke to him, and said the war would be soon over and ended, and the Rebellion would be "squashed."

Q. What else had been said before that?

A. Nothing else. That was all the particulars.

Q. Had you not been talking about other things?

A. No, sir.

Q. When Mr. Downing came in, did not Dr. Mudd say any thing about what had been said while he was out?

A. No, sir: he did not say a word. I just got up, and asked Mr. Downing one or two questions,—if he had taken the oath; and he said he had taken the oath, and he said he was no more loyal than before,—he always was a loyal man; that his feeling was for State rights; but still he did not consider that oath as binding upon any person.

Q. How came you to ask Mr. Downing whether he had taken the oath?

A. Because I told Dr. Mudd, a man like him, that had taken the oath—

Q. Was that Dr. Mudd or Mr. Downing?

A. Mr. Downing, as I have stated; but then I had said to Dr. Mudd, before that, that he had taken the oath, and he ought not to have said such things about the President, and so on, in such a way. He said he did not consider the oath worth a chew of tobacco.

Q. How came you to ask Mr. Downing whether he had taken the oath?

A. From some expressions of Dr. Mudd. I wanted to see whether Downing considered it binding. I considered it binding upon any person as much so as any oath; but he said it was not. As he used to be a justice of the peace, I wanted to hear what he thought about it; and he said he did not consider it binding.

Q. Mr. Downing was justice of the peace?

A. He used to be, but is not now.

Q. Did you say any thing to Mr. Downing about your being a marshal or deputy-marshal?

A. No, sir; never a word.

Q. Did you not say any thing to him about your having a commission from General Wallace?

A. Never a word.

Q. What day was that on which you say you met Mr. Downing in the road and told him about this?

A. I do not remember what day it was precisely.

Q. About how long was that after this conversation?

A. I think, about two weeks: I do not remember the precise day.

Q. Exactly where in the road was it that you met him?

A. If I stated it to you exactly, you would not know it exactly.

Q. State where it was.

A. I think it was between his place and my place, — right in the road, before you get out to the public road. It was in the public road altogether; but the public road lies right through my place.

Q. Try and think of somebody else, besides those you have named, you made this statement to before the assassination.

A. No, sir: I don't think I did tell it to any one else that I could name.

Q. Name over again those to whom you stated it.

A. My brother, Mr. Samuel Watson —

Q. State when you told your brother of it.

A. I do not know precisely what time it was.

Q. Where was it?

A. At his own house: no, it was on Sunday, at church, or before church. I walked over from his house to the Episcopal Church. I am a member of the Episcopal Church; I belong to that church; and I went to his house with him from church.

Q. When did you tell that to Mr. Watson?

A. It was at my mother's. He was at my mother's one day, and I mentioned this to him; and he laughed heartily.

Q. Did you laugh?

A. Yes: after he laughed, I could not help laughing. He said, "Dr. Mudd only did that to scare you, to frighten you. Everybody knows that such a thing is never going to come to pass." And, after Mr. Watson laughed, I laughed myself.

Q. You think you did not say it to anybody else?

A. No, sir.

Q. Did you say any thing at Mr. Downing's house about your having correspondence with General Wallace in Baltimore at that time?

A. No, sir. I never had a correspondence with General Wallace in my life, and did not mention it.

Q. You did not mention having any letters from him?

A. No, sir; never in my life.

Q. What did you say you were a candidate for?

A. A candidate for a seat in the House of Delegates of the State of Maryland, — the Legislature.

Q. Do you recollect how many votes you got?

A. I got sixty votes.

Q. Do you know how many votes were polled in that district?

ASSISTANT JUDGE ADVOCATE BINGHAM. I object to that question. I do not see what it has to do with this case.

JOHN HOPPMAN,

a witness called for the prosecution, being duly sworn, testified as follows: —

By the JUDGE ADVOCATE:

Q. [Submitting to the witness a telegraphic despatch.] Look at that paper, and state whether you have seen it before.

A. I have.

Q. Read it.

A. It reads: —

<blockquote>
"WASHINGTON, March 13, 1864.

"To M. O'LAUGHLIN, Esq.,

"No. 57, North Exeter Street, Baltimore, Md., —

"Don't fear to neglect your business. You had better come at once. [Signed] "J. BOOTH."
</blockquote>

[The original of the foregoing despatch was offered in evidence.]

Q. How are you engaged?

A. I am a clerk in the telegraph-office in this city.

Q. State whether this despatch was sent from this city by telegraph to O'Laughlin at its date.

A. Yes, sir: it was. It ought to be March 13, 1865, instead of 1864. We used the old printed forms of the year before.

Q. Do you know the handwriting of Booth?

A. I saw him write that message.

Q. And you knew the man, J. Wilkes Booth?

A. Yes, sir.

Cross-examined by Mr. Cox:

Q. Can you say whether this is a question or a command: "Don't you fear to neglect your business"?

Assistant Judge Advocate Bingham objected to the question. The writing must be its own interpreter.

The Commission sustained the objection.

Edward C. Stewart,

a witness called for the prosecution, being duly sworn, testified as follows:—

By the Judge Advocate:

Q. Are you a telegraph-operator in this city?

A. I am: at the Metropolitan Hotel.

Q. [Handing to the witness a telegraphic despatch.] Look at that despatch, and state whether you have any knowledge of its having been sent over the wires to Baltimore.

A. Yes, sir. I sent it myself.

Q. Read it to the Court.

A. It is,—

"Washington, March 27, 1864.

"To M. O'Laughlin, Esq.,

"57 North Exeter Street, Baltimore, Md.,—

"Get word to Sam. Come on, with or without him, Wednesday morning. We sell that day sure. Don't fail.

"J. Wilkes Booth."

[The despatch was received in evidence without objection.]

Q. You state that that despatch was sent over the wires by yourself?

A. Yes, sir.

Q. Do you know the handwriting of Booth?

A. That is the despatch he gave me.

Q. Did you know J. Wilkes Booth?

A. I did not.

Q. By whom was that given to you?

A. I cannot tell. The one that gave it to me wrote it, and asked me to send it.

Q. Would you know the man if you were to see his photograph?

A. I think I should.

Q. [Exhibiting the photograph of Booth.] Is that the man?

A. That is the gentleman who sent it.

By the COURT:

Q. Was that telegram sent last March, or last March a year ago?

A. Last March.

By the JUDGE ADVOCATE:

Q. Then the true date is 1865, and not 1864?

A. Yes, sir.

Cross-examined by Mr. COX:

Q. Do I understand you to say that that telegram was sent in March, 1865?

A. Yes, sir.

Q. Have you any recollection independently of seeing the paper itself?

A. I have not.

Q. The paper itself does not show that it was sent this last March, does it?

A. It is dated 1864; but that was because we used last year's blanks.

Q. How do you know it was not last year? You do not remember any thing about it?

A. Yes, sir : I remember that it was sent this year.

Q. Do you remember sending this very message ?

A. Yes, sir.

Q. Who gave it to you to send ?

A. The gentleman whose photograph has been shown me gave it to me.

By the COURT :

Q. How long have you been an operator at the Metropolitan Hotel ?

A. I have been there about ten months.

Q. Were you there on March, 1864 ?

A. I was not.

The Commission then adjourned until to-morrow (Friday), May 19, at ten o'clock.

The Commission on Friday continued the examination of witnesses, as follows : —

COLONEL JOSEPH H. TAYLOR,

a witness for the prosecution, being duly sworn, testified as follows : —

By the JUDGE ADVOCATE :

Q. Are you connected with the Provost Marshal's office of this city ?

A. No, sir : I am not. I am on duty at the headquarters of the Department of Washington.

Q. [Exhibiting to the witness Exhibit No. 7, containing a cipher.] Look at that paper, and state whether you have had it in your hands heretofore, and from whom you received it.

A. I had it in my hands. I received it from Lieutenant Tyrrell, an officer on duty in the Provost Marshal's office, on the night of the 14th of April last. I gave it in, on the 15th of April, to Colonel Wells.

Q. You received it from Lieutenant Tyrrell as one of the papers found in the trunk of J. Wilkes Booth?

A. Yes, sir; for which I had sent him.

No cross-examination.

CHARLES H. ROSCH,

a witness called for the prosecution, being duly sworn, testified as follows : —

By the JUDGE ADVOCATE :

Q. State whether you know the prisoner Edward Spangler.

A. I do not know him personally.

Q. Do you know him when you see him?

A. No: I was not there at the arrest. I went to his house, and secured the rope.

Q. You were not present at his arrest?

A. No, sir.

Q. Did you go to his house after the arrest?

A. Yes, sir.

Q. What did you find there?

A. We found a carpet-bag at the house where he takes his meals, on the corner of Seventh and H Streets. The man in charge of the house handed us a carpet-bag, in which we found a piece of rope, which I measured afterwards, and found to contain eighty-one feet; and the twist was very carefully taken out. There was nothing else in the carpet-bag, except some blank paper and a dirty shirt-collar. When we inquired for his trunk, we were told he kept it at the theatre.

Q. When was that carpet-bag with the rope left there?

A. It was left at the house where he generally took his meals.

Q. When?

A. That I do not know.

Q. When did you take it?

A. I took that rope from the house on the evening of Monday, the 17th of April since, between nine and ten o'clock, in company with two military detectives.

Q. Who were with you?

A. Two of the Provost Marshal's detectives.

Q. Do you know their names?

A. I do not.

Q. You did not see Spangler himself then?

A. I did not. I was to have gone with the other officers for the purpose of securing papers; but I missed them, and consequently I was not present when he was arrested.

Q. Did you find the carpet-bag open? Had it been opened?

A. No, sir: we made out to open it between us. It was locked. We found keys to unlock it.

Cross-examined by Mr. Ewing:

Q. Where is the house at which you got the carpet-bag?

A. It is on the north-west corner of Seventh and H Streets.

Q. Who gave it to you?

A. We took it when we found that it belonged to Spangler.

Q. Who was there?

A. A man called Jake, who works at the theatre in company with Spangler, told me that was Spangler's carpet-sack, and that that was all he had at that house.

Q. What was the man's name?

A. He is commonly called Jake; that is all I know: he is apparently a German.

Q. What persons in the house that lived or staid there did you see?

A. A couple of the boarders, I presume they were. I did not know any of the other parties that were in the house.

Q. What room was it that you got it out of?

A. The bed-room up stairs.

Q. What part of the house?

A. As near as I could judge, on the south side.

Q. On the south side of the house?

A. Yes: the room was facing to the south.

Q. Describe the room.

A. It was on the north side of the room itself where the bag was, right near where Jake — the man I referred to — had his trunk.   He was working, as he said, in the same theatre with Spangler.

Q. Look at that coil of rope, and state whether or not it is the same that you found in Spangler's carpet-bag.

A. I am satisfied and believe that is the same rope.

Q. What did you do with the monkey-wrench ?

A. I found no monkey-wrench in that carpet-bag.

Q. Did you find any anywhere else ?

A. No, sir.

The witness added : I beg leave of the Court to correct my statement as to the locality of the house, not being fully posted as to the latitude.   Since reflecting on it, I think it is the north-east corner of Seventh and H Streets.

By Assistant Judge Advocate Burnett :

Q. On what floor is the room ?

A. On the second floor.

Q. Was the room numbered ?

A. Where we were taken to, where the carpet-bag was found, there was no number on the room.

William Eaton

recalled by the prosecution.

By the Judge Advocate :

Q. State to the Court whether or not you arrested the prisoner Edward Spangler.

A. I did.

Q. At what day, and under what circumstances ?

A. I do not recollect the date.

Q. State the day as nearly as you can.

A. I cannot state the date.   It was the next week after the assassination.

Q. Where did you arrest him ?

A. In a house on Seventh Street, near the Patent Office.

Q. The corner of Seventh and which Street was it ?

A. I think it is between G and H.

Q. Was it at the corner of Seventh and H?

A. It was.

Q. Which corner? Can you state?

A. The right-hand side of Seventh Street.

Q. Is it the north-east corner or not?

A. It must be the south-east corner.

Q. Do you know whose house it is?

A. I do not.

Q. Did you find any weapons in his possession?

A. No, sir: I did not search him. My orders were to arrest him.

Q. Was that his boarding-house?

A. I think it was.

Q. Who was with him?

A. I do not know: the ladies who were in the house.

Q. Are you certain as to the corner on which that house stands? Reflect, and see whether you are right in your recollection.

A. I know it is in the corner building: I do not know whether it is on the corner door.

Q. Is it on the north-east or the south-east corner?

A. I think it is on the south-east corner.

No cross-examination.

WILLIAM WALLACE,

a witness called for the prosecution, being duly sworn, testified as follows : —

By the JUDGE ADVOCATE:

Q. Will you state whether or not, some time after the assassination of the President, you arrested the prisoner O'Laughlin?

A. I did: on the 17th of April.

Q. Where?

A. At the house of a family named Bailey, in Baltimore City, High Street.

Q. Was that his boarding-house?

A. I think not. I think his boarding-house, or the house where he stopped, was with his brother-in-law in Exeter Street, No. 57.

Q. Did you ask him why he was there, instead of at his boarding-house?

A. I did. He said, that, when he arrived in town on Saturday, he was told that the officers had been looking for him; and that he went away to a friend of his, and stopped on Saturday and Sunday night.

Q. Did he ask you for what he was arrested?

A. He seemed to understand what it was for.

Q. Did he ask you no question in regard to it?

A. Nothing that occurs to my mind at present.

Cross-examined by MR. Cox:

Q. Did the brother-in-law of the prisoner send for you, or go for you to arrest him?

ASSISTANT JUDGE ADVOCATE BINGHAM objected to the question.

MR. COX. The object is to show that the prisoner voluntarily surrendered himself by sending for the officer.

ASSISTANT JUDGE ADVOCATE BINGHAM. The brother-in-law is not the prisoner; and I object. The proposition is to show a declaration of the prisoner on his own motion, and at another time and place.

MR. COX. The evidence offered on the part of the prosecution was designed to show that O'Laughlin was avoiding the arrest. In cross-examination, I desire to show that the arrest was made at the instance of the brother-in-law; and I propose to follow that hereafter by proof that the prisoner himself sent his brother-in-law to communicate his whereabouts to the officer. I think that is legitimate on cross-examination.

ASSISTANT JUDGE ADVOCATE BINGHAM. It is not cross-examination: it is new matter altogether. We have not offered any evidence of what the prisoner said to his brother-in-law: this witness's testimony was as to what the prisoner said to him. It is in proof already by one of his associates, that he said he was not going to be taken at home, but was going to change his boarding-place. Now, it is proposed to prove declarations of the prisoner on his own motion, at another time and place, through his brother-in-law.

18

Mr. Cox. Not exactly that. The object of the prosecution, I suppose, in the examination of this witness, was to show that O'Laughlin was avoiding arrest, by showing that he was found at another place than his lodgings. One witness for the Government has already testified that the prisoner gave as a reason for leaving his lodgings, that, if he was arrested there, it would be the death of his mother; and, this witness having testified that he was found elsewhere, I desire to ask him, on cross-examination, whether he went there to find him at the instance of the prisoner's brother-in-law.

Assistant Judge Advocate Bingham. It is the declaration of a third person. That is what I object to now.

Mr. Cox. It is not the declaration of a fact that I offer, but of an act done by the brother-in-law, on which the officer acted.

The Commission overruled the objection.

Q. [By Mr. Cox.] Now state if Mr. Maulsby came after you to make the arrest.

A. Mr. Maulsby I am well acquainted with. He was recommended to me on Sunday evening, as being a good Union man, and that I could put implicit confidence in him. He knew I was looking for Mr. O'Laughlin. I then told him that I wished him to assist me in getting him. He said any thing he could do to assist me he would; and, if he got any information as to his whereabouts, he would inform me. That was Sunday evening. On Monday morning he came to me, and told me, that, if I would go with him, he thought he could find O'Laughlin. I went with him in company to the house in which I got him.

Q. You were asked whether the prisoner made any remark about the assassination. Did he say any thing about having received information that the detectives had been at his house?

A. I think he said, when he got to his brother-in-law's house on Saturday afternoon, he heard they had been there.

Q. Did he protest his innocence of the crime?

A. He said he knew nothing of the affair whatever.

Q. Did he say any thing about its being impossible for him to have participated in it, because he was in company with other persons all day Thursday and Friday?

A. He said he could account for his whereabouts during all his stay in Washington by parties who were there with him.

Q. Did he say why he left home after being advised that the detectives had been there after him?

A. I do not remember that he said so.

James J. Gifford,

a witness called for the prosecution, being duly sworn, testified as follows : —

By the Judge Advocate :

Q. Will you state to the Court whether or not you have been connected with Ford's Theatre, in this city?

A. Yes, sir.

Q. In what capacity?

A. I was the builder of it.

Q. In what capacity afterwards?

A. I have taken care of the building, keeping it in order, and working on the stage.

Q. You have been the carpenter there?

A. Yes, sir.

Q. Were you the carpenter there on the 14th and 15th of April last?

A. Yes, sir.

Q. Did you observe the President's box in the theatre on that day?

A. No, sir : I did not look at it that day. I was not in it.

Q. Do you know who decorated that box on that occasion?

A. I saw Mr. Harry Clay Ford in the box, putting flags out.

Q. Who else?

A. At one time I saw Mr. Raybolt, I think, with him : I am not certain.

Q. Anybody else?

A. No, sir.

Q. Did you see the prisoner Spangler in the box at any time during that day?

A. No, sir: I did not.

Q. Did you observe a large rocking-chair which was in the President's box in the theatre on the 14th of April?

A. I observed it afterwards: I did not take notice of it on the 14th.

Q. When did you see it?

A, I saw it on Saturday, the 15th.

Q. Where?

A. In the box.

Q. Do you know when it was placed in the box?

A. No, sir.

Q. Nor by whom?

A. No, sir.

Q. Do you know whether it had ever been there before?

A. I do not think it had this season. I saw it there last season.

Q. To whom did it belong? and where had it come from?

A. It belonged to Mr. John T. Ford. It was part of a set of furniture, — two sofas and two high-backed chairs, one with rockers and one with castors. I have sometimes seen the one with castors in the box this season; but I never saw the rocking-chair in it. The last I saw of the chair before this was in Mr. James R. Ford's and Henry Clay Ford's room.

Q. In the theatre?

A. Adjoining the theatre.

Q. You say it had not been in the box in the theatre during the past season?

A. Not this season, that I have seen. I saw it last season; not this season.

Q. When did you see it in Ford's room?

A. I suppose it must be three or four or five weeks before the occurrence.

Q. When did you see it again?

A. Not until Saturday morning, April 15.

Q. Did you see it after that anywhere?

A. No, sir: except on Sunday and Monday, when I came away from there?

Q. Do you know who took it away?

A. No, sir.

Q. Do you know whether the scenes of the theatre remain as they were the moment of the assassination?

A. I set a scene for a gentleman there to take a view for the Secretary of War. At the time I left the theatre, the scene was then set as it was the night of the assassination. The back flats in the three back grooves had been pushed off. I do not know whether they were pushed back since. They had been pushed off so as to give a view for the occupants of the side box. I pushed them off the box to assist in making the pictures.

Q. Have you examined the condition of the locks on the doors of that box?

A. No, sir: I have not.

Q. Did you examine the wall where there is a mortise made?

A. Yes, sir.

Q. When did you examine that first?

A. I think I first saw it on the Monday morning after the assassination.

Q. You had not seen it before?

A. No, sir: I was trying to find out where the door had been closed, when I first saw it. The Secretary of War came down to the theatre, and examined the box; and he told me to bring a stick, and fit it in the door. I found that a stick about three feet six inches long, if pressed against it, would keep the door from opening on the outside; but, if they had shook it, the strip would have dropped.

Q. When had you been in that box last before the 14th of April?

A. I cannot tell positively what time I was in there. I judge I was in there a week before.

Q. Do you think, if the mortise had been there then, you would have observed it?

A. Yes, sir: I should think so. I am generally particular in looking around to see that the place is clean, and see that the chairs are in their places, and the same number of chairs there.

Q. Had it the appearance of being very recently made?

A. It looked so to me.

Q. With what instrument do you think it was probably made?

A. I should think it was made with a knife, from the looks of it. It looks as if it had been scraped down.

Q. It would require a good deal of time to make it with a knife, would it not? It is quite a large mortise?

A. It would require a man some ten or fifteen minutes, I should judge. After the plaster on the outside was broken, it would be easy to get the inside off. The facing of the plastering, when it is faced over with the trowel, is hard, pressed.

Q. If the three doors that open into that place were all closed, it would be entirely dark there, would it not?

A. Yes, sir.

Q. Do you not think, therefore, that one or more of those doors must have been open when this mortise was being made?

A. It might have been so. It would have required some sort of light, I should think, if they had the strip.

Q. Would not such an operation made with an open door be likely to attract the attention of persons connected with the theatre?

A. If they used a knife, it would not: if they used a chisel or hammer, it would make a sound.

Q. What were the duties of the prisoner Spangler in connection with that theatre?

A. He worked on the stage, making scenery, fixing up the scenes, and working them at night.

Q. Did the decoration of this box come within the range of his duties?

A. No, sir: there is a gentleman there by the name of Raybolt, who is an upholsterer. It was his duty to have decorated the box; but he had a stiff neck, he said.

Q. That he had, on that evening, a stiff neck?

A. Yes, sir; and he got Mr. Clay Ford to do it for him, — so he told me afterwards. I asked him if I did not see him in the box; and he said, " Yes; but I did not decorate it."

Q. Where were you at the moment of the assassination of the President ?

A. I was standing about ten feet from the centre, where the big lamp is, just at the edge of the platform.

Q. On the stage ?

A. No, sir.

Q. Where ?

A. In front of the house.

Q. Outside ?

A. Yes, sir : I had come out of the front of the house. I had been in the front of the house, I suppose, maybe three or four minutes.

Q. You mean the front part of the theatre ?

A. Yes, sir.

Q. Had you been behind the scenes ?

A. Yes, sir.

Q. How long before ?

A. I had been behind there, I suppose, maybe about twenty minutes before.

Q. Did you see the prisoner Spangler while you were there ?

A. Yes, sir.

Q. What was he doing ?

A. He was on the left-hand side. I came out as the curtain went up. He was waiting for his business to change the scene.

Q. Is it, or is it not, a usual thing for the passage-way which leads to the back door, while a piece is being played, to be entirely free for persons to pass ?

A. The passage on each side, outside of the entrances, is always kept free, — it is a small stage, — so that the actors can pass from the dressing-room down underneath the stage, and come up on the other side. The entrances are always more or less filled with tables, chairs, and set-pieces. It depends altogether on the business they are doing, — whether it is a heavy piece or a light piece. Sometimes they have pieces with a great many sets in ; and then the entrances are generally jammed, but around the scenes is always kept open. At times, when there is a large number of people on, they are crowded with peoplo, but not with set-stuff or chairs or tables, or any thing of that, kind.

Q. Have you seen the bar which was found there?

A. No, sir : the night after the assassination, the police went up there; but I did not go up until Saturday morning.

Q. Did you say that you do not know who made the mortise for the bar that you spoke of?

A. No, sir; I do not.

Cross-examined by MR. EWING :

Q. [Submitting to the witness a plan of the theatre.] Will you examine that plat carefully, and state whether it is or is not an approximately correct plat of the theatre?

A. The lines in the orchestra are not correct. They are all curved lines : these are straight lines.

Q. [Exhibiting another plan of the theatre to the witness.] Examine this map, and state if you think it to be correct.

A. The front line of this plan is not correct. The side line on the south side is not correct.

Q. State in what it is incorrect.

A. This line on the stage curves out. It is just the reverse of what the gentleman who drew this has intended for it. Then, on the south side, there is a projection of about three feet. The stage is that much narrower on that side than it is on the other, and that much narrower than the front of the house.

Q. State what other defects, if any, you see in that map.

A. The fronts of the private boxes are straight : in this they have got a sweep. On the centre of the east wall there is a very large opening, some fourteen feet, which is not marked here at all. Those are all the defects I see in it at present. I do not know what is the meaning of these lines on one side unless they are intended for packs of scenes. The scenes are as they were when I left it. There are three packs here.

Q. They appear to represent the scenes as they were when you last saw them?

A. Yes, sir.

. Q. State whether, in other respects, the map is substantially correct in your opinion.

A. It shows the grooves and the entrances all correctly. The only difference in that respect is, that they have made the first entrance a little smaller, in proportion to the others, in laying them down. I do not know the scale of this drawing, and therefore cannot tell.

[The map was offered in evidence without objection.]

Q. How wide is the first entrance?

A. About four feet six inches.

Q. Is that the entrance by which Booth passed off from the stage behind the scenes?

A. That is the way they told me he passed: that is the entrance he must have gone through.

Q. How wide is the passage-way that he passed through going to the outer door?

A. I judge it is about from two feet eight inches to three feet; in some places a little wider, and in some a little narrower. It is not a regular straight entrance.

Q. Now tell the Court as to whether that passage-way is obstructed during the plays ordinarily.

A. Never, except by people when they have a large company on the small stage. There are never any chairs or tables or scenery put in the way there, so that they can have free access to go under the stage, and come up on the other side.

Q. Is it not also necessary to keep the passage-way clear in order to allow the actors and actresses to pass without obstruction from the green-room and the dressing-rooms on to the stage?

A. Yes, sir: that is what it is intended for.

Q. How is the small back door usually kept?

A. It is always left open until the performance is over; and then it is locked until morning.

Q. Do you mean that the door is swung open, or left unlocked merely?

A. It is left unlocked. The only door that is locked is the door leading from the stage to the front of the house on the side underneath the box where the President was assassinated.

Q. State what position upon the stage Mr. Spangler had during a performance.

A. His business was on the left hand of the stage, — the right hand from the audience, — to run the flats, as we call them, on that side.

Q. Was that the side the President's box was on?

A. Yes, sir.

Q. State at what times during the performance you were on the stage that night.

A. I was on the stage until the curtain went up at each act. When the curtain was down, I would go around on to the stage to see that every thing was right, and then go out again.

Q. State at what times during that evening, when you came on the stage between the acts, you saw Mr. Spangler.

A. I could not state the time. I should judge, the last time I saw him was at about half-past nine o'clock.

Q. State whether you saw him each time you came on the stage.

A. Yes, sir : I saw him each time.

Q. He was your subordinate, I believe?

A. Yes, sir.

Q. State where you were during that play, when you were not on the stage.

A. I was in the front of the house. I walked down to D and Tenth Streets, to look at a big lamp I had put up there, while the first act was going on. I walked up to the next corner, Tenth and F Streets, and took a glass of ale, and stood and talked a moment or two, during the second act. During the third act, I did not leave the house at all.

Q. You were then in front of the theatre a part of the time between the second and third acts?

A. Yes, sir.

Q. How much of the time?

A. I was on the stage between the acts.

Q. You were in front of the theatre during the performance of the second act?

A. During the performance of the second act, I was in front, I think, to the best of my knowledge.

Q. All the time?

A. No, sir : not all the time.

Q. How much of the time?

A. I do not know. I would walk in, and maybe stay five or ten minutes, and then walk out again.

Q. State whether or not you saw the prisoner Spangler at any time during that play in front of the theatre.

A. I did not see him in front of the theatre. I do not think he could have been there in front of the theatre without my knowing it, because the scenes would have gone wrong if he had left the stage any length of time.

Q. Did you ever see Spangler wear a mustache?

A. No, sir : he has never worn one since I have known him.

Q. Do you know how he was dressed that evening?

A. No, sir : I do not. I did not take particular notice.

Q. How was he ordinarily dressed during that period?

A. Just about the same as he is now, as far as I have seen. Lately, during the last four or five weeks, he has been wearing the clothes he has on now.

Q. Was not the play of the " American Cousin " a play in which the scenes were shifted a good deal?

A. They were what we call " plain-sailing," running-on scenes. There is but one set-scene in the piece.

Q. There was not much shifting, then?

A. In one act, the most of the scenes are changed : but that is in the first groove ; and therefore it only takes two men to change them until we get to two, and then it takes four men.

Q. Were the scenes shifted much in the play?

.A. I believe there are some five or six scenes in each act. I do not know — I cannot call to mind now — how many scenes are in each act.

Q. Then Spangler's presence there would have been indispensable to the performance?

A. Yes, sir. If he had not been there, his scene would not have gone on.

Q. Who was with him on duty on that side that night?

A. Ritterspaugh — I think that is the name — was with him at that time.

Q. Did you hear Booth call Spangler that night?

A. No, sir.

Q. What was Spangler's connection with Booth? what had he to do with him?

A. Nothing that I know of, further than friendly. Everybody about the house was friendly with him.

Q. With Booth?

A. Yes, sir; actors and all: they were all friendly with him. He had such a very winning way, that it made every person like him. He was a good-natured and jovial kind of man. The people about the house, as far as I knew, all liked him.

Q. Was he not very much in the habit of frequenting the theatre?

A. Sometimes I have seen him there for a week; and then he would go off, and I would not see him for a couple of weeks. Then he would come again for a week, perhaps; and after that I would not see him for a couple of weeks or ten days, or something of that sort.

Q. Did he not have access to the theatre as one of the *employés* would have?

A. Yes, sir.

Q. And had access by the back entrance?

A. Yes, sir.

Q. At any time?

A. Yes, sir; at any time, except when the door was locked.

Q. At any time when an *employé* of the theatre might go in?

A. When the house was open, he had free access all through the house.

Q. Day and night?

A. Yes, sir; except when the house was locked up, and the watchman was there: he had no access to it then.

Q. Was not Spangler a sort of a drudge for Booth?

A. He appeared so. He used to go down, and help him to hitch his horse up, and such things, I am told: I have seen him once or twice hitching the horse up myself.

Q. Was that hole in the wall cut into the brick?

A. No, sir: I believe not. To the best of my knowledge, it was not: it was only cut into the plaster, I should judge, about an inch or an inch and an eighth.

Q. You say it might have been done with a penknife?

A. Yes, sir: I think it might have been done with a penknife.

Q. [Submitting to the witness the wooden bar heretofore offered in evidence, marked Exhibit No. 44.] Will you examine that stick, and state whether you saw any sticks like that about the theatre about that time?

A. No, sir, I did not. This is the first time I have seen any thing of this kind.

Q. State whether those nails in the end would probably have been put in there for any purpose connected with the fastening of the door?

A. They might have been put in there to keep it from slipping down, — one end against the wall, and the other with the bevelled edge against the moulding of the door.

Q. State whether the nails in that end [a detached piece which had been sawed off the wooden bar] would probably have been put in for any purpose connected with that object.

A. I do not know what they could have been done for.

Q. You think they could not, in any way, have facilitated that object?

A. They might have. If this strip was too short, this block would fit in behind there, so as to make an abutment for it.

Q. But that was a part of the stick: it was on the stick, and was sawed off by a curiosity-hunter. Would these nails have been put in there for any purpose connected with the fastening of the door?

A. No, sir: I see no use for them there. This bevelled edge would keep it from slipping down the door; and, the other end being in the mortise, it would not require any thing to keep it from slipping down.

Q. How long would it have taken, with an ordinary penknife, to cut that hole in the wall you speak of?

A. I should suppose a man intent on mischief would do it in

some ten or fifteen minutes. After the face of the plastering is broken, the sand and lime run out very easily.

Q. I believe you have said that you do not know how the lock on the door of the President's box came to be loose?

A. No, sir: I do not.

Q. When did you first hear that the President was coming to the theatre that night?

A. I judge it was between eleven and twelve o'clock.

Q. Do you know whether he was invited to the theatre?

A. I do not know.

MRS. MARTHA MURRAY,

a witness called for the prosecution, being duly sworn, testified as follows: —

By the JUDGE ADVOCATE:

Q. Will you look at the prisoners at the bar, and see if you recognize either of them as having seen them before?

A. No, sir: I do not see any there that I know. If I have seen any, I have seen that man [pointing to Lewis Payne, one of the accused]. I think I have seen him; but I cannot say whether I did or not. If I did, he does not present the appearance that I have seen.

Q. I do not speak of his dress; but look at his features, and see whether you recognize him as the same person.

A. I think I have seen that man: I think his features are familiar to me; but I could not say for certain.

Q. Was the person of whom you speak a boarder in your house?

A. The one that is alluded to, perhaps, was a boarder in my house.

Q. By what name did he pass?

A. I do not know the name. A gentleman came to our house to inquire about him; and I brought him to the register, and showed him back to the date that I thought he came. I told Mr. McDevitt that I thought he entered that name: it was about the date he came to our house; and Mr. McDevitt cut the name out of the book.

Q. You do not remember what it was?

A. No, sir: it was on the book; but I cannot recollect it.

Q. How long did he remain there?

A. He came of a Friday, and left on Friday two weeks after. He was two weeks in our house.

Q. You keep the Herndon House, do you?

A. My husband does.

Q. Was the Friday on which he left the 14th of April last?

A. Yes, sir: it was the day that this unfortunate circumstance occurred.

Q. The day that the President was assassinated?

A. Yes, sir.

Q. At what hour did he leave?

A. About four o'clock. We have dinner at half-past four; and this gentleman came into the sitting-room, and said he was going away, and wanted to settle his bill; and he wished to have dinner before the regular dinner. So I gave orders for the dinner to be cut off, and sent up to the dining-room for him. He went into the dining-room; and I have never seen him since.

Q. Did he come to your house as an invalid?

A. No, sir: he said he came from the cars at eleven or twelve o'clock. I do not know the time exactly; but I know it was in the forenoon.

Q. Did he come alone, or with others?

A. Alone.

Q. Was he visited while there by others?

A. I expect he was.

Q. Would you be able to recognize any of the persons who visited him?

A. Yes.

Q. Look at the prisoners, and say if any of them visited him while he was there.

A. No, sir: I do not see any one there I could recognize. I never noticed but one little thing; and that was at supper-table. I was sitting at tea one evening, when he came in with two gentlemen to supper. I had got nearly through my tea, and got up and left, without paying any further attention to him, leaving them at the table with several others.

Q. Had anybody else spoken to you for a room for this man before he came ?

A. No, sir ; never to my knowledge. So many have spoken to me on different occasions for rooms, that I could not recollect any particular one. Some one may have done so ; but so many have applied, that I could not recollect any particular one.

Q. Do you remember whether John H. Surratt and Miss Ward, or either of them, called at your house, and spoke for a room for this man ?

A. I never saw or heard of this man until this circumstance.

Cross-examined by Mr. DOSTER :

Q. Will you state to the Court where the Herndon House is situated ?

A. On the corner of Ninth and F Streets, opposite the Patent Office, cat-a-cornered.

WILLIAM H. BELL (colored),

a witness called for the prosecution, being duly sworn, testified as follows : —

By the JUDGE ADVOCATE :

Q. Will you state whether or not, on the 14th of April last, you were living in the house of Mr. Seward, Secretary of State ?

A. Yes, sir : I was.

Q. In what capacity were you ? — at the door ?

A. Yes, sir.

Q. Will you look at these persons at the bar, and see whether you recognize either of them ?

A. There is the man that I recognize [pointing to Lewis Payne, one of the accused].

Q. Did he not come to the house of Mr. Seward on the night of the 14th of April ?

A. Yes, sir.

Q. Will you state all the circumstances connected with his entrance into the house ?

A. It was my night on that night; and the bell rang, and I went to the door; and this man [Payne] came in. He had a little package in his hand; and he said it was medicine for Mr. Seward, from Dr. Verdi, and that he was sent there by Dr. Verdi to direct him how to take it; and he said he must go up. I told him he could not go up. Then he repeated the words over, and was a good while talking to me there in the hall about he must go up, he must see him, he must see him. I told him he could not see him; that it was against my orders to let any one go up; that if he would give me the medicine, and tell me the directions, I would take it up, and tell Mr. Seward how to take it. That would not do; and he walked up the hall towards the steps. I had spoken pretty rough to him, and then I asked him to excuse me when I found out that he would go up. He said, " Oh, I know that, I know that : that is all right, sir ! " When I found out that he would go up, I got up on the steps, and went up in front of him. The reason I asked him to excuse me was, that I thought perhaps he might be sent by Dr. Verdi; and he might go up, and tell Mr. Seward that I would not let him go up, or something of that kind. When he went up, he walked pretty heavy. I asked him not to walk so heavy. He met Mr. Frederick Seward on the steps this side of his father's room, and had some conversation with him up there in the hall.

Q. Did you hear their conversation? If you did, state it.

A. Yes, sir. He told Mr. Frederick that he wanted to see Mr. Seward. Mr. Frederick went into the room, and came out and told him that he could not see him; that his father was asleep at that time; and to give him the medicine, and he would take it in to him. That would not do : he must see Mr. Seward, he must see him ! — he said it just in that way. Mr. Frederick said, " You cannot see him." He kept on talking to Mr. Frederick, saying that he must see him; and then Mr. Frederick said, " I am the proprietor here, and his son : if you cannot leave your message with me, you cannot leave it at all." Then he had a little more talk there for a while, and stood with the little package in his hand. It was just about the size of that little box there [pointing to a small box on the table]. Mr. Frederick would not let him see Mr. Seward no way at all; and then he started towards the step, and said, " Well, if I cannot see him " — And then he mumbled some words that I did not understand, and started to come down. I started in front of him. I got down about three steps, I guess, when I turned around to him, and said, " Don't walk so heavy." Then, by the time I turned around to make another step, he had jumped back, and struck Mr. Frederick. By the time I could look back, Mr. Frederick was falling : he threw up his hands, and fell back in his sister's room ; that is two doors this side of Mr. Seward's room. Then I ran down stairs, and out to the front door, hallooing " Murder !" and then ran down to General Augur's headquarters. I did not see the guard, and ran back again. By that time, there were three soldiers who had run out of the building, and were following me. When I got half-way back to the house, turning the corner there, I saw this man run out, and get on his horse. He had on a light overcoat and brown hat ; but he had not his hat on when he came out and got on his horse. I did not see his horse when he came to the house, and did not know he had a horse until I saw him get on it. I hallooed to the soldiers, "There he is, going on a horse !" They slacked their running, and ran out into the street, and did not run any more until he got on his horse and started off. I followed him up as far as I Street and Fifteen and a Half Street ; and he turned right out into Vermont Avenue.

Q. You lost sight of him there, did you ?

A. I lost sight of him there.

Q. Did you see with what he struck Mr. Frederick Seward ?

A. I did not exactly see it ; but, whatever it was, it appeared to me to be round, and to be mounted all over with silver. It was that long [about ten or twelve inches]. I had taken it to be a knife afterwards ; but they all said he struck him with a pistol : but that I cannot tell.

Q. How many times did he strike him ?

A. I saw him raise his hand twice. I did not wait to see how many times after he hit him. He hit him twice before I could turn around, and while I was looking at him ; and then I ran down stairs.

Q. Mr. Frederick Seward was on the floor when you left ?

A. Yes, sir : he had fallen.

Q. Did this man Payne say any thing when he struck him ?

40*

A. When he jumped back again, he just said, "You"—and commenced hitting him over the head. That is all I understood him to say. I came down stairs when I saw him hit him; but I hardly missed him from behind me until I heard him say that word.

Q. Dr. Verdi was Mr. Seward's family physician, was he?

A. Yes, sir : he said he had a package of medicine from him, and was sent there to give Mr. Seward that medicine, and direct him how to take it; and he must see him. He talked very rough to me in the first place when he came in.

Q. Did he abuse you for not letting him in?

A. No, sir : he did not say much out of the way; only he said he must see Mr. Seward; and walking very slowly all the time, listening to what I had to say. I told him I would not let him up; but, if he had any package of medicine for Mr. Seward, I would take it up, and tell him how to take it. But that would not do : he must see him. He had his right hand in his coat-pocket, and his medicine in his left hand.

Q. Had you ever seen this man about the door before?

A. I never saw him before, that I know of.

Q. When you came out, did you observe any persons about the door or the pavement?

A. No, sir : no one at all.

Q. You say you did not observe his horse?

A. I did not see his horse at all then.

Q. Did you see him when mounting on that horse?

A. I saw him run out of the door, and get on his horse.

Q. How far did he ride from you when nearest to you?

A. I must have been behind him, as far as from here to that door [about twenty feet], until he got to I Street.

Q. Could you by the light see the color and appearance of the horse?

A. His horse was a bay horse. I saw that when he started off from the tree-box; and I was behind all the way to I Street.

Q. Was it a stout or small animal?

A. Very stout, and did not appear to be a very high horse : he did not go very fast until he got near I Street; and then he got away from me altogether.

Q. You say he was bareheaded when he left the house?

A. Yes, sir.

Cross-examined by MR. DOSTER:

Q. How old are you?

A. I do not know: I guess I am between nineteen and twenty.

Q. Do you not know exactly?

A. No, sir.

Q. How long have you been at Mr. Seward's?

A. Near nine months.

Q. Have you ever been at school?

A. Yes, sir.

Q. How long?

A. Four or five years.

Q. What was your duty at Mr. Seward's?

A. I am second waiter.

Q. Where was this man, that you had the conversation with, standing, precisely, at that time? Was he outside or inside the door?

A. Inside. He came inside; and I closed the door.

Q. Did he hand you the package of medicine at any time?

A. No, sir.

Q. You say you talked rough to him?

A. He did not talk rough: he only spoke to me, and told me that he must see Mr. Seward. He had a very fine voice at the time coming in.

Q. You say you recognize that man to be the prisoner at the bar?

A. Yes, sir.

Q. Will you state what there is about this man that resembles the one you saw?

A. I noticed his hair, I noticed his pantaloons, and I noticed his boots, that night. He talked to Mr. Frederick at least five minutes while up there near his father's door, in the third story. He had on very heavy boots at the time, black pants, light overcoat, and a brown hat. His face was very red at the time he came in; and he had very black, coarse hair.

Q. Have you seen the same boots on this man?

A. Yes, sir: I saw him the night they captured him.

Q. Have you seen the same boots on him?

A. Yes, sir.

Q. What else have you seen on him the same? Have you seen the same clothes on him?

A. No, sir: I never saw the same clothes. I have seen the pantaloons he had on.

Q. What was the color of those pantaloons?

A. Black.

Q. Was the fact that he wore black pantaloons one of the reasons from which you inferred that this was the same man?

A. I knew his face.

Q. What points about his face besides his hair? You have told us that his hair was black.

A. I had a very good mark on him from his lip. When he talked to Mr. Frederick, he kind of raised this lip like [the upper one] when he talked; and he had a little wrinkle in his jaw: it appeared as if he had his teeth very tight on them. I knew him the moment I saw him again. They sent for me when they got him; and I went there, and put my finger right on him.

Q. You say he made that motion when he talked. Did he talk when you recognized him the second time?

A. He did not talk any the night I went down to look at him.

Q. But still you said just now that you recognized him by a certain wrinkle in his cheek when he talked?

A. By raising his lip. That I had taken notice of when he was talking to Mr. Frederick Seward.

Q. When have you seen the prisoner before, since between this and the assassination?

A. I saw him on the 17th of April.

Q. Where did you see him?

A. At General Augur's headquarters, on Fourteenth Street.

Q. How did you happen to go there and see him?

A. They sent for me at the house. Mr. Webster and another gentleman came after me about three o'clock that night.

Q. What did they say to you? Describe the circumstances that occurred.

A. They sent a man up to my room where I was; and he asked me to get up. I asked him what he wanted.

Q. What time of day was that?

A. It was in the night, between two and three o'clock : I did not notice the time particularly. I asked him what he wanted. He said Mr. Webster wanted me. I had been getting up every night at all hours since the thing happened ; and I told him to ask Mr. Webster to come up to my room; that I was tired of getting up of nights. I had been out two or three times. When I got up and came down, and saw Mr. Webster, he told me he wanted me to go down to General Augur's headquarters. I went down there. They asked me if the light was very bright in the hall at the time this man came in. I said it was not very bright, because the light in our hall does not go up very high, —it is only a little light ; but it was bright enough to read by : you could see good all over ; but it was not like the light they had in the room down there. A gentleman asked me what kind of hair he had, and what kind of a looking man he was. I told him as near as I could.

Q. Who was that gentleman?

A. I do not know him ; but I saw him here a little while ago, — a colonel, with large whiskers and a mustache.

Q. He asked you to describe him?

A. Yes, sir.

Q. What did you say?

A. I told him he had black hair, a thin lip, very fine voice, very tall, and broad across the shoulders, I took him to be. I told him as near as I could all about him. There were twenty or thirty gentlemen in the room at the time ; and he asked me if there was any one there had hair like him. I told him, " No, sir : not one had hair like him." Then he asked me if there was any one there looked like him ; and I told him there was not.

Q. That was at General Augur's?

A. Yes, sir : after he got through with me, he said, " I will bring a man in here, and show him to you." There were two rooms between. The light was shoved up very high ; and I was leaning down behind the desk, so that he should not see me if he came in. Then they opened the middle door ; and a good many came walking in that door together. I walked right up to this man, raised my hands and put my finger right here [on the lip], and told him I knew him: that was the man.

Q. Had you been shown any other man before that?

A. Yes, sir.

Q. Who else? — do you know?

A. I did not know the men.

Q. How many were shown you before?

A. Two.

Q. Did they look any way like this man?

A. No, sir.

Q. How did they look?

A. One had a mustache, and one had whiskers under the chin.

Q. Were they as tall as this man [Payne] is?

A. No, sir.

Q. Neither of them?

A. No, sir.

Q. You were not shown anybody looking at all like this man?

A. No, sir.

Q. Was there any thing else happened then at General Augur's?

A. That is all.

Q. You went off then back to Mr. Seward's?

A. Yes, sir.

Q. Had you at that time heard of any reward for the apprehension of the supposed assassin of Mr. Seward?

A. Yes, sir: I heard that there was a reward for different ones; but I did not hear, and have not heard yet, that there was a reward for him.

Q. You heard, then, of rewards offered for the apprehension of some?

A. Oh, yes! I saw the bills posted up on the street. I saw a bill posted up the very next morning, offering a reward of $10,000 from General Augur's headquarters; but I did not see any for him alone like there was for the rest of them.

Q. Had anybody offered you any money beforehand for the information?

A. No, sir.

Q. Did anybody threaten you beforehand ?

A. No, sir.

Q. You say, that when the prisoner, or the person that you saw, struck Mr. Frederick Seward, you went away ?

A. Yes, sir : I came down stairs.

Q. Did you find any soldiers there in the passage ?

A. No, sir : the passage was free ; nobody was there ; the door was closed. I came down and opened the door, and ran on down to the corner.

Q. Did you not notice the horse there when you came out ?

A. No, sir : I did not know he had a horse until I saw him run out, and get on the horse.

Q. You say you saw the horse turn out Vermont Avenue : did you run after him ?

A. Yes, sir : I followed him up to I Street.

Q. At what sort of a pace was he riding when he started off from the door ?

A. It seems to me he went very slow, because I kept up behind him until he got to I Street.

SERGEANT GEORGE F. ROBINSON,

a witness for the prosecution, being duly sworn, testified as follows : —

By the JUDGE ADVOCATE:

Q. Will you state to the Court whether or not, on the night of the 14th of April last, you were at the residence of Mr. Seward, Secretary of State ?

A. I was.

Q. In what capacity were you there ? What were you doing ?

A. I was an attendant, — nurse upon Mr. Steward.

Q. Look upon the prisoners here, and see whether you recognize either of them as having been in that house on that evening.

A. I see one that I think looks like him.

Q. Which one do you think looks like that ? Do you mean Payne ?

[The prisoner, Lewis Payne, stood up for identification.]

A. He looks like him, to me.

Q. Will you state all the circumstances attending the encounter between the person of whom you speak and Mr. Seward that evening, beginning with his first appearance as you saw him?

A. The first that I saw of him, I heard a disturbance in the hall, and opened the door to see what the trouble was; and, as I opened the door, he stood close up to it; and as soon as it was opened he struck me with a knife, knocked me partially down, and pressed by me to the bed of Mr. Seward, and struck him, wounding him. As soon as I could get on my feet, I endeavored to haul him off the bed; and then he turned upon me. In the scuffle, there was a man came into the room and clinched him. Between the two of us, we got him to the door, or by the door; and he, unclinching his hands from around my neck, struck me again, knocking me down, and then broke away from the other man, and ran down stairs.

Q. What did he strike you with at the door?

A. With a knife. When he struck me the last time, it was with his fist.

Q. Where did he stab you?

A. In the forehead.

Q. Did he say any thing when he struck you?

A. Not that I heard.

Q. Did he pass immediately to the bedside of Mr. Seward?

A. He did.

Q. Did you see him strike him?

A. I did.

Q. With the same weapon?

A. Yes, sir.

Q. How often?

A. I saw him cut him twice that I am sure of.

END OF VOL. I.

Press of Geo. C. Rand & Avery, No. 3, Cornhill.

www.ingramcontent.com/pod-product-compliance
Lightning Source LLC
Chambersburg PA
CBHW031813270326
41932CB00008B/412